TRUE NORTH

For Lilly —
with great admiration
for your skills &
work .

TRUE NORTH

Canadian Essays
for
Composition

JANICE MACDONALD

Addison-Wesley

An imprint of Addison Wesley Longman Ltd.

Don Mills, Ontario • Reading, Massachusetts • Harlow, England
Melbourne, Australia • Amsterdam, The Netherlands • Bonn, Germany

Publisher: Brian Henderson
Managing Editor: Linda Scott
Cover Design: Anthony Leung
Cover Images: Copyright © Corel Corporation
Page Design and Layout: Heidy Lawrance Associates
Production Coordinator: Alexandra Odulak
Manufacturing Coordinator: Sharon Latta Paterson
Printing and Binding: Webcom

The acknowledgements on pages vii–x are an extension of this copyright page. The publishers will gladly receive information enabling them to rectify any errors in references or credits.

CANADIAN CATALOGUING IN PUBLICATION DATA

Main entry under title:
True North : Canadian essays for composition

ISBN 0-201-61373-5

1. English language—Rhetoric. 2. College readers. 3. Canadian essays (English).* I. MacDonald, Janice E. (Janice Elva), 1959–   .

PE1417.T78 1999   808'.0427   C99-930396-1

ISBN 0-201-61373-5

Printed and bound in Canada.

A B C D E—WC—03 02 01 00 99

CONTENTS

ACKNOWLEDGEMENTS

Chapter Two

Jane Urquhart, "Returning to the Village." Copyright © Jane Urquhart. Published in *Writing Away: The PEN Canada Travel Anthology*, ed. Constance Rooke, published by McClelland & Stewart, Inc. *The Canadian Publishers,* 1994. Reprinted by permission of the author.

Sid Marty, "In Bird-Brained Spring," from *Leaning on the Wind* by Sid Marty. Published by HarperCollins*PublishersLtd.* Copyright © 1995 by Sid Marty.

Andreas Schroeder, "Fragment 6," from *Shaking It Rough* by Andreas Schroeder. First published by Doubleday Canada Limited. Copyright © 1976 by Andreas Schroeder.

Maria Campbell, "Chapter 3," from *Halfbreed* by Maria Campbell. Copyright © 1973 Maria Campbell. Used by permission, McClelland & Stewart, Inc. *The Canadian Publishers*.

Timothy Findley, "Remembrance," from *Inside Memory* by Timothy Findley. Published by HarperCollins*PublishersLtd.* Copyright © by Pebble Productions Inc.

David Carpenter, "Minding Your Manners in Paradise." Reprinted by permission of the author.

Chapter Three

Scott Young, "Polio Was a Killer—and Neil Had It," from *Neil and Me (Revised Ed)* by Scott Young. Copyright © 1984. Used by permission, McClelland & Stewart, Inc. *The Canadian Publishers*.

Thomas King, "The Open Car," © 1994 by Dead Dog Café Productions Inc. Reprinted by permission of the author.

Margaret Atwood, "Under the Thumb: How I Became a Poet." © Margaret Atwood, 1996. Originally published in *This Magazine* (Mar/Apr 1996). Reprinted by permission of the author.

Anonymous, "Drifting Into It," from *Six War Years* by Barry Broadfoot. Published by Doubleday Canada, 1974. Copyright by the author.

Nancy Gibson, "The Road to Freetown." Reprinted by permission of the author.

Chapter Four

Candace Savage, "Aurora: Myth and Mystery," from *Aurora* by Candace Savage, © 1994, published by Greystone Books, a division of Douglas & McIntyre. Reprinted by permission of the publisher.

Marg Meikle, "Who Invented New Year's Resolutions?" from *The Return of the Answer Lady* by Marg Meikle, © 1993, published by Douglas & McIntyre. Reprinted by permission of the publisher.

Andy Russell, "A Way of Life," from *Men of the Saddle* by Andy Russell. Copyright © 1978 by Van Nostrand Reinhold Ltd.

June Callwood, "Why Canada Has to Beat Its Literacy Problem." Reprinted by permission of the author.

Will Ferguson, "America Is Sexy," from *Why I Hate Canadians* by Will Ferguson, © 1997, published by Douglas & McIntyre. Reprinted by permission of the publisher.

Nora Abercrombie, "Which Ship Shall We Sail?" Copyright by Nora Abercrombie. Reprinted by permission of the author.

Chapter Five

Frank W. Epling, "Rats," from *Alberta Magazine*, Volume 1, Number 2, pp. 75-81. Edmonton: University of Alberta Press, 1989. Reprinted with permission.

W. P. Kinsella, "Nuke the Whales and Piss in the Ocean," from *British Columbia: Visions of the Promised Land* by W. P. Kinsella. Copyright by W. P. Kinsella. Reprinted by permission of the author.

Henry Kreisel, "Problems of Writing in Canada," from *Another Country* by Henry Kreisel. Copyright © 1985 Henry Kreisel, published by NeWest Publishers Limited.

Mordecai Richler, "Gretzky in Eight-Four," extracted from *Belling the Cat* by Mordecai Richler. Copyright © 1998 by Mordecai Richler Productions Limited. Reprinted by permission of Knopf Canada.

M. Nourbese Philip, "Why Multiculturalism Can't End Racism." First published in *Fuse Magazine*. Copyright © 1992 M. Nourbese Philip. Reprinted by permission of the author.

Jacqueline Dumas, "V Day," from *Other Voices* 11.1 (Spring 1998). Copyright by Jacqueline Dumas. Reprinted by permission of the author.

Chapter Six

Marni Stanley, "Wasp Waists and Lotus Buds: The Corset Looks at Footbinding." Copyright by Marni Stanley. Reprinted by permission of the author.

Marian Engel, "Twins and a Typewriter," from *Women and Words/Les Femmes et Les Mots Conference*. Copyright © 1985 Estate of Marian Engel.

Peter C. Newman, "Slouching Toward the Millennium," from *The Canadian Revolution* by Peter C. Newman. Copyright © 1995 by Power Reporting Limited. Reprinted by permission of Penguin Books Canada Limited.

Sally Armstrong, "Veiled Threat : The Women of Afghanistan," from *Homemaker's Magazine* Volume 32, Issue 5, (Summer 1997), pp. 16-30. Reprinted with permission from *Homemaker's Magazine*.

Gail de Vos, "Once Upon a Tabloid," excerpt from *Tales, Rumors and Gossip: Exploring Contemporary Folk Literature with Grades 7-12*, pp. 39-40. Copyright © 1996 Gail de Vos, published by Libraries Unlimited, Littleton, Colorado, 1996. Reprinted by permission of the author.

Chapter Seven

Myrna Kostash, "Creative Non-Fiction and Me," from *Arts Bridge* (Fall 1994).

Sharon Butala, "Belonging," from *Perfection of the Morning* by Sharon Butala. Published by HarperCollins*PublishersLtd*. Copyright © 1994 by Sharon Butala. Reprinted by permission of the publisher.

Caterina Edwards, "Where the Heart Is," from *The Second Bite: Eating Apples II*. Published by permission of the author.

David Layton, "Irving Layton, Leonard Cohen, and Other Recurring Nightmares," from *Why Are You Telling Me This?* Published Banff Centre Press, 1997. Copyright by the author.

Paul Quarrington, "Epilogue," from *Fishing with My Old Guy* by Paul Quarrington, © 1995, published by Greystone Books, a division of Douglas & McIntyre. Reprinted by permission of the publisher.

Sheldon Oberman, "Garage Sales Sailing," Copyright Sheldon Oberman. Reprinted by permission of the author.

Chapter Eight

Tommy Douglas, "Capital Punishment," from *Prose Models* ed. Gerald Levin. Copyright © 1989 Harcourt Brace Jovanovich Canada Inc. Originally a speech to the House of Commons.

Robert Fulford, "Mary Pickford, Glenn Gould, Anne of Green Gables and Captain Kirk: Canadians and the World's Imagination." Originally from a lecture at The Hebrew University, Jerusalem, 5 June 1997. Copyright by Robert Fulford. Reprinted by permission of the author.

Mel Hurtig, "A Dream of Canada," from *At Twilight in the Country: Memoir of a Canadian Nationalist.* Copyright by Mel Hurtig, published by Stoddart, 1996. Reprinted by permission of the author.

Robert Kroetsch, "Eulogy for Mort Ross." Copyright © Robert Kroetsch. Reprinted by permission of the author.

Maude Barlow, "Canada by Design: Using New Media and Policy to Build a Knowledge Nation." Copyright by Maude Barlow. Reprinted by permission of the author.

Chapter Nine

Randy Williams, "Dialling In for Dollars." Copyright by Randy Williams. Reprinted by permission of the author.

Janice MacDonald, "Brave New Neighbourhoods: Net Communities." Reprinted by permission of the author.

Marshall McLuhan, "The Role of New Media in Social Change." © Corinne McLuhan. Reprinted by permission of Corinne McLuhan and the Canadian Speakers' and Writers' Service.

Chapter Ten

Rita Donovan, "A Fine Romance." A review of *The Republic of Love* by Carol Shields from *Books in Canada*, Volume XXI, No. 3 (April 1992). Reprinted by permission of the author.

Robertson Davies, "An Unlikely Masterpiece," from *The Merry Heart* by Robertson Davies. Copyright © 1996 by Pendragon Ink. Reprinted by permission of Penguin Books Canada Limited.

Janice MacDonald, "Murder Most Foul Ball." A review of *Prairie Hardball* by Alison Gordon. Reprinted by permission of the author.

Robert Kroetsch, "Sitting Down to Write: Margaret Laurence and the Discourse of Morning," A review of *The Diviners* by Margaret Laurence from *A Likely Story* by Robert Kroetsch. Reprinted by permission of the author.

Candace Fertile, "Alberta Author Creates a Buzz." A review of *A Recipe for Bees* by Gail Anderson-Dargatz. Reprinted by permission of the author.

Kelly Hewson, "To Dream the Authentically Canadian Dream." A review of *The Whirlpool* by Jane Urquhart from a paper for *The South-western American Association of Canadian Studies Conference*, February 1993. Reprinted by permission of the author.

Chapter Eleven

George Orwell, "Politics and the English Language." Copyright © George Orwell, 1946. Reprinted by permission of Mark Hamilton as the Literary Executor of the Estate of the Late Sonia Brownell Orwell and Martin Secker & Warburg Ltd.

E. B. White, "Once More to the Lake," from *Essays of E. B. White*. Copyright © 1941 by E. B. White.

Dorothy Parker, "Good Souls." Copyright 1944 by Dorothy Parker, copyright renewed 1972 by Lillian Hellman, from *The Portable Dorothy Parker*. Used by permission of Viking Penguin, a division of Penguin Putnam Inc.

James Thurber, "University Days." Copyright © 1933, 1961 James Thurber. From *My Life and Hard Times*, published by Harper and Row. Reprinted by arrangement with Rosemary A. Thurber and the Barbara Hogenson Agency.

NOTE TO INSTRUCTORS

Welcome to *True North*. This essay reader has been constructed with certain concepts in mind. First of all, you will likely notice that there are no "leading questions" at the end of the essays. This is for two reasons. The first is that the aesthetic properties of the essays themselves are diminished in the eyes of the reader if they are treated as fodder for exams rather than as literary constructions. If we are not properly respectful of the merit of these works, how can we expect someone with less learned appreciation of literature to react in a positive manner? We mustn't forget, either, that students are coming to these essays "having" to read them, rather than necessarily "wanting" to read them. Letting them stand alone will in some way diminish that initial chip on the reader's shoulder.

The other reason for leaving the "notes" out of the arena of the reader is that oftentimes an instructor will have his or her own concepts of how to tackle the essay at hand. To either have to feel led by, or to have to counter, the editorial notes is a difficulty I hope, in this way, to circumvent. However, since sometimes it is helpful to see how others might approach a work, and since I cannot resist throwing in suggestions if given an iota of a chance, there will be accompanying material on each essay in the *Instructor's Manual*, should you want to check it out.

Aside from the five essays found in the Appendix (which are there for all of us who have marvellous teaching notes on "A Modest Proposal" and don't intend to drop it from the syllabus), all the writers featured in this text are Canadian. You'll notice, however, that not all the essays are patriotic in nature, or even about Canada. The topics have been chosen to be of interest in generating class discussion, before moving into the writing processes featured. The fact that this is a Canadian reader is one whose time has come. We are blessed with myriad gifted writers in this country. Not only are there more than enough to fill several readers, but also it is about time that students discovered names that they might eventually run across in periodicals in their own daily life.

1

While the essays have been grouped into dominant rhetorical modes, there is quite a bit of cross-over, as there is in all writing. Links between essays are noted in the *Instructor's Manual*, should you wish to structure your course in a content-driven manner.

Some sections in this book are unique to this reader, although the types of essays found within them can be found in other texts. These sections include: one on creative non-fiction, which goes beyond the form of personal essay; a section on speeches, which differ in many ways from essays written solely to be read (and many courses on communication require an oral component); a section on new media and cyberwriting, offering some ideas on what is indeed becoming a new rhetorical mode; and a section demonstrating the differences between a review and a critique.

The final critical rationale for choosing the essays and articles found in this text is that they are all writings I enjoy, written by writers I respect. I enjoy teaching them for the discussions they generate, the topics they touch on, and the quality of writing they demonstrate. I hope you find them equally energizing to teach. Have a lovely term.

NOTE TO STUDENTS

W elcome to *True North*, and welcome to an adventure in reading and writing. This text has been compiled with two aims: to
make you more aware of the ways in which words can be used
to influence you as a reader (and to give you some tools to use in influencing others with your words in turn); and to give you some exposure
to many of the terrific writers within your own country.

The essays in this book have been arranged into sections, which
you will soon realize are rather arbitrary. No essay can be completely singular in its use of rhetorical modes. The groupings are made by
determining the "primary" rhetorical mode used within each essay.

At the beginning of each section, I will be popping in with an
overview of the rhetorical mode that somehow connects the essays
that follow. Your instructor may or may not assign these prologue
essays for your reading. It would make me very happy, though, if you
were to read them in your spare time, anyway.

Sitting here, thinking of you reading these opening words, I am
overcome with envy. There is nothing quite like the feel of a brand
new book, the smell of the crisp new pages opening like some time-
lapse flower before you. What is more, this is the beginning of a new
class for you, perhaps even the first college course you've taken. The
whole wonderful world of post-secondary education is ahead of you.
You likely even have a new binder and backpack. Admit it, this is
just as exciting as preparing for any first day of school, be it Grade
One or Grade Ten.

Here's a bit of advice from a former perpetual student. Jump whole-
heartedly into this and all your courses. It doesn't matter whether
you've just come from high school, or you've been out of school for
years; as they say, these will be the best years of your life. Luxuriate
in the time you have to discuss ideas, get involved in debate, think.
All too soon, the real world will take over and insights and abstract
concepts too often get pushed aside when the main thing is to balance your chequebook. Enjoy your chance to think for yourself. If
you get hooked on it, you may never give it up. And wouldn't that be
wonderful?

CHAPTER ONE: READING, WRITING, AND RHETORIC

Welcome to this book. I have to say that, because this is a book of Canadian writing, and I am a Canadian, and we are unfailingly polite. In fact, that is all that most people seem to know about us, except that we live in igloos in that big pink place on the map.

A contemporary joke goes, "Question: How do you get a football team of drunken Canadians out of your pool? Answer: You say, 'Would you please get out of the pool?'"

Perhaps there is more to bind us in similarity than just our good manners, our ability to whistle the tune to "Mr. Dress-up," and the fact that we all have at one time or another shopped at the Bay. However, this book is not an attempt to find an "authentic Canadian voice." Instead, this book is a celebration of the variety of Canadian voices to be found around us.

It is called *True North* because that is one of the only lines I remember in the English version of our national anthem. I thought it appropriate because, being a collection of non-fiction Canadian writings, it seemed to fit the bill. Everything you read here is true. Except the bits that are made up.

I'm going to go out on a limb here, and guess that you are reading this book only because it's the required text for a required course, right? Don't be afraid to admit this, it's not going to hurt my feelings. I have no guilt at all about the fact that you will *have* to read some of these essays. Some of our greatest inventions and works of art came about because of demands and requirements.

Michelangelo would likely have been just as happy doing a mosaic on the floor of the Sistine Chapel, but an awkward pontiff pointed at the ceiling during the commission. Alexander Graham Bell was searching for a communication device for his beloved, deaf wife, when he invented the telephone. Jonas Salk was revered by anxious parents all over the world for discovering the polio vaccine. Creating something just for the heck of it results in inventions like pet rocks and the Spice Girls. I rest my case. Sit still and read; this will be good for you.

Try to forget that you had to wait in a monumental lineup to buy this required text, or that you haven't been registered in an English class in recorded geological time. You are embarking on an adventure into the art of the essay. If you can separate the horrors of a late night session of cramming-everything-you-know-on-a-topic-into-three-pages-to-meet-a-deadline from the works you are about to read here, you will see there is an elegance and beauty to the essay that is different from any other genre of literature. The essay is where the writer shows his face, where the connection between writer and reader is closer than any other form, except perhaps for poetry.

The French verb "essayer" means "to try." The essay is called such because it is "an attempt" to give one's viewpoint in a well-reasoned and finely crafted argument. Regardless of whether there is merely an individual reminiscence, or a debatable issue, one can see the essay as an argument. The writer is attempting, by use of various rhetorical strategies, to bend you, as the reader, to the writer's point of view.

Rhetoric, another word that will be bandied about with glee in this text, is the art of using words to get your own way. There are various ways and means available to a writer to woo, berate, seduce, convince, or fool the reader into believing that what she is saying is the right and true message. Now, while it is likely that most people are sincere in what they write, what they write may not always be the truth. It becomes the reader's responsibility to recognize how he or she is being manipulated.

Letting people read without an understanding of rhetorical strategies is like letting a four-year-old child watch unrestricted commercial television for two months before Christmas. Everything sounds good. To keep the child's wish list from becoming a mile long, and the reader's own moral, aesthetic, and ethical position from changing drastically with every new article she reads or speech he hears, one has to educate both in the ways of rhetoric.

One Christmas my daughters were captivated by a doll advertised on TV that twirled about and sparkled, to the delight of two little girls in the advertisement. Both my daughters wanted this doll desperately. We went to see it at the store, in plenty of time before their letters to Santa were mailed off. They were astonished to discover that said doll was only three inches tall. We came home and set out a three-inch-tall ornament on the table and tried to see if we could approximate the advertisement. One girl put her head next to the ornament while the other stood back, and then they reversed positions. They discovered that somehow camera trickery had to be involved in the ad to have made the girls' heads appear near the doll without dwarfing her down to her actual size. My girls were outraged to think they'd been fooled. Needless to say, Santa was petitioned for something else that year, and they are now much warier of tinsel and hype.

Just think about all the advertising that you are bombarded with daily. Is every product exactly what you need to make your life complete? Think of political speeches you've listened to from the campaign platforms. Are they making promises that can be followed through? Have you ever bought something because of its advertisement? Have you ever voted for the politician who resembled a "man of the people" because he campaigned in a denim shirt? Have you ever gone to see a movie based on the promotional trailer, only to discover it was nothing as it appeared to be in the mini-clip? In those cases, the rhetoric of the promotion manipulated you. Sometimes you may be won by the rhetoric, because it speaks to your own deep-held beliefs. Again, I repeat, not every piece of writing is fraudulent; most people do believe in what they are saying or writing. However, if you don't question and thoroughly examine what you are being sold, you deserve who you vote for.

You may find yourself marginally more cynical after contemplating the various ways rhetorical strategies can be used to manipulate you, the reader; but never fear. Recognizing them is only one step away from using them yourself. Soon, with what you learn in this book and this course, you will be winning arguments, convincing people of your acumen and knowledge, persuading the person of your dreams to marry you, becoming the youngest CEO of a Fortune 500 company, and selling all the new, improved, sterling-plated, multi-pronged widget sorters you care to (this particular rhetorical strategy is called *hyperbole*).

Still don't believe that writing is the most powerful tool invented, and a mastery of words places you in the driver's seat? Well, let's look at what you've just been reading, the *Introduction* to a college reader. The purpose behind such an essay (for that is what it is, if you pull it out of the context within which you find it) is to offer you an overview of what to expect within the text. It discusses the concepts of the essay genre and rhetoric. The underlying focus is to persuade you of the importance of studying essay styles to make you both a stronger writer and a more informed thinker. Now, while I am fascinated by this topic and enjoy reading and teaching essays, I am the first to admit that this isn't necessarily the most gripping topic in the world. Very deliberate rhetorical strategies have been employed to keep you reading this far (you are still there, aren't you?).

The conscious choice made here was to approach you as reader in a friendly manner, with a deliberate attempt to make you laugh as a way to lull you into submission prior to clobbering you with information in the rest of the book. The use of the *first person voice* creates a more intimate connection between reader and writer. I told a joke almost immediately, much the way a politician or preacher would, to break the ice (remember that old line, "A funny thing happened to me on the way here this evening."?). *Humour*, if used judiciously, can disarm a wary reader and create a closer link between writer and reader. When we were discussing the concept of studying rhetoric, which is a rather abstract subject, I moved into a concrete *analogy*, that of examining an advertised Christmas toy. A comparison can often enable a reader to relate to a strange concept if you twin it with a known quantity. The analogy was written as a *narrative*, or a story, much as if I was talking with you over coffee. We all tell stories, and can relate to narrative naturally. I used *examples* to reinforce my thesis. As you can see, there are plenty of strings attached to this seemingly simple introduction. Just be happy I wasn't trying to sell you a car.

So, in the last few pages, we have developed a relationship of a sort. You have grudgingly acknowledged that this text may not be as much of a headache as you'd anticipated. Heck, it might even be fun. Any topic is more interesting when you find someone who demonstrates a passion for it. (If their passion seems to be for sharp objects, however, I would advise you to back away slowly.) So, again, welcome to this book. If you haven't smiled once while reading this, either you're already a cynic, and will sail through this course with skeptical ease, questioning everything, *or* you need a good dictionary.

That last bit wasn't really a joke. You *do* need a good dictionary. You also should have a good writing handbook on your reference shelf. I keep both, right next to a dictionary of famous quotations, the complete Shakespeare, and the Oxford Annotated Bible. Believe me, I've never lost at Trivial Pursuit. The other thing that should go on that reference shelf for all time is *this* book. Again, I'm not joking. My advice is, bring along a pencil to class and jot things down in the margins while your instructor mentions them. There will come a time when you can look back on this text and find immediate answers to questions on how to document, how to tear apart a fallacious argument, how to insert a quotation seamlessly into the body of your work. Like apprentice painters copying paintings hung in the Louvre, you can learn to write more effectively by studying the masters.

Speaking of masters of their art, let's examine some of the reasons behind the choices in this book. As stated before, all these writers are Canadians (except for the writers whose essays are found in the Appendix; those are in here because you're not entitled to call yourself an educated person without having read them). The essays have been chosen to illustrate various strategies and styles of format, and have been grouped accordingly. Along with the general categories of *descriptive, narrative, expository, comparison*, and *persuasive* essays, we are also going to examine essays that were written to be presented orally, and essays written specifically for the Internet, as each of those forms requires specialized rhetorical strategies.

You'll find a short introduction to the organizing rhetorical technique at the beginning of each chapter. You may be bouncing around in the text, according to the course structure determined by your instructor, but it would be worth your while to read the introduction to each section as you move forward in the course (after all, we've already established how much fun introductions can be).

When reading an essay, try to read it in one sitting. This is a good rule of thumb for any work of literature, although your muscles might atrophy if trying this while reading *War and Peace*. Read with a pencil in your hand. If you don't understand a word, underline it, or put a tick in the margin. If something strikes you as relevant, important, or interesting, mark it with a line in the margin. Look up words you don't know. Determine which meaning, if there are more than one, the writer had in mind. Try to read the essay more than once, if you are going to be discussing it in class.

After reading, try to rephrase, in your words, what the essay was trying to impart. Aim for twenty-five words or less. If you can, you have likely uncovered the essence or *thesis* of the essay. Then ask yourself if the writer was convincing; have you accepted what she said? What sort of strategies has he used to sell his point of view? Have they succeeded in communicating?

Communication. Remember in your high school biology classes how the teacher spoke reverently of the highly formed communication patterns of bees and ants? Well, we humans too live in close proximity to each other. We are community-based creatures. To be fully functioning members of our society, it behooves us to learn the intricacies of our system, because we have more to impart than "I've already been to that flower but there is some great pollen in the next yard." Enjoy this adventure in rhetoric. In the beginning was the word. In the end, words are all we've got.

CHAPTER TWO: DESCRIPTIVE ESSAYS

Y ou've heard the adage, "A picture is worth a thousand words," but I would like to state for the record that I'll always choose that thousand words over the picture. Why? Because with a picture, you are given a flat, two-dimensional vision. With the right thousand words, however, you have everything.

Description has been likened to a "still life," a portrait in place. It is the rhetorical device that produces the setting for whatever the author has in mind to show us. The advantage is that, as writers rather than photographers, we have *all* the senses to pull from, not merely sight. We can transmit textures of velvet or burlap; smells as disparate as fresh baked bread and wet skunk on the same page; the jangling sounds of the crowded market place or the soft whisper of the breeze through aspens; the taste of rich Belgian chocolate sliding down the throat or bitter, angry bile rising up the gorge. A few choice words can deliver the reader *into* the picture we create, not leaving her merely standing on the sidelines, viewing our creation.

Description in an essay is used to advantage when giving readers a glimpse of a place they've never been, or a place they're otherwise familiar with, from a different perspective. Napoleon said, "An army marches on its stomach." Well, an essay marches on its details. Those details are provided through description. This is not to say you have to load down every sentence with ponderous, effluent adjectives. There is nothing more cloying than too many adjectives gumming up an otherwise picturesque landscape. Avoid general terms when you can use specific nouns, and you'll cut down on the need for adjectives.

As you have seen above, thorough description uses all the senses. This is not done merely for show, but to bring the reader into the scene in the best way for each individual reader. While some people's memories are visually stimulated, it has been clinically proven that the strongest sense for activating memory is the sense of smell. One whiff of new plastic can evoke distant Christmas mornings, a scent of mildew can recall the horrors of junior high gym class showers, a drift of aftershave can recall an old love affair in its entirety. Your

11

object is to involve the reader in your writing; a committed reader will not put down the text.

When should you use description in an essay? Any time you want to create an image for your reader, to clarify a situation, elucidate an unknown, implicate your reader by making him party to your memory or vision, description will serve the purpose.

What details should you highlight? This is a good question; it is a danger in descriptive essays to go "overboard," getting microscopically detailed over something inconsequential, letting the big picture get hazy and out of focus in the meantime. There are a few general tips for choosing what to detail. Things your readers may not be familiar with would be a good start; by describing them you bring your readers closer to an understanding of your vision, and give them a new experience. Don't forget, however, that a certain attention to shared concepts will reinforce a bond between you and your reader. Quirky details—like the wacky names people have given their cottages, dotting your drive to the lake; the combination of smells that accost you as you detail a visit to the circus; the disparity of the opulence of the Taj Mahal in comparison to the poverty surrounding it— are the features that bring alive your writing to your reader. Once you begin to paint with words, the likelihood is that you will find yourself waxing on indiscriminately, rather than not having anything to say.

However, if you keep in mind that each word you use is costing you a word you don't use, you can begin to make value judgements for yourself. Think in terms of sending your essay via telegraph, each word costing you ten cents. There is nothing like having to pay per word to make you a judicious self-editor. Weigh each word carefully. If your description is just as clear with one phrase as two, say it in one. The economy with which you paint your vision will be appreciated and admired.

The order in which you describe something is also worth paying attention to. It really doesn't matter whether you begin to the left of the doorway and work your way around the room clockwise or counter-clockwise, as long as your reader understands that there is a pattern. A system of any kind shows that you are in control of your material. This will make the reader far more comfortable going along with your writing, much the same way it is easier to be a passenger in a car where the driver knows where he is going. Think about your detail pattern, though; underlying messages can be transmitted in what gets described first and next. For instance, while it would seem to be a simple pattern, it is not a wise move necessarily to describe a woman from the feet up. Your reader might accuse you of subliminally objectifying her, in which case your description might back-fire. Patterns can be as simple as left to right, least significant to most significant, or highest to lowest. It's your canvas, and you can choose which focus the reader takes.

An objective description can be a rather clinical piece of writing, but if you move into a subjective, or personal, description, you have to decide on the voice you intend to offer your reader. There are certain aspects to consider when you apply a *point of view* to your description. Try to describe your childhood home (this presupposes you aren't one of those lucky people who hasn't moved seventeen times in your life). Will your voice become that of the child you were, to describe the windows as very high from the floor, so that you are only able to see over the sill by standing on tip-toe? Or will you look back on it from an adult's perspective and see the house through a filter of the ensuing years? Either is a valid choice, but as you can imagine, two different places will be described. It is possible to maintain a distance when using description, but if you are making value judgements, the reader has a right to know something about the person passing judgement. If your descriptions don't reflect some of your own choices in them, why are you including them? Just as you can learn a lot about people by examining their music collection, readers will find out quite a bit about you by noting what details you decide to include.

This thought that your reader will be psychoanalysing you as he reads might tend to inhibit you at the beginning, causing you to attempt to whitewash things to make yourself appear better, or at least more interesting. While you are, of course, in charge of your description, it is important to remain truthful to your vision. The reader will sense when the picture you paint is reflecting the actual, and when touch-ups have occurred. While it may be tempting to air-brush out those stray pimples or unattractive architectural features, letting them appear in your text will only add verisimilitude to your writing, and allow the reader to accept other factors that might seem more unbelievable.

Very few essays can be considered solely descriptive in their intent. In fact, none of the selections in this section would be classi-fied as solely descriptive. They have been chosen for their strong use of description as a primary rhetorical device. "Returning to the Village" is a vision of Ireland that Jane Urquhart presents. After an absence of several years, she returns for a visit to the village where she first became a writer. Old memories combine with new, showing a portrait of a place that resists change. Sid Marty, writer and park warden, takes us to the mountains with "In Bird-Brained Spring," giving us an insider's vision of the Rockies, but moreover, an insider's view to raising chickens. His account shows us how strong the surrounding wilderness can be, when an attempt is made at civilizing it. Andreas Schoeder lets us visit him in jail, giving a fascinatingly non-judgemental portrait of the Inside. And Maria Campbell gives us a portrait of the wonderful, strong people surrounding her as she grew up in a Métis community. As you can see, none of these essays are "just" descriptions; there is an ulterior thesis at work in all of them, whether it be political or rhapsodic.

Description is never used just for description's sake. It's a tool you use judiciously as a writer, to enhance your objective, or sometimes even to camouflage your objective, which is always to bring your reader around to your way of thinking. Use it as a means, not an end in itself.

I spoke earlier of the danger of over-adjectivizing your description. I cannot stress this enough. Think of adjectives as sugar. Then think about the dangers of sugar on teeth and waistlines. Put your writing on a strict diet. The last thing you want is your reader gagging on an overdose of treacle. Instead of describing the "feel of teeth piercing the skin and releasing the sweet, juicy flavour of Eve's fall from grace," why not opt to depict the "joy of biting into a hard Delicious apple"? By stuffing the chinks of your writing with adjectives, you deny any room for readers to enter the picture. Much as a healthy building requires some natural ventilation, healthy writing needs spaces for the reader's imagination to flourish.

Your mission, in a descriptive passage, is to let the reader experience, through your eyes, whatever you have in mind to show him. When you are successful, it will be an unencumbered reader who travels with you, one who allows you to show him, without hauling along his own preconceptions, whatever your vision determines. This is the real value of description; once a reader has become complicit in your vision, she is much more likely to absorb and agree with whatever argument your essay is postulating.

The greatest object of any essay is to present an argument and have your reader become aware, or indeed, change his way of thinking to yours. The danger of any rhetorical strategy is becoming wound up in the joy of the device itself. Never let description get the better of you. It is always used for an underlying purpose, which is to make your argument as palatable as possible. The essay writer's deep-rooted desire is to conquer the world, one reader at a time.

Jane Urquhart

Jane Urquhart was the winner of the 1997 Governor General's Award for her novel *The Underpainter.* She is also the author of three previous internationally acclaimed novels: *The Whirlpool,* which won France's Prix du meilleur livre étranger in 1992; *Changing Heaven;* and *Away,* which co-won the Trillium Award in 1993 and was shortlisted for the prestigious International IMPAC Dublin Literary Award. She has also published a volume of short stories and three collections of poetry. She lives in a small village in southwestern Ontario.

"Returning to the Village" is taken from the PEN anthology, *Writing Away.*

Returning to the Village

I wanted to be in a place that was both familiar and foreign, a place distant from the dailiness of life and yet filled with the warmth of domesticity, and I knew I could only do this by returning to the village.

The village was across an ocean, deep in the green heart of a country whose larger landscape I had come to understand by collecting a series of bright, startling images and whose language I knew only superficially. The village, however, I knew well. I lived there seven years before with my husband and two-year-old daughter for one serene year. I had walked its narrow streets and gazed down into the valley from its gates. I had followed the paths that branched out from its walls towards an ancient cross, a medieval forest, a wash house, an enclosed garden. I had bought bread each morning at its single *alimentation* and lit candles in its dark, cold church. Because my husband worked each day in a studio which was separate from the house and my daughter attended *École Maternelle*, I had been, during the daylight hours, always alone in my explorations. It was the place where the in me—such as she is—was born.

The following few years had been filled with excitement and activity: people, parties, bouts of blurred travel. Now I wanted separation from the world, solitude, wanted to rediscover what it was that had set the words spinning in the first place. I needed to begin another book, and for this reason I felt it was necessary that I return to the village alone.

Because I chose late November to make this pilgrimage, it was already dark when I arrived in the village on a Thursday afternoon. I collected the key and six brown eggs from the farming family across the street, and opened the familiar oak door. The interior of the house was just as I remembered it; the tiles in the kitchen, the cream-coloured walls, the old stone sink, the crack in the bedroom ceiling. I lit room after room, expecting to be confronted with some evidence of change. There was none. Spoons in drawers, goblets in cabinets, the grain on the oak stairs, the pattern on the salon rug, mirrors and pictures on walls, the figures of birds worked into lace curtains were just as they had been.

This was a privilege and I knew it; to bring one's own altered body and psyche into a space, architectural or natural, that has remained constant over the passage of almost a decade is not an experience easy to come by in the last quarter of the twentieth century. I thought of Wordsworth's "Tintern Abbey," of Yeats' "Coole Park and Ballylee"; poems of memory and reassessment that had needed the reassurance of familiar visual stimuli to trigger them. I had had to travel thousands of miles to get to the remembered, abandoned place, but I was blessed in that I had access to the return. I counted my blessings as I faced the fireplace.

The idea of the fireplace as a theatre had been planted in my mind seven years before by the owner of the house when he had left instructions regarding the fires which were to be lit there. "Use lots of paper, lots of kindling," he had written, "and place the logs slightly to stage right." So began my relationship with this small corner of the universe, a corner which would grow in importance when the winds of January rattled the shutters and removed loose tiles from rooftops. Never housing a predictable entertainment, often difficult to cause to perform, this hearth and its fire became, over the course of that distant year, my own territory. I cursed the fire and I coaxed it. Often it had sent me choking to the windows or scrambling through outbuildings searching for materials which would guarantee flame. It was seldom well behaved, its unfolding plot rarely uncomplicated until I had been at it for some time. It wasn't until the winter was almost over that I realized that I had been working at the fire in precisely the same way that I had been working on my writing, experiencing, each day, the frustration, the fascination.

I awakened on the first morning of my return, as I had awakened every morning years before, to the sound of the family across the street beginning their day—the moan of a cow, the sound of a milk pail striking cobblestone—and to the bells of the monastery on one side of the village and the convent on the other. In the intervening years I had thought a great deal about the convent, which had remained a hidden and mysterious female alternative, its activities made known only by the songs I had heard when I passed by its walls, or by a glimpse of its garden through a locked iron gate. Now I was grateful for its regularity: the fact that I knew that its bells would ring at the time of the day when bells should ring, that rituals were being performed, rituals I had never witnessed, mere steps from my door. All around me, I realized, a symphony was celebrating the sanctity of industry, continuity, inevitability. A tractor was fired up in a stone barn; children departed, chattering, for school; a milk truck arrived, picked up the fruits of the farmer's daybreak labours, and pulled away again; and I, the only pulse in the house, placed my bare feet on a familiar floor. Then I wandered through the house, pushing back the shutters, while behind me a series of rooms opened itself to the light.

After breakfast I took my remembered spiral walk around the village: outside the walls, inside the walls, through narrow streets, down alleyways, ending at the church square in the village's heart. I had brought along a basket which I filled at the *alimentation*. The woman there remembered me, mostly because of the "petite fille" who had sometimes accompanied me in the past. "Elle est comme ça," I said, holding my hand in front of me at shoulder level. The woman raised her eyebrows in astonishment.

In the early afternoon, after I had washed my few lunch and breakfast dishes, I entered the salon and began my daily struggle with the fire. Then I turned to the round walnut table, pulled out the green chair, sat down and opened my notebook. Behind me was a case filled with English books—a good thing because I knew I was not ready to write. I pulled the two large volumes of *Scott's Last Expedition* from the shelf and spent the remainder of the afternoon attempting to survive the sea voyage to Antarctica on the one hand, and on the other trying to encourage the reluctant fire. Blizzards swept pages, huge waves crashed over the icy decks of the *Terra Nova*, familiar fire tools clanked against marble, the wind banged in the chimney. Two decorative female faces looked solemnly up at me from the end of the andirons, twin girls I had become intimate with a decade before. A large log, eaten through the centre by fire, collapsed between them and was replaced by a chunk of softwood which burst almost immediately into flame. During the ocean storm, Scott was sick with anxiety concerning the fate of the animals on board. In the end he reported, sadly, that two ponies had been lost and one dog.

On the third day I decided to clean the house, which had been vacant for some months and was, as a result, somewhat dusty. This was a great pleasure in that it allowed me to run my hands over the surfaces of desks and cupboards, bureaus and tables that I hadn't consciously thought about for a long time but which, nevertheless, had remained in my memory so that the act of cleaning them, now, became a sort of ceremonial reunion. I recognized wood grains—sometimes even the reflections of windowpanes in wood grains—that I had known well in the past. I reacquainted myself with several small pieces of statuary; sad, resigned gestures and vulnerable expressions. In the kitchen I was able to see again the way a damp cloth caused the old blue-and-red tiles to shine until an opaque tide rolled over them from the direction of the radiator. All of this calmed and comforted me.

In the afternoon, and at a respectable distance, I followed a party of dark-robed, contemplative seminarians on their daily walk out the narrow road that led eventually to the Camp de Caesar. They could not possibly have been, but they looked the same as the clusters of their brothers I had seen bicycling down poplar-lined lanes into the valley or taking this exact walk seven years before. I turned around, however, and began the trek back, stooping down now and then to collect sticks for the fire. There were several wonderful views of the village from this road, particularly now that the low winter sunlight shone on its walls. At one point a path I remembered plunged into the now leafless forest, and I walked down it to the place I had called my secret thicket. Here, there was an ancient stone bench and a view of the valley, the monastery, and, on the next ridge of hills, the neighbouring village. I sat down, and, not for the first time since my arrival, I confronted my former, younger self: her fantasies, expectations, disappointments, and obsessions.

That evening, while the fire behaved admirably, I sat in the gentleman's chair, stage right, and did not even look at the round walnut table where so much writing had taken place in the past. Things were not going well in *Scott's Last Expedition*; shrieking winds, frostbite, snow blindness. But none of this stopped Ponting from taking his glorious photographs or Scott himself from reporting both disasters and triumphs in his clear, eloquent prose. But after he had left Cape Evans, the tone of his writing changed, became more forced and practical. Poetic images disappeared and at times the sentences became harsh, almost brutal. The weather, it seemed, was always against him, and he wasn't progressing as quickly as he had hoped. Sometimes he and his men were trapped for days inside tents while something white and furious took hold of the rest of the world.

At Camp Shambles the rest of the beloved ponies had to be shot.

It was almost midnight. Before finishing this tragic history I wanted to clear my head, so I left the house for the village streets. All lamps were extinguished, except mine; all shutters were closed, including mine. The streetlights, in the interests of economy, had always been and were still switched off at nine P.M. There was a partial moon, and this, plus a carpet of brilliant stars, was my only source of illumination. But unlike Scott and his party I was safe, surrounded by a culture and civilization that had been left to me like a gift by preceding generations. Some of the narrower streets were so dark that I couldn't see my own feet, but I realized by my sure-footedness how intimate I had become with their surfaces, their dimensions, their distances. There was frost in the air; I could see its minimal shine on rooftops. But there was no ice underfoot. When I entered the house again, all the furniture seemed to greet me. I cut myself a chunk of bread on the old board in the kitchen, adding another incision to the thousands etched there, some by my own previous, younger hand.

After great hardship Scott and his men eventually reached the Pole only to discover that they had been pre-empted by Amundson and the Norwegians. Returning, they found the weather had worsened. Petty Officer Evans had died, and Oates, sensing that his weaknesses were slowing the party's progress, had staggered off into a blizzard in order to relieve the others of the burden he felt he was becoming. And Scott, himself, would never again walk into familiar rooms or gaze out windows at familiar landscapes. After penning his last few feeble words, he lay down in his tent and prepared to freeze to death.

The following morning I opened my eyes to shafts of strong sunlight, which penetrated the shutters and made narrow golden bars on the floor beside the bed. I had slept through the convent bells and the morning activities of my neighbours. When I opened first the windows, then the shutters, I was amazed to see that while everything in the village was crisp, frosty, and clear under a cloudless sky, the whole valley surrounding it was filled with a thick fog. I imagined what the village would look like from a distance, perched like a heavenly city on a prairie of soft cloud. The rest of the world, I realized, had simply disappeared.

In the afternoon, after setting a log slightly to stage right, I opened my notebook on the round walnut table and began to write.

Sid Marty

Sid Marty is the author of *Men for the Mountains* and *Leaning on the Wind*, from which "In Bird-Brained Spring" is taken. His commitment and practical experience as a conservationist dates back to his park warden days in the Rockies. He is a well-anthologized poet and singer/songwriter as well. His articles have been published in numerous magazines, including *Canadian Geographic* and *Equinox*. He lives with his family in the foothills of the Rockies.

In Bird-Brained Spring

Over the years we have learned that if a chinook blows in around March 1, it seems at first to break the winter's back. Snow turns into a flood of meltwater; the roads are running freshets. But March is just a battleground between Pacific and northern fronts. The ground may quake underfoot as the warm wind blows. But during the night, the wind backs up as the cold arctic air pours south like water. Warm and cold air mix up a low fog that oozes west toward us off the prairie, a grey blanket being drawn upslope. In the morning there is a fairytale landscape of lacy hoar frost on every twig and stem. Underfoot, the frost has tightened yesterday's quaking pudding into a drumhead again.

More than snow and cold, winter (between chinooks at least) is a silence, and the night is the heart of it. There are long intervals when the only sound you hear is your own pulse. This is the night that the first homesteaders knew, the night of forgotten centuries. In the daylight hours what is most noticeable by its absence is birdsong. All winter we have had no avian company on the ranchette except for rascally magpies stealing the dog's food, and faithful chickadees around the feeder, cracking sunflower seeds and singing "Here, pretty" to each other. These little grey-and-black birds have to feed constantly to keep their metabolic fires burning. They fluff out their feathers and hole up in old woodpecker nests at night, surviving temperatures of –40°F with ease.

But then comes a March morning when our front deck is a tussle of chattering slate-coloured juncos, usually duelling with an irate downy woodpecker who ruled the roosts all winter. They seem to squabble as much as they eat. This is promising, but a true Frostback (what Montanans call us Canadians) stays sceptical. I have looked up through driving snow on March 5 and heard the wild cries of returning Canada geese that I could not see though they were flying at treetop height. Unearthly voices, they speak of the annual wedding of

heaven and earth. I almost believe their boasts of an early spring.
See them next morning, though, waddling clownishly over the frozen
surface of a pond where they expected open water. Soon they take
wing again, headed east for the Oldman River, where they can find a
pool to swim in until the ice goes out on our creek.

By the middle of the month a few impatient crocuses may stick
their purple heads up on the hillside above the house. Comes the
vernal equinox and covers them with snow again. It was still March
when I heard the song of a meadowlark from the caragana hedge
behind the house. Impossible, this early in the season. And there
was no lark in sight when I looked, only some beady-eyed starlings
shining like blue-black streaks of coal in the hedge. Cheeky little
imitators, birds of false hope. Not even the robins can persuade me,
because often as not they spend their first week huddled in the treetops like small, orange baseballs, embarrassed to silence by a spring
snowstorm. Watching as I shovel runways in the snow for them so
the sun can thaw out a worm or two. I am waiting for something
much more tangible even than robins, a song that will finally shatter
the brooding incubus of winter.

Over the years, I have come to expect the song in early April. But
that first year it came to my astonished ears on March 31, when the
chinook had melted all the snow in the wetlands below the house. I
thought I was hearing crickets, and then realized it was dozens of
tiny chorus frogs creaking out their mating song. The wind was
breezy and mild, and the night was a black, shining pool smeared
with stars, filled with their cricketing exultation. A little bit of last
year's summer had sprung loose from the frozen muck.

On April Fools' day I was sent for: "Your chicks are in." I picked
them up at the Cowley Co-op, two cardboard boxes full of animated
yellow fluff. They would grow into large white adult birds in only six
weeks. This variety was a meat producer, with a preponderance of
cockerels. But the hens, when mature, would produce large, tasty
eggs. Back home, the chicks crowded together under our heat lamps,
peering out at the universe of the garden shed. Soon they scattered
out to line up at their tiny feeder, made from a length of eavestrough.
They played the anvil chorus on the tin trough with their bills. The
boys were thrilled with the cute things, glad to feed them and change
their woodchip bedding. But after a few weeks, the teenaged chicks
had a gangly, reptilian look as they shed their down and started
fledging. The boys' interest began to wane.

As spring descended, the aurora borealis made its last appearance of the season in a fiery band of ghostly dancers. Gazing north we observed a symptom of progress that the pioneers never bargained for: the toxic-pink glow of light pollution from the distant city. A shimmering airborne oilslick in the heavens, it was a tawdry imitation of the glorious aurora.

On April 15, the ice went out on Livingstone Creek. Valley nights were slap-happy with beaver tails echoing across the flats. Ducks came whirling in landing cycles over our yard and geese gabbled and honked in cacophony. This constant singing by night and by day— this is spring at the mountain foot. It woke us from the sleepy ennui of the cold days. We hurried around the place tending to chores, sung to, squawked at, our lives registering on all those others. One evening we stood on either side of the creek, watching a beaver repairing a dam. "Don't move," hissed Myrna. A shadow came in over the treetops and a great blue heron wafted down over the creek, its pterodactylian wings whoofing the air in such regular beats, they might have been drawn up and down on puppet strings. "It's that damn herring!" I said, delighted. This is a joke we had, occasioned when a neighbour said to us, "Used to be plenty of trout in the crik, but them damn herrings ate 'em all."

Back home, a murder of crows threatened the aspen trees like a black net thrown down. They lifted in a quarrelsome mesh after a red-tailed hawk, like fishwives nagging the butcher's boy. The first yellow tulips, planted by our predecessors along the south wall of the house, had long since bloomed. The red curls of the rhubarb poked up through the thawing earth. The first mountain bluebird made a brilliant exclamation point on a fence post. There came a flight of swallows, in and out of the workshop, furiously gluing mud to the sides of the house and barn, starting three nests for every one they finished. There was at last an exaltation of larks to claim the east fence line, and the red-winged blackbirds flashed their red chevrons over a meltwater pond.

All the wild birds sang of new life in the land, and as they sang, the chickens began to die.

Lefty, who dragged his right leg awkwardly behind him, was the first. We discovered him one morning, unable to stand, but fighting gamely for a space at the feeder while stronger birds employed him to their advantage as a stepping stool. It seemed to us that Lefty's leg must be broken. At the Pincher Creek library, Myrna got a book on how to care for our feathered friends. Equipped with this, we took the game little fellow into the house, and cleaned him up, then set him on some newspaper on the kitchen table, and opened the book. There was a diagram showing how to splint the broken leg of a budgie with toothpicks. This inspired us to make a larger version for Lefty's leg out of popsicle sticks. Lefty seemed to resent our attention, however, and refused to try out the leg. Sated with food and drink in his infirmary box, he preferred to crawl on his belly like a reptile.

I hiked upstream to visit my agricultural consultants. Over coffee, I described Lefty's problem and our first-aid efforts. Frank suddenly convulsed, and expelled a sip of coffee halfway across his kitchen table. "Splinted his leg! You never did."

"I did. I felt I owed it to Lefty. He's a trooper."

Amy handed Frank the dish cloth, giggling wildly.

"What's next, you figger?" demanded Frank after a moment of hilarity that left him gasping for breath. "Crutches?"

"Well, I thought I'd ask you guys."

"Well, now you finally done the right thing. Got a hatchet?"

"Of course, but —"

"Well, if you bring the pointy end down on that chicken's neck with sufficient force, that'd be the best first aid you could give it. Just don't cut your thumb off while you're at it."

"There's no hope for him, then?"

Frank blinked owlishly at me. "Know what, kiddo? It ain't really the chicken that I am worried about."

We sipped our coffee. "It's the feed, Sid," said Amy sympathetically. "It's too hot. They grow too fast, and the leg can't support the weight of the body, so it gets all bent. It's called slipped tendon. They're not really bred for people like us, for free-range use. It's kinda the fast-food market they aim the damn things for. ..."

People like us. I grinned, pleased that Amy had included me in the description. "Maybe you could whittle him a cane," suggested Frank. "Use one of them twigs from them oval poplar trees of yours. Keep him aerodynamic."

We changed to a feed mixture Amy recommended to try to subvert the madcap speed of growth programmed into the chicks. Later we would learn that one must control the postmodern chicken environment and feed quantity in a more scientific manner, so that the skeletal development stays in balance with the body growth. But it was too late for Lefty. He sulked in his cardboard box in the kitchen while I broke the sad news around the supper table. "Boys, I'm afraid that Lefty must be terminated—with extreme prejudice."

"All right!"

"Outstanding."

They took the news a little too well, I felt. The noble bird was given a final meal before the sentence was carried out. The grim task fell to me. I elected to dispatch him with the same small-calibre weapon I had previously used to finish off scores of crippled big game animals—deer, elk, moose and bighorn sheep—mangled by cars, trucks and trains, when I worked in Banff National Car Park, protecting the wildlife from poachers. (For every deer killed by a poacher, we probably lost about fifty to the internal-combustion engine.)

Lefty declined the blindfold; he died like a real chicken. Unfortunately, we could not dine on his undersized carcass, because he was too recently on the medicated feed. We gave him a tree burial like a true warrior instead; we fed him to the sky. In due course, several more birds were found dead whose legs had suddenly given out under the strain. Their bodies were pounded into the woodchips by their voracious fellows. Learning how to raise chickens was obviously more complicated than greenhorns might assume. But even among experts, losses will occur. Chickens, we would discover, are extremely inventive when it comes to dying.

We cleaned out the ancient log chickenhouse, repaired the dilapidated wire pen and moved the newly fledged chickens into their new home. During the day, they were left out to range around the premises. They were fat and healthy, and already bigger than the chickens one usually sees in the market. They were about as happy as a chicken ever gets. Some juvenile crowing identified potential roosters. But as butchering day approached, they began to drop dead again, sometimes singly, sometimes in pairs. We would find them lying on the ground, feet in the air, wings outspread, grinning. The district agriculturalist had a look at our facilities, but found nothing amiss. He sent two victims in to the lab. The report that came back was enigmatic: "Specimens died of rollover or SDS." It sounded more like a traffic accident than an avian disorder.

"What is rollover or SDS?" I asked the Local Oracle, when we chanced to meet on the road one day.

"Ha! Sent some chickens to the lab, didja?"

"Yes."

"I figured. Well now—S-D-S; that stands for Sudden Death Syndrome. Not even them eggheads in Edmonton know what causes it."

"In other words, these chickens died of death."

"That's about the size of it. And take my advice, kiddo. Hurry up and kill those chickens, before they all die."

"Kill them before they die?"

"You said it, kiddo. You said a mouthful there."

We weren't looking forward to butchering day, however, so we tended to find reasons to postpone it. I had a good excuse. May found me back in Banff after a long absence from the place. Instead of riding the trails, however, I rode herd as resident editor to a group of writers at the Banff Centre for the Arts. I tried to get home every weekend to get some work done, but had no time for the great chicken kill.

As May came on, hearty with sun, Myrna switched to gardening mode. The chickens took to digging her garden seed faster than she could plant it. The garden contained earthworms, which they loved. The robins were very miffed and took to dive-bombing them. Myrna was opposed to fencing the garden with chickenwire. She loved the log fence that the old couple had left us.

"Those birds are looking good," I said one Saturday morning, as she returned yet again from shooing them out of her seed beds.

"Yes," she said plaintively. "Gee, I sure wish they were dead."

"Hush," I cautioned. But it was too late. Another one rolled over within the hour.

The Great Chicken Massacre finally took place. It was a stinky, gory day of wet feathers and tubs of guts that had the boys reconsidering a vegetarian diet. For a week afterward I could not close my eyes without picturing, as if on a screen, the puckered-up anus of a chicken. Our rate of loss had been high. We started out with seventy-five chicks. In the end, we wound up with one rooster and twelve laying hens in the chickenhouse, and fifty birds, each weighing from six to eight pounds, stashed in our freezer. Our family got a lot of value out of one chicken, however. Each one represented three meals, such as roast chicken, chicken casserole and chicken soup.

Over the years, I have learned that chickens, despite their tendency to drop dead if looked at crosswise, are very popular creatures. Hawks love them, coyotes love them, mink love them. The least weasel will drink their blood like wine. Coons very wisely wash them in the watertrough before partaking. Coyotes, however, are too clever to get caught stealing a chicken. It will have to stray quite a ways from home before the little wolf will nab it. Skunks are reasonable though dedicated killers. A mother skunk will whack out one free-range chicken per day. Like a burglar with a sack, she throws the booty over one shoulder and carries it back to her kits.

The predators that first season robbed us blind. Lion, the beloved mountain hound who had practically raised Paul as one of her pups, was old and ailing, and unable to attend to business. Her life would soon be over. The solution was to purchase another dog. This was Mojo. Colour her ink blot. Billed as a pure bred labrador before purchase, Mojo developed, after the cheque was cashed, the head shape of a golden retriever and the body of a Newfoundland water dog. Nature had apparently designed her for retrieving lobster traps. I built her a beautiful dog house, which she never entered.

Her assignment, as she saw it, was to avoid conflict. When threatened by the least weasel on its commutes to the henhouse, she would whine anxiously, and later moan sadly, deploring the carnage. Her main interest, when young, was barn cats. She collected them—sometimes going so far as to cat-nap kittens from god knows which empty culvert—and carry them home, in her mouth, for us to feed. The cats aroused her maternal instincts, and she soon learned to steal eggs from the henhouse to share with her little ones. The cats slept on top of Mojo, under the porch. By all appearances, she was a very comfortable cat mattress.

Mojo despised mink, and kept well clear of them when they visited, though she would quietly moan or groan an alert whenever she glimpsed one approaching. Hence the mink that hiked over from Livingstone Creek one night was the most extravagant assassin. It managed to burrow under the chickenwire while Mojo was cuddled up with her barn cats. Once inside, it killed seven chickens and our new additions that season—two beautiful white ducks of great size and impeccable dignity.

I had loved those ducks. They'd ridden herd on the entire flock, including the rooster. We had only a child's plastic wading pool, dug into the ground, for a duckpond back then. But every day, those ducks had herded the little flock to the pool and, quacking hysterically, tried to teach those chickens to swim—to no avail, alas.

The mink had munched its victims' heads to get at the blood, and ate a few mouthfuls of breast meat. The chickenhouse looked like a slaughterhouse the next morning; the rooster refused to come down from his roost until well after lunch, and the laying hens went on strike for two weeks.

This same rooster became psychotic as a result of the mink incident. Roosters are probably a bit crazy to begin with, it's true. They make interesting alarm clocks, but unless one wants the hens to go broody and raise chicks, the only other use a rooster has is to die on the job, if necessary, protecting his hens from predators. This one was too clever for the job, wise enough to hide from mink and skunks while they were murdering our hens, but happy to fly at us when we went out to feed him and his wives.

One night during that same year of the predators, Nathan, aged eight, went out to pick eggs. In the dim light of the chickenhouse, the rooster flew at our little one. It lit on his head, sinking one of its ugly yellow talons right inside his mouth, and just missing one eye with the other set of meathooks. Beating its wings around his ears, it drummed its beak on his head like a woodpecker from hell. The pain was terrific; he groped upward at the thing, felt a talon nail scrape at the roots of his front teeth, tasted blood and acrid chickenshit, his terrified scream choked in his throat. He pulled the bird off, pushed, punched it away from him, made for the door, tripped over the feed bucket and went down, while the rooster circled the place squawking his fury. Nathan got to his feet as it came running back and launched up at him again, outlined against the moonlight pouring through the chickenhouse door. With a frenzied yell, Nathan delivered a roundhouse kick in midair that accelerated the bird's flight, and sent it crashing through the window out into the pen. Nathan rushed into the house and scared hell out of us; his mouth poured blood, and he had a bloody cut over one eye. The cut in his mouth was deep and nasty. Thank heavens, the talon had not come back out through the lip. But the mouth is wonderful at cleaning and healing such wounds. Nathan soon recovered. The rooster was not injured; he wound up in the stewpot.

It takes an optimist to plant a garden at 4,700 foot altitude, which may be hit by frost, as we discovered, at least three times before the end of August. But by the last weekend in May of our first year in the valley, the aspen trees were leafing out and winter had begun to fade in memory as we planted the last row of potatoes.

Now the days came on with serious heat, and a dark green tinge stained the skin of earth under the old autumn colour of the desiccated grass. Then a sudden storm dumped eight inches of snow on the green grass. Snow caught in the new leaves bowed the aspen saplings and the willow boughs right down to the ground. But such a snow makes the farmer smile as it melts into the cultivated fields. As it melted in these southern foothills that first season, we saw something new to us.

The high slopes and ridges blazed with big yellow flowers of the balsam root. These plants are beloved by the Stoney and Blackfoot

people, who still dig the gnarled roots and use them for cold medicine. Now the montane flowers burst forth in all their extravagance.
The meadow turned to bright yellow as buttercups erupted. On the
hillsides were scarlet clouds of three-flowered avens and scattered
along the deer paths were fiery shooting stars.

Our boys made the best of the warm days and cool nights. They
pitched our old canvas tourist tent deep in the woods. I went to wake
them for breakfast. The trembling aspen had covered their tent with
catkins. They smelled of canvas and sunlight as they tumbled out
into the green grass, and jumped on my back, wrestling me to earth.
I remembered my own father, who could not remember J.C. offering
a fatherly embrace, and I hugged them to me, fiercely.

"What's for breakfast?" asked Paul.

"Eggs. Poached, boiled or scrambled."

"Yech. We had eggs three days in a row now."

"You got a better idea?"

"I do," said Nathan.

"Yes?"

"A nice, piping hot bowl of lovely swill."

"Swill, swill," I chanted, "beautiful swill. If we don't eat it the
chickens will...."

Andreas Schroeder

Andreas Schroeder has proved himself a versatile and talented writer. He is a novelist *(Dustship Glory)*, short story writer ("The Late Man"), poet *(File of Uncertainties)*, essayist *(Shaking It Rough)*, literary politician (his personal efforts are largely responsible for bringing public lending right funds to authors), radio personality (a regular on CBC's *Basic Black* show), and translator *(The Eleventh Commandment)*. This only proves that sometimes a "jack of all trades" can be master of all.

Fragment 6 from *Shaking It Rough*

There were forty-seven of us on that tier, two to a cell and you couldn't trade, but I was amazed how quickly we all banded together. We were an improbable bunch, everything from failure to pay alimony to attempted murder, we were Indians, Chinese, Hungarians, East Indians, Italians, you name it. We would probably never have given each other the time of day if we'd met on the Outside.

In here, it was a different story. It was us against them, not active warfare but a cold war, each side keeping as much to itself as it could. If communication was necessary you kept it short and loud; loud because secrets were dangerous commodities to have in prison. To be labeled a rat was the kiss of death; rats were stoolpigeons and they had something to hide. So the apparent antagonism between inmates and guards was rarely anything but impersonal, each person simply maintaining the party line for his own safety and comradeship. And if comradeship was essentially a pact between strangers to agree extravagantly on one or two items and forget the rest, we certainly had it made; a simple settling back on one's haunches and baying at the institutional moon, at the injustice, the oppression, the outrage, etc., invoked an instant clamor of agreement all around; one sat marvelously bathed in the wash of so much concord.

Even our speech reflected this will to solidarity. Cursing and general foul language was no accidental characteristic of prison jargon. When an inmate kicked irritably at an uncooperative piece of machinery and announced succinctly that "the fuckin fucker's fucked, fer fuck sakes!" he had neatly sandwiched two separate statements into one outburst; one direct (the machine malfunctions), one implied (jail is hell). He could always count on unanimous agreement because at least one of those statements was always correct, automatically ensuring safe passage for the other.

The guards, for their part, tacitly respected this solidarity in a very practical way; they never entered our rabbit warren in groups of less than three, and if an inmate was wanted by Administration for any reason, one of them simply cupped his hands and hollered through the entrance bars down the tier: "Sinclair! Four-Right-Nine!" I was quite startled the first time I heard that call, because after a brief silence a voice far down the tier distinctly hollered back: "You'll never take me alive, copper!" I quickly slid off my bunk to watch the ensuing hassle, but nothing happened and after a while Sinclair was summoned again: "Sinclair! Four-Right-Nine!" Later I found out that this was actually an old ritual, the inmate being summoned automatically hollering his defiance (which varied from the above to responses like "C'mon try and get me, asshole!" and "Try an' make somethin of it, bullmoose!") and settling back for the obligatory second call. That call having been made, and after a decent delay to indicate the appropriate lack of cooperation, the inmate would shuffle down the tier to be administrated unto.

So we spent our days not unpleasantly. Since none of us had as yet been classified,* we could not be given regular jobs and so had a lot of time on our hands. While the cells were open (from 9:00 A.M. to 12:00 noon; from 2:00 P.M. to 4:30 P.M.; from 6:30 P.M. to 10:30 P.M.) we played chess or cards or read books; people drifted in and out spreading the daily rumors or joining the bull sessions that were always under way in one cell or another. At noon we queued up at the "kitchen hole" with our plastic cups and our spoons (no forks or knives permitted), picking up our trays from an unseen hand, which pushed them at us through a slot in the wall. The food generally consisted of potatoes (mashed) and starchy fodder, canned vegetables, salad (sometimes), some form of cheap meat (meat loaf, wieners, hamburger) plus canned or bakery dessert and coffee or tea or powdered milk. As a rule the food was overcooked to the point of falling apart but otherwise it seemed life-supporting enough. As soon as we had returned to our tiers the cells were locked, and we

---

*When a man is first sentenced by the courts, he is automatically sent to the highest-security prison in the Corrections system. Once there, he is watched and interviewed, his record is analyzed, and if he is in consequence deemed sufficiently harmless and stable he is transferred (classified) to a lower security jail, sometimes right down to a minimum-security prison camp, which has no surrounding fence or cells. Unacceptable behavior in any minimum- or medium-security prison generally results in a reclassification back to maximum.

had to slip the emptied trays out under the cell doors for a flunky to pick up.

Two hours later they opened the drums again, and also a heavily fenced-in yard where we shot some of the best basketball games I've ever played. After yard came supper, then movies or gym or simply free time to write letters, read or sleep. Aside from the odd counseling or classification interview, or visits, there was no special claim on our time during those first few weeks.

Something that impressed me particularly at that time was the rapidity with which inmates seemed to unpack their psychic baggage before each other. With a casualness and frankness that struck me as nothing if not quite dangerous, they exchanged confidences and intimacies within minutes of meeting each other, often before it even occurred to them to ask each other's names. It was a catching habit and somehow exciting; there seemed in all of us a willingness, almost an urge to throw away the old rules, a need in some strange way to celebrate our descent into this underworld with a reckless psychical potlatch. Instant friendships sprang up everywhere, alliances were forged and tested, it was all a little like having newly arrived in a foreign country with new papers and a new name. There were many of us on that tier who had never been in jail before.

And yet, as I grew more accustomed to being Inside, I began to discern an underlying pattern that eventually alerted me to the survival techniques at play in this phenomenon. The older or more experienced inmates offered only "stock" or "standard" confidences, things (when you really looked at them) not particularly compromising at all, while the newcomers babbled away facts about former criminal acts, other contacts or friends, home addresses and information about their families—of which the more experienced inmates quietly noted and "filed"; you never knew when you might need the edge over a man who at the moment was not being dangerous, but who could turn into an opponent as quickly as he'd become a friend. Many months later I watched one of these newcomers pay for such indiscretion when he was blackmailed by two lifers into using his visits to bring heroin Inside. As for myself, I learned very quickly to falsify enough details about my Outside life to make it improbable that I should meet any unwelcome ghosts from the past at my door. But if I didn't end up playing directly into someone's hands it was due to sheer luck rather than brains; of the standard list of newcomers' mistakes in prison (whistling in jail, talking to guards, obeying staff commands too promptly, admitting to all your job skills indiscriminately, answering all psychiatrists' questions truthfully, believing more than 10 percent of what you're told and putting non-coded information about your emotional state into letters to the Outside, etc.), I'm sure I committed most of them at one time or another.

And there was another phenomenon, which, concurrent with all our abandon, I could already see becoming increasingly defined: a hierarchy, a rigid pecking order was already relentlessly sorting itself out, eventually floating an elite to the surface which few challenged and even fewer successfully defied. By the time I had been Inside for a week, I had already developed an uncannily sure sense of where a newcomer would eventually come to rest on the social scale; in fact, most of us had done so. There was no distinct pattern to the selection, but one characteristic was unquestionably a major asset: if you clearly didn't *care*, if you could convince inmates and guards that you had absolutely nothing to lose and that your countermeasures to even the most trivial provocation would be totally unrestrained and pursued to the utmost of your abilities—then you were given respect and a wide berth, and people looked to you for leadership and advice. "He's crazy," they'd say admiringly, even longingly, when the name came up. "He's just totally, completely insane."

Maria Campbell

Maria Campbell is best known for her autobiography *Halfbreed*, which relates her struggles as a Métis woman in Canadian society. Considered a sociological tract as well as a moving historical account, the book has been praised for its humour, its documentation of Métis patois and rituals, and its tender portrait of Campbell's loving relationship with her grandmother, Cheechum.

Campbell is additionally known for such children's works as *People of the Buffalo: How the Plains Indians Lived* and *Riel's People*, which relate Métis traditions and history, and for *The Book of Jessica: A Theatrical Transformation*, which documents her attempt to produce a stage adaptation of *Halfbreed* with Linda Griffiths.

Chapter 3 from *Halfbreed*

I was born during a spring blizzard in April of 1940. Grannie Campbell, who had come to help my mother, made Dad stay outside the tent, and he chopped wood until his arms ached. At last I arrived, a daughter, much to Dad's disappointment. However this didn't dampen his desire to raise the best trapper and hunter in Saskatchewan. As far back as I can remember Daddy taught me to set traps, shoot a rifle, and fight like a boy. Mom did her best to turn me into a lady, showing me how to cook, sew and knit, while Cheechum, my best friend and confidante, tried to teach me all she knew about living.

I should tell you about our home now before I go any further. We lived in a large two-roomed hewed log house that stood out from the others because it was too big to be called a shack. One room was used for sleeping and all of us children shared it with our parents. There were three big beds made from poles with rawhide interlacing. The mattresses were canvas bags filled with fresh hay twice a year. Over my parents' bed was a hammock where you could always find a baby. An air-tight heater warmed the room in winter. Our clothes hung from pegs or were folded and put on a row of shelves. There were braided rugs on the floor, and in one corner a special sleeping rug where Cheechum slept when she stayed with us, as she refused to sleep on a bed or eat off a table.

I loved that corner of the house and would find any excuse possible to sleep with her. There was a special smell that comforted me when I was hurt or afraid. Also, it was a great place to find all sorts of wonderful things that Cheechum had—little pouches, boxes, and cloth tied up containing pieces of bright cloth, beads, leather, jewelry, roots and herbs, candy, and whatever else a little girl's heart could desire.

The kitchen and living room were combined into one of the most beautiful rooms I have ever known. Our kitchen had a huge black wood stove for cooking and for heating the house. On the wall hung pots, pans and various roots and herbs used for cooking and making medicine. There was a large table, two chairs and two benches made from wide planks, which we scrubbed with homemade lye soap after each meal. On one wall were shelves for our good dishes and a cupboard for storing everyday tin plates, cups and food.

The living-room area had a homemade chesterfield and chair of carved wood and woven rawhide, a couple of rocking chairs painted red, and an old steamer trunk by the east window. The floor was made of wide planks which were scoured to an even whiteness all over. We made braided rugs during the winter months from old rags, although it often took us a full year to gather enough for even a small rug.

There were open beams on the ceiling and under these ran four long poles the length of the house. The poles served as racks where furs were hung to dry in winter. On a cold winter night the smell of moose stew simmering on the stove blended with the wild smell of the drying skins of mink, weasels and squirrels, and the spicy herbs and roots hanging from the walls. Daddy would be busy in the corner, brushing fur until it shone and glistened, while Mom bustled around the stove. Cheechum would be on the floor smoking her clay pipe and the small ones would roll and fight around her like puppies. I can see it all so vividly it seems only yesterday.

Our parents spent a great deal of time with us, and not just our parents but the other parents in our settlement. They taught us to dance and to make music on the guitars and fiddles. They played cards with us, they would take us on long walks and teach us how to use the different herbs, roots and barks. We were taught to weave baskets from the red willow, and while we did these things together we were told the stories of our people—who they were, where they came from, and what they had done. Many were legends handed down from father to son. Many of them had a lesson but mostly they were fun stories about funny people.

My Cheechum believed with heart and soul in the little people. She said they are so tiny that unless you are really looking for them you will never find them; not that it matters, because you usually only see them when they want you to.

The little people live near the water and they travel mostly by leaf boats. They are a happy lot and also very shy. Cheechum saw them once when she was a young woman. She had gone to the river for

water in the late afternoon and decided to sit and watch the sun go
down. It was very quiet and even the birds were still. Then she heard
a sound like many people laughing and talking at a party. The sounds
kept coming closer and finally she saw a large leaf floating to shore
with other leaves following behind. Standing on the leaves were tiny
people dressed in beautiful colours.

They waved to her and smiled as they came ashore. They told
her that they were going to rest for the evening, then leave early in
the morning to go further downstream. They sat with her until the
sun had gone down and then said good-bye and disappeared into
the forest. She never saw them again, but all her life she would
leave small pieces of food and tobacco near the water's edge for
them which were always gone by morning. Mom said it was only a
fairy tale but I would lie by the waters for hours hoping to see the
little people.

Cheechum had the gift of second sight, although she refused to
forecast anything for anyone. Once in a while if someone had lost
something she would tell them where to find it and she was always
right. But it was something over which she had no control.

Once, when we were all planting potatoes and she and I were cutting out the eyes, she stopped in the middle of a sentence and said,
"Go get your father. Tell him your uncle is dead." I ran for Dad, and
I can remember word for word what she told him. "Malcolm shot
himself. He is lying at the bottom of the footpath behind your mother's house. I'll prepare the others. Go!" (Malcolm was Dad's brother-
in-law.) Dad took off, with me right behind him. When we reached
Grannie Campbell's no one was home. While Dad went to the door I
sped down the footpath. Just as Cheechum had said, my uncle's body
was lying there just as if he was sleeping.

Another time, late at night, Cheechum got up and told Dad that
an aunt of ours was very sick and that he should go for Grannie
Campbell as there was no time to waste. They arrived a few minutes
before the aunt died.

She often had this kind of foresight and would tell Mom and Dad
days before someone died or something happened. I wanted to be able
to see things as she did, but she would reply that it was a sad thing to
know that people who are close to you are going to die or have bad fortune—and to be unable to do anything to help them because it is their
destiny. I am sure that she could see what was in store for me but
because she believed life had to take its course she could only try to
make me strong enough to get through my difficulties.

Qua Chich was Dad's aunt, Grannie Campbell's older sister, a widow, and a strange old lady. She had married Big John when she was sixteen. He had come to the Sandy Lake area before it was made a reserve. He brought with him two yoke of oxen, an axe and a beautiful saddle horse. He settled beside the lake, built himself a large cabin and broke the land. After the first year there was a home, a crop, a garden, and the saddle horse had a colt. He traded one ox for a cow and a calf, the other for another horse, and then went hunting for a wife.

He visited all the nearby families and looked over their daughters, finally settling on Qua Chich because she was young and pretty, strong and sensible. Some years later, when the treaty-makers came, he was counted in and they became treaty Indians of the Sandy Lake Reserve instead of Halfbreeds. Then the great flu epidemic hit our part of Saskatchewan around 1918 and so many of our people died that mass burials were held. Big John went first and a week later his two children.

Qua Chich never remarried; half a century later she still wears widow's clothes: long black dresses, black stockings, flat-heeled shoes and black petticoats and bloomers. She even wore a black money-bag fastened with elastic above her knee, as I discovered one day when peeking under the tent flaps. A small black bitch, blind in one eye from age, went everywhere with her. She scolded it continually, calling it bitch in Cree and accusing it of running around shamelessly with the other dogs.

She was considered wealthy by our standards as she owned many cows and horses as well as a big two-storey house full of gloomy black furniture. She was stingy with money, and if someone was desperate enough to ask for help she would draw up formal papers and demand a signature.

Qua Chich visited her poor relations, the Halfbreeds, every year in early May and late September. She would drive up to our house in a Bennett buggy pulled by two black Clydesdales and set up her own tent for a week. The first afternoon she would visit Mom and Dad. Her black eyes never missed anything and when she focused them on us we would fairly shrink. Sometimes I would catch her watching me with a twinkle in her eye but she would quickly become her usual self again.

The second day of her visit she would rouse Dad and my uncles out of bed early so that they could take her horses to plough and rake our large gardens. In the fall we could haul our supply of wood for the winter. When this was done, she would rest the horses for a day and then go on to visit other relatives. Our people never had strong horses and few had good ploughs, so this was her way of helping. When one of the family married she gave them a cow and a calf, or a team, but the calf was usually butchered the first year and the cow often suffered the same fate. The horses just ended up as Halfbreed horses—fat today, skinny tomorrow.

Once a year we all went to Qua Chich's house, usually when the cows came fresh. She would line the young ones all around the table and bring a pudding from here oven made from the first milking. She would say a prayer in Cree before we ate that awful pudding, and then we were not allowed to talk or make a sound all day, which was very difficult for us noisy, rowdy children. Dad said he had to do this too when he was little.

Once the old lady told me never to look at animals or people when babies were being made or else I would go blind. Of course, this was repeated with great authority among the rest of the kids. About a week later one of my boy cousins looked at two dogs and screamed that he was blind. By the time we helped him to the house we were all hysterical. Cheechum finally calmed us down and found out what had happened. She told us all to be quiet and said, "No one goes blind from seeing animals make babies. It is a beautiful thing. Now stop being so foolish and go and play."

When World War II broke out many of our men were sent overseas. The idea of travelling across Canada was unbelievable enough, but the sea was frightening for those who had to let loved ones go. Many of our men never returned, and those who did were never the same again. Later on, I'd listen to them talk about the far-off places I'd read about in Mom's books, but I never heard any of them talk about the war itself.

Daddy signed up but was rejected, much to his disappointment and everyone's relief, especially Cheechum's. She was violently opposed to the whole thing and said we had no business going anywhere to shoot people, especially in another country. The war was white business, not ours, and was just between rich and greedy people who wanted power.

We also acquired some new relatives from the war: war brides. Many of our men brought home Scottish and English wives, which of course didn't go over very well with our people. They marry either their own kind or Indians. (It is more common among Indians to marry a white.) However, these women came and everyone did their best to make them welcome and comfortable.

What a shock it must have been for them to find themselves in an isolated, poverty-stricken, native settlement instead of the ranches and farms they had believed they were coming to!

Two of the war brides I remember very well. One was a very proper Englishwoman. She had married a handsome Halfbreed soldier in England believing he was French. He came from northern Saskatchewan's wildest family and he owned nothing, not even the shack where a woman and two children were waiting for him. When they arrived, his woman promptly beat the English lady up and gave her five minutes to get out of her sight, and told the man she'd do what the Germans didn't do (shoot him) if he didn't get his ass in the house immediately. Mom brought the woman home and because she had no money and too much pride to write home and ask for some, the people in the settlement got together and collected enough money to pay her way to Regina, where they were sure the government would help her. She wrote Mom a letter from England a year later and was fine.

The other bride was a silly blonde. She married a sensible hard-working man who provided well for her, but she drank and ran around, and was so loud and bawdy that she shocked even our own women. In spite of everything she was kindhearted and likeable, and eventually settled down to raise a large family.

I grew up with some really funny, wonderful, fantastic people and they are as real to me today as they were then. How I love them and miss them! There were three main clans in three settlements. The Arcands were a huge group of ten or twelve brothers with families of anywhere from six to sixteen children each. They were half French, half Cree, very big men, standing over six feet and over two hundred pounds. They were the music-makers, and played the fiddles and guitars at all the dances. We always knew, when arriving at a party, if there was an Arcand playing. They were loud, noisy, and lots of fun. They spoke French mixed with a little Cree. The St. Denys, Villeneuves, Morrisettes and Cadieux were from another area. They were quiet, small men and spoke more French than English or Cree. They also made all the home brew, of which they drank a lot. They were *ak-ee-top* (pretend) farmers with great numbers of poor skinny horses and cows. Because they intermarried a great deal years ago, they looked as scrubby as their stock.

The Isbisters, Campbells, and Vandals were our family and were a real mixture of Scottish, French, Cree, English and Irish. We spoke a language completely different from the others. We were a combination of everything: hunters, trappers and *ak-ee-top* farmers. Our people bragged that they produced the best and most fearless fighting men—and the best looking women.

Old Cadieux was always having visions. Once he saw the Virgin Mary in a bottle when he was pouring home brew, and prayed for a week and threw all his booze out, much to everyone's dismay. The priest had given his daughter a bottle with the Virgin inside to try to scare him our of making home brew and she had put it beside the other empty bottles. Poor old Cadieux! He was very religious and never missed Mass, but he was back making booze again in a week. He made what we called *shnet* from raisins, yeast bran, old bannock and sugar. He kept it in his cellar where we once saw a swollen rat floating in it. He just scooped it out and strained the brew. His wife was a French woman who spoke no English and was almost too fat to move. One daughter, Mary, was tiny, with one of the most beautiful faces I ever saw. She was very religious and wanted to become a nun.

In the Cadieux family was Chi-Georges, son of Old Cadieux. He was short and round with extra-long, skinny arms. He was near-sighted and slow-witted and always drooled. He walked everywhere because he didn't trust horses, and wherever he went he had a bannock under his arm. When he got tired he would climb up a tree, sit on a branch and eat his bannock. If someone asked what he was doing up there he would say, "Hi was jist lookin' 'round to see hif hi could spot a hindian. Don't trust dem hindians!" It was nothing out of the ordinary to go somewhere and see Chi-Georges up in a tree.

He died some years ago after a party with his father. He had been missing for six days when Pierre Villeneuve, out setting rabbit snares, came running to the store all bug-eyed and screaming in French, "He's laughing at me!" The men in the store followed him and found Chi-George lying on a footpath with his head on a fallen tree, his eyes and mouth pecked off by birds. His whole body was moving with maggots. Poor Pierre, who was the local coward, prayed for months, and if he had to go anywhere at night he always carried a rosary, a lantern, a flashlight and matches so he would have a light. He was afraid Chi-George would haunt him.

Then there were our Indian relatives on the nearby reserves. There was never much love lost between Indians and Halfbreeds. They were completely different from us—quiet when we were noisy, dignified even at dances and get-togethers. Indians were very passive—they would get angry at things done to them but would never fight back, whereas Halfbreeds were quick-tempered—quick to fight, but quick to forgive and forget.

The Indians' religion was very precious to them and to the Half-breeds, but we never took it as seriously. We all went to the Indians' Sundances and special gatherings, but somehow we never fitted in. We were always the poor relatives, the *awp-pee-tow-koosons*.* They laughed and scorned us. They had land and security, we had nothing. As Daddy put it, "No pot to piss in or a window to throw it out." They would tolerate us unless they were drinking and then they would try to fight, but received many sound beatings from us. However, their old people, "Mushooms" (grandfathers) and "Kokums" (grandmothers) were good. They were prejudiced, but because we were kin they came to visit and our people treated them with respect.

Grannie Dubuque's brother was chief on his reserve and as they loved me, I often stayed with them. Mushoom would spoil me, while Kokum taught me to bead, to tan hides and in general to be a good Indian woman. They had plans for me to marry the chief's son from a neighbouring reserve when we grew up. But the boy was terrified of me and I couldn't stand him.

They took me to pow-wows, Sundances and Treaty Days, and through them I learned the meanings of those special days. Mushoom would also take me with him to council meetings which were always the same: the Indian agent called the meeting to order, did all the talking, closed it and left. I remember telling Mushoom, "You're the chief. How come you don't talk?" When I expressed my opinion in these matters, Kokum would look at Mushoom and say, "It's the white in her." Treaty Indian women don't express their opinions, Halfbreed women do. Even though I liked visiting them, I was always glad to get back to the noise and disorder of my own people.

---

*Awp-pee-tow-koosons: half people.

Timothy Findley

Timothy Findley is best known as the author of novels such as *The Wars, Famous Last Words, Not Wanted on the Voyage, The Telling of Lies*, and *The Pianoman's Daughter*. This essay comes from his deliciously personal memoir, *Inside Memory*. He has also been an actor and playwright, and short-story writer. To hear him read from his own work is a theatrical event in itself, full of mellifluous tones and distinct voices, and always the warmest of smiles.

Remembrance

Stone Orchard
November 11, 1970
Radio

In the plays of Anton Chekhov, there is always a moment of profound silence, broken by the words: "I remember...." What follows inevitably breaks your heart. A woman will stand there and others will sit and listen and she will say: "I remember the band playing and the firing at the cemetery as they carried the coffin. Though he was a general, in command of a brigade, yet, there weren't many people there. It was raining. Heavy rain and snow."

Or some such thing. And she is transformed, this woman, by her memories—absolutely transformed. And as you watch her and listen to her, you are transformed, too—or something inside you is. You change. Your attitude changes. In a way—if it has been well done— your life changes. Why should this be?

I think one reason must be that Chekhov discovered the dramatic value of memory—that a woman in tears remembers happiness; that a smiling, laughing man remembers pain. This gives you two views in one: depth and contrast. But, there's more to it than that. Memory, Chekhov also discovered, is the means by which most of us retain our sanity. The act of remembrance is good for people. Cathartic. Memory is the purgative by which we rid ourselves of the present.

Because memory is what it is, the first thing we tend to "remember" is that time passes. In going back, we recognize that we've survived the passage of time—and if we've survived what we remember, then it's likely we'll survive the present. Memory is a form of hope.

If the memory is a bad one, say of pain or of a death—then it's clouded. The sharpness is blunted. We remember that we were in pain. But the pain itself cannot be recalled exactly. Not as it was. Because, if we could recall it, then we'd have to be in pain again—and that, except where there's psychological disorder, is a physical and mental impossibility. If you've ever had a bad accident, then you'll remember that you can't remember what happened. But you can recall joy. You can make yourself laugh again and feel again something joyous that happened before.

Of course, you can make yourself cry again, too. But the tears aren't as valid as the laughter, because the tears you conjure have as much to do with the passage of time as with the sadness you remember. Still, a sad memory is better than none. It reminds you of survival.

Most of the activity in your brain relies on memory. That takes energy. Have you ever noticed that when you're tired and there's silence in your brain, you begin to sing? That's good health taking over. The tensions of serious thought are being released through play.

Today is Remembrance Day, and it's a strange thing to me that we confine ourselves to remembering only the dead—and only the war dead, at that. If they were able, what would *they* be remembering? Us. And we're alive. Here we are. Maybe it's sad—I suppose it is—that the dead should be remembering the living and the living remembering the dead. But the main thing is, we all remember when we were together. We remember what we were in another time. Not now, but *then*. Memory is making peace with time.

They say that loss of memory is not to know who you are. Then, I suppose, it has to follow that we *are* what we remember. I can believe that. I mean, it's very easy for me to imagine forgetting my name. That wouldn't worry me. And it wouldn't worry me to forget how old I am (I wish I could!) or to forget the colour of my eyes and have to go look in a mirror to remind myself. None of that would worry me. Because I can skip all of that. None of those things are who I am.

But it would worry the hell out of me if I couldn't remember the smell of the house where I grew up, or the sound of my father playing the piano, or the tune of his favourite song. I remember my brother, Michael, as a child. And the child I remember being myself is as much a remembrance of him as it is of me. More, in fact—because I saw him every day and did not see myself. I heard him every day—and did not hear myself (except singing). So, to be a child in memory means that I conjure Michael, not the child in photographs who bears my name.

I am my Aunt Marg, for instance, telling me not to lean into the cemetery over the fence at Foxbar Road. I am not me leaning over the fence, I am her voice—because that is what I remember. And I am all the gravestones I was looking at when she called me. And the fence boards that supported me. And the sun on my back. But I am not that little boy. I don't remember him at all. I remember him falling and being picked up—but I am the distance he fell and the hands that lifted him, not the bump in between. I remember the sound of my own voice crying—but not the feel of it. That voice is gone. And I am the gloves my mother wore when she held my hand and the tones of her laughter. And I remember and will move forever, as all children do, to the heartbeats of my mother. That remembrance is the rhythm of my life. So memory is other people—it is little of ourselves.

I like Remembrance Day. I'm fond of memory. I wish it was a day of happiness. I have many dead in my past, but only one of them died from the wars. And I think very fondly of him. He was my uncle. He didn't die in the War, but because of it. This was the First World War and so I don't remember the event itself. I just remember him. But what I remember of my uncle is not the least bit sad.

I was just a child—in the classic sense—a burbling, few-worded, looking-up-at-everything child. Uncle Tif—who died at home—was always in a great tall bed—high up—and the bed was white. I would go into his room, supported by my father's hands, and lean against the lower edge of the mattress. There was a white sheet over everything, and I can smell that sheet to this day. It smelled of soap and talcum powder. To me, Uncle Tif was a hand that came down from a great way off and tapped me on the head. He smoked a pipe. And there was something blue in the room—I don't know whether it was a chair or a table or my father's pant legs—but there was something blue and that has always been one of my favourite colours.

And high above my head, there was a tall glass jar on a table and the jar was full of hard French candies. They had shiny jackets and were many colours. And Uncle Tif's hand would go out, waving in the air above my gaze and lift up the lid of the jar and take out a candy and slowly—it was always slowly—he would pass the candy down into my open mouth. Then I would lean against the bed, or fall on the floor, and taste the candy for about two hours—or what, to a kid, just seemed two hours—while the adult voices buzzed above my head.

I know he sacrificed his youth, his health, his leg and finally his life for his country. But I'd be a fool if I just said *thanks—I'm grateful*. I might as well hit him in the mouth as say that. Because my being grateful has nothing to do with what he died for or why he died. That was part of his own life and what I am grateful for is that he had his own life. I am grateful he was there in that little bit of my life. And I am grateful, above all, that he is in my memory. I am his namesake. He is mine.

Remembrance is more than honouring the dead. Remembrance is joining them—being one with them in memory. Memory is survival.

David Carpenter

David Carpenter writes (more and more) and teaches (less and less) in Saskatoon. He brought out his second collection of essays in the fall of 1997, a book about seasonal rituals entitled *Courting Saskatchewan*. His fourth book of fiction, a novel entitled *Banjo Lessons*, came out in the spring of 1997. He sleeps nightly and fishes daily and paddles his boat with a ukulele.

Minding Your Manners in Paradise

When I was a little boy, I had no trouble imagining Paradise in very specific terms. No angels and saints for me. My Paradise would look just like Johnson Lake, a small reservoir fifteen minutes drive from Banff, Alberta on the Lake Minnewanka Road. It was stocked with rainbow and brook trout that grew prodigiously fast on big nymphs, snails, and freshwater shrimp and spawned spring and fall in the feeder stream. I caught my first trout there and my brother hauled in a 6 pound rainbow at the age of six.

When I was in my late teens, I used to fly fish there with my friend Peter Hyndman. We came to Banff to work in the summer partly because of the fly fishing. We were just out of high school and convinced that at the secret heart of the unfolding cosmos was nothing but fun. There were more parties here in one month than we had ever gone to in a year, more unattached girls than we had ever seen. And one or two nights a week, we would declare a health night and go casting on the banks of Johnson Lake. In my first summer in Banff I landed a four pound brook trout and Hyndman brought in a 5 1/2 pound rainbow. We were becoming legends in our own time, at least among the trout. The girls were another thing entirely.

Each summer we returned and took the well worn trail around Johnson Lake. Always there was wildlife. One night a very large black bear came down to the lake to drink, or perhaps to stare at the bizarre fly lines whipping through the late summer air. The bear came right up to me. I think I detected an air of disapproval. This was 1960 or '61, and bears were still so common and innocuous, we hadn't learned to fear them. The bear and I looked at each other from a distance of perhaps 20 feet. It saw that I wasn't going to feed it, and so it lumbered into the jackpine. Hyndman and Carpenter returned to their casting.

A big rainbow was rising just beyond my fly, so I waded in and tried again. Night was falling and Hyndman had brought in his line.

"One more cast," I tell him.

This is the most commonly spoken promise by a fisherman, and the least likely to be honoured. I threw out a big bucktail right where the trout had been rolling in the sunset. I let my line sink and began a slow retrieve. My bucktail became an escaping minnow. Jerk jerk jerk, and suddenly the tip of my rod plunged down. A tailwalking olympian had grabbed my fly. He leapt high out of the water, paused for a moment to defy gravity, and plunged back in. He took off for the middle of the lake and my reel whined high and frantic.

"Should I get the net?" Hyndman yelled to me.

"Yes," I must have said to Hyndman, "get the net."

Hyndman got the net and waded over to me while the rainbow cavorted and leapt and took shorter and shorter runs.

"Don't lose him."

Any non-fisher might think that this advice was labouring the obvious. But an angler knows that this is a good luck spell one casts for another.

The rainbow seemed to be tiring. It was pointed down and tailing feebly into the gravel. This passive stance allowed me to ease it closer and closer to the net. Hyndman stretched toward the fish. Dark blue on the back, silver on the sides with a long stripe of pink. It was more than two feet long. It was bigger than Hyndman's 5 1/2 pound rainbow. It was going to be gutted and filled with wild mushroom stuffing and baked for a gathering of at least a dozen friends. It was going to ingratiate me with a half dozen mountain beauties and be bragged about for years to —

Snap!

A side to side motion of its head, the rainbow's way of saying NO to the dreams of a young man intent on becoming a legend. Gone. The king of the rainbows tailed its way back into the deep water as uncatchable as the great white whale.

One of the differences between old anglers and young anglers is in what they tell their friends. We told our friends everything about Johnson Lake. We even took them there. We took our girlfriends there, baiting their hooks with big juicy worms and nymphs. Our friends told their friends and their friends told their friends. By the mid-sixties, this lake, which I felt Hyndman and I had owned, became host to dozens of anglers a day and one or two wild parties each night in the campground. You could hear the voices of folksingers and the sound of guitars and bongos. Always those plaintive undergraduate voices puling about the misfortunes of picking cotton in the hot sun or mining for coal. I was one of those folk-singers.

I even remember once throwing a half finished bottle of wine into the lake. Someone had noticed the approach of an R.C.M.P. patrol car, and I was still under age. I threw the bottle into the lake in panic and stumbled off into the woods. The wine in question was pink, cheap, and bubbly. It was called *Crackling Rose*. Does anyone else remember *Crackling Rose*?

The problem with Paradise is always the people who go there.

Johnson Lake declined rapidly as a fishing spot, and by the mid-70s, it was only good for a few trout of the pan-sized variety. By and by, the parks people stopped stocking it.

By the 1980s I had given up on Johnson Lake. It was overfished, and the only catchable trout at this time seemed to be spawners. And then an incredible thing happened. I was driving by one evening for a nostalgic look at the lake of my youth. At most I'd hoped to get a glimpse of an osprey or a rising trout. I parked my car in a newly constructed parking lot with signs and fancy latrines and picnic benches. I took our old path to the rise overlooking the lake. I looked at the lake.

More accurately, I looked *for* the lake. In the evening light, it appeared to be gone. Perhaps I blinked or shook my head. It *was* gone. The dam at the near end of the lake had burst, leaving behind an ugly grey scar. A prank, I was told later. I raced down to what had been the shore of the lake. I leapt into the muddy cavity. I walked all the way down to the middle of the lake to what would have been one of the deepest holes. All I could find was a trickle from the feeder stream.

How many magnificent memories had that lake held? Standing in the muddy bottom, I had a last look and slowly trudged back. Perhaps a hundred feet from shore my foot dislodged something that made me look down. A wine bottle. It was unbroken and it had no label. But I could tell at a glance from the shape and colour that it had once been a bottle of *Crackling Rose*. I suppose it could have been the bottle of some other folksinger, equally drunk and irre-sponsible, but I think it was mine. I took the bottle, communed with it for a while, and threw it into the garbage container next to my car. But the bottle wouldn't go away. It contained messages from those carefree years. 1960, 1961, 1962, 1963, 1964, 1965 ...*Michael row your boat ashore, Hallelujah ...*

This story began with the discovery of my wine bottle. The lake of all memories seemed to disgorge a sad and bounteous flow of them. I had heard often enough that the mind is like a lake that harbours memories in the great Unconscious. But now it seemed to me that the lake was like a huge mind. The more I looked at its vast muddy grey container, the more it poured out the ghosts of its former life, and mine. I was saddened by the usual things. The loss of youth. The loss of that feeling that said the sky was the limit. The inevitable comparisons between the bounteous past and the fishless present. But I think what bothered me most of all was that I had betrayed my lake. I'd made it known to mobs of people unworthy of its great gifts. I'd conspired against my lake by leaving my trash behind and using it merely for my pleasure. I had not taken the time to become my lake's custodian.

Stories like this are legion, and they almost always end in a sad nostalgic sigh. But this one doesn't. A few weeks ago I was in Banff on business. The town had transformed from a place where families came to stay and see the wonders of nature to a place where wealthy foreigners come to shop. Walking down Banff Avenue was an agony. I decided to get out of town and go for a drive. It was more habit than intention that took me out to Johnson Lake, and there I made *another* amazing discovery: it was once again brim full of water and trout! If there's a god that presides over this earthly Paradise, he works for the fisheries department and stocks fish for a living. He is the Johnny Appleseed of the freshwater kingdom. God bless him wherever he goes.

If you should happen to come upon my new old lake, you'll have no problem recognizing me. I'm the balding guy in the belly boat who floats like a frog and hums old folk songs. I'll watch how you dispose of your garbage, if you stick to your limit, whether you bring a ghetto blaster to drown out the sounds of the wilderness, whether you tear up the trail with your ATV. If you fail any of my tests, I will be unforgiving. If you're foolish enough to throw a bottle into the lake, beware. You may not see me *do* anything, but if a huge bear should amble down to your campsite and send you up a tree, don't say I didn't warn you.

CHAPTER THREE: NARRATIVE ESSAYS

This section could be subtitled "Why I Am More Interesting Than My Neighbour." As E.B. White once said, the essayist is probably the ultimate egotist of all writers, and nowhere is it more obvious than in a narrative essay. "Sit back and allow me to tell you what happened to me, because it is worth listening to." Of course, given the observation and facility with language of good writers, this is most often the case. Narrative is perhaps the most familiar form of writing we can come across, since we all instinctively understand the construct. We tell stories with beginnings, middles, and ends, and have done so even before we were inundated with those conjuring words "Once upon a time." When we have coffee with our friends between classes, our escapades of the previous weekend come out as narratives.

If, as we spoke of in the last section, a descriptive essay is a "portrait in place" or a verbal still life, then a narrative is a "portrait in time." To extend the visual art metaphor, a narrative is a verbal movie. The most important decisive factor about a narrative essay is chronology. How do you order your story? Do you "start at the very beginning," like Maria von Trapp in *The Sound of Music,* or do you backtrack to fill in the blanks for your reader only when necessary, beginning with the results and moving back into the history of the event to show how it came about? However you decide to order your narrative, be sure to indicate the destination for your readers. You may want to do this with an opening paragraph stating where you intend to go with the essay ("To fully appreciate why I am thinking of donating my liver to the Smithsonian Institute, you have to be privy to how I spent my first few years of University"), or you may just want to lead your willing reader along with signpost terms like *before, after that, as soon as, a few days later, while the elephant was eating my Tilley hat,* and hope they follow you along your merry narrative path.

Of course, there has to be a purpose to the telling of your tale. This purpose should become obvious to readers as they read; it needn't necessarily be hammered into place with a neon-lit thesis statement. With any luck, we've advanced past the "how I spent my summer vacation" stage, and your narrative essay will enlighten the world by means of a telling incident in your life. It may entertain, it may inform by shedding light on an event or situation out of the ordinary, it may offer a new point of view on a seemingly ordinary happening.

The great advantage a narrative essay has over telling your tale at the coffee break is that there is no rude person with a better story about to break in on you. This means that you don't need to fill the air with meandering, unnecessary words while holding the floor, trying to think of what to say next. You can be to the point, lingering only on the passages that you wish to highlight, skipping through the dross ("it happened last Tuesday, no, maybe it was Wednesday, well, Wednesday was the day I had the cat de-wormed, so it must have been Tuesday, well, not that it matters, anyway…."). Your readers can be amused, horrified, brought to tears, elated or diverted by your story if you offer it to them as a honed and crafted version of the truth as you know it. What's more, they won't put down your essay and head off to do something more interesting, like bleaching the grouting between the tiles in their bathrooms.

Just because your essay is within the realm of "non-fiction" and thus, by extension, has to be "truthful" doesn't mean that every minute section of your life has to be recorded within the construct. You are the writer, you are the one who gets to decide what moments are the important moments. This is the only perk to being a writer, to tell you the truth. Otherwise it's just a life of sitting alone in front of a computer monitor, interspersed with people asking you what you do for a "real job."

Let me illustrate the concept of choosing one's narrative moments. A few months ago I bought a new car, which is one of those once every decade or so "when the struts crack" sort of impulse buy for me. I was driving my lovely new car home from an evening class down a rather dark residential street. Coming toward me was a car without its headlights on. Instinctively, in that international signal known to all to indicate that "your lights aren't on," I reached for my brights to flick at the approaching car. Instead, I politely washed my windshield at him (the international signal for "I have no idea where things are on my new car"). I had to pull over and stop because I was laughing too hard to drive safely.

At the same time as I was automatically storing the incident for future retelling, the voice of a friend accompanying me on a similar silly incident (my life is a cabaret, I tell you) recurred to me. Just at this aftermath point, she had turned to me and said, "I can't wait to hear just how you're going to tell this one!" Now, I hasten to swear to you that I *never* lie when I relate the strange and funny things that happen to me. I do admit, however, to embroidering, winnowing, and teasing things into a presentable package. In the previous anecdote you didn't need to know what sort of car I had bought, what sort of car I used to drive, what class I was teaching, whether it was winter or summer, what colour my new car is, whether the approaching car even knew what I was up to, what my driving record is, or if I have figured out yet how to set the clock in the car to get the gist of the story. So, I left all that out. (However, for all of you who hunger for truth, it's red, and no, but my ten-year-old child showed me how.)

The interesting rhetorical thing about narrative, like description, is that we can use it to advantage within the format of essays which are not predominantly narrative in structure. Sometimes all that is required within a persuasive or comparison essay is a short anecdotal section to illustrate a point you are trying to make. For ease of understanding, however, I've grouped together a few essays that are mainly narrative in their format, so you can pick narrative structure out every time on a "blind taste test," should one occur.

The essays chosen in this section are all similar in that they use the first person to bring the reader closer to the incidents depicted. Scott Young's offering is from his autobiographical work *Neil and Me*, where he writes of his other claim to fame beyond being one of Canada's foremost sports and mystery writers: being rock star Neil Young's father. I once heard Scott read this passage to a group of hardened, embittered, anti-social indigents (i.e., writers) and we were all in tears at the poignant and vulnerable emotion obvious in the deceptively simple phrasing. Before you snort derisively at my seeming sappiness, let me add that I have never cried at any of my viewings of *Bambi*.

Novelist Thomas King also uses simple phrases and situations but in his essay, "The Open Car" (from the PEN collection entitled *Writing Away*), he deals with two narratives, which both feature different versions of an "open car." An examination of the two stories, in tandem, sheds light on each narrative. It is of interest to see how he transmits political anger with a deceptively mild voice. Polemic is often easy to avoid, when hammered at us from a self-appointed pulpit or soapbox, but when it is delivered within the disguise of a witty story, it tends to find its mark.

Margaret Atwood wrote "Under the Thumb: How I Became a Poet" with her tongue firmly in her cheek, and yet, there is likely more there for aspiring writers to take to heart than in many how-to books. Humour and invention can often be a disarming strategy to make your point to your reader. Check out in particular the way in which she uses the stereotypes we've developed about poets and explodes them to her advantage.

The section from Barry Broadfoot's *Six War Years* has an anonymous credit, for self-explanatory reasons, being that it is the narrative of how a young woman slid into prostitution during the early 1940s here in Canada. The chronology is so effortlessly clear, that it is a stunning example of simple narrative structure. This was written by a "non-professional" writer, which is also one of the reasons it was chosen. Remember as you read it, however, that it is only her writing style I am advocating you consider adopting.

Nancy Gibson spent a year in Sierra Leone, after a twenty-six year absence. She had returned to conduct research for her PhD in Anthropology, but found herself enmeshed in a terrifying and incomprehensible war. This section of her memoir, *War and Rumours of War*, deals with a frightening evacuation from Kenema, which was being overrun by rebel forces, to Freetown, the capital of Sierra Leone. The choices of which details to highlight, and where dialogue becomes the best mode of narrative over description, makes it a useful example of narrative strategy.

While dealing with a study of narrative, it is useful to look around beyond the context of the material assigned. Can you find narratives in the journalism you read in the daily newspapers? How do radio interviews come across? As mere question and answers? Or as mini-narratives? And go for coffee; listen carefully to the weekend escapades of your friends. How have they structured them to their most entertaining advantage?

Moreover, think of something that has happened to you recently. How can you tell it to someone to get all the nuances of emotion, delight, importance, or interest across to another reader? Sit down and write it out. And then send it to your mother. She would love to hear from you.

Scott Young

Scott Young is a writer, broadcaster, and journalist. He won his first National Newspaper Award in 1959 and has never looked back. His non-fiction titles include *Gordon Sinclair: A Life ...*, *And Then Some*, and *The Boys of Saturday Night: Inside Hockey Night in Canada*. He has also turned his hand to mystery writing with élan, and produced the Inuit detective, Matteesie Kitologitak, who has appeared in the novels *Murder in a Cold Climate* and *The Shaman's Knife*.

His other claim to fame, of course, is being the father of the renowned singer/songwriter Neil Young. That experience is described in *Neil and Me*, from which the following is taken.

Polio Was a Killer—and Neil Had It

You have to be a certain age to remember the polio epidemic in the late summer of 1951, before there was Salk vaccine to control the disease. In Omemee, as elsewhere in Canada, the headlines every day gave the statistics, usually using the phrase "infantile paralysis" because the killer disease most often struck the young. News reports explained the different types. One form could kill a person in a few hours. Another could result in paralysis and leave a person crippled for life. People that August stayed away from fairs and exhibitions and were urged to avoid mingling in crowds anywhere. In cities the ultra-cautious walked instead of taking streetcars, and kept their distance from everyone else. City or country, the fearful woke in the night wondering if that back pain was the polio back pain, or that sore throat was the polio sore throat. There was, however, no polio in Omemee as the summer wore on into early September and the ducks began to flock up on the lake and partridges in farm wood lots began to feed in late afternoons under the apple and hawthorn trees.

Then Omemee did have its first case, and ten days later in September I went up to my third-floor study and wrote something, not for sale, but just so I would remember. It sat in my files for nearly thirty years, unpublished. Here it is, exactly as written in 1951:

The night that polio first made my younger son groan sleepily in his bed, I was reading. It was past one o'clock and I was the only one awake in the house. I waited for a minute or two after the first sound I heard from Neil's room. He seemed to be mumbling to himself. I got out of bed, trying not to disturb my wife, and opened his door. In the dim light that shone across the hall from my reading light I could see that he had squinched (as he called it) down to about the middle of his bed, as usual, and that he was awake.

"What's the matter, pally?" I asked.

"Nothing," he said. He's a noisy enough kid in the daytime, but at night, or when he is sleepy, he has a soft, clear voice and always is very polite. He is five years old.

"Want to go to the toilet?"

"No, thank you."

I went over to the side of his bed and started to tuck the covers around his neck and he said, with sort of a protesting whine, "Hey!"

"What's the matter?"

"My back hurts."

I touched his forehead and he seemed a little too hot. "Where?" I asked.

He reached around exploringly with his left hand and indicated the middle of his back. But when I touched him there, he said no, it was over farther. Finally we settled on his right shoulder blade. I noticed in the dim light that there were tears in the corners of his eyes. He had a round, tanned face; a crew cut, very big eyes.

"Did you fall and hurt yourself today?" I asked.

"No."

"Bang it on anything?"

"No."

I stood by his bed for a minute. As parents know, we all live with the word *polio* for months every year. I got an aspirin and some water and he moved very gingerly when he sat up to take the pill, but he took it.

"Good night, pal," I said from the doorway.

"Good night. See you in the morning," he said in his small, formal night voice.

I went along the hall for a minute and listened outside Bob's door. Bob is nine. He was sleeping peacefully. I looked out at the village street. It is very quiet in the country at night. Just seven or eight hours earlier, Neil and I had been at the village swimming hole together and he'd had a great time riding on my stomach while I swam on my back across the river. I seem to pray a lot more easily in the polio season than at other times of the year. Quite often I'd been one of God's requestmen in the middle of the night when my wife or one of our boys was sick. So I was one of His requestmen again, there at the window, before I went back to bed.

Rassy stirred and said, "What's the matter?"

"Neil's a little restless," I said. "I gave him aspirin."

He was quiet the rest of the night. I was up first in the morning, still the cook because my wife was just about three days out of hospital, where she'd had a minor operation. She said she'd come down. I went along the hall to call Bob and paused when I heard Neil's voice.

"I don't want any breakfast," he said.

I opened his door. "How's your back?"

"It hurts."

I got a thermometer and took his temperature. It was 100°F. Downstairs, while the coffee water boiled, I got some honey in a dish, and a spoon. Neil has a tendency to acidosis, which complicates every illness he has. He protested, but not too much. He took three teaspoons of honey. That, or syrup, or anything sweet, fights acidosis. Then I closed his door. Downstairs I told Rassy his symptoms and his temperature. Neither of us said the word we both were thinking, because so often before we'd been scared by false alarms.

"We'd better phone Bill," she said.

Bill Earle is our doctor, known in the village as Dr. Bill to distinguish him from his father, Dr. George. I phoned him at his summer cottage twenty miles north. He came a little before noon. I was out. When I got back I asked Rassy, "How's Neil?"

She was very pale. Her face sort of broke up when she started to cry. "Bill thinks he's got it," she said. She said a minute or two later, into my shoulder, "He's coming back about four." She told me that Neil couldn't touch his chin to his chest, and had cried out when his knees were bent and moved upward towards his chest. Dr. Bill had given him a penicillin injection, which the British found useful in polio although they are not sure why. Neil was sleeping now.

It was a grim afternoon. Even Bob, who usually spent these last days of the summer holidays swimming or swiping apples or boiling corn from farmers' fields down by the river with his pals, stayed around home. I just kept putting the thought of polio out of my mind. I thought of having a drink but we didn't, for no particular reason. When Bill came again at four, after his office hours, I went upstairs with him to Neil's room and watched.

All his reflexes seemed good. But when he got up to go to the bathroom he moved like a mechanical man, jerkily, holding his head in a tense position. And when he was back in bed he cried out when his head or neck was touched, and also when his legs were bent too far. Bill covered him up and beckoned me into the bedroom across the hall.

"He's a little worse," he said.

"What do we do?"

"One of two things. Either we can take him into Peterborough and do a lumbar puncture to confirm it, or you can take him into Toronto. If you take him to Toronto they'll do a lumbar puncture there." He explained that a lumbar puncture was the practice of taking off a small amount of spinal fluid and testing it for the presence of white cells, which would mean polio, for sure.

"Which is best, Peterborough or Toronto?" I asked.

He lit a cigarette. "I hate to say this," he said, "but you'll understand that it's better to look at the darkest side. There's only one iron lung in Peterborough and it's in use. The chances are good that he won't need one, but if you're taking him any place you may as well take him where there are a lot of iron lungs. That's better than having him go bad suddenly in Peterborough and having to be taken to Toronto in the middle of the night in an ambulance."

"When should we take him?"

"How about an hour and a half?" he asked. "Eat something, bundle him up well. I'll phone Toronto and tell them you're coming. I'll give you some disinfectant. After you get him into the hospital, whisk out your car. I'll also get him a surgical mask. Put him in the back seat."

"Do you think Rassy could stand the trip?" I asked.

"I think so. Better for her to be along and know what's going on than sitting here seven or eight hours wondering. Bob could go along, too. You won't be able to stay in Toronto overnight, though. You're quarantined."

"Okay," I said. "Let's tell them."

So we went downstairs and told Rassy and Bob.

That morning I had bought Neil a toy locomotive that gave off a clacking noise when pulled on a flat surface. He held it, but didn't clack it very much on the way into Toronto. For the ninety miles he lay on the back seat and watched the lightning of the harsh storm through which we travelled. Bob counted cars. It was the Friday night of the Labour Day weekend and we had a lot of traffic to buck. He counted 154 cars in one five-mile stretch, got the count to 1,000 in another twenty miles, and then quit. Rassy was quiet, keeping her face averted from Bob and me. Neil grumbled some about the surgical mask, but Rassy leaned over into the back seat occasionally and spoke soothingly. At 8:30 we pulled up at the admitting entrance for the Hospital for Sick Children. I went inside. A couple of women were standing by the admitting desk, talking to the nurse there.

"I have a boy in a car outside," I said. "Neil Young. Dr. William Earle of Omemee phoned about him."

The nurse looked through some notes she had, found nothing.

"What is it that's the matter?" she asked.

"Polio," I said.

The two women standing there moved swiftly, sidelong, away from me. The nurse said quickly, "Bring him in."

Writing this now, I keep asking myself, what were you thinking? I don't know what I was thinking. One of the bad things about having polio in the family is the sound of the term. There is so much dread and fear and helplessness in the word that if a man wants to do the things he has to do, the things I was doing, he has to keep it from his mind. I had kept it from mine fairly well until I had to say the word. Then when the women cringed away from me in the modern hospital in a city wet and fresh from rain, with the cars zipping over the black pavement outside and the lights of the taverns flicking on and off in promised pleasure, it was like a scene from the Middle Ages when a man spoke the name of the plague.

I carried him in. The poor little guy was stiff and it hurt him to move, but I got him comfortably into my arms, him and his toy locomotive, and I carried him through the door. A second nurse was waiting. An attendant got a wheelchair, and without any pause for paperwork at the admitting desk I pushed him along the corridor behind the nurse and into a tiny room and lifted him from the wheelchair to a high rubber-tired table. The nurse donned a mask before she went near him.

During all this time, Rassy had done well. She had broken down only once, and that time when we were alone, the two of us. But now, when the admitting doctor began to give Neil the tests for pain and stiffness, she couldn't stand it. She went back to the car. And she couldn't stand that either, and came back at the wrong time, when Neil was screaming behind a closed door while the doctor and nurse did the lumbar puncture. That time she fled and

I couldn't see her face. The doctor came out in a few minutes with the sample of spinal fluid, and said, "He wouldn't take the sedative. We had to do it without."

He hurried away. I waited. I went in and talked to Neil and tried to calm him down. He said he wished Dr. Bill was here. "Dr. Bill wouldn't stick a needle in me," he said, although Dr. Bill often had given him shots in the past. "I want to go to sleep," he moaned, over and over again.

We waited.

About fifteen minutes later the doctor came back. He walked in, took a deep breath, and said, "The test is positive. That means he has the disease."

Arrangements were started immediately to have Neil admitted to the isolation ward. The doctor who wrote down Neil's medical history (a series of questions including such items as: Was he breast-fed or bottle-fed? What was his formula as a baby? Was condensed milk used or whole milk? When did he walk? Talk? Get his first tooth?) told me that Neil would be in isolation for seven days. If paralysis or weakness developed he'd then be moved to a surgical ward for therapy. If not, he'd be sent home. He said that as long as Neil had a temperature there was danger of paralysis, and that weaknesses had developed as long as six months after the first signs of the disease. He said we'd have to spend the next seven days waiting. By that time the temperature usually was gone.

So we waited. The waiting began immediately. Neil was wheeled off by a masked nurse from the isolation ward. On the drive home that night, we tried to reassure ourselves with the fact that the speed with which the disease had been diagnosed was a good sign, and that he had the best possible chance of coming out of this whole. After all, we argued to ourselves, some victims of polio die in a few hours. Others have paralysis almost from the beginning. I suppose the thought occurred to all of us that we had been exposed to the disease as much as anyone ever could be, if it was contagious. Only Bob mentioned it, and that briefly. "I hope Neil is all right," he said. "I hope we don't get it."

That week was hellish. Each day we phoned the hospital. The first day the nurse said he had spent a bad night, in considerable pain, and that he had a temperature. She wouldn't tell us what temperature. The next day the report was better. I can't remember much about that week. I was the only one of the family allowed out of our yard, and only to buy groceries. The white quarantine sign greeted me each time I returned to the house. We got used to it. Or rather we got so that we could keep our minds blank, or almost blank, trying to ignore the lifetimes of fear of the words on the sign, "Poliomyelitis. Infantile paralysis." We talked to the doctor on Wednesday and he assured us that Neil was coming along fairly well. That was the fifth day. On the sixth we got a phone call from the hospital.

"Mr. Young?" the nurse said. "I'm glad to say that you can come and take Neil home with you now."

I remember when I typed that last line I started to cry and couldn't go any further. By that time Neil had been home two or three days and was in his bed downstairs, very weak. All of us spent a lot of time in there with him, talking. Remember, he was only five years old then and his scope of experience was narrow. "Polio is the worst cold there is," he confided to me one day. It was years later before he told me he could still remember sitting in the hospital cot half upright, holding the sides to keep himself there because it hurt his back so much to lie down. But then he would fall asleep and let go, and when he fell back the pain would waken him again, crying.

The first thing he said when we picked him up at the hospital was "I didn't die, did I?"

Thomas King

Thomas King was born in 1943 in Sacramento, California, and is of Cherokee, Greek, and German descent. He obtained his PhD from the University of Utah in 1986. He is known for works in which he addresses the marginalization of American Indians, delineates "pan-Indian" concerns and histories, and attempts to abolish common stereotypes about Native Americans.

He taught Native American Studies at the University of Lethbridge in Alberta, Canada, and since 1989 has been associate professor of American and Native studies at the University of Minnesota. King has become one of the foremost writers of fiction about Canada's Native people. He received the Governor General's Award in 1992 for *Medicine River*, and other titles by King include *Green Grass, Running River*, *All My Relations*, and *A Coyote Columbus Story*. *The Dead Dog Café Comedy Hour*, which King writes and co-stars in, can be heard on CBC Radio.

"The Open Car" appears in the PEN anthology, *Writing Away*.

The Open Car

My brother and I grew up in a small town in central California. My mother ran a beauty shop out of our house. She worked long hours, and what I remember most was that we were the only family in the neighbourhood who didn't have a television or a car.

That's what my mother wanted. A car. A convertible. When we got a car, she told Christopher and me, we could put the top down and get away. We could go on a trip. We could travel.

Three weeks ago, I had to go from Toronto to New York, and because I had some time before and after my meetings, I persuaded Helen that we should travel by train. I pointed out that a train trip would give us a chance to relax and see the countryside. She reminded me that I was simply terrified of flying and would do anything to stay off a plane.

Which is true.

Nonetheless, I prevailed on her generous spirit and bought two rail tickets for New York. It was a twelve-hour trip, and Helen was sceptical.

"What are we going to do for food?"

"They have food on the train," I told her. "It's got to be as good as anything you get on a plane."

Helen packed apples, grapes, ham and cheese sandwiches, water, juice, cookies, yogurt, crackers into two plastic bags, lugged them on the train, and arranged them like small pillows around our feet. Just as the train pulled away from Union Station, she remembered we had to cross a border.

"We have to eat all the apples before we get to Niagara."

"How many do we have?"

"Eight."

My mother believed that travelling was broadening, that by visiting other people and other places you became more tolerant and understanding. And she believed that travel was magic.

I ate two apples. Helen ate one. When we arrived at Niagara Falls, and the American border guards came on the train, we still had five apples.

The border is the part of the trip that Helen doesn't like. Leaving Canada and crossing to the States. She is a staunch nationalist, and the only pleasure she takes in going from one country (home) to the other (the evil empire) is in telling the guards (when they ask) that she is Canadian. She was hardly in a mood to give up five perfectly good apples, I can tell you that.

Outside the train, two station wagons pulled up with German shepherds in the back seat. These were not pets. At the time, I supposed that they were drug-sniffing dogs, but I wasn't sure, and I wasn't going to ask.

The guards worked their way through the train in twos, coming along the aisles slowly, checking passports, asking questions. There was a young black man sitting in front of us. He was, from the sound of his voice, from the Caribbean, and when they got to him, the guards stopped.

My mother travelled through her music. Every Sunday morning, she would stack records on the phonograph spindle, and, when they had all dropped onto the turntable, she would lift them off, turn them over, and begin again. They were musicals, for the most part, and operas—*Carmen, La Traviata, The Desert Song, South Pacific*.

There was a globe in the living room, and while the music played and my mother sang along with each piece, Christopher would find Spain and Italy and Arabia and Tahiti on the map.

One of the guards began asking the man a series of questions—where he was from, where he was going, how long he was going to stay.

And more questions.

Did he have any cigarettes. Any liquor. Any drugs. How much

money was he carrying. Did he have a job. The guard asked the man about marijuana several times, each time hooking his lips around his fingers and sucking on an imaginary joint with practised ease to demonstrate exactly what they were looking for.

The man's responses were low and flat, so much so that neither Helen nor I could hear the answers even though we leaned forward in our seats on the pretext of looking out the window.

Evidently, the first guard couldn't hear the man either, for he became irritated and then angry. The man continued in his low, patient way, until finally the guard stopped him and motioned for him to stand up.

"Get your bags and your identification," the guard told the man, "and see immigration in the open car."

The man got his duffel bag from the overhead, smiled at the guard, and walked slowly towards the back of the train. The guard watched the man go. Then he took two steps forward and leaned in to Helen and me. Helen settled into her seat and locked her feet around the food.

"Citizenship?"

"Canadian."

"Canadian."

"Where are you going?"

"New York."

"New York."

The guard smiled at Helen as if she had just told him she thought he looked spiffy in his uniform and then he tipped his hat, just the way the sheriff always did in the Westerns I saw as a kid.

"Have a nice day," he said.

That was it. No liquor, no cigarettes, no drugs, no money, no job. No apples. No open car. As the guard stood by our seats, just before he moved on to the next person, I had two competing emotions.

First, I was appalled that they had not taken us to the open car, where Helen could have told them what they could do with our five apples. And, second, I was relieved.

We stayed at the border for about an hour. Just before the train rolled out of the station, the black man returned to his seat. He was still smiling as he slung his bag into the overhead. He sat down next to the window, put his head against the glass, and went to sleep.

I was about fifteen when my mother got her first car. It was a pink Plymouth Fury convertible with enormous fins and a cutaway at the headlights that made it look a little like a shark. My mother was proud of that car. On days when she finished work early, she would put the top down and drive it around town, slowly, as if she were in a parade. She always wore dark glasses and a long yellow scarf that floated above the back seat.

Just as soon as the car was broken in properly, my mother told us, we would pack up our stuff and go on a trip.

New York was fun. Not as clean as Toronto and a little scarier—and Helen pointed these differences out to me—but fun. Even Helen had a good time, though she was not unhappy when we got back on the train to come home.

We did not take much food with us on this part of the trip. Helen forgot about it until all the stores near our hotel had closed. We walked around the area, but nothing was open.

We were reduced to boarding the train early the next morning with nothing more than a pitiful bag of bran muffins, four little bottles of orange juice, and six bananas.

About six months after she got the car, my mother announced that we were going to take a trip. She got a road map from the gas station and laid it out on the table. Christopher and I watched as she worked her way down the coast and through the mountains, circling places as she went. Later, she took a ruler and measured out the distance, converted it into miles, and figured out how much the gas would cost to get there and back.

Then she folded the map up and put it away.

When we got to the border at Niagara for the second time, we were met by Canadian border guards.

"Watch this," Helen told me as the guards came on the train.

Actually, the Canadian guards looked pretty much the same as the American guards.

"Look around," Helen said. "Do you see any dogs?"

There were no dogs, at least none that I could see. But there were people standing on the platform taking pictures of the train.

"Maybe they can't afford dogs."

Why do we travel? Obviously, because we can afford to. Time. Money. Time and money. Perhaps it is a particular inclination curiosity, romance, distraction. Perhaps it is nothing more than that.

I have friends who travel regularly, and when they say travel, they

mean trips that involve great crossings—oceans, continents, hemi-
spheres—and visits to great cities—Paris, Rome, Bombay, Tokyo,
London. They leave home with vaccinations and visas and return
with colour slides and colds.

As I recall, the Canadian guards had guns. Helen disputes this vigorously. In any case, they came through the train in twos, asking the
same questions that the Americans had asked. And when they got to
an East Indian couple, they stopped.

Every week, on Saturday (as long as the weather was good), we
would get up early and wash the car. We washed it twice with deter-
gent and then rinsed it gently with the garden hose, so we wouldn't
get water on the upholstery or hurt the finish. Christopher and
I crawled around under the seats, picking up twigs and leaves,
little stones, lint, and pieces of a bubble-gum wrapper, while my
mother took an SOS pad to the whitewalls and scrubbed them until
they glowed.

We told her we'd like to go to Donner Lake or to the ocean, and
my mother said that that was a great idea.

The East Indian man told the border guard that he and his wife were
Canadian citizens.

"Do you have any proof of citizenship?"

The man smiled and nodded his head and handed the guard two
passports. The first guard looked at the passports for a moment and
then handed them to his partner, who flipped through the pages,
looking at each one in great detail.

"What's the purpose of your visit?"

"We live in Toronto."

"How much liquor are you bringing back into Canada?"

"None."

"Cigarettes?"

"No."

"Presents?"

"Nothing."

The first guard turned to his partner. Then he turned back to the
couple.

"Get all your bags and your identification," the guard said, "and
take them to immigration in the open car."

One day, my mother walked over to my aunt's house and left the car sitting in the carport. I grabbed the keys from the hook and Christopher got the map and we jumped in the car and put the top down, just the way we had seen Mom do it.

Then I started the car, left it in park, and revved the engine a couple of times. It was exciting sitting there behind the wheel, with the top down, Christopher calling out the towns we were passing and the towns we were coming to.

We had only been driving for about five minutes, when the car suddenly shuddered, coughed a couple of times, and died. I tried starting it, but it was no use. Christopher and I got out of the car and put the top back up. I hung the keys back up on the hook and Christopher put the map away.

The next day, my mother tried to start the car, but nothing happened. Later Mr. Santucci came by. He poured some gas into the tank and tinkered around under the hood, and in about an hour the car was running just fine.

When the guard got to us, I was ready for him.

"Citizenship?"

"Canadian."

"Do you have any cheese?"

I must admit, the question threw me, and had I had my wits about me, I am certain I could have come up with a clever response.

"No," I said.

"Have a nice day," said the guard.

My mother never travelled. She stayed home. I think she would have liked to travel, but she had my brother and me and the beauty shop. My father travelled. He started travelling just after Christopher was born and never came back. Perhaps he is still travelling.

Customs cleared the train, and the East Indian couple returned to their seats. As we pulled away from Niagara, I went back to the open car to see what we had missed, which, as it turned out, wasn't much. The open car was a cramped affair with a bar off to one side where you could get frozen hot dogs, pizza, hamburgers, nachos (microwaved while you waited), and a variety of drinks.

It had all the ambience of a small bus station. There were no tables or chairs, nothing convenient for an intimate conversation or an interrogation. Whatever you wanted to eat or do had to be managed standing, and I wondered what the immigration people could have done to the black man and the East Indian couple in a room like this.

When I got back to my seat, I told Helen about the open car.
"Did they have any yogurt?"
"They had pizza."
"Salads?"
"Hot dogs."

My mother no longer wants to travel. At least that's what she tells me. When Helen and I went to New York, my mother flew to Toronto to watch the kids. Have a good time, she told us. If you want to stay a few extra days, don't worry about anything.

So I told her about the car and what Christopher and I had done. When I finished the story, she looked at me and shook her head. The Plymouth was a hardtop, she said. The Pontiac was a convertible. And the Plymouth hadn't run out of gas, it had been a problem with the alternator. John Varris fixed that, she told me, not Mr. Santucci. If you're going to tell a story, she insisted, at least get the facts right.

We waited and ate when we got back to Toronto. A nice little restaurant on Queen. As we sat there waiting for the server, Helen began to laugh.

"What do you think the Americans would have done to us if they had found the oranges?"
"You mean apples."
"What apples?"

After we ordered, Helen slid a guidebook across the table. "We should go there next," she said, and she spread a map of Ireland out across the table and began running the coastline with her finger, stopping here and there to read a description from the book.

My mother was right. The Pontiac was the convertible.

Margaret Atwood

Margaret Atwood was born in 1939 in Ottawa and grew up in northern Ontario, Quebec, and Toronto. She received her undergraduate degree from Victoria College at the University of Toronto and her master's degree from Radcliffe College. She is the author of more than twenty-five books. Her most recent works are the novels *Alias Grace*, *The Robber Bride*, and *Cat's Eye*, the story collections *Wilderness Tips* and *Good Bones and Simple Murders*, and a volume of poetry, *Morning in the Burned House*.

Among the many honours she has received are the Governor General's Award, The Sunday Times Award for Literary Excellence in the U.K., and Le Chevalier dans l'Ordre des Arts et des Lettres in France. Ms. Atwood's work has been published in more than twenty countries.

This essay appeared in *This Magazine*.

Under the Thumb: How I Became a Poet

I recently read an account of a study that intends to show how writers of a certain age—my age, roughly—attempt to "seize control" of the stories of their own lives by deviously concocting their own biographies. However, it's a feature of our times that if you write a work of fiction, everyone assumes that the people and events in it are disguised biography—but if you write your biography, it's assumed you're lying your head off.

The latter may be true, at any rate of poets: Plato said that poets should be excluded from the ideal republic because they are such liars. I am a poet, and I affirm that that is true. About no subject are poets tempted to lie so much as about their own lives; I know one of them who has floated at least five versions of his autobiography, none of them real. I, of course, am a much more truthful person than that. But since poets lie, how can you believe me?

Here, then, is the official version:

I was once a snub-nosed blonde. My name was Betty. I had a perky personality and was a cheerleader for the college football team. My favorite color was pink. Then I became a poet. My hair darkened overnight, my nose lengthened, I gave up football for the cello, my real name disappeared and was replaced by one that had a chance of being taken seriously, and my clothes changed color in the closet, all by themselves, from pink to black. I stopped humming the songs from **Oklahoma!** and began quoting Kierkegaard. And not only that —all of my high-heeled shoes lost their heels, and were magically transformed into sandals. Needless to say, my many boyfriends took one look at this and ran screaming from the scene as if their toenails were on fire. New ones replaced them: they all had beards.

Believe it or not, there is an element of truth in this story. It's the bit about the name, which was not Betty but something equally nonpoetic, and with the same number of letters. It's also the bit about the boyfriends. But meanwhile, here is the real truth:

I became a poet at the age of 16. I did not intend to do it. It was not my fault.

Allow me to set the scene for you. The year was 1956. Elvis Presley had just appeared on the **Ed Sullivan Show**, from the waist up. At school dances, which were held in the gymnasium and smelled like armpits, the dance with the most charisma was rock'n'roll. The approved shoes were saddle shoes and white bucks, and the evening gowns were strapless, if you could manage it; they had crinolined skirts that made you look like half a cabbage with a little radish head. Girls were forbidden to wear jeans to school, except on football days, when they sat on the hill to watch and it was feared that the boys would be able to see up their dresses unless they wore pants. TV dinners had just been invented.

None of this—you might think, and rightly so—was conducive to the production of poetry. If someone had told me a year previously that I would suddenly turn into a poet, I would have giggled. (I had a passable giggle, then.) Yet this is what did happen.

I was in my fourth year of high school. The high school was in Toronto, which in the year 1956 was still known as Toronto the Good because of its puritanical liquor laws. It had a population of 650,509 people at the time, and was a synonym for bland propriety, and although it has produced a steady stream of chartered accountants and one cabinet minister, no other poets have ever emerged from it, before or since—or none that I know of.

The day I became a poet was a sunny day of no particular ominousness. I was walking across the football field, not because I was sports-minded or had plans to smoke a cigarette behind the field house—the only other reason for going there—but because this was my normal way home from school. I was scuttling along in my usual furtive way, suspecting no ill, when a large invisible thumb descended from the sky and pressed down on the top of my head. A poem formed. It was quite a gloomy poem; the poems of the young usually are. It was a gift, this poem—a gift from an anonymous donor, and, as such, both exciting and sinister at the same time.

I suspect this is why all poets begin writing poetry, only they don't want to admit it, so they make up explanations that are either more rational or more romantic. But this is the true explanation, and I defy anyone to disprove it.

The poem that I composed on that eventful day, although entirely without merit or even promise, did have some features. It rhymed and scanned, because we had been taught rhyming and scansion at school. It resembled the poetry of Lord Byron and Edgar Allan Poe, with a little Shelley and Keats thrown in. The fact is that at the time I became a poet, I had read very few poems written after the year 1900. I knew nothing of modernism or free verse. These were not the only things I knew nothing of. I had no idea, for instance, that I was about to step into a whole set of preconceptions and social roles that had to do with what poets were like, how they should behave, and what they ought to wear; moreover, I did not know that the rules about these things were different if you were female. I did not know that "poetess" was an insult, and that I myself would someday be called one. I did not know that to be told I had transcended my gender would be considered a compliment. I didn't know yet that black was compulsory. All of that was in the future. When I was 16, it was simple. Poetry existed; therefore it could be written. And nobody had told me—yet—the many, many reasons why it could not be written by me.

At first glance, there was little in my background to account for the descent of the large thumb of poetry onto the top of my head. But let me try to account for my own poetic genesis.

I was born on November 18, 1939, in the Ottawa General Hospital, two and a half months after the beginning of the Second World War. Being born at the beginning of the war gave me a substratum of anxiety and dread to draw on, which is very useful to a poet. It also meant that I was malnourished. This is why I am short. If it hadn't been for food rationing, I would have been six feet tall.

I saw my first balloon in 1946, one that had been saved from before the war. It was inflated for me as a treat when I had the mumps on my sixth birthday, and it broke immediately. This was a major influence on my later work.

As for my birth month, a detail of much interest to poets, obsessed as they are with symbolic systems of all kinds: I was not pleased, during my childhood, to have been born in November, as there wasn't much inspiration for birthday-party motifs. February children got hearts, May ones flowers, but what was there for me? A cake surrounded by withered leaves? November was a drab, dark, and wet month, lacking even snow; its only noteworthy festival was Remembrance Day, the Canadian holiday honoring the war dead. But in adult life I discovered that November was, astrologically speaking, the month of sex, death, and regeneration, and that November 1 was the Day of the Dead. It still wouldn't have been much good for birthday parties, but it was just fine for poetry, which tends to revolve a good deal around sex and death, with regeneration optional.

Six months after I was born, I was taken in a wooden box to a remote cabin in northwestern Quebec, where my father was doing research as a forest entomologist. I should add here that my parents were unusual for their time. Both of them liked being as far away from civilization as possible, my mother because she hated housework and tea parties, my father because he liked chopping wood. They also weren't much interested in what the sociologists would call rigid sex-role stereotyping. This was beneficial to me in later life, as it helped me to get a job at summer camp teaching small boys to start fires.

My childhood was divided between the forest, in the warmer parts of the year, and various cities, in the colder parts. I was thus able to develop the rudiments of the double personality so necessary for a poet. I also had lots of time for meditation. In the bush, there were no theaters, movies, parades, or very functional radios; there were also not many other people. The result was that I learned to read early— I was lucky enough to have a mother who read out loud, but she couldn't be doing it all the time, and you had to amuse yourself with something or other when it rained. I became a reading addict, and have remained so ever since. "You'll ruin your eyes," I was told when caught at my secret vice under the covers with a flashlight. I did so, and would do it again. Like cigarette addicts who will smoke mattress stuffing if all else fails, I will read anything. As a child I read a good many things I shouldn't have, but this also is useful for poetry.

As the critic Northrop Frye has said, we learn poetry through the seat of our pants, by being bounced up and down to nursery rhymes as children. Poetry is essentially oral, and is close to song; rhythm precedes meaning. My first experiences with poetry were Mother Goose, which contains some of the most surrealistic poems in the English language, and whatever singing commercials could be picked up on the radio, such as **You'll wonder where the yellow went / When you brush your teeth with Pepsodent!**

Also surreal. **What yellow?** I wondered. Thus began my tooth fetish.

I created my first book of poetry at the age of five. To begin with, I made the book itself, cutting the pages out of scribbler paper and sewing them together in what I did not know was the traditional signature fashion. Then I copied into the book all the poems I could remember, and when there were some blank pages left at the end, I added a few of my own to complete it. This book was an entirely satisfying art object for me, so satisfying that I felt I had nothing more to say in that direction, and gave up writing poetry altogether for another 11 years.

My English teacher from 1955, run to ground by some documentary crew trying to explain my life, said that in her class I had showed no particular promise. This was true. Until the descent of the giant thumb, I showed no particular promise. I also showed no particular promise for some time afterwards, but I did not know this. A lot of being a poet consists of willed ignorance. If you woke up from your trance and realized the nature of the life-threatening and dignity-destroying precipice you were walking along, you would switch into actuarial sciences immediately.

If I had not been ignorant in this particular way, I would not have announced to an assortment of my high school female friends, in the cafeteria one brown-bag lunchtime, that I was going to be a writer. I said "writer," not "poet"; I did have some common sense. But my announcement was certainly a conversation stopper. Sticks of celery were suspended in mid-crunch, peanut butter sandwiches paused halfway between table and mouth; nobody said a word. One of those present reminded me of this incident recently—I had repressed it—and said she had been simply astounded. "Why?" I said. "Because I wanted to be a writer?"

"No," she said. "Because you had the guts to say it out loud."

But I was not conscious of having guts, or even of needing them. We obsessed folks, in our youth, are oblivious to the effects of our obsessions; only later do we develop enough cunning to conceal them, or at least to avoid mentioning them at parties. The one good thing to be said about announcing myself as a writer in the colonial Canadian fifties was that nobody told me I couldn't do it because I was a girl. They simply found the entire proposition ridiculous. Writers were dead and English, or else extremely elderly and American; they were not 16 years old and Canadian. It would have been worse if I'd been a boy, though. Never mind the fact that all the really stirring poems I'd read at that time had been about slaughter, battles, mayhem, sex, and death—poetry was thought of as existing in the pastel female realm, along with embroidery and flower arranging. If I'd been male I would probably have had to roll around in the mud, in some boring skirmish over whether or not I was a sissy.

I'll skip over the embarrassingly bad poems I published in the high school yearbook (had I no shame? Well, actually, no), mentioning only briefly the word of encouragement I received from my wonderful grade 12 English teacher, Miss Bessie Billings: "I can't understand a word of this, dear, so it must be good." I will not go into the dismay of my parents, who worried—with good reason—over how I would support myself. I will pass over my flirtation with journalism as a way of making a living, an idea I dropped when I discovered that in the fifties, unlike now, female journalists always ended up writing the obituaries and the ladies' page, and nothing but.

But how was I to make a living? There was not then a roaring market in poetry. I thought of running away and being a waitress, which I later tried but got very tired and thin; there's nothing like clearing away other people's mushed-up dinners to make you lose your appetite. Finally, I went into English literature at university, having decided in a cynical manner that I could always teach to support my writing habit. Once I got past the Anglo-Saxon it was fun, although I did suffer a simulated cardiac arrest the first time I encountered T. S. Eliot and realized that not all poems rhymed anymore. "I don't understand a word of this," I thought, "so it must be good."

After a year or two of keeping my head down and trying to pass myself off as a normal person, I made contact with the five other people at my university who were interested in writing, and through them, and some of my teachers, I discovered that there was a whole subterranean wonderland of Canadian writing that was going on just out of general earshot and sight. It was not large: In 1960, you were doing well to sell 200 copies of a book of poems by a Canadian, and a thousand novels was a best-seller; there were only five literary magazines, which ran on the lifeblood of their editors. But while the literary scene wasn't big, it was very integrated. Once in—that is, once published in a magazine—it was as if you'd been given a Masonic handshake or a key to the Underground Railroad. All of a sudden you were part of a conspiracy. People writing about Canadian poetry at that time spoke a lot about the necessity of creating a Canadian literature. There was a good deal of excitement, and the feeling that you were in on the ground floor, so to speak.

So poetry was a vital form, and it quickly acquired a public dimension. Above ground, the bourgeoisie reigned supreme, in their two-piece suits and ties and camel-hair coats and pearl earrings (not all of this worn by the same sex). But at night, the bohemian world came alive, in various nooks and crannies of Toronto, sporting black turtle-necks, drinking coffee at little tables with red-checked tablecloths and candles stuck in Chianti bottles, in coffeehouses—well, in the one coffeehouse in town—listening to jazz and folk singing, reading their poems out loud as if they'd never heard it was stupid, and putting swear words into them. For a 20-year-old, this was intoxicating stuff.

By this time, I had my black wardrobe more or less together, and had learned not to say "Well, hi there!" in sprightly tones. I was publishing in little magazines, and shortly thereafter I started to write reviews for them too. I didn't know what I was talking about, but I soon began to find out. Every year for four years, I put together a collection of my poems and submitted it to a publishing house; every year it was—to my dismay then, to my relief now—rejected. Why was I so eager to be published right away? Like all 21-year-old poets, I thought I would be dead by 30, and Sylvia Plath had not set a helpful example. For a while there, you were made to feel that, if you were a poet and female, you could not really be serious about it unless you'd made at least one suicide attempt. So I felt I was running out of time.

My poems were still not very good, but by now they showed—how shall I put it?—a sort of twisted and febrile glimmer. In my graduating year, a group of them won the main poetry prize at the university. Madness took hold of me, and with the aid of a friend, and another friend's flatbed press, we printed them. A lot of poets published their own work then; unlike novels, poetry was short, and therefore cheap to do. We had to print each poem separately, and then disassemble the type, as there were not enough a's for the whole book; the cover was done with a lino block. We printed 250 copies and sold them through bookstores for 50 cents each. They now go in the rare-book trade for $1,800 a pop. Wish I'd kept some.

Three years or so later—after two years at graduate school at the dreaded Harvard University, a year of living in a tiny rooming-house room and working at a market-research company, and the massive rejection of my first novel, as well as several other poetry collections—I ended up in British Columbia, teaching grammar to engineering students at eight-thirty in the morning in a Quonset hut. It was all right, as none of us were awake. I made them write imitations of Kafka, which I thought might help them in their chosen profession.

In comparison with the few years I had just gone through, this was sort of like going to heaven. I lived in an apartment built on top of somebody's house, and had scant furniture; but not only did I have a 180-degree view of Vancouver harbor, I also had all night to write. I taught in the daytime, ate canned food, did not wash my dishes until all of them were dirty—the biologist in me became very interested in the different varieties of molds that could be grown on leftover Kraft dinner—and stayed up until four in the morning. I completed, in that one year, my first officially published book of poems and my first published novel, which I wrote on blank exam booklets, as well as a number of short stories and the beginnings of two other novels, later completed. It was an astonishingly productive year for me. I looked like **The Night of the Living Dead**. Art has its price.

This first book of poems was called **The Circle Game**. I designed the cover myself, using stick-on dots—we were very cost-effective in those days—and to everyone's surprise, especially mine, it won the Governor General's Award, which in Canada then was the big one to win. Literary prizes are a crapshoot, and I was lucky that year. I was back at Harvard by then, mopping up the uncompleted work for my doctorate—I never did finish it—and living with three roommates named Judy, Sue, and Karen. To collect the prize, I had to attend a ceremony at Government House in Ottawa, which meant dressups— and it was obvious to all of us, as we went through the two items in my wardrobe, that I had nothing to wear. Sue lent me her dress and earrings, Judy her shoes, and while I was away they all incinerated my clunky, rubber-soled Hush Puppies shoes, having decided that these did not go with my new, poetic image.

This was an act of treachery, but they were right. I was now a recognized poet and had a thing or two to live up to. It took me a while to get the hair right, but I have finally settled down with a sort of modified Celtic look, which is about the only thing available to me short of baldness. I no longer feel I'll be dead by 30; now it's 60. I suppose these deadlines we set for ourselves are really a way of saying we appreciate time, and want to use all of it. I'm still writing, I'm still writing poetry, I still can't explain why, and I'm still running out of time.

Wordsworth was partly right when he said, "Poets in their youth begin in gladness / But thereof comes in the end despondency and madness." Except that sometimes poets skip the gladness and go straight to the despondency. Why is that? Part of it is the conditions under which poets work—giving all, receiving little in return from an age that by and large ignores them. Part of it is cultural expectation: "The lunatic, the lover, and the poet," says Shakespeare, and notice which comes first. My own theory is that poetry is composed with the melancholy side of the brain, and that if you do nothing but, you may find yourself going slowly down a long dark tunnel with no exit. I have avoided this by being ambidextrous: I write novels too.

I go for long periods of time without writing any poems. I don't know why this is: as the Canadian writer Margaret Laurence indicates in **The Diviners**, you don't know why you start, and you also don't know why you stop. But when I do find myself writing poetry again, it always has the surprise of that first unexpected and anonymous gift.

Barry Broadfoot

Barry Broadfoot compiled *Six War Years* from conversations begun with "What did you do during the war?" In its entirety, the book is a moving account of a country at war, in the best of oral history tradition. Broadfoot's other books in this vein include: *Ten Lost Years: Memories of Canadians Who Survived the Depression, The Immigrant Years: From Europe to Canada, My Own Years, Years of Sorrow, Years of Shame: The Story of Japanese-Canadians in World War II, The Veterans Years: Coming Home from the War,* and *Next-year Country: Voices of Prairie People.*

This selection from *Six War Years* was retrieved in 1974, from a woman who shall remain nameless.

Drifting Into It

In 1941 I was just 16 when I suddenly grew up and boy, did I ever grow up. Betty Grable had nothing on me. All over. I still have some pictures of me at Centre Island, me in a bathing suit on the beach and I was, as they say, stacked. And that's where I met my husband.

His name was Gary and his family had a small farm somewhere near Peterborough. Gary was a good-looking cuss and soon I was meeting him about three times a week because he was training just outside Toronto and could get the mail truck or some truck every night and go back out with it. When I took him home my dad was in one of his good moods that night and he took to Gary. I should say my mother was sick most of the time, lying on the chesterfield or in her room, but she met Gary and said he was a nice boy. From those two, that was a compliment and a half.

Okay, quickly. I married him, at City Hall, on a Friday afternoon, and we went to Niagara Falls for the weekend and that was just about my married life. He got notice, it was posted that his bunch were going to New Brunswick for final training, and when it came time for him to come back on his embarkation furlough, he just didn't show up. I guess he found another girl in Halifax or somewhere.

Anyway, no Gary—and I can't really say I was heartbroken. Nothing like that. I guess I was more pissed off—excuse me, angry— than anything. I wasn't jilted, because he was my husband, but I guess you could say I was abandoned, but I kept telling myself I didn't care. I wasn't pregnant—those three days at Niagara Falls hadn't taken, and I was getting my allowance and the twenty bucks he signed over. I'd quit school, of course, and was working in a restaurant on Yonge Street and, all in all, you might say, I wasn't doing too bad. I got a letter from him saying he was going overseas. Just that. Not love and kisses, just so long. Maybe I should have been suspicious about a guy that my dad and mother liked. But remember, I was only sixteen.

From then on it was the same old story, you might say. I started going to dance halls downtown with my girlfriend Maggie Smythe, just looking for fun. All the boys were in uniform and everybody had a lot of money and there was fun around.

The first time. It was in a dance hall on the second floor and it was painted green. I always remember that. The Beer Barrel Polka was big stuff then, everybody danced it, and I think the Lambeth Walk. There were a whole lot of new dances, and all these good-looking boys. One I got to like, he was an air force something or other at the manning pool, he asked if I would go to a hotel with him and I didn't even think it over too much. I just said yes. Yes, just like that. I wanted to. I wanted him and he wanted me. So we went to this hotel just down the street. It might have been the Ford Hotel, but I'm not sure. We made love and then he took me to a nice restaurant and we had fish and chips, and that was the first time I ever tasted that kind of sauce they put on the side of your plate. I always remember that.

The next night or the next time I was there we went again and this time he gave me a cashmere scarf. Soft. I won't say that's the way it started, but a cashmere scarf, that was something. So the next time a fellow asked me I said yes, and this one gave me 3 dollars. When we came back, Maggie and I went into the little girls' room and she said, "Are you doing it?" I said I had and she asked how much and I said 3 dollars. Three dollars was not enough, she said. Five dollars, that's how much I should get.

You just seem to drift into these things. Quite honestly, cross my heart, I didn't think of it as prostitution. I wasn't hanging around the Union Station or the hotels or, well, those places. These were just real nice guys, mostly air force, who were at this dance. Oh ho, what a dumb little girl I was.

I guess it got through my thick skull what I was doing when I wasn't getting a meal or a scarf but 10 or 15 dollars a night, from the two or three guys taking me out. One night I did four fellows and I found out, I noticed, about the third guy that it was the same hotel room all the time. These fellows had come in from Trenton or someplace and took a room just for a good time.

Then Maggie came to me and she said we should rent a room by the month, the two of us and she would use it half an hour and then me, and then she would, and we couldn't get our times mixed up and there would be the rent and the hotel clerk, he'd be paid off and we'd give him some more for the police, the cop on the beat, if he got suspicious. She said, "Mary, remember, this is a business. You're not selling fountain pens in Woolworth's, you're selling your body, so you got to keep clean. Keep clean and pretty"—and remember, I was only seventeen at the time.

I think I was making about 700 dollars a month within a couple of months, working with Maggie, and I was away from home and living over near Jarvis and dressing well, and I never solicited. Just the dance halls and if some guy, usually an officer, wanted me to go down to London or up to Ottawa with him, well I did. I was a prostitute but I don't feel I was a whore. A whore, I've always thought, stands on street corners.

This went on for two more years. We never had a pimp, and when Maggie left for Halifax I kept on alone. I was never lonely and I was never arrested. You can't think of me as doing this alone. I knew lots of girls, oh hell, dozens of them whose husbands were away, overseas, everywhere, and they did it, and some right in their own homes. Some with their own kids in the next room.

Look at me. Do I look as though I had a terrible time? The prostitute all beat up by some drunks? That never happened to me, but it did to some of the other girls but I was just lucky, and I always let them know two things. One, that I was a lady, and the other was that I was the boss and no funny stuff.

We were a club too. Like on Fridays, afternoons, we'd often get together at one of the girls' apartments and paint each others' legs. You know, leg paint. They didn't have nylons then, the war, so you used leg paint. I think there were seven colours you use and we'd paint each others' back seams and drink coffee or tea and talk and mend clothes and giggle. We'd never talk men. We weren't professionals in the sense I'd heard that kind of girl talk in cafés when I'd be in there. We were just kids, and every moment seemed to be excitement. Pure excitement. You might say, though, you had to like going to bed with a feller. You would have to say that.

Then Gary got killed in England. His plane was in an accident. I never did get the details. The chaplain's letter just didn't make too much sense, just that there had been an accident and everybody died as brave men. Some nonsense like that.

I thought it over—and remember I wasn't more than nineteen at the time—and I had nearly 5,000 dollars in the bank and 4,000 in Victory bonds and so I just quit. I just quit and I stayed away from downtown Toronto and moved into another apartment and read a bit and learned to cook and had one friend who I'd let come in. He was an officer, a nice guy. After the war I took a trip across the country and on the train coming back, the C.P.R., I met this guy who got on at Banff and we hit it off and I married him a month later. I told him my money came from my aunt's estate and I had no other relatives, and really I didn't, far as I was concerned, and that's about all there is to say about it. I'm happy now.

Nancy Gibson

In 1994, Nancy Gibson and her daughter Carolyn travelled to Sierra Leone, Africa, at the invitation of Dr. Sama Banya (presently Minister of Foreign Affairs and International Cooperation), to conduct research for Nancy's PhD in Anthropology. They went to Kenema, where twenty-six years earlier, Nancy had helped Sama to develop the Nongowa Clinic when she worked as a nurse with CUSO. Instead of being able to conduct research within a familiar environment, they discovered themselves caught up in a unruly and confusing "civil" war. Added to this was an unfamiliarity with a country that had much of its former social structures sadly eroded. This essay deals with their evacuation from Kenema to the relative safety of Freetown. Nancy's memoirs are soon to be published under the title *War and Rumours of War*. Dr. Nancy Gibson is the Chair of Human Ecology at the University of Alberta, in Edmonton, Alberta.

The Road to Freetown

Journal entry: March 13th

Yesterday morning Dr. Ellco knew that it was time to leave the Panguma hospital altogether. So he loaded up his family, the priest, another volunteer doctor from New Zealand, Ann Greeling, and several African nuns, in a couple of Land Rovers. As they were leaving the hospital compound his car was ambushed. His wife and baby and the priest were killed immediately, but he was wounded, and continued to drive toward the gate. The rebels shot the car tires and the car stopped. Ann Greeling, the volunteer doctor from New Zealand, was hiding on the floor of the back seat. She managed to slip out of the car and into the bush. She hid there for a while, and then when she thought the rebels had gone, she came back to help anyone still alive in the car. But the rebels were still there and chased her back into the bush again, firing at her.

In despair, from where she was hiding behind a rock, she raised her hand.

"New Zealand," she shouted. They stopped firing.

They took her prisoner and held her while they killed the wounded Dr. Ellco and burned his Land Rover. Then a rival group appeared, and began firing on Anne's attackers. She managed to escape once more, and some of the second group took her to a near by barracks, from whence she was taken to Kenema, and then on to the Mission House in Bo, and eventually to Freetown.

Before what came to be known as the Panguma incident, the war was still being described as factional. Now, with the deaths of international aid workers and missionaries, it was definitely something else. This incident, widely reported in the local newspapers, and even in the international media, forced a refocusing, an acknowledgement of the arbitrary nature of the banditry. There was a brief rumour, quickly lost in the pain and sorrow of the atrocities, that the murders resulted from resentment from a staff firing. Too simple. But we were still seeking logical explanations for the unexplainable, reasons for the irrational.

The rumours of Panguma reached us that day in Kenema, but were unsubstantiated till the next day, when Ann Greeling passed through and visited briefly with Emad the pharmacist. We did not see her, but he sent for us just after she left for Bo. From his apartment I telephoned to Canada, telling our family that we were thinking of leaving Kenema. We packed quickly that night, prepared by our practice session after the Eastern Motel attack.

The road to Freetown had been closed except to daily military convoys which sometimes included civilian vehicles. Geoff and Judy from British WaterAid came to our apartment once again to offer us a place in the military escort leaving for Freetown that afternoon. This time I reluctantly accepted. We had an hour to get ready.

We went to see the staff at Nongowa Clinic. All night there had been gun fire near by.

I listened to Aniru Conteh's earnest advice. "We know how to hide in the bush, Nancy. You don't. Leave now, take Carolyn and go to Freetown." After Panguma we had become a liability to the Clinic.

Ada, Mary, Dr. Conteh, the rest—they all stood along the porch, watching us walk away. I was shamed. I was abandoning them. Is this how Dr. Ellco had felt?

"It is impossible not to get involved." Carolyn spoke quietly. "This is our war now, Nancy." She took my hand and we walked back across Kenema town, the mother and daughter relationship eclipsed by our equality in the face of uncertainty.

Geoff met us at the apartment at eleven with a Land Rover. We bade Hawa a casual farewell, betrayed by our tears. I asked Hawa and her family to live in our apartment while we were away. Not only would that provide a measure of security to our home, but it would give that family some relief from the crowding of the Banya compound. We promised to return soon, even as doubt floated all around us.

It took another two hours to gather up the people in the WaterAid compound into two Land Rovers, a small pick-up truck driven by

Cameron, a Scottish mechanic, and two huge open lorries laden with over a hundred Sierra Leonean employees of WaterAid and their families, their bundles, chairs and chickens. Directed by the determined calm of Geoff and Nigel, the young regional director, our part of the convoy left the WaterAid compound at 2 P.M. with Carolyn and I in the back seat of Nigel's Land Rover. There were two other WaterAid men with us. We drove to Bandama at the edge of Kenema, the junction with the main highway to Freetown, to meet the ECO-MOG army escort. The local troops guarding the highway had been largely replaced by the West African peace keeping forces. Confidence in the local army had vanished.

Another long wait. The soldiers, our guards, were reluctant to take us over the road between Kenema and Blama, the site of the attacks and burnings of the past week. They had a very practical excuse—they were afraid they might run out of gas. Or so they said. Nigel offered them petrol. Still they stalled, repairing a supposedly flat tire.

We were all restless as the hot afternoon wore on. Nigel was rearranging the luggage in the back of the Land Rover.

"Carolyn, is the strangely shaped box among your essential baggage a guitar, by any chance?" Carolyn's face became guarded.

"Why?" She was afraid she'd be forced to leave it behind.

But Nigel asked, "Can you play it?"

"Sort of." Her voice betrayed her relief. "Can you play it, Nigel?"

"May I try?"

"Of course, please do!" Carolyn laughed.

Nigel unpacked the guitar from its case, and climbed up onto the hood of the Land Rover. "Come on, Carolyn." He pulled her up beside him.

For the next hour or so they sang Cat Stevens, John Denver and Beatles songs, many of them 1960s peace songs. I listened to the John Lennon refrain, "I dreamed the world had all agreed to put an end to war," as I walked back and forth among the vehicles, singing some of the words to myself. Incredulous, I watched some of the soldiers dancing beside their tent at the check point.

Suddenly the escort was ready and the atmosphere changed. Everyone quietly got back into the cars. Nigel said, "Good luck, everyone," reaching out his hand. We all touched his hand, then sat back as he steered us into the line up. And we entered a vacuum of timelessness.

Nigel, as driver of the lead car, had made a pact to drive only as fast as the slowest vehicle, Cameron's pick-up truck, with its excessive load of people. I looked back at the truck and the lorries. They were filled to the brim with people, children and belongings hanging over the sides, completely unprotected from the gun fire. We passed over the road at a crawling 45 km/hour, always keeping the open trucks behind us in sight. I felt so much safer behind the roof and windows of a Land Rover, even if they are not protection from bullets. The armed escort was firing to scare off potential rebels. I don't think we were ever fired at directly, but I am not sure. That stretch of road between Kenema and Bo normally takes only forty-five minutes or so—twenty with Mohammed just last week. My eyes burned from scanning the brush for rebels. I saw the burnt villages, and the frames of the taxi and the two Red Cross trucks and other abandoned vehicles. I couldn't see the bodies still inside some of them, unclaimed as yet by their frightened families. I wondered fleetingly what they'd look like now. Inside our vehicle the silence was broken only by the gunfire. I remember being suddenly furious with Carolyn for being so tall. I kept pushing her down in the back seat of the Land Rover, trying to force her to fit below the seat at my knees, out of sight. Her voice reached me, softly.

"Mum, I can't go down any further."

Then, from where I sat behind the driver's seat, I massaged Nigel's rigid shoulders. I had a desperate need to soothe him, us, everyone.

At one point the narrow red road bed had been cut between two high bluffs, towering twenty feet on either side above the vehicles. All of us looked up, scanning the grass at the top. The convoy stopped. We watched the soldiers descend from their vehicles to scout the bushes along the edge.

"A great place for an ambush." But no one said it out loud.

The hundreds of hours of this passage ended at the check point just before Bo. Nigel released his grip on the steering wheel to hold his palm in the air once again. We touched his hand and each other, relief bonding us with a warmth that fear had not.

In Bo we stopped at the Catholic mission house to make some phone calls to Freetown to assure others that we were safely through the dangerous part of our journey. We listened to the stories of the nuns who had comforted Ann Greeling as she had passed through the day before, the New Zealand doctor who by some miracle had escaped from the ambush in Panguma. Then we spoke of the road, of Kenema, of the displaced. We carry our own newscasts.

The delay in Bo stretched into several hours. Nigel eventually came back to the mission to bring us up to date.

"The soldiers at the check point won't let the large lorries with the WaterAid employees pass." Nigel's fatigue was etched on his face, aging him far beyond his thirty or so years.

"What is the problem?" I knew that none of us would leave Bo until all of us could.

"They want some document that proves that they all work for WaterAid. I never thought of that before we left. I should have known."

"Do you have your computer and printer along, Nigel?"

"Of course," he replied.

"Then let's make them the document they want," I suggested.

The lorries were released within half an hour of receiving the "official" documentation.

The images of Panguma were so terrible that, for some time, I could not tuck them safely away in my subconscious. Instead, the memory and the horror became linked to something that Sama had said which provided a tenuous sort of understanding and acceptance. We had been talking of the gunshot wounds of the patients.

"It is the preceding fear that is so terrible. Once you are shot it is over," he explained, from experience. "The aftermath is really quite simple. You are wounded, or you are dead."

Like the Ellcos and Father McAllister, I thought.

Carolyn knew more about that than I did. If I had any fear it was still securely locked away. She had been terribly afraid for weeks, and her anger was very close to the surface now. She was angry at me for containing my fear, thus negating hers; angry that we stayed so long in Kenema; angry at the rebels, at the soldiers, at the government. Deeply angry. And deeply frightened. But for the moment we were out of danger.

Once we the convoy left the mission, we sang all the way from Bo to Freetown. We still traveled very slowly, staying with the other vehicles although it was no longer necessary. We all felt vulnerable, and the likelihood of a flat tire was omnipresent, disproportionate to its likelihood. But it was more than that. The convoy had become a stable unit in our minds, the image of the other cars behind us engraved in our memories.

We reached Freetown well after midnight and dropped the others off at a hotel. Then Nigel and Carolyn and I went to the beach, and all of us quietly walked into the water, the dark places in our hearts lightened by the moonlight glistening on the shining surface of the sea. We slept that night in a hotel near the ocean.

Chapter Four: Writing to Explain

"**D**id you know?"

This phrase has probably introduced more juicy sessions of gossip than any other. We live to impart knowledge, which is why secrets are so hard to keep. There is nothing better than having information at your fingertips and an eager ear to pour it into. Well, perhaps chocolate is better, but little else can compare. That is why the explanatory essay is such a popular form of writing.

There are various subcategories of explanatory essays, depending on the type of material you are trying to impart. If your object is to explain HOW something works, you may opt for a *step-by-step* method of organization, moving chronologically along the directions. If, however, the predominant question is WHAT, you would choose to write a *definition* form of essay. You might even move into a *classification* mode, pulling apart the big picture to give your reader a view of all the working parts. Perhaps the motivating question is WHY, in which case a form of *cause and effect* organization would be best. There are examples of each of these essays within this section. As well as learning something about the rhetorical strategies available to you in writing an explanatory essay, you will also learn quite a bit about the Northern Lights. In "Aurora: Myth and Mystery," Candace Savage explains the background mystique of the aurora borealis. The history of New Year's Resolutions becomes clearer after reading Marg Meikle's short, definitive essay. Andy Russell's "A Way of Life" gives an informal classification of the life of real cowboys. And in "Why Canada Has to Beat Its Literacy Problem," June Callwood utilizes aspects of cause and effect to order her argument to its best advantage.

All these essays are inordinately informative, and you may know far more than you wanted to about any number of topics after reading them. That is, after all, the intent: you write an explanatory essay to impart knowledge of some specific subject. What then is the difference between these explanatory essays and general news articles? Both give factual information. The main difference is the *voice* used. In an explanatory essay, there is still a narrator's voice to consider—

the one telling the story—and, within the context, that voice is one of relative authority on the topic.

You have two loyalties when writing such an essay; the first and continuous loyalty is to your reader. You have to make information easy to attain and your prose worth reading. In the same vein, you have a loyalty to your information. You need to present it in a way that will make the reader entranced, amazed, informed, and pleased.

Beyond the quality of your information, the most important rhetorical strategy you must create in an explanatory essay is a voice of authority. In some cases it may be enough to allow the material (if you are certain that you have all the facts and figures at your fingertips) to speak for itself. However, if there is a level of subjectivity—a level of interpretation—to the topic, and there often is, it might be helpful to present yourself to the reader as a worthy authority.

It's not part of our normal makeup to proclaim ourselves as authorities; however, there are ways of doing so that won't abuse any small voices telling you it's not polite to "brag." One has to delineate to the reader WHY it is valid to listen to your comments on a topic. This might be as specific as "Having lived all my life as a diabetic..." or as general as "After some careful study of the case...." Both of these phrases proclaim your right to speak on the topic at hand.

How does one achieve a flavour of the personal while retaining the formality that suggests authority? Various rhetorical possibilities spring to mind. One can leaven formality with an *analogy* that explains an abstract concept along concrete lines; one can sprinkle a little *humour* into the mix to lighten the weight of information; one can structure the explanation to include a *narrative* or story aspect. The sheer act of personalizing the essay may make otherwise difficult material more accessible.

Let's examine the *analogy*. It's a useful rhetorical strategy, although you must never run the risk of using analogy as a focal part of your argument. Analogies are used to clarify, not to support an argument.

Suppose you have an argument that relies on some very abstract concepts to bring it all together. Much of the knowledge base necessary for someone to grasp your argument is either difficult to articulate, or is laden with technical language, too much to constantly define. This is the perfect situation for an analogy. Find a common experience, a concrete example, that most readers will understand, that can be likened to the concept you are trying to impart.

Think about explaining your present course of studies to your Great-Uncle Hector. Where he can see the usefulness of a general education, he cannot see the need of such esoteric courses as one in "communications." How will you explain the need for learning rhetoric? Indeed, how will you explain how to spell "rhetoric"? Searching for something Uncle Hector will understand, your eye strays outside to the fine stone fence he built surrounding his property. An analogy occurs to you, and you sit Uncle Hector down.

"Writing well is very much like building a good stone wall. If you think of words and thoughts as stones for the essay/wall, you can see my meaning. First there is the gathering and selection of rocks. Some, no matter how beautiful they appear on their own, just will not hold up under the weight and have to be discarded in favour of the larger structure. Some of the strongest rocks have to be unearthed; an onerous task, but necessary to bolster the entire structure. Gathering your materials takes time, and only the best will do if you want the wall to last, and not topple at the first push. Once you've found all the stones you require, the real task begins. You have to piece them all together into a unified structure. There can't be any gaping holes, an aesthetic balance must be achieved, and the design has to be suitable for the terrain and the materials used. While there is a certain amount of instinct at work, in that few people will set a boulder on top of three pebbles, it helps to learn some technique before beginning any project requiring craftsmanship and expertise. Rhetoric is this technique."

Now, Uncle Hector may not know much about essay structure, but he knows his wall-building. If you've worded your analogy properly, he will pat you on the hand smilingly, and likely be bragging about you down in the Legion Hall later that evening.

Humour is another useful rhetorical strategy to use when dealing with information-laden essays. However, there are people who equate levity with insincerity. You therefore need to be both very conscious of your writing situation—the audience for your piece and the purpose of your humour must match this situation. One rule of thumb is to resist anything that might require underlining or exclamation marks. (Snickering remarks in parentheses should also be eschewed.) However, a light-hearted style may be appropriate for some situations, especially the more personal essay, but generally not for an academic paper. Be very careful to be properly respectful of your information. Usually you have to sacrifice a really great joke to maintain your reader's understanding that you are serious about your subject matter (like, for instance, the one I just edited out of here).

The choice of *narrative* works well if you are explaining something that allows for a chronological progression. We are creatures of habit, and our habit is to start at the beginning. A strong story will often provide a showcase for what you wish to say. Consider this possibility when ordering your information. Likewise, don't forget the choice of descriptive sections to bring your material fully focused to the reader. These are devices and strategies that work in conjunction with each other and are not always separate and distinct forms of essays.

A last bit of advice: don't let your research run away with you. Chances are you will choose a topic that fascinates you, something you wouldn't mind learning a bit more about yourself. Some of the information you may deal with may be "anecdotal," that is, not proven, but true for your particular instances. Other information will be "empirical," statistical and proven. In order to create a worthwhile paper, nothing will be "general," or not backed up by some sort of proof. Depending on your subject, this may require a great deal of research.

There is a risk of spending more time on the research than the writing of your essay. Make specific deadlines for yourself, and stick to them. Sometimes you have to begin writing to realize what information you still require, just as Uncle Hector might need to find some smaller stones to fill in the gaps in his wall. If you leave your writing to the eleventh hour, you will have no time for this. As pragmatic as this may sound in a text devoted to the beauty and integrity of the language, there is no point in creating the most wonderful essay in the world if it isn't going to get read. Furthermore, should you continue as a writer professionally, you will soon realize that an editor, choosing between a brilliant writer who requires countless extensions for a deadline and a respectable writer who brings her work in under deadline, will go with the deadline-meeting writer every time.

But enough cautionary dictates. Enjoy the knowledge imparted in the next few essays. Check to see what method of organization each writer utilizes. Learn something.

Candace Savage

Candace Savage was born in northern Alberta, and graduated from the University of Alberta in Edmonton. She is the author of nine internationally acclaimed books of natural history, including *Wild Mammals of Western Canada, Eagles of North America, Wolves, Grizzly Bears, Wild Cats*. Not to mention other non-fiction books like the fascinating and frothy *Beauty Queens*. She has also written several children's books as part of a series on environmental issues. She lives in Saskatoon, Saskatchewan, with her daughter Diana.

This piece is taken from *Aurora*.

Aurora: Myth and Mystery

"They're scary," my daughter said. Yes.

The aurora is both wondrous and alien. In its presence, we may feel delight or dread or some uneasy mixture of conflicting emotions. These responses give us a living connection to the powers that are at work in the heavens. At the same time, our feelings offer us an important connection to other members of the human tribe. Through countless millennia, people have stood and wondered under the polar lights. In different places and times, our ancestors created radically different interpretations of what was going on. But their contradictory emotional responses seem always to have been much the same as our own.

On the one hand, the lights appeal to people with their loveliness. Under their spell, the universe may come to life with gaiety and benevolence. Thus, the Eskimos of the lower Yukon River in Alaska described auroras as the dancing souls of their favourite animals: deer, seals, salmon and beluga whales. The Finns were put in mind of magical "fire foxes" that lit up the sky with sparks that flew from their glistening fur. In a similarly joyful mood, the people of the Hebrides thought they could make out a tribe of shining fairies known as the "nimble men." To the Scots the lights were "merry dancers" and to the Swedes a polka, or folk dance. Old-timers in French Canada knew them as "marionettes." A tale from Estonia imagines them as the glow from a celestial wedding, in which the horses and sleds of the guests all shine with a mysterious radiance.

In Scandinavia tradition has it that the lights are the final resting place for the spirits of unmarried women who busy themselves above the mountain Konnunsuo by making fires, cooking fish, dancing and waving their white-gloved hands. "The women of the North are hovering in the air," the Finns used to say, or "Sibylle is burning her woollen blanket." In a less decorous spirit, the Samis of Sweden some-times addressed the aurora as "Girls running around the fireplace dragging their pants."

And if there are half-naked women up there, perhaps there will be childbirth. The Chuvash people of central Asia identified the lights as the god (or goddess) Suratan-tura (Birth-giving Heaven); it was said that the sky gave birth to a son when the lights rolled and writhed. Fittingly, this deity could be called upon to ease women through the pains of labour. There was also a suspicion in some cul-tures that the lights were connected to the life-giving mysteries of conception. The Lakota Sioux thought the aurora might be the spir-its of future generations waiting to be born, and there is an old Chinese record of "the mother of the Yellow Emperor" who, in 2600 B.C., "saw a big lightning circulating around the Su star of Bel Don [in the Big Dipper] with the light shining all over the field" and "then became pregnant." To this day, dozens of Japanese honeymooners visit northern Canada each year, persuaded that children conceived in the spell of the lights will be fortunate.

The aurora has also been thought to enhance the fruitfulness of the earth. A Swedish tradition has it that "when the northern light is burning, the seed will be abundant." Some Nunamiut Eskimos believe that if the sky is divided in half by auroral displays, animals will be plentiful in the area the next day. Dene elder Alexis Arrowmaker says the lights are there to show hunters where they can find the most game. Similarly, Scandinavian fishing people used to interpret the lights as sunshine glinting off schools of herring in the northern sea and, hence, as a welcome omen of rich catches in the offing.

The power of the lights could also be invoked to cure disease. When Knud Rasmussen visited the Inuit of the central Canadian Arctic in the 1920s, he found the aurora to be "in great demand as a helping spirit for the best shamans." It was a basic responsibility of all Inuit healers to make "spirit journeys" into the lights, to obtain advice about treatments and to rescue souls from death. As recently as the 1950s, a healer on Kodiak Island, Alaska, relied on the lights to cure heart ailments. A boy who experienced this procedure remem-bered that "his mother sent for a woman who held him up to the northern lights and then pulled something out of his chest." Unfortu-nately, we are not told if he was healed by this treatment.

But we do know of an instance in which the aurora provided reli-gious guidance and spiritual healing to an entire community. It hap-pened among the Lakota Sioux in 1805, when the people wished to revive an important ceremony that had been abandoned several years earlier. Performing the ritual correctly was a matter of life and death, and the leaders were not sure exactly what to do. So, as John Blunt Horn recalled in the early years of this century, the elders and shamans "said they would counsel and make medicine and talk with the spirits and find out about this thing":

> They went into the council lodge and stayed there two days and two nights. ... And many persons saw ghosts the first night. The second night the ghosts danced so that it was light like the moon (the Aurora Borealis). While the ghosts were dancing, the old men and the wise men and the medicine men came out of the council lodge and danced in a circle around it. Many saw ghosts dancing with them. So all were afraid and went into their tipis.
>
> In the morning one of the old men called aloud to the people to come out of the tipis and look on the sun when it was rising. And all the people came out and stood looking at the sun, and while it was rising, the old man cried in a loud voice that the spirits were pleased, [and] that they had told them how to perform the ceremony ...

And, indeed, after that, the ceremony was revived in a new form, following the auroral spirits' instructions.

Even Christians could sometimes benefit from the aurora's spiritual help. In 1397 a Russian monk named Kirill heard a voice urging him to establish a monastery. When he went to the window, he saw a great aurora radiating over the northern sky and pointing with its fingers towards the chosen location. Guided by this instruction, Kirill established the Kirillo-Beloszerskij monastery at White Lake, near Novgorod, a strategic location in which he and his community enjoyed both influence and wealth.

So it seems, in large ways and small, that the aurora can reflect the favour of heaven to humans watching below. The Ottawas of Manitoulin Island in Lake Huron expressed this thought in the form of a myth. According to a tradition recorded in the 1850s by Francis Assikinack, the lights are a message from the creator-hero Nanahboozho, who restored the earth after the Flood and then went to live in the North. Before he left, he told his people that he would always take a deep interest in their well-being. As a sign of his good will, he promised to light large fires that would glow against the sky and appear to the people as the northern lights. Thus, like the rainbow in the Old Testament, the aurora stands as a sign of harmony and trust between humans and their creator.

The Dogrib people have a similar belief—but with a crucial twist. According to their mythology, the hero Ithenhiela first laid out the landscape of northwestern Canada and then journeyed to his rest in the Sky Country. He is up there still and sometimes beckons to his people with long, gauzy fingers of light, calling them to the home he has found for them in the land beyond the sky. But it is a decidedly double-edged message, since to join him you first have to die.

That's the rub, in life and in auroral traditions. *You have to die*, and people have long harboured a suspicion that the lights are somehow implicated in this tragedy. Indeed, the whole of the North has often been mythically linked with death and dying. As mythologist Uno Holmberg points out, since the night is the time when spirits move about, it follows "that the underground world of the dead lies towards the sunset, or towards the dark north." In old Scandinavian texts, the road to Hel always leads "downward and northward," and the way is barred by a "trembling road" and a "flaming whirlpool"— both possible references to the aurora at the boundary between the worlds. "I seemed to be lost between the worlds, while around me burned the fires," laments the shaken narrator of the Hervarar Saga. And while the cold flame of the aurora flickered in the North, cold flames of the same ghastly fire flickered above the graves of the old Norse ancestors.

The Iroquois people were troubled by similar intimations. They imagined the aurora as the entry point into the Land of Souls, where the sky rose and fell to let spirits into the world beyond. For many other northern aboriginal peoples, the lights were seen as the actual spirits of dead ancestors. Sometimes their progress across the sky was interpreted as a torchlight procession or a joyful dance (perhaps inspired by the "cheerful" thought of relatives who would soon die and join them), but more often their erratic movements conjured up alarming images, especially when the lights were tinged a lurid red.

According to a circumpolar tradition shared by Eskimos in Alaska, Inuit in Canada and Greenland, Samis in Scandinavia and Russia, and various Siberian peoples, the northern lights are the souls of those who have died through loss of blood, whether in childbirth, by suicide or through murder. Elevated to the frozen snowfields of the sky, these spirits dash to and fro playing a macabre game of soccer. Sometimes the ball they kick is a human skull; sometimes it is a walrus head. In certain traditions, the head is alive and can be heard chattering its jaws in pleasure or roaring viciously as it slashes at the players with its tusks.

According to the Chukchi people of Siberia, spirits who have hanged themselves are honoured spectators at the auroral game. On the rare occasions when they join in the sport, they play awkwardly because of the ropes that still dangle from their necks. The souls of dead infants can be seen up there, too, trailing their long, gory ribbons of afterbirth.

But to many other observers, the violent play of the lights did not resemble a game of ball, however bizarre. To them it looked like war. Sometimes the heavenly battle was bloodless and abstract, as in the Finnish belief that the Archangel Michael stood arrayed in light to fight with Beelzebub. In that case the aurora was understood to be a fiery warning to resist one's own sinfulness. But usually the conflict was pictured as a literal combat among the souls of those who had died through violence, especially warriors who continued fighting after death. The Samis sometimes referred to the lights as *runtis-jammij* ("some who are killed by the use of iron") and described them as quarrelsome spirits that lived together in a large hall. When a brawl broke out among them, they stabbed each other to death, and the floor of their quarters was stained blood red. If blood from an auroral battle rained down over the Hebrides, it might congeal into the coloured pebbles that are known as blood stones or fairy blood. As recently as 1871, an auroral observer in London declared that he had heard the distant clash of weapons when the lights raged overhead.

Bad enough that the very heavens should be aflame with battle; worse yet to know that this sign foretold calamity on earth—death, pestilence, assassination, political upheaval and armed combat. Not surprisingly, this portent was most troubling for people who lived outside the auroral zone, where strange lights in the night sky were a rare and terrible occurrence. (As it happens, the great auroras that appear at low latitudes are also more likely to be red, which gives them an even more threatening appearance.) Thus the Roman author Pliny the Elder declared in 112 B.C. that "there is no presage of woe more calamitous to the human race" than "a flame in the sky," or a display of northern lights.

Who could doubt it then or since? In 507 A.D. the citizens of Rome awoke to the sight of glowing armies in the sky and the sounds of ghostly trumpets, just as their empire crumbled under an attack by the

Longobards. Several hundred years later, Henry of Huntingdon saw the skies of Northumberland, England, aflame with light and sparks and took it as a sign of terrible bloodshed and conflagrations to follow—predictions that were tragically confirmed during an ill-fated rebellion in 1138.

By the late Middle Ages, a brilliant display of aurora caused total, pathetic panic among Europeans. People fainted and went mad at the sight. Even in the sixteenth century, country people were so alarmed by these signs of divine displeasure that they poured out of their villages to make penance at major cathedrals. Thus, as auroral scholar Alfred Angot reports,

> in the month of September 1583 eight or nine hundred persons of all ages and both sexes, with their lords, came to Paris in procession, dressed like penitents or pilgrims ... "to say their prayers and make their offerings in the great church at Paris; and they said that they were moved to this penitential journey because of signs seen in heaven and fires in the air, even towards the quarter of the Ardennes, whence had come the first such penitents, to the number of ten or twelve thousand, to Our Lady of Rheims and to Liesse." The chronicler adds that this pilgrimage was followed a few days afterwards by five others, and for the same cause.

More than three centuries later, on 13 October 1917, Our Lady of the Rosary, Mother of God, appeared miraculously to three children in Fatima, Portugal, and warned of "a night illuminated by an unknown light" when a "terrible war will begin." And, just as prophesied, on 25 January 1938, the heavens over western Europe "filled with a strange and terrible crimson fire" that, to some, presaged the Nazi invasion of Austria three months afterwards. Four years later, violent displays of aurora flared over the United States for three nights straight, as far south as Cleveland, Ohio—an awful portent, it was later said, of the Japanese assault on Pearl Harbor.

By treating the lights with holy dread, people have traditionally attempted to keep their evil influence at a distance. The auroral spirits can be spiteful and easily irritated. A folktale from Norway tells of a boy who dared to chant at them —

> The northern light is running lip, lip, lip
> with fat in its mouth lip, lip, lip

with a hammer in its skull lip, lip, lip
with an axe on its back lip, lip, lip —

whereupon the lights zoomed down and burned him to a crisp.

Although some traditions suggest the aurora can be placated by singing, most northern peoples agree that whistling and singing at the lights are highly risky. The lights get aroused when they hear these sounds and think they are being teased. At the very least, they run faster and writhe into new forms; at worst, they take offense and come plunging down. People are said to have been blinded, paralyzed and decapitated by these assaults; others have been abducted into the lights' cold brilliance. In French Canada, a fiddler who charmed the lights with his music was seized by the rays and bewitched.

"When the Aurora Borealis falls," warns a Gwich'in text, "when it runs close to man, the human brain goes mad and man is seized by the Heart and killed. That is why we are frightened of it and why we reject it utterly and have done for a long time."

To people who lived in the spirit-filled world of traditional cultures, one fact was clear. The forces that dance in the polar dark are awe-inspiring—alien, uncontrollable and immensely vigorous. With that conclusion, at least, modern science would have no argument.

Marg Meikle

Marg Meikle is known as the Answer Lady, having fulfilled that function on CBC Radio on the former Vicky Gabereau Show. Her well-researched and lively answers to some odd questions have since been gathered into several volumes, including *Return of the Answer Lady*, from which this selection is taken. In addition to this role, she also writes magazine articles, does freelance research, and is an avid player of croquet, which she considers to be a blood sport.

Who Invented New Year's Resolutions?

Hey Answer Lady: I want to know about making New Year's resolutions. Whose idea was this annual deal in the first place?
                                                    Vicki Gabereau
                                                    Vancouver, B.C.

Personally, I don't bother with January 1 any more. Call me blasphemous, but I think the better new year is in September, the day after Labour Day. New season, new pencils, new courses, a fresh start. What's January 1 but a new date and a new tax year? It's not much of a change of daily routine. There are even calendars now that start in September.

Like many people, I make resolutions all the time, especially on Sunday nights, resolving to start the week right, and Monday is universally the most popular day to start a diet. Longfellow said, "Resolve and thou are free." But there's also an old German proverb that says the way to hell is plastered with good resolutions. I'm wary.

No one knows exactly when New Year's resolutions began, but our modern ritual (read: big bash) to welcome in the New Year certainly has roots in ancient times. Our resolutions started as ancient purifications and confessing of sins at end-of-the-year festivals. Ancient peoples did wild things, all in aid of constructing order out of the chaos of their lives. They would beat drums and shout to scare off demons and indulge in alcoholic and sexual excess to create the chaos that would soon be banished. There were fights too, but people saw them as ceremonial battles between the old year and the new. Definitely the same idea we have now. You can put out of your mind what has passed. You no longer have any control over the past, but the new year—it's a whole new period of life; it's a time of promise; the world is your oyster. And you can make all of these solemn vows about what you will do with your life and start afresh.

Rituals associated with resolutions and the new year often involve this fresh start. In ancient England you cleaned your chimney on New Year's Day so that luck could descend and remain all year. We "clean the slate," and if we make good our resolutions, the slate will stay clean all year.

I particularly like this order-out-of-chaos notion because it seems so many resolutions have to do with getting organized: doing a better job of accounting, answering letters promptly, remembering to look in one's daytimer (writing in it is only half the process). The most common resolutions, though, are rather mundane and predictable. In order, they are: losing weight, exercising, cutting down on or cutting out smoking and alcohol.

Four thousand years ago the two favourite resolutions of the ancient Babylonians were to pay off outstanding debts and to return all borrowed farming tools and household utensils. They were pretty boring then too.

Louisa May Alcott once made a great resolution that any of us could use today. She resolved to take fate by the throat and shake a living out of her. Frances Marion said that promises that you make to yourself are often like the Japanese plum tree: they bear no fruit.

And what of resolutions unkept? Psychologists say you've got to make deals with your subconsciousness for resolutions to work. A simple "I will stop eating" won't work. So try "if I cut down on my eating then I can ..." (buy a new dress, go to a movie, get my hair cut or whatever). There is an old joke that one swallow doesn't make a summer, but it breaks a New Year's resolution.

Oscar Wilde had a few things to say about resolutions: "The fatality of good resolutions is that they are always too late," and "Good resolutions are simply checks that men draw on a bank where they have no account."

You know what they say: Father Time is something that goes in one year and out the other.

Andy Russell

Andy Russell has long been considered the voice of the Canadian cowboy. A mountain man, cowboy, writer, photographer, film-maker, and conservationist, Andy Russell is one of the most engaging storytellers in Canadian history.

Born in 1915, his first publication about a cattle-killing bear in a 1945 edition of *Outdoor Life* magazine was followed by books including *Grizzly Country*, *Memoirs of a Mountain Man*, and *The Canadian Cowboy*.

Mr. Russell's career has spanned 50 years, gone through seven typewriters, and produced 12 books. He has received honorary degrees from the Universities of Calgary, Lethbridge, and Alberta. His writings at all times display a passion for nature and its conservation. He actively fought the Oldman River dam project and is a recipient of the Order of Canada for his work.

"A Way of Life" comes from Russell's book, *Men of the Saddle*.

A Way of Life

There have been changes. No longer does the cowboy or his boss spend the long hours in the saddle covering hundreds of miles of open range. Nor is the cow business quite so much of a poker game with the weather. It is a rare thing now for cattle to be caught starving in a killing winter storm. The ranchers know how much feed it takes to winter a cow and they work hard to keep enough on hand with some surplus to take care of the unexpected.

But the weather hasn't changed; it is as unpredictable as ever with winter cold and blizzards just as fierce. Where teams of horses hitched to bobsleds and basket racks were once the only way of spreading hay, now tractors and four-wheel-drive trucks are the transport on almost every ranch. Where it once took a man all day to feed 200 head of cows, it can now be done in two or three hours. But still, some ranchers keep a team in reserve for times when wheels are bogged by snow conditions.

Hay is no longer stacked loose in big stacks for it is too slow to handle; it is now baled, which makes feeding much easier and quicker. Thus, every animal gets its quota of feed per day with guesswork pretty much eliminated.

There are still a few of us around, however, who remember the old ways in the hard, cold days of winter. When I was growing up on a small cow and horse ranch at the foot of the mountains in southwest Alberta, there was a time when I came to know what it was like to work long hours in the bone-chilling cold. It was mid-January when a blizzard hit the country dropping two feet of snow. Then it cleared and the temperatures dropped to forty below zero. My father came down with flu and was flat on his back in bed. So it was up to me to see that the cattle were fed. I was thirteen years old.

Up well before daylight, I threw hay and oats into the manger in front of our big team and then wrestled the heavy harness onto them. Leaving them to feed, I went to the house where mother had a hot breakfast ready. Then I hitched up and drove to a stack on the other side of the ranch, picking up on the way an old cowboy who lived in a tiny log cabin with his wife and daughter. He was a tough, stringy old Irishman, by the name of Phil Lucas, with a crippled hand. Together we forked loose hay onto the rack and spread it for the cattle, while sundogs glittered coldly in the steely sky. Then we loaded the rack again.

That work filled the morning. After lunch we fed the cattle being kept close to the buildings, then I took Phil home. By the time the team was fed, watered and put in the barn for the night, the woodbox filled and the other chores done, the stars were out. At night I did more than sleep, I passed out. It seemed as though I had just closed my eyes when the alarm clock would cut loose. Sometimes I slept through its clamor and then mother would come to shake me awake.

The days were a blur of unending cold, tired muscles, creaking hooves and sleigh runners, and the steamy smell of the horses. One night the thermometer dropped to fifty-two below, but it didn't seem to be much colder when I went out next morning.

On the way to the haystack old Phil told me, "Your nose is freezing. You'd better thaw it out with your hand." I took a look at him to see that his beaky nose was white as bone. "Yours is froze solid," I told him. He felt it gingerly and cussed, "Damn if it ain't! Hard enough to peck holes in a board!"

I couldn't help laughing and he looked hard at me with sharp blue eyes past the hand that was holding his nose, in a way that shut me up. Then he chuckled and remarked, "We can still laugh anyway. Things could be worse."

Like almost every boy in the country, I had aspirations to become a cowboy, but this part of it I could do without. There seemed to be no end to the cold. Dad was up and around again, but too weak to do very much. I couldn't remember what it was like not to be tired.

Then one evening just as we were finishing supper, the house suddenly cracked. Dad went to the door and looked out. "It's a chinook!" he exclaimed. "It feels warm as summer!" Next morning it was forty above and water was dripping from the eaves. The temperature had risen about eighty degrees in fourteen hours. In three days the hills were bare on the south slopes and the stock was lazing about enjoying the warmth. The wind continued to blow soft and warm, and apart from a few short snow storms the back of the winter had been broken.

Winter weather in wintertime is one thing, but when cold and snow hold on stubbornly into spring and the calving season, the life of a cowman can be tough. In the old days on the open range the cows were pretty much alone when it came to calving. If one got into trouble and was lucky enough to be spotted in time, she got help, but much more often she was on her own. It was a stark matter of survival of the fittest. Consequently, genetics had arranged that they didn't have trouble nearly as often as the more pampered cattle of today. Vets were few and far between and such things as caesarean operations were unknown. It is amazing what a cow can stand and even more impressive how newborn calves manage to survive, though there is a preponderance of bobbed tails and cropped ears from being frozen in a bad spring.

I remember a miserable night twenty odd years ago, when our phone rang at midnight and a neighbor was on the line. One of his heifers was in trouble calving and would I give him a hand? I put on some warm clothes and tied on my snowshoes, for the roads were blocked by drifts. When I arrived at his place, it was to find him out among his cattle with his Land Rover. The heifer had a calf stuck in her pelvic opening with its front feet showing, and she was so spooky that he couldn't get her into the barn. A good-looking, strong Aberdeen Angus, she was in no mood to be pushed around. While I watched she lay down and heaved on the calf, but it was being just as stubborn as its mother and didn't budge.

I got a lariat and a short piece of sashcord, then sat on the hood of the vehicle, while my friend eased it up to the heifer. She jumped up and started to move off, but I got a loop over her head and snubbed her to the bumper of the truck.

Closer examination showed the calf's head was where it should be, so I looped the sash cord over its feet like short hobbles and pulled. Seeming to realize that I wanted to help, the heifer lay down. Sitting down and bracing my feet against her rump, I timed my pulls with her heaves and in a few moments the calf was out in the snow. I picked it up and put it on some dry straw, then turned its mother loose. While we watched, she went to it and began to lick it vigorously and before long it was up on wobbly legs and busy sucking a bellyful of warm milk.

Even there in the dark with snow spitting on the wind there was something wonderful about it—an inert, wet, little thing suddenly blossoming into life and responding to its mother's care. The tired lines of my friend's face softened and smoothed out as he watched. "He'll make it now," he said. "Let's go have a drink. I got a bottle of Old Stump Blower for times like this."

Sometimes a birth can be a lot more complicated when a calf is coming backwards or has its head or a front leg bent back. Then it is hard work being a midwife—working with an arm buried in the cow's uterus against her straining muscles as one tries to rearrange the calf so it can get out of the gate of her pelvis. It is always messy and difficult, but heart-warming when it works out right. It is miserably discouraging when it doesn't.

In these times of high expense and low returns in the cow business, the ranchers work hard at all hours of the day and night to save every calf they can. Family teams work in shifts, so the cows have someone watching them closely almost every hour of the day and night, particularly in bad weather. There are vets on call to help with complicated cases. The survival of the fittest is not the rule any more.

After a miserably cold, wet spring, it is particularly pleasant to ride out at last across green meadows, warm under the sun, among contented cows with new calves at their heels. Their old winter hair is slipping; they are "slicking up" and there is lots of milk for the calves. Sometimes this promotes scours, which can be a virulent intestinal infection that will kill calves. So even then the owner is watchful.

With the coming of warm weather, there are miles and miles of fences to repair and branding to be done. As always, the ranchers help each other with the branding. Now the cattle are worked in corrals, but the methods haven't changed much. A roper still heels the calves and drags them to the fire. There teams of wrestlers throw them and hold them down for dehorning, branding, castrating of the bulls, vaccination and ear tagging. Some outfits heat the irons with propane gas, but many still use a willow-wood fire.

The modern cowboy always has a vaccine syringe close at hand to administer an injection of antibiotics in case of infection and to immunize the cattle against such diseases as blackleg, brucellosis and redwater. Now practically every herd is treated against redwater twice a year. In the fall the cattle are chemically treated to discourage the warble fly.

When the branding is done, the cattle are put on summer pasture, sometimes on big fenced leases on the prairie or far up various mountain valleys. Salt is scattered and the bulls turned loose—generally one to every thirty or forty cows. While artificial insemination is being practiced by some ranchers, it is by no means universal, for it is a time-consuming and expensive process, not altogether practical in rough, brushy country.

On the bigger summer pastures cowboys are hired to ride among the cattle keeping an eye on fences and watching for rustlers, disease and predators. As in the early days, it is a lonely life, although now pick-up trucks and CB radios give the men advantages of communication and transportation such as their forebears never dreamed about. Many of the cowcamps even have telephones.

Meanwhile, back on the ranches hay is irrigated, and when ready it is cut, baled and stacked for winter feed. It is a time of long hours and hard work there too.

By the time the aspen leaves are turning gold, the cattle are rounded up, various herds cut out and then trailed or trucked back to wintering pastures. It is market time, when yearlings or calves are shipped out to feedlots or sold by auction at various sales centres to feeders who route them in the same direction.

With the return of winter, the whole cycle begins another revolution.

Some of the changes from the old ways have been immense. But ranching people are still as enterprising and adventurous as ever. They are at once innately conservative and yet the greatest gamblers upon earth—anyone who stakes his future against the vagaries of weather and markets has to be a gambler to the marrow of his bones. Ranching is a business that brings bank account riches to very few people; it is a way of life. It is a challenge to make the best use of the good earth without abusing it. It is an art in its dealing with animals, where one must mix a strong back with a wise head and a warm heart. It involves many things, from training a skittish colt to the careful study of bloodlines, from welding a broken piece of machinery to the intricate plaiting of a hackamore from thin strips of rawhide.

Above all, ranchers have to be practical. Their spirit has not changed even though the vast, open ocean of grass has gone forever. It is good to pause once in a while to contemplate how much we owe those oldtimers who blazed the trails and showed the way. They worked hard and played hard and through their sacrifices made it easier for their great-grandchildren.

June Callwood

June Callwood is an author, journalist, humanitarian, and outspoken activist championing ever-needier causes. For decades now she has made it her business to help those in trouble. She has founded and co-founded more than fifty social action organizations. In the beginning there was Diggers in Yorkville (a safe haven for Hippies in the '60s). Today there is AIDS hospice Casey House (founded 1988), where some 750 people have lived and died with dignity when no medical cure was available; Jessie's Centre for Teenagers (founded 1982), which is a drop-in and education centre for teenage moms and their babies; and finally, Nellie's Hostels for Women, serving homeless women.

Throughout her 28 books Callwood combines her journalist's abilities with her humanist's desire to understand human motivation. Ms. Callwood asserts altruism from a single individual can make a substantial difference in the lives of others. All change starts with small individual efforts, made because one human being can't bear to watch bad things happen to another.

Why Canada Has to Beat Its Literacy Problem

Carole Boudrias shudders when she remembers the time she almost swallowed Drano because she thought it was Bromo. Even more painful to recall is the time she mistook took adult pain-killers for the child-size dose and made her feverish child much sicker.

"When you can't read," she explains, "it's like being in prison. You can't travel very far from where you live because you can't read street signs. You have to shop for food but you don't know what's in most of the packages. You stick to the ones in a glass jar or with a picture on the label. You can't look for bargains because you can't understand a sign that says 'Reduced.' I would ask the clerk where is something and the clerk would say aisle five. Only I couldn't read aisle five. I'd pretend that I was confused so they'd lead me right to the shelf."

Carole Boudrias is able to read now, at last. She's a 33-year-old single parent who lives with her five children in a handsome townhouse on Toronto's harbourfront and holds a steady job. But her struggle with illiteracy is all too vivid in her memory. "You can't get a job," she says earnestly. "You can't open a bank account. You have to depend on other people. You feel you don't belong. You can't help your children. You can't help yourself."

Six years ago when her oldest child started school, the boy floundered. Because he had been raised in a household without books, print was strange to him. He would point to a word in his reader, that classic, endearingly silly *Dick and Jane*, and ask his mother what it was. She was as baffled as he, so he'd check with the teacher the next day and that evening would proudly read the new word to his mother. She began to absorb the shape of the words he identified. She found she could recognize them even days later.

That was astonishing. As a child she had been labelled mentally retarded and confined to "opportunity classes" where reading wasn't taught. She grew up believing that she wasn't intelligent enough to learn. Nevertheless, she was learning. The vocabulary of words she could read in her son's reader was growing. She began to think maybe the experts were wrong. Then, one miraculous day, she realized she was learning to read even faster than her son was.

"My son was my first teacher," she grins. She had never allowed herself to believe that it was possible that she could learn to read. She hadn't even tried: no one whose life is made up of poverty and failed relationships is ready to take on, voluntarily, the potential for another defeat, another kick in the self-esteem. She hesitated a long time but the evidence was persuasive—she was beginning to read. Her welfare worker had always been kind, so she summoned the nerve to ask her where she could find help.

That led her to Beat the Street, a program that helps people who are illiterate for all the reasons that befall sad children: unrecognized learning disabilities, emotional stress, too many schools, scorn and belittling, terribly bad teachers. She was linked with a volunteer tutor, and they came to admire each other deeply.

"Now I can read, I can read books, anything. I can write. In English and French."

Carole Boudrias has written a book, *The Struggle for Survival*, which tells of her tortured childhood lacerated with incest and violence, and her triumphant recovery from illiteracy. Last summer she was the poet laureate of the annual golf tournament hosted by Peter Gzowski, the beloved and respected heart of CBC Radio's Morningside. He has befriended the cause of literacy in Canada and over the past four years has raised a quarter of a million dollars for Frontier College, one of the first organizations in the country to tackle the problem of illiteracy.

"Learning to read," Carole Boudrias says quietly, "was like a second birth, this time with my eyes open. Before I could read, I was a blind person."

Canada has nearly five million adult citizens who are described as functionally illiterate, which means that they can recognize a few words, such as washroom signs and exits, but they can't read dense print at all. They can't decipher directions, for instance, or application forms, or warning labels. The world of newspapers, posters, advertising, books, menus, recipes, and instructions for assembly that literate people take for granted is barred to them; they lead a life of bluff, anxiety, embarrassment, and isolation.

A good many Canadians are as profoundly illiterate as Carole Boudrias was. People who meet illiterate adults are struck by the similarity of their textural experiences. All of them liken the inability to read and write with being disabled or chained in a prison. Edwin Newman, a U.S. broadcaster who writes about language, calls illiteracy "death in life."

The sense of being caged and blinded is not morbid fantasy. People who can't read may be able to walk freely but they can't go far. Subway stops rarely have pictures to guide them and the destinations bannered across the front of buses and streetcars are meaningless. If they ask for directions, well-intentioned people tell them, "Go along Main Street to Elm and turn left." Consequently, they must travel by taxi or stay home, even though they usually are the poorest of the poor.

Almost every job, even simple manual labour such as street-cleaning, requires an ability to read. Personnel managers don't take kindly to people who can't fill out an application, or when asked, can't spell their own addresses.

The divide between the literate and illiterate has never been wider. In this half of the century North America has become a world of forms and documents and instructions, written warnings, posted rules, leaflets, and vital information circulated in brochures. Two generations ago, illiteracy was prevalent but not such a great disadvantage. Someone functionally illiterate could fake it through an entire lifetime and still hold a good job. Employment skills were acquired by watching someone else; apprenticeship was the accepted teacher, not two years in a community college.

Today inability to read is a ticket to social segregation and economic oblivion. A poignant example is the skilled house-painter who turned up one day in the crowded quarters of the East End Literacy Program in Toronto. He said he wanted to read. The counsellor asked him, as all applicants are asked, what he wanted to read. "Directions on paint cans," he answered promptly. "I'm losing jobs. I can't read how to mix the colours."

Many who are illiterate can't read numbers. When they are paid, they don't know if they are being cheated. Because she couldn't fill out bank deposit slips, Carole Boudrias used to cash her welfare cheque in a storefront outlet which clips poor people sharply for no-frills service. To pay for goods, she would hold out a handful of money and let the cashier take what was needed—and perhaps more, she never knew. Once she would have been short-changed $50 she could ill afford if a stranger who witnessed the transaction hadn't protested.

The common emotional characteristic of people who can't read is depression and self-dislike. All feel at fault for their situation: with few exceptions, they went through school with bright little girls exactly their age who leaped to their feet to recite and smart little boys who did multiplication in their heads. Everyone else in the world, it seemed, could learn with ease; for them, even C-A-T looked a meaningless scribble. Teachers called them stupid. Worse, so did other children.

"Stupid" may just be the cruellest word in the language. It consumes confidence, on which the ability to learn relies. Seven-year-olds having trouble with reading will frolic at recess with an edge of glee; 11-year-olds who can't read have bitter faces and scarred souls.

Loss of hope for oneself is a descent into desolation without end. It causes men to rage in fury and women to wound themselves. People who can't read come readily to view themselves as worthless junk, and many feel they must grab what they can out of life and run. Canada's prisons are full of young men who can't read. The Elizabeth Fry Society estimates that close to 90 per cent of the women in Kingston's infamous prison for women are illiterate.

Because Canada has five million people who can't read, the political shape of the country and the priorities of governments are not influenced greatly by the needs of the poor. Since illiterates are effectively disenfranchised, the political agenda is written by the more powerful. Candidates rarely find it advantageous to uphold the causes that matter most to Canada's illiterate—an end to homelessness and the need for food banks, welfare payments that meet the poverty line, and better educational and job-training opportunities. Few votes would follow any politician with such a crusade. The electorate that can't read won't be there to ruffle the complacent on election day.

Their silence costs this country severely. Education is free in Canada because it was recognized that democracy isn't healthy unless all citizens understand current events and issues. Five million Canadians can't do that. Voters, most of them literate, choose can-

didates who help their interests; those who don't vote, many of them
illiterate, by default get a government that does not need to know
they exist.

The result is a kind of apartheid. The government has lopsided
representation, which results in decisions which further alienate and
discourage the unrepresented. The gap between the haves and have-
nots in Canada is already greater than at any time in this century,
and widening. Urban apartment houses are the work places of crack
dealers, the streets are increasingly unsafe, and households have
installed electronic security systems. The poor, if asked, would have
better answers than guard dogs. The best, most lasting responses to
crime and addiction and violence are literacy programs, coupled
with job training and full employment.

Schools are a disgrace, with a failure rate of fully one-third of all
high school students. A soup company with such a record would be
out of business in a day. The educational system has managed to
exacerbate the class differences which are developing in this country.
Canada's millions of illiterates went through school the required number of years, give or take time-out for truancy, illness, running away
from abuse, and confinement in detention homes. These human dis-
cards, identified promptly in the first years of elementary schools,
will ever after drift around disconsolately. They are surplus people,
spare parts for which society has no use. Unless there is a war.

Carole Boudrias is working on a project, Moms in Motion, to help
young mothers to get off welfare rolls. She says to them, "What do
you want?" They reply, "To go back to school."

Another chance. Five million Canadians need another chance.
Maybe they can become literate. Maybe they can become healed and
whole. What a lovely goal for the 1990s.

Will Ferguson

This essay, a section from Will Ferguson's best-selling second book *Why I HATE Canadians*, offers a thought-provoking argument against mindless nationalism, and makes us question previous assumptions. It would be a mistake to let the fact that you will likely be laughing out loud throughout the reading of this essay keep you from seeing the serious intent of Ferguson's message.

Why I HATE Canadians is a scathingly funny tribute to Canada with admonishments to us all. It asks the question: "Do we as Canadians deserve a country as great as Canada?" Ferguson is also the author of *The Hitchhiker's Guide to Japan* and *I Was a Teenage Katima-Victim*.

America Is Sexy

The three great themes of Canadian history are as follows:
1. keeping the Americans out
2. keeping the French in, and
3. trying to get the Native to somehow disappear.

These three themes represent the political/social mission of Canadians. Americans: *out*. French: *in*. Natives: *invisible*. If Canada were a hockey team, this would be our chant.

These three forces push us and pull us, they haunt us with doubts, they enrage us, they engage us, they *are* us. They are so fundamental as to be embedded right in our DNA.

There are other minor themes as well: Sucking Up to the Royal Family; Waxing Poetic About Nature While Huddling Inside Shopping Malls; Electing Boneheads; Trusting Authority; Avoiding Extremes; and Resenting Success. All of which are played out against the larger Myth of Niceness.

Of our three great themes, I began with the Americans. Why? Because without the Americans there would be no Canada, at least not in the political sense. I imagine the people living on the northern half of this continent would be an odd, introspective, stir-crazy bunch no matter what course history had taken, but the fact remains that *two* nations were created by the American Revolution. It was the Revolution that drove the final stake between Us and Them.

Bloodied but still standing, the U.S. of A.—last of the Superpowers— is at once obnoxious and enticing. Love them or hate them, and Canadians manage to do both, Americans are impossible to ignore.

My brother Ian is a playwright. He is talented and intensely patriotic. "We live in an occupied country," he says bitterly whilst eating a French cruller in Tim Horton's at three o'clock in the morning. If there were a Liberation Underground, Ian would have joined. He once beat the living hell out of a *USA Today* news box, which he saw as a symbol of the stifling pillow of American culture pressed up against our face. "We live in an occupied country," he says, and he may be right. And he may be wrong.

"But you would be better off beating up the Canadians who read *USA Today*," I said. They didn't appear at random, these advance-guard news boxes, they were summoned. Summoned by a yearning. My brother Ian is a proud Canadian. He is a die-hard fan of the Edmonton Oilers, Gordon Pinsent and Gabriel Dumont. He is also a fan of Clint Eastwood and Arnold Schwarzenegger, who are the very epitome of American values, and he never misses the Academy Awards. "Long after the U.S. dies," says Ian, "and long after capitalism goes tits up, Hollywood will still rule the planet."

This American presence is so pervasive we often have trouble recognizing it. It surrounds us like air, as unavoidable as gravity, as unfathomable as identity. Unfortunately, when the average Canadian does react to it, it is often in a nasally voiced, whiny way.

In *Last Train to Toronto*, American author Terry Pindell chronicles his journey across Canada in the twilight of the Age of Rail, culminating in the melancholy January 14, 1990, run from Vancouver to Toronto, the last passenger train along the old CPR line, the one that first bound Canada together as a nation.

Throughout his travels, Terry runs up against nasty anti-American comments and paranoia. He takes it all in stride. "Every province has grievances against some other, and all distrust the dominant Ontarians," he notes. "There is only one neighbor that unites Canadians in a national prejudice—Americans. We are mean, rapacious despoilers of the continent—somewhat akin to Ontarians."

When a group of tourists are identified as Americans—in a searing *Invasion of the Body Snatchers* scream, I imagine—Terry writes, "Having been immersed in the Canadian milieu for some time now, I am struck by how [the American] presence changes the atmosphere of the train."

At one point a man holds up a Canadian five-dollar bill and insists that the tiny, illegible flag depicted over the Peace Tower is in fact the Stars and Stripes. An American flag on Canadian money, a conspiracy!

The supreme, delicious irony of it all is that the very people who rant and rave to Terry about Americans never realize that Terry himself is in fact an American. They cannot tell the difference. But I can.

The Canadians are the ones carping on and on about Americans. And what they are saying is so familiar and so very petty, it is embarrassing to read. (It is to Terry's credit that he didn't throw half a dozen or so Canadians from the back of the caboose.)

Which brings me to the infamous Skis on the Car Roof Mentality. Memo to any Canadian nationalist muttonheads out there: No American has ever—*ever*—shown up at the Canadian border in the middle of July with skis strapped to the roof of his car, asking "Where's the snow?"

I must have heard this stupid story a hundred times. If I hear it one more time, I'm going to scream. Or puke. Or both. Either way, it won't be a pretty sight. So the next time some whiny Canuck bastard starts in with the old "skis on the car roof" story, I reserve two boots to the head. And while we are at it, Americans do not think we all live in igloos. No one thinks we live in igloos. These folk legends reveal more about Canadian insecurities than they do about American attitudes.

Our feelings towards America are complex, but they can be summed up in the following five (5) axiomatic propositions of Canadian Nationalism *vis-à-vis* the Americans:

1. Boy, we hate Americans.
2. We really do.
3. Really.
4. I'm not kidding. We really hate them.
5. So how come they never pay us any attention?

It is a classic love/hate obsession, and it defines us in ways we can never transcend. We measure ourselves against Americans. We crave their attention and their approval, we revel in their ignorance of us, and we take masochistic glee in slights, perceived or real. It is a form of neurosis, one step away from a compulsive high school crush. We pout, flirt, throw pencils, pass notes and talk maliciously about the object of our fears and desires. And they ignore us.

There are two examples, two thin books, each written by an icon of Canadian culture, that best illustrate this: the first is *My Discovery of America* by Farley Mowat, and the second is *Why We Act Like Canadians* by Pierre Berton.

Farley's book is a blow-by-blow account of his "war" with the U.S. Immigration and Naturalization Service (INS) back in 1985, when he was denied entry into the United States on vague charges of possible communist links. Throughout the book, Farley seethes in righteous indignation—as Farley is wont to do, righteous indignation kind of being his shtick. Squeeze any book by Farley Mowat and righteous indignation oozes out from between the pages. He suffers, but not—alas—in silence. The book even begins with Farley's own version of the "skis on the car roof" tale, as he explains why a professor in California invited him to America in the first place:

> [H]e thought I would be a good person to help dispel the myth of the Great White North. This is a delusion afflicting many Americans, one that makes them shiver apprehensively on those rare occasions when they acknowledge the existence of a frozen wasteland lying mainly to the north of the 49th parallel of latitude, inhabited by a meagre scattering of beer-drinking, parka-clad bacon-eating lumberjacks, polar bears, and scarlet-coated stalwarts of the Royal Canadian Mounted Police.

That second sentence is quite a marathon, but Farley eventually does come up for air, just short of saying "And they think we all live in igloos! Boy, I hate Americans. I really do."

What happened to Farley was a minor bureaucratic adventure, wherein stale McCarthy-era sentiments were used to justify barring writers whose ideas differed from the reigning Reaganites of the 1980s. Big deal. The U.S. has been excluding suspected commies and anarchists for years, and the list includes such luminaries as Pierre Trudeau, George Woodcock, at least one Attorney General, and even a classical violinist—and we all know how dangerous they can be. The Uninhibited States of America tends towards paranoia. So what? It's their country, they can do what they want. And no matter how much we like to assume otherwise, when Canadians cross into the U.S. *we* become foreigners.

The odd thing, and one that Farley notes with genuine surprise, is that throughout his "ordeal" his strongest support—and the sharpest criticism of the INS—came from south of the border. Newspapers across the U.S. ran editorials denouncing the decision to exclude Farley. They mocked the INS and sent letters of apology and support to Canada. The issue even worked its way up to Capitol Hill and was championed by U.S. senators. Of the hundreds of letters Farley received from Americans, only three thought the INS was justified in their actions.

It also turns out that the information used to bar Farley probably came from Canadians: those scarlet-coated stalwarts, the RCMP. Later, Farley writes, "We Canadians are hardly more than house slaves to the American Empire."

And therein lies the crux of the Canadian neurosis. Not that we are actually "slaves;" to argue this is to demean the very real suzerainty of the economic slave-states of the Third World. No, we are not slaves. But we *feel* like slaves, or more accurately, like underappreciated housewives in prefeminist days.

Canada's intense preoccupation with America reminds me of nothing so much as those old black-and-white 1940s flicks where the heroine beats her fists on the man's chest, sobbing "I hate you, I hate you, I hate, I hate you," only to collapse into his embrace.

Let's face it, America is sexy. It is exciting, dangerous, crass, brash and violent.

The problem is not that America is screwing us daily—which they are—but that they never send flowers or call afterwards. They barely remember our name. "See you around, doll. Here," as they toss us a coin, "buy yourself something nice." It is intercourse without foreplay, when all we needed was a little respect. (Cue the sobbing, chest-beating litany of "I hate you's.")

Farley Mowat was thrown into a foot-stomping tirade because the Americans wouldn't let him in. There was a party planned, but he couldn't get past the front gate. In this, then, *My Discovery of America* is a key book understanding something deep in the Canadian psyche, something I call "the Angst of the Spectator." As the United States careens by like a parade on crack cocaine, amid fireworks and gunplay and racially sparked riots, we watch from the sidelines, from the curb, thankful we are not caught up in it and yet—and yet, somehow wishing we were.

Existing as we do, somewhere between Voyeur and Spectator, we know in our hearts that we will never he invited to actually participate. We will never be the biggest or the strongest or the richest.

So why should we care? There are many quiet, backwater countries that have attained a degree of civility and social order that the Americans can only dream of. Sweden. Switzerland. Singapore. The problem is that Canada is still very much a *North American* nation, a New World country; we are a frontier-bred people and we will never be satisfied with mere comfort and security. We are nagged by dreams of greater things, a promise of something more. It is a state of mind we share with the United States, Mexico and the separatists of Québec. For all our angst, it is a resolutely optimistic and materialistic world view, one based on the idea that we can be anything, dream anything, achieve anything. And therein lies the problem. Deep inside, we are not satisfied with the safety of the suburbs. We have grasped the brass ring: security, peace, prosperity. But we were bred for bigger things, and this knowledge gnaws away at us like a rat on a bone. We have settled for less. We have made our peace with the world, but not with our dreams. Canadians, under the cottage calm and the down-filled comforter blankets, are restless.

If Farley Mowat really doesn't give a shit about the United States, then why does he expend so much emotion and energy when they won't let him in?

The other book, and one that ought to be standard reading for every Canadian citizen, is Pierre Berton's succinct inventory of our national traits entitled *Why We Act Like Canadians*. Whatever you may think of Pierre Berton the celebrity/institution, you have to admire Pierre Berton the author. As a popular historian, he has done more for Canadian self-awareness than any other writer.

He is also a nationalist of the Old School, and it was in this capacity that he set out in 1982 to explain what exactly makes us Canadians. With all due respect to Mr. Berton, this is one of the biggest nonmysteries ever. If he only thought to give me a call, I could have cleared it up for him in a few minutes. What makes us Canadians? The answer is both paradoxical and self-evident: *Canada makes us Canadians. Canadians are what we all are. Simply put: I am. Canadian.* But that would have made for a very short and very esoteric book. And anyway, a beer company already had dibs on it. Instead, Pierre focussed on law and order, the French, the Loyalists and our lack of blacks. Other than that last somewhat disturbing assumption, Pierre's book is fairly straightforward.

What is unsettling is how it is presented. *Why We Act Like Canadians* is in the form of an open letter. And to whom is this letter addressed? Is it addressed to new Canadians seeking to learn more about the land they have chosen? Or landed immigrants who have just begun the journey to citizenship? Or to young Canadians? Or Native Canadians? No.

It is revealing that Pierre chooses to address not his fellow Canadians, but the people of the United States.[1]

"Dear Sam," he writes (Sam as in *Uncle* Sam, get it? Get it?) "Today is Constitution Day in Canada! That doesn't mean much to you, I know—I doubt if it will make your front pages—but it's a big thing for us."

Farley rants and raves over American ignorance of Canada, Pierre tries to enlighten them, but the message is still basically the same.

---

[1]Like they care.

We hate you, we hate you, we hate you. Why don't you pay us more attention?

I remember one book exclusively devoted to the Americans' lack of understanding of Canada. The author, Walter Stewart, travelled across the U.S., asking average Americans what they knew about Canada and then recording the often flip remarks with a martyr's fastidiousness. The book managed to be both masochistic and smug. Stewart also ransacked archival sources to quote celebrities such as Al Capone saying things like "Canada? I don't even know what street Canada is on." The basic theme was, *Americans sure are dumb, huh?*

I tried to imagine another nationality that would undertake such a project—New Zealanders travelling across Australia to record Australian lack of knowledge about New Zealand; or Scots travelling through England, seething whenever an Englishman asked "What's a haggis?"—and the only one that seemed possible was Japan.

The Japanese, like Canadians, love to be misunderstood and underappreciated. I could perfectly imagine Japanese commentators travelling across the United States, recording with painstaking accuracy American ignorance of Japan. I can even imagine the book doing quite well.

At best, this inbred anti-Americanism of ours is a survival technique. At worst, it is petulant and petty. In many ways, our relationship to the United States is remarkably similar to Québec's relationship with English Canada. No matter how much Québec nationalists would like to deny it, English Canada *defines* Québec. Just as America defines Canada.

Nationalism, as a force, often relies on the fear of outsiders, and this reveals itself in paired antagonism: Greece and Turkey, Japan and Korea, France and England, Québec and the RC, the United States and the Soviet Union. For English Canadians, anti-Americanism renders the world into easy opposites. Unfortunately, it takes two to play, and the Americans don't realize they are being cast as the Bogeyman of Canadian nationalism. Even worse, it is getting harder and harder to hate them, especially now that they have that big marshmallow in the White House havering away about bridges to the twenty-first century.

There is, however, some good news in all of this. The United States acts like a forerunner for our own fears and apprehensions. In many ways, the Americans are not an invasion force, but are in fact our first line of defence, an Early Warning Line where the consequences of ideological decisions are played out in graphic detail: gun laws, private medicine, unchecked capitalism, the complete ghettoization of minority groups, and allowing too few people to get too rich too fast. We learn from their mistakes.

Unfortunately, as well as using the United States as a harbinger of things to avoid, we also use it as a measuring stick by which we judge Canada's place in the world. And this is where we run into trouble.

Whenever Canadians describe themselves as being kind, cautious, timid and nice, what they are really saying is that they are kind, cautious, timid and nice *when compared to Americans*. Christ, who wouldn't be? When you are comparing yourself to the wildest saloon in the West, of course you will end up appearing soft and angelic. This is the heart of the Canadian Myth of Nice. Just as we seem quieter when compared to the Americans, we also seem more modest, more polite and more self-deprecating. This is utter rot. We may not have an edge, and we may err constantly on the side of caution, but overall we are a loud, brash, gregarious people. Ask any northern European who has travelled in Canada.

I remember my Scottish cohort Marion saying with a mock Canadian accent, "Everything is bigger 'n' better in Canada!" She couldn't believe how relentlessly handshaking and back-slapping Canadians were. An English traveller said, "It was aggravating how the cashiers would smile at me as though we were dear friends and ask *How ya doing?* as though I were dying for their acknowledgement." There is nothing bookish or morose or European about us. We are North Americans, through and through. True, we are not as bad or as extreme as the citizens of the United States, but then, the only person as bad or as extreme as an American is another American.

My Japanese friends think Canadians are hopelessly slothful, slovenly, unreliable and fun. My Ecuadorian friends think Canadians are hopelessly uptight, punctual and obsessed with schedules. They can't both be right. Or can they?

In *Hello World!*, Jacques Hébert's chronicle of Canada World Youth, a young volunteer recalls the shock of coming home after a stint in the Dominican Republic: "I realized Canadians live at a frantic pace and don't take the time to enjoy life's simple pleasures. Though Canadians are very sociable, their use of time is too rigidly structured and makes no allowance for the unexpected." However, when my friend Kerry returned to her hometown of Victoria after an extended stay in Japan, she found Canadians intimidating.

"Everyone was wearing dirty clothes. The men were hairy and huge, and I felt threatened."

It all comes down to your standard of comparison. Canadians appear tidy, timid and soft-spoken only when standing next to Americans, in much the same way that I look slim when standing next to a sumo wrestler.

And while we are hammering away at popular delusions, let's take on another one: that Canada is facing cultural annexation by the United States, that we are in imminent danger of being absorbed, *Protozoa*-like, into the American soul. This is a vestigial fear, born of what was once a very real, very ominous possibility. The Americans have coveted our land for centuries. The annexation of Canada was official policy in the United States for over 150 years. They invaded us twice, encouraged sedition several times and were involved in endless border skirmishes. Canada regarded the United States as its biggest territorial threat right up until World War I. Until then, our major military plans involved defence against an American invasion. The United States themselves did not relinquish their pro-annexation sentiments towards Canada until 1923! So our suspicions that the Yanks are waiting to gobble us up are well-grounded in history.

But the old-style "annex and plunder" imperialism is dead, and it's time we got over it. Even if Québec goes, Canada will not be absorbed piecemeal into the United States. Why? Because Canadians do not want to become Americans. This is what created us in the first part, this desire *not* to be American, and it is a sentiment that is getting stronger, not weaker. In *Nationalism Without Walls*, columnist Richard Gwyn writes:

> Not a scrap of evidence exists that Canadians want to become Americans. In April 1995, a survey by Decima Research for the Canadian Council of Christians and Jews found that just 3 per cent polled favoured "union with the United States." This was down from a 5 per cent tally measured by an Angus Reid survey in 1991. It's entirely possible that fewer Canadians want to become Americans than do the citizens of almost any other country in the world.

Three per cent! That is less than the percentage of naturalized and second-generation Americans living in our fair land. Even our own domesticated Yanks are not big on the idea. Surely, three per cent does not represent any kind of Fifth Column threat, yet still the breakup and cannibalization of Canada is trotted out every time we face a domestic crisis. Let's lay this demon to rest. It isn't going to happen. The Americanization of Canada is a shadow-puppet spectre conjured up by intellectual nationalists and their ilk. Indeed, nationalists never shut up about the Americans in much the same way that fundamentalist preachers never shut up about Beelzebub and the Day of Judgement.

There is, of course, a flip-side to all of this: *pro*-Americanism. This is manifest in the ease with which Canadians have surrendered their autonomy, their economy and their confidence to the American juggernaut. Hate is only one half of any love-hate relationship, and Canadians have all too often crawled on their bellies for American approval. Again, this has got nothing to do with the Americans themselves. Just as Americans do not really deserve our hatred, neither do they deserve our love.

Yet there was Smilin' Brian up on stage, singing away to Cowboy Ron at the Shamrock Summit. It was March 1985 and Ronald Reagan was visiting Québec City, where—live on stage—our prime minister sang a warbled version of *When Irish Eyes Are Smiling* to the president. "The general impression you get," noted commentator Eric Kierans, dryly, "is that our prime minister invited his boss home for dinner." Heck, it was all Brian could do not to give Ronnie a big wet smooch right then and there on national television.

Canadians have long since disowned Mulroney, but in doing this we are shirking our responsibility. We voted that man into office twice—*twice mind you!*—so in a very real sense that was *us* up there on stage, crooning away like an infatuated schoolboy.

Brian Mulroney's serenade was a low point in Canadian pride. For those of you too young to remember, consider yourself lucky.

The key point is that Brian's performance, like the free trade that followed, was done with our approval—and usually on our initiative. Don't blame the Americans. They aren't the real threat—the real threat comes from our own insecurities and ambivalent feelings.

We worry far too much about America.

Why should we give a tinker's damn about how we stack up against the U.S.? Whether our gun laws are more civilized than theirs or whether our medicare is more humane doesn't really matter. We have nothing to gain by using the United States as our yardstick. We should be setting our standards by who we are and who we *could* be—not by what we aren't. And that is the heart of the matter: we must stop defining ourselves in terms of negation.

Let us put an end to the wailing, hair-pulling, woeful lamentations about our impending Americanization. That we share many similarities with those foreigners to the south is not a cause for despair. Given the similarities in geography, history and background, the surprising thing is that we are different at all. And we are. Whether we can agree on what makes us Canadian, whether we can articulate something so near the bone, is irrelevant. The deep silent chasm that separate us from the United States of America is one of the miracles of North American history—one of the *enduring* miracles. That Canada exists at all is remarkable, that we have made a damn good show of it is even more impressive. So let's stop treating the Americans like the Bogeyman. Let's stop blaming them. Let's stop admiring them. Let's stop hating them. Let's stop loving them.

We will always be something more—and less—than American. In the twilight of the twentieth century, we will have to redraw old maps and realign outdated thoughts. It is time we stopped looking, with a mix of fear and longing, across the river to that dark wooded shore.

Nora Abercrombie

Nora Abercrombie started writing professionally in 1976. Over the years she has been a successful writer of non-fiction, fiction, and screenplays. Her periodical credits include *Saturday Night* magazine and *Books in Canada*. She is former editor of *The Edmonton Bullet*, *The Visual Art Newsletter*, *Prairie BookWorld*, and *Arts Bridge*. In 1986, she co-authored (with Candas Jane Dorsey) *Hard-Wired Angel*, the winner of the Pulp Press International Three-Day Writing Competition. Her screenplays include "The Girlfriend's Guide to Hockey" and "Morning, Joan." Nora has served on the executive of the Periodical Writers Association of Canada and continues to work for rights for writers.

Her examination of the need for new cognitive models is laced with both anecdotal and empirical proofs and her clear, reasonable voice is heard throughout.

Which Ship Shall We Sail? Workplace Values and the Models That Bear Them

> *There will be little drudgery in this better ordered world. Natural power harnessed in these machines will be the general drudge. What drudgery is inevitable will be done as a service and a duty for a few years or months out of each life; it will not consume nor degrade the whole life of anyone.*
>
> — H.G.Wells (*Outline of History*)

My great-grandmother came to Alberta in a covered wagon and lived long enough to see a human being walk on the surface of the moon. Despite witnessing two global wars and the needless extinction of millions of lives, she felt comfortable and hopeful about her future, and the future of her children. But now change asserts itself with increasing speed—so much so that very few of us are willing to bet on what our lives will look like in ten years.

Technology was supposed to release humanity from poverty, ignorance and overwork. But instead of the leisure and security we expected to accompany the computer age, we experience fear. Workloads are increased 20 to 40 per cent from five years ago. "Downsizing" is still a staple management buzzword. Longer working hours have resulted in greater absenteeism and basement-level morale. Employees feel it's useless to bother suggesting improvements, and plan to "coast" to retirement.

Robert Logan, a physicist and communications theorist, describes even scarier scenarios emerging in the future: "We face the possibility of electronic sweatshops, unemployment, and displacement.

Computing and automation, for all their efficiencies, have increased the length of the workweek, not reduced it. Many workers whose skills are overtaken by technology find themselves suddenly unemployed and, at a certain age, unemployable"(Logan, 1995).

It appears that the combination of good intentions and technology has failed to produce the kind of society we want. As we enter a new millennium, we must step ahead of technology and the changes it engenders to ensure that the values we cherish are preserved in the choices we make.

The key question is: how do we *do* that?

THE LACK OF A GOOD TOOL

> *To be conscious that you are ignorant is a great step to knowledge.*
>
> Disraeli

A few years ago I was on a three-month long canoe trip that took my partner and me along the shore of a remote lake in northern Canada. We had not laid eyes on another human being in weeks and were therefore surprised to encounter another canoeist, moreso to discover that he was an English zookeeper who had been paddling his canoe alone for some months. Quentin Rose was an appealing character; his activities as a zookeeper had resulted in him being hurled over a high wall by an African elephant, his skull cradled between the teeth of a growling Bengal tiger and having his ear temporarily removed by a leopard. Quentin related these stories and electrifying tales of high adventure in the bush by campfire light as the sun descended over the lake, his fingers deftly untangling fishing line as he spoke. I was profoundly impressed, and curious about how an urban Englishman might learn enough to stay alive in the Canadian outback.

He read a lot of books, he said, fingers busy with his line

Eventually he stood up and, slapping his legs with the palms of his hands, declared, "Well, that's that until tomorrow night." I asked him what he meant and he replied that the action of his fishing lure spinning in the water twisted his line into a mess so he spent approximately two hours untangling his fishing line every evening before he went to bed. My jaw dropped.

"Don't you use swivels?" asked my partner, incredulous.

Quentin looked puzzled. "What's a swivel?"

All that knowledge and bravery, yet his evenings are ruined for the lack of a simple tool.

The effects of using inadequate technology for a physical task are immediately apparent. People don't use shovels to hammer nails or look backward through binoculars because the ineffectiveness of doing so is immediately apparent. To continue to look backwards through a pair of binoculars is obviously idiotic.

But then, quite a lot of the things people do, especially in the work-place, are equally idiotic. Some years ago I was employed as a researcher in a bureaucracy. I took the job because I felt very strongly that I wanted to support the goals of the organization and because the pay was great. The two managers chose me, they said, because they wanted their employees to operate like private contractors and they hoped that my "entrepreneurial approach" would spread to other workers. For the first six months they were thrilled at the speed of my work and how little help I required. At six months into the job I felt fully trained, keen to learn more and ready to take on new respon-sibilities. My request to work harder was denied. At first I thought they didn't understand. Look, I said, as a private contractor I always chose work that would enable me to keep improving my skills. I didn't accept work that I already knew how to do because it didn't teach me anything. That's how businesses grow, I said. That's how they expand their market. The goals of this organization will be better met if you let me off the leash. The more I voiced my desire to contribute to the professed goals of the organization, the less I was supported. I was given an arduous task that would have taken six weeks to com-plete but which could have been performed effectively by a high school drop out. That was a slap, intended to put me in my place. I came to suspect that our mission statement was not what was actually running the organization.

Other employees concur. "What they said they wanted was rarely what they wanted," says "Tina", one of my former colleagues (who chooses to remain anonymous). "They said they valued hard work but what they rewarded was loyalty. They said they valued indepen-dence but they punished workers who acted autonomously. They were always angry at somebody in the office, and deliberately sabo-taged that person's work, but we couldn't figure out why. Doing so did not meet the needs of the organization, nor did it meet the needs of the people our organization served. Actually, they were pretty well nuts."

I lasted 13 months. I was openly scornful and hostile the last three, and quit just as they were about to "let me go". Within a few years none of my colleagues were there and, while the managers were promoted into a different division, the organization folded. The cherished goals of the organization melted into mist and disappeared.

I've gained some perspective over the years and can now see that these managers probably wanted to achieve the goals of the organization. They probably wanted that elusive "entrepreneurial approach". I can also see, clear as day, the model they employed to get it. Both managers were childless women who treated us as if we were their daughters, employing tools like silent disapproval, favouring one of us over the others, withholding rewards (such as more responsibility) from those of us who refused the childish role. Wherever those two are, they probably continue to employ these tools not because they are effective but because of the muck in their heads. They are not alone. The number of managers with heads full of muck is legion. Wherever they flourish, the competent, mature worker is forced out, leaving the goals of the organization to the immature and the neurotic.

COGNITIVE MODELS AS "TOOLS"

The other day my eight-year-old daughter philosophized to her father about the nature of the world. Wriggling on the couch as only an eight-year-old can, she held forth about the status of human beings on the "food chain".

"We are at the top because we eat everything else and nothing eats us," she announced, feet waving in the air.

I couldn't let such a piece of misinformation pass unchallenged, so inquired as to the relative status of spinach on the food chain.

"At the bottom," replied my daughter, confidently, balancing a cushion on her head.

"Okay," I said, "but we eat spinach and coyotes don't, so does that mean we're lower on the food chain than coyotes?"

"No," said my intelligent daughter as she snuffled her socked toes, "because coyotes don't eat *us*."

"But mice eat spinach and we eat spinach, and we don't eat mice and coyotes do," I said. "So what does that mean?"

"But we *could* eat mice if we *wanted* to," said my daughter, irritated.

"Oh," I said. After a few minutes of watching her snake around the couch, I inquired as to where plants and microbes fit on the "food chain".

"Lower than spinach," said my daughter.

"But they should be higher."

"No."

"Microbes and plants eat us, so...."

"No they don't!"

"They do when we're dead and rotted and leaking into the ground."

"But they don't *kill* us."

"Sure they do." I listed poisonous plants, viruses and bacterial infections until my daughter sat up straight and glared at me. Parents of emphatic eight-year-olds know when to shut up. But our discussion bounced around in my head long after my daughter bounced off the couch. She is exploring her world and, in the process, acquiring and developing models that will assist her to store, process, transform and apply information. It occurred to me that my daughter's incomplete understanding of ecosystems was very much like Quentin Rose's incomplete tackle box. If Quentin Rose wasted two hours every night for the lack of a swivel, what behaviours might humanity engage in for lack of an appropriate *cognitive* tool? My daughter's understanding of the food chain is a legacy of an old model of the universe: god on top, closely followed by men (clones of god, but flawed), followed by women (who, unable to achieve being god-like by virtue of their gender, serve men because otherwise this model can't explain what else women might be for) and children. And everything else falls into a slot based on our limited understanding of who eats who, or who we like best. I wondered if we saw the ecosystem as a magnificent swirling, uncontrollable concert of energy—shape shifting from sunlight to a leaf to a bug to a bird to birdshit to grass to a cow to milk to a child to an adult to ashes and dust to start all over again—would we be so eager to mess with the system? I thought about what cognitive tools might have been operative during the Nazi Holocaust, and what industrialists could have been thinking when they strapped children to carts and sent them down coal mines.

No sane human being desires a brutal future. But our best intentions have not saved us from a brutal past. So here's a key question: are there invisible qualities imbedded in cognitive tools that cause unintended results?

THE VALUES INHERENT IN TOOLS

> *Let us cling to our principles as the mariner clings to his last plank when night and tempest close around him.*
>
> Adam Woolever

Communications theorist Marshall McLuhan introduced the world to the idea that, just as hand tools are extensions of our bodies, cognitive tools are extensions of our psyche. More importantly, he postulated that no technology is value-neutral: "The medium is the message."

Robert Logan writes, "Like most good aphorisms, McLuhan's famous dictum has more than one meaning. Two of its principal interpretations form an integral part of the philosophy of the Toronto School of Communication. One is the notion that, independent of its content or messages, a medium has its own intrinsic effects on our perceptions which are its unique message. 'The message of any medium or technology is the change of scale or pace or pattern that it introduces into human affairs.'" (Logan, 1995)

Decoding and interpreting McLuhan's aphorism has occupied theorists for decades. But, simply applied, the "message" of any technology is the effect it has on our lives. And if cognitive tools hold intrinsic values, then perhaps the unintended disasters of history and the befuddling vicissitudes of the workplace are simply what happens when the invisible values inherent in our cognitive tools conflict with our personal values. Because the "messages" are invisibly imbedded, they are not easily confronted.

Some workplaces operate in a militaristic hierarchy. Some operate in competitive "hunting parties", some are structured in "teams". Each structure is a cognitive model and each carries intrinsic messages which are invisible or apparent in varying degrees.

Management theory offers advice and information to people struggling to facilitate their employees' performance: body language, confrontational techniques, performance measurements, rewards, removing barriers, and so on. Lots of good technologies and strategies—but they may be wasted if the organizational design—the cognitive model—conveys unintended messages. The challenge, then, is to illuminate the messages imbedded in a cognitive model, to sift organizational structures for invisible values.

AN INADEQUATE EXPERIMENT

I asked three friends to join me in an experiment based on the assumption that our primary cognitive model is hierarchy. Most of us, whether we apply the model of hierarchy to our families, our workplaces, our nations, or even the cosmos, can—like my little daughter—pinpoint our exact status. I suspected that at least some values cherished by my colleagues are not congruent with the values intrinsic in hierarchy.

Assuming that the "message" is the extent to which a technology affects human perception and affairs, I suggested that our group of intrepid investigators reflect upon hierarchies they had participated in, then sort a list of words that reflect values, behaviours and feelings into three groups: those their hierarchy rewarded, those their hierarchy punished, and those their hierarchy did not react to. My theory was that each hierarchy, regardless of whether it was a workplace, an organization or a family, would react consistently to at least some of these words. And that is generally what happened. The results of our experiment revealed that the message of hierarchy is that it rewards security, effectiveness, money, success, cooperation, stability, competence, quality, the acquisition of personal power, loyalty, efficiency, trust and comfort. Those are all good things. But we also found that our hierarchies punished self-esteem, self-actualization, reflectiveness, taking risks, youth, expertise, autonomy, socializing, originality, independence, openness, integrity, adventure, excitement, happiness, pleasure, personal health and family life.

Uh oh.

I was curious to see if the participants in my experiment could think of a place where the behaviours and values they cherish found full expression. They could. I proposed that they might draw a "picture" of that organization. I was hoping that their "pictures" might be visual representations of a different kind of cognitive model. I was also hoping that there would be some similarity among the models. If there was, I could postulate that *this* model held its own intrinsic messages.

Again, that's generally what happened. When asked to draw a "picture"of organizations in which our cherished values and behaviours are fully expressed, three of us drew circular diagrams. Another drew a network of "nodes". I asked if these diagrams were mobile. The consensus was yes, they were very dynamic and therefore difficult to represent in a static picture. I asked if their hierarchies were as changeable or adaptable as the circles and nodes. All four of us said: No. Were the "circles"responsive to change? The answer was an emphatic: Yes.

So I wonder if hierarchy is an appropriate cognitive model to support the values we want to take with us to the next millennium. I wonder if some of the devastation our species has caused and experienced is not a failure of values or a lack of will, but an intrinsic fault in the cognitive models we have employed to implement those values. Perhaps it's not only what we want that counts, but the way we plan to get it.

CEO OF THE FOREST?

Management theorist Dee Hock says that the command-and-control models of organization that had grown up to support the industrial revolution "were not only archaic and increasingly irrelevant. They were becoming a public menace, antithetical to the human spirit and destructive of the biosphere. I was convinced we were on the brink of an epidemic of institutional failure (Waldrop, 1996)." Hock's track record adds enormous credibility to his ideas. In 1966, the bank card industry was near collapse. Hock provided the vision for a group of people who, over a period of years, came up with an innovative structure for VISA, a nonstock, private, for-profit membership corporation. Since 1970, the company has grown 10,000 per cent. Annual profits exceed $1 trillion. (Waldrop, 1996)

VISA is composed of 20,000 financial institutions, operates in more than 200 countries and, according to Hock, is "bound by no political, economic, social or legal theory." The participating financial institutions compete with one another but cooperate for their mutual benefit. The system is decentralized, nonhierarchical, evolving, self-organizing and self-regulating. The term Hock uses to describe such a system is "chaordic."

Hock says chaordic organizations resemble actual natural systems rather than the intellectual construct of hierarchy. "Show me the chairman of the board of the forest," Hock exclaims. "Show me the chief financial fish of the pond. Show me the chief executive neuron of the brain!" Natural systems are far more able to handle complexity and swift change—the primary elements in the emerging workplace—than hierarchy. When a simplistic, static hierarchical model is imposed on a system that strains toward complexity and change, you get institutional failure. Given the unprecedented complexity and rapid change in our society, Hock says mass institutional failure is what we can expect if we don't overhaul not only our institutions but our thinking. (Durrance, 1997)

"The important thing to remember," says Hock (reflecting on what he calls the Age of Management that Newton's assumptions ushered in) "is not that we became a society of expert managers but that the nature of our expertise became the management of constants, uniformity, and efficiency while our need has become the coordination of variability, complexity and effectiveness—the very process of change itself." (Durrance, 1997)

WE HAVE THE TOOL...DO WE HAVE THE PROCESS?

VISA is not the only organization to adopt the "network" or "node" or "chaordic" structure. One of the most powerful structures on the planet today is the Internet: clusters of computers cooperating to form a global self-renewing, self-regulating, self-organizing information network All attempts to regulate, privatize or limit the Internet have failed because the primary ethic of the Internet is the freedom to evolve. Other organizations, such as twelve-step programs and some religious institutions, are structured to support autonomy and cooperation around a set of commonly held values and principles.

Our institutions can be no more or less than the sum of the beliefs of the people drawn to them, Hock says. "An organization's success has enormously more to do with clarity of a shared purpose, common principles and strength of belief in them than to assets, expertise, operating ability, or management competence, important as they may be.... All organizations are merely conceptual embodiments of a very old, very basic idea—the idea of community." (Waldrop, 1996)

Hock refuses to supply a "plan" to implement his radical ideas. He says that every organization has to agree upon its own values and principles, then create modes of working that reflect those shared values. Hock tells the groups he works with that getting consensus on purpose, values and principles "is going to be the hardest work you'll ever do... Most of you will want to quit. And before it's over, quite a few of you will.

"... getting there is going to be downright excruciating," says Hock. "You're going to struggle to articulate things you never even knew you felt. How do you really feel about power, for example, or autonomy, or job security, or how the money flows? Executives and secretaries alike are going to find themselves breaking down in tears. It's going to take a year—or more. But it's absolutely essential. Because what we're trying to do is build a community. And it's only when that community has solid agreement on purposes and principles that you can start talking about the concept and structure of the organization (Waldrop, 1996)."

CONCLUSION

I welcome change and the opportunities it brings. I approve whole-heartedly of the flattening of organizations and the demise of "command-and-control" management style in families and schools as well as workplaces. And yet I see the potential for enormous harm. People cannot be expected to embrace change if they lack the tools to cope with it. Just as Quentin Rose cannot be blamed for not knowing what a swivel is, we cannot expect ourselves to be nimble, self-directed and responsible while we see the world with inadequate cognitive tools.

Are our tools all that inadequate? I think it is quite obvious. To me, the acceptable number of children living in poverty is zero. The acceptable level of unemployment? Zero. The acceptable level of inflation? Zero. The acceptable number of dictators, wars, little kids weaving rugs or making running shoes in sweatshops? Zero. And that's just me. Other people have their own concerns—about the environment, human rights, world health, preserving culture and so on. There is a long list of convictions people routinely devote their lives to.

I go mental when people shrug and say ridiculous things like, "that's just the way things are." If Charles Dickens had agreed, he might never have written *Oliver Twist* and we might still be sending children down coal mines. If Copernicus had agreed, he would never have discovered the model of the universe that made it possible for us to get to the moon. At one time, the moon was a distant fantasy. What's our fantasy? Which ship will we build to sail there? Will there be room for everybody (including the sick, the lazy and the untalented)? Comfortable berths? Freedom, equality, health and justice? I hope so. Can we create the tools, cognitive and otherwise, we need? I believe it. Like astronaut Jim Lovell says in the movie Apollo 13: "From now on we live in a world where man has walked on the moon. It's not a miracle. We just decided to go."

References

Durrance, Bonnie. *"The Evolutionary Vision of Dee Hock: From Chaos to Chaords."* Training and Development. The American Society for Training and Development. Vol. 51, Number 4. April, 1997.

Logan, Robert K. *The Fifth Language: Learning a Living in the Computer Age.* Stoddart, Toronto, 1995.

Waldrop, M. Mitchell. *"The Trillion-Dollar Vision of Dee Hock"* FastCompany, 1996 http://www.fastcompany.com/ (November, 1997).

CHAPTER FIVE: PERSUASIVE ESSAYS

E ssentially, all communication is a ploy to convince someone of your position on any given issue. Every essay in this book is trying to persuade you, as reader, to follow the writer's train of thought to his or her conclusions. Each outfit you don is an attempt to persuade the people who see you as to what type of a person you are: casual suburban, professional power-suited industrious type, preppie, goth, free spirit. Even people who deny a conscious attempt to create a "statement" manage to wear appropriate clothing for weddings, job interviews, and outdoor rock concerts. With all these indicators and every nuance being one of persuasion, imagine what happens when you deliberately try to place words in a pattern to sway someone.

When you are attempting to truly persuade someone to your way of thinking, you have to spend some forethought on your readers. Are they likely to be already in synch with your way of thinking, and as a result just in need of being moved to action on a particular issue? Or, are they possibly already entrenched in an opposing viewpoint, and your mission will be to topple that way of thinking in order to make room for your argument? These considerations are vital, as they will influence the ways in which you decide to appeal to your reader.

There are various ways to persuade your readers. You can appeal to their sense of logic and reason; you can pull on their emotions; and you can play to their sense of ethics. There are other things you can appeal to as well, though we won't be dwelling on them here. It would be wise to understand, however, that some writers may try to appeal to your baser senses, those of greed, bigotry, or insecurities. As you achieve more power in your own concept of how rhetoric works, you will likely be able to spot these ploys much more easily.

If you think that your argument may be one which will require some fundamental change of position for your readers, or that they will already hold a contrary opinion, it is best to use as much reason and logic as possible to present your argument. This is usually the case in formal and college essays. Back up all your statements with proof, in some form or other. This can be achieved through statistical facts, expert opinion which supports your argument, or strong anecdotal evidence from your own research and observations.

If, on the other hand, your argument is one which you consider to be a "motherhood and apple pie" issue, (in other words, something that no one would dispute) but you wish to incite your reader to some form of action on said issue, an appeal to their emotion might be in order. Offer more figurative language, paint telling descriptive pictures, and provide insightful narratives to bolster your argument and create a powerful message to your reader. This is not to say you should avoid reasoning and logic in such an essay. However, if your reader is likely to be on your side from the beginning, you must question your rationale for your essay and playing upon the heartstrings of your reader is a good way to create a groundswell supportive attitude for your cause, whatever it may be.

An appeal to ethics is something that one can use to a certain extent in any form of persuasive essay. Within this form, you tend to highlight your own attitudes, showing yourself to be a decent, right-thinking sort of person who would not steer your reader wrong. In equal measures will come the subtextual argument that people who agree with you can also be considered decent, right-thinking people. This, in its most abject form, is akin to the homespun car salesman who uses his own personality to sell you a beater. If you achieve the right tone, this strategy can be incredibly effective, but it can also decimate your argument, no matter how logical, if your reader senses he is being snowed into believing you. Be very wary of sounding like someone's Uncle Ernest when using this ploy.

Now that you've determined how to appeal to your reader, it is useful to look at the two ways of laying out your argument for your reader. There are two forms of argument: deductive and inductive. Either one is effective, depending on the basis of your argument and the implied reader you have in mind.

The deductive argument is one in which you present several facts which line up to create your argument infallibly. A logical syllogism is a simple form of deductive argument, and can be considered the basis of all logical thought. A syllogism is an argument in which two facts are presented (a major and minor premise) and, from them, a third supposition (a conclusion) is arrived at. One famous syllogism goes:

> Socrates is a man.
> All men are mortal.
> THEREFORE, Socrates is mortal.

In order for the conclusion to be true, both premises must be true. There cannot be a false conclusion which is supported by two premises which are true. However, one must investigate to ascertain that the premises are indeed true. Think of this syllogism:

George Eliot wrote sensitive characterizations of women.
Many male Victorian writers were dismissive of female characters.
THEREFORE George Eliot was an unusual man of his times.

Do you recognize anything wrong with this argument? The conclusion is very wrong. This is because George Eliot, aka Mary Ann Evans, was a woman. When creating a deductive argument, be very careful of your facts. When examining a deductive argument that you find troubling in its conclusions, pay careful attention to the premises on which it is founded.

An inductive argument goes beyond deductive fact, and often relies on the reader's ability to make cognitive leaps with the writer. The argument, while founded in fact, will push beyond known provable argument, and venture into some hypothetical extensions, which, if argued properly, can be very effective. An analogy that might help elucidate this form of argument is the scientific community's trials on lab rats to ascertain what might be equal reactions in humans. While the rats and humans differ in various respects, there are some similarites (they are mammals, they all look pretty much alike to people who don't work with them on a daily basis, very few of them bother to vote) that allow the scientists to hypothesize from their research onto possible human consequences. These hypotheses are inductive up to the point where they are actually tried on humans. Likewise, an inductive argument will provide enough fact in some respects to allow the writer, and by extension, the reader, to make conclusions about hitherto unproven areas.

Most college essays will be of the deductive variety. You will choose a position to defend, and then provide proof of your conclusions. Eventually, you may move into more inductive arguments, requiring more rhetorical skills to lead your reader to make the leaps of logic you require to fulfill your argument.

When persuading a reader of your position, there are two things to remember, which both your mother and Emily Post have tried to inculcate in you from an early age. Never insult the reader, is the first thing to remember. People who have been put on the defensive rarely have the largeness of spirit to retain an open mind. The other thing to keep in mind is that "present company" is never excepted. This statement, often prefacing rather biased or prejudicial statements, is not enough to bring your reader on to your side against the world. Suppose a student's paper was to contain the sentence, "All English lecturers have big noses (present company excepted)." I know that, however objective I might try to be, I would not likely think myself a nasal anomaly in my chosen profession. I would be off to the mirror to check my nose, just before finding and circling every nitpicking error in the essay to ensure that the student's grade would be swimming with the fishes.

Your task is to persuade. It is a line of diplomacy and reason which you wish to walk. Plan your argument to highlight its most cogent aspects; appeal to your reader's sense of logic, emotion, or ethics. Demonstrate your own authority, without undermining the humanity of any opponent you may have to tackle. It is their argument you are disputing, not their character. Even if the character of the opponent is questionable (a pornographer, a criminal, a politician), it would behoove you to recall at all times that you must be perceived as the "good guy." Thrown stones tend to rebound in print. They also don't win you readers, although they may occasionally garner a laugh or two. All in all, it's not worth it. Let your argument speak for itself, without denigrating the personality of any other person. Remember, if people are not worth treating with a modicum of respect, perhaps their argument isn't really worthy of your time at all. If it is, then treat them as you would a colleague. Let your reader make up her own mind about their character. You walk on higher ground. You are a writer, after all.

W. Frank Epling

Frank Epling is a Professor of Psychology at the University of Alberta. This essay first appeared in the now defunct *Alberta*, Vol 1, #2, in 1989. It speaks to the controversy of animal testing. It is especially significant to hear from a scientist from Alberta, since the province is proud of its "rat-free" state.

Humour is the strategy used to bring us into this essay, which is dealing with issues that normally create strong emotions in debaters.

Rats

I am an animal researcher and I work with rats. Now, for most people, the rat is an animal that does not elicit great sympathy. In fact, most people would hit a rat with a shovel if it dared to run across their basement floor. Of course, in Alberta, rats do not run across basement floors because the province is "rat free" and proud of it. This is not, however, exactly correct because some rats manage to sneak in from British Columbia and Saskatchewan, and I have some in my laboratory. Nonetheless, the Alberta Rat Patrol does an excellent job, and only very sneaky rats survive the border crossing. Since most of these are new arrivals and don't have a home, the Alberta winter usually gets what the Rat Patrol misses.

There are good rats and there are bad rats. I know this sounds absurd but stick with me and I will explain. Some time ago I was preparing a twelve page written document that was an ethics justification for some proposed research with rats. I had to make certain that my rats got the very best food, shelter, and medical care. I also had to convince the local committees that I had the overall welfare of my rats foremost in my mind. This proposal took several days to write. The reason for all this is that I have good rats. Good rats live in laboratory cages.

Following the second day of work on my ethics proposal, I went home, opened a beer, put up my feet and flipped on the tube. "Fifth Estate" or "W5" was on, I don't remember which. Also, I can't recall the first news item but I certainly can the second—it was about the Alberta Rat Patrol. On this show the dedicated people of the Rat Patrol were keeping the cities, fields, and houses of Alberta rat free. This was not a fun time for those creatures who tried to invade the province. The documentary focused on the Alberta/Saskatchewan border. There are lots of rats in Saskatchewan. Well, let me tell you, the members of the Rat Patrol were shooting, hitting, and poisoning rats; these were bad rats. Bad rats do not live in laboratory cages.

There are other ways to be a bad rat. Rats that escape from their cages are not protected by ethics proposals. As soon as their feet hit the laboratory floor they become pests and are subject to traps, poison, and so on. Shotguns are not used because of damage to walls, noise, and the possibility of shooting a student or researcher. Believe me though, these rats are not held in high esteem. This is particularly true in Alberta because they could get out of the building and infest our rat-free province.

Another way that rats lose their good status is to be food. There are animals, like some very large snakes, that will not eat unless their prey items are alive. In order to keep these animals, they must be fed. Food is not protected by ethics committees.

All of this makes me wonder why I am spending a significant amount of time writing ethics proposals for rats, rather than doing research with them. Don't misunderstand me. I happen to like rats and I do not advocate mistreating them. I am against the use of these animals for testing cosmetics and for repeating research where the findings are well established and rats are made to suffer. I am, however, convinced that research with rats (and other animals) can lead to findings that promote human welfare, and I am in favour of doing that research. In order to understand why I am spending a fair amount of time writing ethics proposals for my rat research, it is necessary to consider the animal rights movement.

Over the past fifteen years, this movement has steadily grown in number of members, and it has received increasing attention from the press. So called "animal activists" belong to a variety of organizations and they range from moderate to extreme in their views. I think it is fair to say, though, that all animal activists think that cute furry animals, are nice animals—even when they are pests or food. Rats have two strikes against them, bad press and a long hairless tail. Also, the black plague did not help their cause. This prejudice for some animals and against others is curious. Not very many people are concerned about the live lobsters found at supermarkets. I think this is because the lobster is very tasty and looks vaguely like a large underwater insect. On the other hand, baby seals look cute, warm, cuddly, and helpless. Thus, the seal but not the lobster gets sympathy. Returning to my point, the animal rights movement has created a public concern for the welfare of animals, and some of this has reached hysterical and absurd proportions.

A few of the more extreme views include stopping all medical research with animals, replacing animal subjects with humans, including animals in the United States Bill of Rights, recognizing specism as a prejudice similar to racism and so on. I don't know about you, but I can't imagine a rat, a lobster, or even a seal with the rights of free speech, assembly, and the pursuit of happiness. How would they know they had these rights? Also what happens when one animal, say a lion, infringes on a deer's right to life? All in all, these views seem a bit whacky to me but they are taken seriously by some people.

One tactic of the more extreme animal activists has been overt violence and intimidation. Some individuals have joined paramilitary animal rights movements. This is an odd development since it is the only revolutionary movement I know of where none of the members are the creatures whose rights are being fought for. Nonetheless, these people are serious, and they have bombed the houses of animal researchers, released laboratory animals, vandalized labs, threatened to inject meat products with poison, organized and promoted letter writing campaigns to stop legitimate research, and harassed reputable scientists with threatening letters and phone calls.

I don't know how many of my fellow citizens are members of, or in sympathy with, the animal rights movement; but I suspect not very many. This speculation is based on the number of steaks on display at my local grocery and the notable lack of concern for pit bull dogs in Edmonton. So, why all the fuss?

A few years ago, the *Edmonton Sun* called and wanted to interview me and several other animal researchers. We were encouraged to participate in this interview in order to "promote the benefits of animal research." Anyway, we had one of the best run and closely supervised facilities in Canada. The reporter and a photographer showed up and asked questions about my projects, photographed my rats, thanked me for giving them time, and left. I looked forward to local fame.

A week or so later, the *Sunday Sun* carried the article. I was not famous. They had so garbled my name that you could not tell whose research they were talking about. This was very fortunate (or perhaps intentional to prevent a civil suit). The first page of the Sunday supplement had a full page picture of a monkey sitting in a restraining chair looking like it had just had a tooth pulled by a student dentist. None of the people interviewed by the *Sun* worked with monkeys and I recognized the picture. The photograph was a famous one that has appeared in antivivisectionist magazines and advertising campaigns for "save the animals." I don't know why the same picture is used over and over, but it is.

Articles like this portray animal researchers as modern day versions of Dr. Mengele. It would seem that we can't wait to torture animals in order to arrive at conclusions everybody knows already. We have not received "good press." I could present a case for doing animal research but I would digress from the point I am trying to make. Writing ethics proposals that defend research with animals that are arbitrarily defined as good is bizarre.

As I have said, there are good and bad rats. At least in Alberta, it appears there are going to be bad rats for some time to come. Being a bad rat seems to depend on "the luck of the draw." Since bad rats are not considered worthy of ethics protection, I could use them in my research. There is, however, a problem. I could ask for bad rats but they would automatically become good when they were placed in cages in my laboratory. To appreciate this it is necessary to understand a few things about universities and public relations.

The people who run universities tend to place great value on "positive press": "negative press" is very much discouraged. This makes sense; the public supports universities and if they don't like what is going on they may withdraw their support. Animal activists would like to stop all animal experiments, and they search for an opportunity to provide unfavorable press. Forcing scientists to justify the ethics of their animal research helps protect the university from this publicity. There are, however, unfortunate side effects. Large sums of money are spent on animal care staff who police laboratories. Time is wasted on writing ethics proposals, sitting on ethics committees, and waiting for ethics approval. This and more for an animal most citizens would stomp on if given the chance.

I am probably more concerned about the welfare of rats than most people. I have known many rats over the years and I have liked more than a few. I am in favor of kind treatment for rats and other animals that are used in scientific research. I do think, however, that a consideration of good and bad rats and lobsters and seals points to a confusion of ethics. So what can I do? Not much, write a commentary like this and then put in another two days writing another ethics proposal. Rats!

W.P. Kinsella

W.P. Kinsella is probably most famous for his baseball novels, and especially *Shoeless Joe*, which spawned the enormously successful movie *Field of Dreams*. Originally from Alberta, he now lives in British Columbia. Kinsella is a highly successful and popular writer. Monumentally prolific, he is often controversial and always entertaining. While essay writing is not his chosen métier, his distinctive voice makes one wish he'd try it more often.

Nuke the Whales and Piss in the Ocean

I am the wrong person to ask for an essay. I hate essays. I seldom read nonfiction because it is so boring. I seldom contribute to books by small presses who have to publish five books a year, no matter how inane or dismally self-serving, in order to keep the Canada Council gravy drooling down their chins. I can only imagine the soulless drivel you will receive for "a book that adds grist to the mill of British Colombians inclined to ask the WHO-AM-I questions."

People with the time and temerity and mush for brains to ask those darling WHO-AM-I questions are already safely locked up in a university, or sleeping fitfully in a cardboard box under a viaduct somewhere in downtown Vancouver.

Upon reading the letter asking me for an essay, I raced into the living room and said to my wife, "I have finally arrived on the Canadian cultural scene. I have been asked to write an essay for 'a book that contributes to existing definitions/expressions of B.C.' Imagine that!" I cried. "They obviously think they've written to someone who gives a shit.

"Try to picture the reams of pretentious intellectual crap they're going to have to sift through," I went on. "The list of potential contributors reads like a *Who's Everybody* in the local artistic community. For some reason these editors seem to think that writers and artists know or care about what is going on in British Columbia. Real writers and artists *create*, they don't give a flying fuck about British Columbia, or any piece of geography, or any simpering small press that wants to publish a timely book in order to cash in on the Expo 86 gravy train. I suppose anyone dumb enough to attend Expo 86 might be dull-witted enough to want to read about 'existing definitions/expressions of B.C.'

"If they want to capture the true British Columbia, the editors should have solicited contributions from any of the province's corrupt labour leaders, or how about Cuddly Dave Barrett, who's the

world's number one St. Louis Cardinal fan? Or maybe Big Bob
Carter, the guy who's turned on by one-legged runners?

"I suppose it was easy to overlook someone as short as Allan
Fotheringham. But what about Clifford Olsen, who is probably
Canada's best-known British Columbian? I've always thought that
anyone with the bad taste to open a cabaret called The Clifford
Olsen Case couldn't help but succeed. The cabaret would be papered
with pictures of the victims as published by the Vancouver *Province*,
as well as reproductions of the $100,000 check the RCMP paid to
Olsen's family. The band could be called Cliffie and the Stranglers.

Then there's Flyin' Phil Gaglardi (is he still alive?). And Ma
Murray (is she still dead?)."

"You lack a certain sense of community," my wife said.

"I sincerely hope so," I replied.

I think it is vitally important, especially for a writer, *not* to have
a sense of community. If a person is going to be creative there is no
time for the pettiness and idiocy that are part and parcel of *all*
organisations.

I am not a person who asks the WHO-AM-I questions. In fact I do
not have a philosophical bone in my body, and I have a good deal of
contempt for people who waste time on philosophical ruminations.
My suggestion to people who worry about things like WHY AM I
HERE is to get a job and they won't have time to worry about such
totally unimportant issues.

I am a writer. Writers write. *So-called writers* spend their time
looking for excuses not to; they join writers' organisations (being
especially happy when they can serve on the executive; if the organ-
isation is small enough *everyone* gets to serve on the executive),
become involved in causes (they campaign for either the poor or the
whales; if they are really desirous of not writing they campaign for
both), teach one or more courses at a university or community college (preferably poetry writing, modern dance, or anything to do with
tofu), mess with politics, serve on committees, go out drinking, start
a small press so they can publish themselves and all their friends who
don't have enough talent to write copy for grocery bags, and have a
lot of other writers as friends. None of the above applies to me.

The editors are obviously looking for contributors who easily get
choked up over matters of patriotism and philosophy. Sorry to disil-
lusion you, but I live in British Columbia for only one reason; White
Rock is the warmest spot in mainland Canada.

Canadian politics, both federal and provincial, is so asinine as to boggle the mind. I try very hard to ignore it; I seldom read local papers, don't own a radio, try never to watch local or even national news. Still, it is impossible not to be angry. I have always been in favour of a separate and independent Western Canada. I was a separatist long before separatism became a force in western politics. If that little weasel Pierre Trudeau had stayed in power a few more months the West might have separated and I might have broken my vow about becoming involved in politics.

I once received a letter from a school in Ontario; a copy had been sent to forty prominent Canadians asking them to discuss the "Canadian Identity" for the benefit of the students. The school promised to display each reply on the walls somewhere in the school. I often wonder if they displayed mine. Behind the furnace probably, because first of all I told them they should be ashamed to be wasting their time on something so pointless. I also told them that *if* there were anything truly representative of Canada it had to be Bob and Doug Mackenzie of the Great White North. Beer-swilling drunks in tuques and parkas with ski lift tickets attached to the zippers seem to epitomize everything truly Canadian.

Having lived in B.C. off and on since 1967, I suppose the dominant impression I have of this province is of strident and greedy union leaders, most of them foreigners, who, after they helped the unions destroy the economy of the British Isles, set sail for Canada to do the same thing here. They must be extremely gratified that they have succeeded in making the B.C. lumber industry noncompetitive in world markets. The image I associate most strongly with British Columbia is overpaid slobs walking picket lines, threatening violence.

To answer the question I get asked most often—I do not write autobiography. My life is not interesting enough to write about. Let me give one short piece of advice to every would-be fiction writer who thinks he or she has an interesting life: "You haven't. Nobody cares about your life. Don't write it down."

What a fiction writer puts on paper should have little or nothing to do with his or her personal life.

Personally, I hate banks, churches, Pierre Trudeau, bilingualism, metric measurement, dogs, seat belts, alcoholics, royalty, the Bay Street thieves who have robbed the West blind for a century, all bureaucrats, the CFL, hockey, snow, skiers, figure-skating, the CBC, all fish, dates, figs, liver, cold weather, people who send out Christmas letters, traffic, Expo 86, unions, house plants, demonstrators of every ilk, Pro-Life fanatics, the dipsticks from Greenpeace, the term "Meaningful Relationship," and binder twine. And I don't like *anybody* very much.

In my fiction, I take frequent shots at my first two hates, for they are after all universals; whenever there is a revolution the bankers are killed first and then the priests, as it should be. I suppose if I could change the world in any one way, I would obliterate the word RELIGION and everything attendant to it from the history of mankind. Suffice it to say that no matter what is professed, religion teaches hate, intolerance, misogyny. The world would be a 1000 percent better place if no one believed in the supernatural.

A fiction writer ultimately writes about what he or she likes to read. There are only two absolute universals, laughter and tears, and I like to read stories that make me laugh and make me cry, ideally both in the same story. Consequently I try to write the same kind of literature. My heroes are rather likable fumblers, who are overmatched by the idiots who surround them. Like it or not the bureaucracy usually triumphs; all the rest of us can do is throw an occasional wrench in its gears. I know from long experience that being highly intelligent is a terrible drawback when it comes to holding a job. Most managers are not there because of their intelligence but because of their ability to follow orders and to suck up to someone in higher management who is of equally average ability. There is nothing a manager fears as much as an employee more intelligent than he is.

About 75 percent of all books published in Canada don't deserve to see the light of day. I would include several of my own books. The Canada Council grant system allows would-be publishers to form incestuous little groups who take turns publishing each other's nonsensical poetry and boring fiction. In the USA even the small presses, unless they are operated by someone rich who doesn't mind losing money, have to consider the market, the sales potential of the manuscript, and marketing, before committing to publish a manuscript. In other words, if no one is going to be interested in reading a book, it does not get published. Still, there are very few talented writers who go unpublished. Even in the USA much of the poetry and fiction published should never see the light of day. Unfortunately, in Canada, once a publisher gets a grant he or she does not have to sell any of the books that are printed. There are many publishers who make absolutely no effort to sell or distribute their books.

I am not arguing that aid to writers and publishers is wrong, just that there must be a better way to allocate the money. In my experience (I have never had a major Canada Council grant), the process is too complicated. Consequently the people who are able to get a long string of grants are the accountant-mentality types who are good at filling out forms but terribly short on writing talent. Instead of supporting writers who are talented and turn out saleable work, we are supporting nitpickers who are good at filling out grant forms.

I am reminded of something that happened to me about ten years ago when I was still writing poetry. I submitted a batch of poems to a literary magazine. I enclosed a photocopied sheet of biographical information, which began, "in the event that you need biographical information, the following will save us further correspondence."

Following is the letter I received from the editor of that magazine, and my reply.

Dear W.P. Kinsella:

Thank you for submitting poems to _____.

It is this magazine's policy to publish the finest creative talents in this country and elsewhere, and this is what we've done. However, implicit in this policy is our dedication to the writing community—that is, to not only provide a quality showcase for poets and writers and artists but also to try and provide a sense of community, of oneness with our fellow artists.

For this reason, I am returning your poems—and they are fine pieces—because I sincerely feel you are either lacking in any genuine sense of what the writing community is, or you simply ignore it. I tell you this out of reaction to your sentence, "the following will save us further correspondence." I see that you have published in several magazines, and I suggest that, if you would like the frequency of your acceptance to increase, then do away with such Goddamn rubbish. Publishing poems is not like—God forbid!—ordering underwear out of a catalogue, though admittedly you *at least* have to sign your name when ordering underwear. No truly dedicated editor would accept any poems from a poet who sent along such a sterile, impersonal note as yourself. Though, in the literal sense, you are quite right: your note will, indeed, "save us further correspondence," sadly enough.

Now, as you can see, I have spent quite a deal more effort in writing you back than yourself in submitting to _____. This is a fundamental error, there is no interaction between us at all.

Yours truly,

Tim _____

Dear Tim:

Your tirade received and noted.

I am both sorry and amused that a simple list of publications and biographical information could elicit such a devastating response. I have been told that my poetry is of such dubious quality as to only be fit for publication after being translated into some little known foreign language, perhaps Bulgarian, but never before have I had my biographical information maligned as sterile and impersonal. It is sterile and impersonal, and as I see it, that is the way it should be. I am not in the habit of enclosing chatty little letters with my submissions to editors. Even if the editor is a personal friend, submissions for publication are on one level, personal letters on another, and I would never try to combine the two.

I'm afraid that your reference to, "a sense of community, of oneness with our fellow artists," leaves me cold. I don't, I feel, lack any sense of what the writing community is; however, I do my best to ignore it.

My experience is that most writers, when away from their typewriters, are vain, egotistical, irksome, opinionated, argumentative, tiresome, and more often than not, ill informed. I rather proudly include myself in each of the above categories, only in my case I can display all of those delightful qualities while at my typewriter, as well as away from it. Writers like free liquor, cigarettes, food, praise (legitimate or otherwise), and enjoy sitting around pretending they know the meaning of words like *juxtaposition*, *ambivalent*, *nebulous*, and *antisyzygy*. The odd one knows how to spell *impersonal*, but most of them spell it *your* way. They'll use any excuse, and create one if none is available, to pat the ass of your wife, girlfriend, mother, daughter, brother, father, or budgie bird. They will also, on occasion, send chatty little letters to editors they don't know in hopes of endearing themselves and thus getting some of their second rate poems printed because they have a oneness with the writing community, while serious, hard working, dedicated writers who only include a list of publications get their poems sent back and their ears boxed in the bargain. (God, I forgot to add thin-skinned to the list of lovable qualities which most writers possess.)

Have you ever considered publishing some of the dandy little covering letters that are submitted to your magazine? Perhaps you could have "Chatty Letter" contest. To qualify, writers would have to include one short story or three poems along with their friendly letter to the editor. It would be just like sending in two box tops and the door off your garage, in care of The Station To Which You Are Listening.

The next time I submit material to your magazine, nothing is holy, I am going to include the kind of covering letter I imagine you are looking for. It would read something like this:

Dearest Timmy: I'm sending you some peachy keen poems I just wrote. Don't you just come at the image of Joachin Murieta going down on the Andria Doria? I do. If you don't grab them up right now, I just know that *Shipbuilder's Semiannual* will.

I haven't been writing much lately because I've been working just so hard out in the writing community trying to attain oneness with my fellow artists. I'm not sure what oneness is, but I'd cut off my left nut if it would get me published in your groovy keen magazine, which I've read and reread and just adore every comma of.

Timmy, I know what a great writer you are personally, not to mention professionally, and I have this friend who is publishing just the most prestigious little magazine. It is a single bark of birch hand painted annually and personally delivered by the editor, a retired Hungarian neo-activist wino, who you have to let live in your bathroom for two weeks between deliveries. I've told him all about you, Timmy, and he's simply dying to see the covering letter *you* send out with your manuscripts. I'm certain that by using my influence I can get you published. You can just send some of your work back with the acceptance letter for my poems, save postage and everything.

Last week I attended this really super keen writer's workshop and welding instructional school, where we all sat around under a railroad bridge and drank muscatel, while we discussed the phallic imagery in *Nancy Drew and the Case of the Dried Up Prune*. Oneness, man, that's the name of the game.

God, Timmy, how time flies. (Terrific metaphor, or is it? I think I'll use it in one of my poems anyway.) It seems like years since the last time I saw you. Hey, man, remember the time we got bombed on aspirin and lemon gin and ended up with that freaky chick who used to walk her pheasant down Second Avenue? Those were the days, eh? TIMMY, IF YOU DON'T PUBLISH MY POEMS I'M GOING TO TELL YOUR WIFE ABOUT THE GIRL WITH THE PHEASANT.

Well, I've got to hurry this up, Dear Timmy, because I have an appointment with just the most talented young author. She doesn't believe in pens or typewriters and is writing her novel by gluing mouse turds on 8 x 10 sheets of plywood. She's having a little trouble with the *O*'s and *S*'s but we are going to try and work that out this afternoon. We figure that if she has a mouse right there and squeezes it at the appropriate moment. ... but, I really must run, my nails are almost dry.

Warmest regards,

Grope**

** Writers always like to sign letters with little pet nicknames when they write to each other.
*** Timmy, for god's sake keep this letter; it will be valuable someday. You can contribute it to my collected letters and probably get your name in the index with an asterisk either before it or after it.

Now, as you can see, I have spent quite a deal more effort in writing back than you originally did in attacking my biographical information for being cold and impersonal. I wonder where that leaves us? I do hope you have a sense of humour and a sense of the ridiculous.

Best regards,

Bill Kinsella

I never heard back from that editor, who obviously wanted pen pals rather than contributors. His magazine died almost immediately after our correspondence. I've always hoped I had something to do with its demise.

Henry Kreisel

Henry Kreisel was born in Vienna, Austria, in 1922. He left for England in 1938 during the Nazi annexation of his country. In 1940 Kreisel was among the many Jews and alleged Nazi sympathizers sent from Britain to internment camps in New Brunswick and elsewhere in Canada. When released a year later, he studied English literature at the University of Toronto where he received his Bachelor of Arts degree in 1946 and his Master of Arts degree in 1947. Kreisel then joined the University of Alberta where he completed his Doctorate in 1954, became a full professor of English in 1959, and eventually head of the Department of English in 1961. In 1970 Kreisel was named Vice-President (Academic) of the University of Alberta. Kreisel wrote two novels, *The Rich Man* (1948) and *The Betrayal* (1964). He also published a collection of short stories, *The Almost Meeting* (1981), and has written many essays and articles on immigration literature and culture. The University of Alberta awarded him the A.C. Rutherford Award for Excellence in Teaching in 1986 and the Government of Alberta awarded him the Sir Frederick Haultain Prize for significant contributions to the Fine Arts.

"Problems of Writing in Canada" comes from Kreisel's book, *Another Country*.

Problems of Writing in Canada

There has been a great deal of talk in recent months about the problems of so-called 'new' Canadians. In the last few years hundreds of thousands of people have come to this country from all parts of Europe in order to settle and begin a new life here, and we have heard and read, in radio talks and in articles in the press, something of the problems which they have had to face, and which they continue to face, in their attempts to integrate themselves into the life of our country. Their problems are economic, but also psychological and cultural, because the transition from one way of life to another is not always easy.

Suppose now that among these new arrivals there is the odd person who wishes to devote himself to literature. A quixotic notion? Perhaps. Assume it, anyway. Suppose further that this man has come to Canada from some Central European country, so that his native language is a language other than English; and yet he decides that, having cut his ties with the old world and the old country, he must adopt this new land, and, above all, its language, and that if he is to express himself at all it must be in English.

That was the decision I made when I came to this country in 1940. I had left Austria, where I was born and partly educated, after Hitler annexed that country in 1938. I was then fifteen years old.

The next two years I spent in England. There I worked in a tailoring factory, but also managed to learn enough English to begin a fairly systematic reading of classic English literature in the evenings and on my days off. I even began to have some notions that I might myself perhaps write something some day. When I reached this country, I made two decisions. I decided that I would stay and work in this country if this country would have me, for such charms and allures as Europe once held for me were gone, and I decided further that I would devote myself to the study of English literature, and that if I were to write anything myself it would be in English. I remember making these decisions very consciously and very deliberately, but without the full realization that in the waters in which I proposed to swim there were submerged rocks. At seventeen one tends to be romantic, and to have exaggerated notions of what is possible. Still, in this case ignorance perhaps was bliss because, blissfully unaware of danger, I did not suffer fright. Not that I was completely blind to the difficulties that faced me. I knew, even at seventeen, that a language is more than a collection of words and grammatical rules, and that to master it one had to understand also the traditions, the attitudes, the frame of mind of the people who speak the language. Could a foreigner do that? Could he change his language as if it were a shirt? And could he simply throw the discarded shirt away? I was troubled and perplexed. And I remember talking the whole matter over at great length with a friend, an older man who had been a very successful journalist in Vienna.

'Perhaps,' he said, 'perhaps it can be done if one is young enough when one starts.'

'How young,' I asked, 'is young?'

But he wouldn't commit himself. 'It has been done before,' he said to me with an amused smile. 'Joseph Conrad did it. Go and see what he did.'

So I went and read Conrad. The result was despair. For how could one hope to emulate that master? But there was also hope. Hope derived from Conrad's despair. 'I had to work like a coal miner in his pit,' I found Conrad writing to a friend, 'quarrying all my English sentences out of a black night.' It was comforting to know that the great Conrad had not come by his triumphs easily. And Conrad also taught one to have respect for one's adopted language, especially because it was an acquired instrument, and one had to **earn** the right to use it, even if one could never hope to use it in so masterly a way as he had done.

I have often heard it said that the writer who changes countries, as it were, has an advantage over the writer who stays put. He observes his new country with fresh eyes, the argument goes, he sees things more sharply because he can view both the old and the new country with a certain amount of detachment, and place people and events in their proper perspective. The argument sounds convincing at first, but it contains at best a half truth. Certainly, the newcomer sees some things more sharply than people who have lived all their lives in one place and have come to take a great many things for granted, and some of his insights may well be perceptive and original and even valuable. But—and this is especially true of first impressions—his observations are often a compound of what he has heard and read about the new country, of preconceived notions, that is, modified by what he now sees and hears at first hand. That is the way most travel books are written, and very often they tell us more about the feelings and prejudices of the writer than they do about the country which he describes. It is only very rarely that the newcomer can give us a really profound picture of a country and its people in a work of art. There are too many things he doesn't know or doesn't understand, and there is often a tendency to make people and things look quaint and picturesque merely because they are different. There are some countries—Mexico, for instance, or Italy—where life seems very highly coloured and exciting, and where people often seem to act out their private lives in public. The exotic surface of life, the rich historical associations, the very climate, thus become sources of drama and therefore act as powerful stimuli to the creative imagination.

Canada is not such a country. The surface of life here seems almost too placid, the tempo of life too even. Canada is not therefore a country that offers a writer—and especially one who comes here from abroad—ready-made dramatic situations. This drawback (if it is a drawback) he shares with the native Canadian writer, of course. In recent years, indeed, the search for the **Canadian** character, for a **Canadian** identity, has been the number one intellectual parlor game of serious-minded Canadians. Hugh Kenner wrote, in a rather snide way, that 'the Diogenes who would shine his torch on the Canadian face is rather in the position of the spinster continually looking beneath the bed and finding nobody,' and Chester Duncan said, 'We haven't discovered what we are or where we're going and therefore we haven't much to say.' Similar views are widely held, I think, and I have often heard them voiced. I am beginning to suspect that to hold them is to take the easy way out, but they do reflect some of the difficulties which writers in Canada have felt they had to cope with.

Certainly it has been my experience that it is only after a long time that one begins to sense, and partly to understand, the strong undercurrents of passion and emotion which exist here as elsewhere in the world, but which are often hidden beneath a rather thick crust of reticent Puritanism. To the man who comes here from abroad, Canada is not an easy country to come to know and to write about.

At any rate, I found that when, after many trials and many errors, I felt confident enough to undertake the writing of a novel, I turned, almost instinctively, to a European experience, although I had very naively thought when I first came here that I had done with Europe altogether. *The Rich Man*, which is, so far, the only long piece of fiction that I have published, begins in Toronto, but the central scenes of the book play themselves out in the Vienna of the 1930s, on the eve of great and catastrophic events—the annexation of Austria, the war, the horror of the Nazi concentration camps.

Soon after I had finished writing *The Rich Man*, I set to work on another novel. Stirred and moved by the experience of those who had survived the torment and the torture of the concentration camps, I wanted to write about a man who returns to the wreck and ruin of his former home. For so, I thought, might I have returned had I been less fortunate. Of this novel I wrote about a hundred pages before I felt forced to abandon it. For I found that a tremendous gulf of experience now separated me from the material I wanted to deal with, and sympathy and imagination alone were not enough to make up for the lack of precise and intimate knowledge.

As a writer I was now standing between two worlds. I no longer really knew Europe, and I did not yet feel that I really knew Canada. And only intimate knowledge can confer authority upon the imagination. It is only now that I am beginning to feel that this country is in me as well as that I am in this country. It takes a long time, much longer than I had thought when I set out upon my journey, to circumnavigate the submerged rocks.

Mordecai Richler

Mordecai Richler is the author of numerous screen plays and ten novels, including the much lauded *Barney's Version*, which won the Giller Prize, The Stephen Leacock Award for Humour, and the Commonwealth Writers Prize. Caustic and slapstick in equal measures, Richler never pulls his punches when it comes to essay writing.

In fact, this particular essay is infamous for Edmontonians, for while we all read it eagerly, knowing it was about our very own St. Wayne of the Puck, we were horrified to see Edmonton skewered so bitingly. Now collected in *Belling the Cat: Selected Essays and Reports*, it still retains its power to wound.

Gretzky in Eighty-Four

Nineteen eighty-four. Edmonton. One day in March, at Barry T's Roadhouse out there on tacky 104th Street—wedged between welding shops and cinder-block strip joints and used-car lots—the city's amiable sportswriting fraternity gathered for its annual award luncheon. The writers were going to present Wayne Gretzky with their Sports Professional of the Year Award again. "I'll bet he tells us it means more to him than the Stanley Cup," one of the writers said.

"Or the Hart."

"Or his contract with General Mills. What do you think that's worth, eh?"

Bill Tuele, director of public relations for the Oilers, joined our table. "Does flying really scare Gretzky that much?" I asked.

"Nah. It doesn't scare him *that* much," Tuele said. "It's just that if we go bumpety-bump, he staggers off the plane with his shirt drenched."

Gretzky, who was running late, finally drifted into Barry T's. A curiously bland twenty-four-year-old in a grey flannel suit, he graciously accepted his plaque. "Any time you win an award, it's a thrill," he said. "With so many great athletes in Edmonton, I'm very honoured to win this." Then, his duty done, he retreated to a booth to eat lunch. And in Western Canada, where civility is the rule, he was not immediately besieged by reporters with notebooks or tape recorders. They left him alone with his overdone roast beef and curling, soggy french fries.

There had been a game the night before, the slumping Edmonton Oilers ending a five-gave losing streak at home, edging the Detroit Red Wings, 7–6, only their second victory in their last eight outings. Even so, they were still leading the league. Gretzky, juggling his crammed schedule, had fit me in for an interview at the Northlands

Coliseum at 9 a.m. Increasingly caught up in the business world, he told me he had recently read *Iacocca* and was now into *Citizen Hughes*. Though he enjoyed watching television soap operas and had once appeared on "The Young and the Restless" himself, he never bothered with fiction. "I like to read fact," he said. "I'm so busy, I haven't got the time to read stories that aren't real."

After the interview, there was a team practice and, following the sportswriters' lunch, he was scheduled to shoot a television commercial, and then there was a dinner he was obliged to attend. The next night, there was a game with Buffalo. It would be the seventieth for the Oilers in the regular NHL schedule but the seventy-second for Gretzky, who had played in two Canada Cup games immediately before the NHL season. There were a further ten games to come in the regular season and, as it turned out, another eighteen in the playoffs before the Oilers would skate to their second consecutive Stanley Cup.

But, at the time, Gretzky, understandably, was in a defensive mood, aware that another undeniably talented club, the Boston Bruins, led by Bobby Orr and Phil Esposito, had promised better than they had paid, faltering more than once in the playoffs. "We've already been compared to the great Boston team of the early seventies, which won only two cups but they still say should have won four," Gretzky said.

I asked Gretzky if he didn't consider the regular NHL schedule, which more than one wag has put down as the longest exhibition season in sport, to be insufferably long and meaningless. After all, it ran to 840 games, from September to April, and when it was over only five of the then twenty-one teams had been cut from what knowledgeable fans appreciated as the real season—the Stanley Cup playoffs. "Well," he said, "this city's not like New York, where there are lots of things to do. In Edmonton in February, we're the only attraction."

When I asked Peter Pocklington, the owner of the Oilers, about the seemingly endless season, he protested, "We're the only show in town. Coming to see Gretzky is like going to watch Pavarotti or Nureyev. What else are you going to do in Edmonton in the middle of the winter? How many beers can you drink?"

The capital of Alberta is a city you come from, not a place to visit, unless you have relatives there or an interest in an oil well nearby. On first glance, and even on third, it seems not so much a city as a jumble of a used-building lot, where the spare office towers and box-shaped apartment buildings and cinder-block motels discarded in the construction of real cities have been abandoned to waste away in the cruel prairie winter.

If Canada were not a country, however fragmented, but, instead, a house, Vancouver would be the solarium-cum-playroom, an afterthought of affluence; Toronto, the counting room, where money makes for the most glee; Montreal, the salon; and Edmonton, Edmonton, the boiler room. There is hardly a tree to be seen downtown, nothing to delight the eye on Jasper Avenue. On thirty-below-zero nights, grim religious zealots loom on street corners, speaking in tongues, and intrepid hookers in miniskirts rap on the windows of cars that have stopped for traffic. There isn't a first-class restaurant anywhere in town. For all that, Edmontonians are a truly admirable lot. They have not only endured great hardships in the past but also continue to suffer an abominable climate as well as isolation from the cities of light. And, to some degree, like other westerners, they thrive on resentments against the grasping, self-satisfied East, which has exploited their natural resources for years, taking their oil and gas at cut prices to subsidize inefficient Ontario and Quebec industries.

Insults, injuries.

For as long as Edmontonians can remember, the biggies were elsewhere. Though they had contributed many fine hockey players to the game, they could only hear about their feats on radio or later see them on television. Hockey was *their* game, damn it, *their* national sport, but New York, Chicago, Detroit, and Boston were in the NHL long before the league's governors adjudged Edmonton not so much worthy as potentially profitable. But in 1984, Canada's hockey shrines were either in decline, as was then the case in Montreal, or in total disrepute, as in Toronto. In those glory days, if easterners wanted to see the best player in the game more than twice a season, if they wanted to catch a dynasty in the making, why, then, they had to pack their fat coats and fur-lined boots and head for Edmonton, home of the Stanley Cup champions and the Great Gretzky himself.

In March 1984, Gretzky the commodity was soaring to new heights of fame and fortune; Gretzky the most famous player ever was struggling, justifiably fatigued.

In a five-week period, Gretzky had been on the cover of *Sporting News*, two Canadian hockey magazines, and *Sports Illustrated* (for the fifth time), and he had shared a *Time* cover with Larry Bird of the Boston Celtics. He had tested his scoring skills against no less a goalie than George Plimpton, and he had been the subject of an article in the *Saturday Evening Post* and an interview in *Playboy*. He had, Gretzky told me, been criticized for submitting to the *Playboy* interview, accused of endorsing pornography. But, as he put it, "You

can't please everybody." Actually, the engaging truth is that his interview with *Playboy* was a triumph of small-town Canadian rectitude
over that magazine's appetite for salacious detail.

PLAYBOY: How many woman have been in your life?
GRETZKY: Vickie Moss was my first girlfriend. I never dated anyone
else.
PLAYBOY: Do you have *any* vices?
GRETZKY: Oh, yeah, I'm human. I do have a bad habit of swearing
on ice. I forget that there are people around the rink. It's a problem.
I hope I'm heading in a direction where I can correct it, but I don't
know if I will be able to.

Gretzky was what athletes are supposed to be, but seldom are—
McIntosh-apple wholesome, dedicated, an inspirational model for
young fans. He was an anachronism, rooted in an age when a date
wasn't a disco, then your place or mine, but rather a movie, then
maybe a banana split at the corner soda fountain. He had owned a
Ferrari for four years but had never had a speeding ticket. He still
phoned home to Brantford, Ontario, to report to his father three
times a week. He struck me as nice, very nice, but incapable of genuine wit or irreverence, like, say, Rug McGraw. What he did tell me,
his manner appropriately solemn, was that he felt it was his responsibility never to refuse to sign an autograph: "For that person, that
kid, it could be the greatest thing that ever happened to him."

Gretzky worked hard, incredibly hard, both for the charities he supported and for himself. He was boffo sales stuff. The hockey stick he
endorsed, Titan, leaped from twelfth to first place in sales in thirty-six
months. Gretzky also pitched for Canon cameras, Nike sportswear,
General Mills Pro Stars cereal, Mattel toys, Travellers Insurance, and
American Express. These endorsements were handled by Michael
Barnett of CorpSport International out of handsomely appointed offices
in an old, converted Edmonton mansion. There was a large portrait of
Gretzky in action on a wall in the reception room as well as the essen-
tial LeRoy Neiman; and a placard with a quotation from Ralph Waldo
Emerson: "Make the most of yourself, for that is all there is of you."

CorpSport International represented other athletes, but for the
past four years Gretzky, who then earned an estimated $1 million
annually in endorsements—about the same as his salary—had been
the major preoccupation of its thirty-four-year-old president.
Barnett, a former minor-league hockey player himself, was in daily
contact with Gretzky's lawyer as well as the firm that handled his

investments. "Though Wayne listens to all his advisers," Barnett said, "he makes his own business and investment decisions. We get some three dozen personal appearance requests for him a month, but he will only speak for charities. Pro Stars cereal advertises the Wayne Gretzky Fan Club on four million boxes. It costs seven bucks a year to be a member, and for that you get four annual Wayne Gretzky newsletters as well as this set of photographs.

"There have been seven unauthorized biographies," Barnett continued. "Wayne gets between two to five thousand fan letters a month. Vickie Moss's mother handles that for him."

Mattel has marketed a Wayne Gretzky doll ("For avid fans, his out-of-town uniform, jogging suit, and tuxedo are also available"), which has led to cracks about the need for a Dave Semenko doll to beat up any kid who roughs up the Gretzky doll.

Late at night, even as he talked business with Barnett, Gretzky autographed coloured photographs of himself. Mattel supplied the photographs, which included its logo, but Gretzky, according to Barnett, paid the postal charges, about $2,000 monthly. Barnett also pointed out that, since the Oilers took their first Stanley Cup on May 19, 1984, Gretzky had only six weeks off the ice before joining the Canada Cup training camp, playing in that series, and then moving directly into the NHL season.

And in March, things weren't going well. Gretzky was playing without his usual intensity. I asked saucy, streetwise Glen Sather, president, general manager, and coach of the Oilers, if he was guilty of overplaying Gretzky. "Wayne," he said, "plays something like twenty-two minutes a game. He thrives on work. The more ice time he gets, the better he is."

Yet Gretzky hadn't had a two-goal game since February 19 or scored a hat trick for two months. He would, however, finish the 1984–85 season with 208 points (73 goals, 135 assists). This marked the third time he had scored more than 200 points in his six seasons in the NHL. A truly remarkable feat, this, when you consider that no previous player in league history had managed it even once.

Records.

The Official Edmonton Oilers 1984–85 Guide lists a modest three records under the heading, "NHL Individual Records Held or Co-Held by Edmonton Oilers (excluding Wayne Gretzky)," and there follows a stunning full page of Wayne Gretzky's contribution to the NHL records. Paraphrasing the guide, here are Gretzky's statistics:

"No. 99, centre: height, 6'0"; weight, 170 lbs.; born, Brantford,

Ontario, Jan. 26, 1961; shoots, left. He is not the fastest or the most graceful skater in hockey, neither does he boast the hardest shot. But he now holds 38 NHL records."

Of course he would, as was his habit, set or tie even more records in the 1985 playoffs, as well as win the Conn Smythe Trophy for most valuable player in that series. But back in March 1984 all I asked him was, did he feel a 100-goal season was possible?

"Sure, it's possible," Gretzky said. "Somebody will do it. The year I got ninety-two, everything went my way." But he had begun to feel the pressure. "Yesterday you got two goals in a game, tomorrow the fans want three." He has said he would like to retire at the age of thirty, after fifteen years in hockey. "When Lafleur retired, it made me open my eyes," he said.

Lafleur, who quit suddenly in 1984 (temporarily, as it would turn out) at the age of thirty-three after four mediocre years, had scored sixty goals in his best season, 1977–78. "I wasn't surprised he retired," Gretzky said. "You wake up, you're no longer in the top-ten scorers, you think, 'Oh, my God,' and you begin to press. When Lafleur was in his prime, it was a much rougher league, but slower. We get hit, but not as much as in the late seventies."

Danny Gare, the Red Wing veteran who had played against Gretzky the night before, told me, "They don't run against him like they did on Lafleur." Acknowledging Gretzky's enormous talent, he added that it had been more exciting to watch Lafleur. Well, yes, so it was. And come to think of it, the same could be said of Bobby Orr.

When either Lafleur or Orr were on the ice, you never took your eyes off them, never mind the puck. Orr could literally establish the pace of a game, speeding it up or slowing it down at will. Lafleur couldn't do that. He was—in Ken Dryden's felicitous phrase—the last of the river-hockey players, who had learned the game outdoors instead of in a rink, a solitary type, often lost in a reverie on ice all his own. Gretzky was something else again. Sometimes you didn't even realize he was out there, watching as he whirled, until he emerged out of nowhere, finding open ice, and accelerated to score. Other times, working out of a seemingly impossible angle in a corner, he could lay a feathery pass right on the stick of whoever had skated into the slot, a teammate startled to find the puck at his feet against all odds.

It's not true that they don't run on him. The hit men seek him here, they seek him there, but like the Scarlet Pimpernel they can't board him anywhere: he's too elusive. Gretzky can fit through a keyhole. Watching him out there, I often felt that he was made of Plasticine. I've seen him stretch his arms a seeming two feet more because that's what was required to retrieve a puck. Conversely, putting a shift on a defenceman, cruising very low on ice, he seemed to shrink to whatever size was necessary to pass. He is incomparably dangerous behind the opposition's net and unequalled at making a puck squirt free from a crowd.

If, to begin with, Gretzky had a fault, it was his tendency to whine. For a while, all an opposing player had to do was to skate past Gretzky thinking negative thoughts for No. 99 to fall to the ice, seemingly mortally wounded, his eyes turned imploringly to the referee. In Edmonton, this had earned him a pejorative nickname: "The Wayner."

In June, Gretzky won the Hart Memorial Trophy, the league's most valuable player award, for the sixth straight time, this in a year in which he had already won his fifth consecutive Art Ross Trophy, for the NHL's leading point scorer during the regular season. One hundred and eighteen years after Confederation, the only thing out of Canada more famous than Gretzky was the cold front.

For a hockey player, it should be noted, this was a grand accomplishment for, as a rule in 1985, NHL Stars had to cope with a difficult paradox. Celebrated at home, they could, much to their chagrin, usually pass anonymously south of the 49th parallel. Not so Gretzky. But for all his fame, he remained something of an enigma, a young man charged with contradictions. Ostensibly modest beyond compare, he had taken to talking about himself in the third person. Speaking of the endless hours he clocked on his backyard skating rink as a child, he said: "It wasn't a sacrifice. That's what Wayne Gretzky wanted to do." Discussing possible commercial endorsements, he allowed, "The thing to look for is ... is there a future in it for Wayne Gretzky?"

Seemingly self-composed, he didn't fly on airplanes easily. Obviously, there was a lot of inner tension bottled up in Gretzky, and at thousand feet it began to leak. In 1981, trying to beat his fear of flying, he tried a hypnotherapist, but it worked only briefly. Come 1984 he flew with pilots in the cockpit as often as possible, which helped only some, because they had to send him back into the cabin once they began landing procedures, and Gretzky had been known to sit there, unable to look, holding his head in his hands.

Sifting through the Gretzky file, it appeared that just about every reply he had ever given in an interview was calculated to oblige. Again and again, his answers were not only boringly proper but taint- ed by what W. H. Auden once condemned as the rehearsed response. Under all the superficial sweetness, however, I suspected there was a small residue of bitterness. This, in remembrance of a boy deprived of a normal childhood, driven to compete on ice with boys four to six years his senior from the age of six.

Gretzky, for example, unfailingly went out of his way to pay obei- sance to his father, his mentor. Walter Gretzky, a thwarted hockey player himself, a man who was mired in Junior B for five years, was still working as a telephone repair man in 1984. In his brash mem- oir, *Gretzky*, written with Jim Taylor, he gloated, "Wayne learned to skate and Walter Gretzky built a hockey star." He had Wayne, at the age of four, out in the backyard skating rink well into the dark evening hours, learning to criss-cross between pylons made of Javex bleach containers. Walter Gretzky wrote: "You can just see them thinking, 'Boy, did he push those kids! That's a hockey father for you!' Actually, it was the most natural thing in the world." But in an epilogue to the book, Wayne, recalling that he had been shipped to Toronto to further his hockey career when he was barely a teenager, noted, "There's no way my son is leaving home at fourteen." At four- teen, he added, he thought Toronto was the greatest thing in the world, "but if there was one thing I could do over again, I'd like to be able to say I lived at home until I was eighteen or nineteen."

Wayne was only eleven years old when he began to set all manner of amazing records in minor-league hockey, even as he would later astound the NHL. But in 1984, even as Gretzky was arguably the best player the game had ever known, a much-needed publicity bonanza for the NHL in the United States, he was also, ironically, a menace to the game.

Imagine, if you will, a baseball outfielder, not yet in his prime, who hits .400 or better every season as a matter of course and you have some notion of Gretzky's hockey stature. Furthermore, since Gretzky's sophomore year in the NHL, there had been no contest for the Art Ross Trophy. Gretzky is so far superior to any other forward, regularly win- ning the point-scoring title by a previously unheard of fifty or sixty points, that he inadvertently makes the other star players appear sadly inadequate. And while the other players tend to tell you, tight-lipped, that "Gretz is the greatest ... he has all the moves and then some," I don't think they really liked him, any more than Salieri did the young Mozart. Effortlessly, he made most of them look mediocre.

Peter Gzowski, in one of the very few intelligent books ever written about hockey, *The Game of Their Lives*, ventured, "Often the difference between what Wayne Gretzky does with the puck and what less accomplished players would have done with it is simply a *pause*, as if, as time freezes, he is enjoying an extra handful of milliseconds." Gzowski goes on to cite experiments done with athletes by a neurologist at McMaster University in Hamilton, Ontario. Based on this and other research, he suggested that Gretzky, like other superstars (say, Ted Williams or Bjorn Borg), benefited from motor neutrons that fired faster than those of mere mortals. Or, put more simply, time slowed down for him. Gretzky also profited from an uncanny ability to react quickly to everybody's position on the ice. "What separates him from his peers in the end," Gzowski wrote, "the quality that has led him to the very point of the pyramid, may well have nothing to do with physical characteristics at all, but instead be a manner of perception, not so much of what he sees—he does not have exceptional vision—but of *how* he sees it and absorbs it."

As Gretzky often emerged out of nowhere to score, so did Peter Pocklington, the owner of the Oilers. The son of a London, Ontario, insurance agent, he parlayed a Ford dealership, acquired at the age of twenty-three, some choice real estate, and a meat-packing firm into a fabled fortune, even by western oil-patch standards. Pocklington got into hockey, he said, because he wanted to be recognized on the streets. In 1984, he not only owned the most talented team in the NHL, a club that boasted such players as Paul Coffey and Mark Messier, but he also had Gretzky tied to a personal-services contract that made him one of the world's highest-paid indentured labourers. It was said to be worth $21 million and to extend until 1999.

In 1981, Pocklington's assets were estimated to be worth $1.4 billion, but the recession got to him, and his holdings by 1984 had reportedly shrunk to a mere $150 to $200 million. Gone, gone, was the $9 million worth of art, the private Lear jet, and the Rolls-Royce. I asked Pocklington about the rumours, rampant at the time, that—such were his financial difficulties—he might be offering his legendary chattel to the nefarious Americans, say Detroit or New York. Looking me in the eye, he denied it adamantly. "There's nothing to it," he said. "You can imagine what they would do to me here if I sold Wayne. It's almost a sacred trust."

M. Nourbese Philip

M. Nourbese Philip is a poet, writer, and lawyer who lives in Toronto. She has published numerous books of poetry including: *Thorns, Salmon Courage, She Tries Her Tongue; Her Silence Softly Breaks* (for which she received the prestigious Casa de las Americas prize), and *Looking for Livingstone: An Odyssey of Silence*. She is a Guggenheim Fellow, a Macdowell Fellow, and was shortlisted for three awards for her children's novel *Harriet's Daughter*. In 1994, she received the Lawrence Foundation Award for her short story "Stop Frame."

Recent non-fiction work includes *Showing Grit: Showboating North of the 44th Parallel*. Her dominant thesis can be summed up in a quotation from a presentation she gave in 1994: "Let us try to keep this country what it has always been, which is a country that has always welcomed people and always treats all her other peoples, based on that first act of hospitality (a welcoming by native peoples), with a loving heart."

This essay on multiculturalism is taken from Philip's book, *Frontiers: Essays and Writings on Racism and Culture*.

Why Multiculturalism Can't End Racism

A national culture is the whole body of efforts made by a people in the sphere of thought to describe, justify and praise the action through which that people has created itself and keeps itself in existence.

—The Wretched of the Earth, *Franz Fanon*

At its most basic, multiculturalism describes a configuration of power at the centre of which are the two cultures recognized by the constitution of Canada—the French and the English—and around which circumnavigate the lesser satellite cultures. Native culture, to date, remains unrecognized by the Constitution.

The configuration of power appears to be designed to equalize power among the individual satellite cultures, and between the collectivity of those cultures and the two central cultures, the French and English. The mechanism of multiculturalism is, therefore, based on a presumption of equality, a presumption which is not necessarily borne out in reality.

Because it pretends to be what it is not—a mechanism to equalize all cultures within Canada—it ought not to surprise us that multiculturalism would be silent about issues of race and colour.

The Ontario government in its official policy on multiculturalism, *Multiculturalism: A New Strategy for Ontario*, recognizes the special concerns that colour and race present, and addresses those concerns within their policy. The new federal bill, Bill C-18, soon to be the Department of Multiculturalism and Citizenship Act, does not even define multiculturalism, let alone mention race or colour.

A long historical overview of the formation of Canada reveals that this country was, as was the United States, shaped and fashioned by a belief system that put white Europeans at the top of society and Native and African people at the bottom. This ideology, for that is what it is, assigned more importance to European cultures and values than those of the Native or African.

The Canadian examples are numerous: its genocidal practices against Natives; its past and present treatment of the Black Empire Loyalists who fled to the Maritimes; the various immigration acts which record Canada's preference for white Europeans; Canada's past treatment of Chinese and Indian immigrants; its refusal to allow entry to large numbers of Africans or Asians until very recently; Canada's treatment of its citizens of Japanese heritage in World War II; its present treatment of Asian refugees; and the present location and quantity of immigration offices around the world. To these must be added Canada's reluctance to allow Jews to seek refuge here during World War II.

These examples all constitute evidence of a nation founded upon a belief in white and European supremacy, of which racism, as we presently know it, is an offshoot. In his study of the right wing in Canada, *Is God a Racist?* Stanley R. Barrett writes that, "racism in Canada has been institutionalized ... as deeply rooted as that in the United States," the difference being that Canada has always put a more polite face on its racism.

Wherever the European went, whether he was English, French, German, Spanish, Dutch or Portuguese, he took with him this particular gospel—that the Native and indigenous peoples he encountered, who were also not white, were to be brutalized, enslaved, maimed, or killed and, where necessary, used to enrich him personally and/or his particular European country.

Wherever you find the European outside Europe, there you will find this particular pattern and method of settlement. The settlement of Canada was no exception to this rule.

The source of this belief—that the light pigmentation of one's skin bespeaks one's superiority and entitles one to destroy those of a darker hue, and/or unjustly enrich one's self at their expense—is a complex one and cannot be explored here. Suffice it to say that this belief system is, historically, an integral part of the cultural fabric of

Canada. It is a belief system that is still with us today in many forms, and of which South Africa presents a telling and modern example.

Some might object to the use of the expression "white supremacy" on the grounds that it is an expression commonly used to describe extreme bigots who, along with other demands, openly advocate anti-Semitism, the repatriation of African and Asian immigrants, and a keep-Canada-white policy.

It is, however, an expression that accurately describes a certain historical and present-day reality as outlined above, and one which we must understand in order to grasp how thoroughly racism—the glue that holds the edifice of white supremacy together—permeates our societies.

What we have in Canada, therefore, are the manifestations of racial and ethnic prejudices between many of the so-called multi-cultural groups, because racism is not restricted only to relations between white and Black people. Depending on whether the variable of power is present, these prejudices may remain just that—prejudices —but prejudices which must be eradicated through a combination of education and legal remedies.

We also have, however, a larger and overarching structure posited on the ideology of white supremacy, one of the foundation stones of this country, and within which these other manifestations of racism function. To complicate matters even further, many of the white groups within the great multicultural pool come from cultures that have espoused these beliefs of white supremacy.

The net result is that Black people of African heritage will be found at the bottom of the multicultural pool. And below them will probably be found Natives.

What do we have when schools perfunctorily dump Black and Native students into dead-end, vocational programs; when police forces in our large urban centres treat their Asian and African communities as a sub-class to be policed differently and more harshly than white communities?

What do we have when justice systems and police forces treat Native people as a sub-class which receives a lesser form of justice than do white people; when statistics reveal that Black people are refused employment three times more frequently than whites?

What is it when publishers refuse to read manuscripts because they contain African Canadian characters, or when a museum under the guise of mounting an exhibition about African cultures, glorifies the imperial conquest of Africa?

What do we have? Racism or white supremacy? Does the difference in terminology really matter? And how, if at all, does multiculturalism affect these practices?

To the Indian, Jamaican or Micmac person on the receiving end of some of the practices described above, it often matters little what words you use to describe the actions that hurt and sometimes kill them. The results, whether we call it the ideology of white supremacy or racism, are the same—poor schooling, high unemployment, and inadequate housing to name but a few. All of which add up to the greatest tragedy of racism—wasted human potential and lives.

When you are black-skinned, it often matters little if the person refusing to rent to you is Polish-, Anglo-, or Italian-Canadian. The result is the same. And multiculturalism, as we presently know it, has no answers to these or other problems such as the confrontations between the police forces in urban areas like Toronto and Montreal and the African Canadian communities that live there; it has no answers for the African Canadian or Native child shunted into a dead-end program in school.

In short, multiculturalism, as we know it, has no answers for the problems of racism, or white supremacy—unless it is combined with a clearly articulated policy of anti-racism, directed at rooting out the effects of racist and white supremacist thinking.

A society or nation such as Canada, founded on the principles of white supremacy and racism, cannot ever succeed in developing a society free of the injustices that spring from these systems of thought, without a clearly articulated policy on the *need* to eradicate these beliefs. And we cannot begin such an eradication by forgetting how one brutal aspect of Canadian culture was formed. It is for this reason that an understanding of the ideological lineage of this belief system is so important to any debate on racism and multiculturalism.

Despite its many critics, multiculturalism will not disappear. Too many people benefit from it, and it is far too fancy a piece of window-dressing for a government to get rid of.

However, unless it is steeped in a clearly articulated policy of anti-racism, multiculturalism will, at best, merely continue as a mechanism whereby immigrants indulge their nostalgic love for their mother countries.

At worst, it will, as it sometimes does, unwittingly perpetuate racism by muddying waters between anti-racism and multiculturalism. It is not uncommon to read material from various government departments that use these words interchangeably so as to suggest that multiculturalism is synonymous with anti-racism. It is not. It never will be.

It is possible that Canadian society may come to accept that racism and white supremacist beliefs must no longer be a part of its culture. But only if there is a collective commitment to such a goal. It cannot do so merely by a policy of multiculturalism, which is a far less difficult task than eradicating those theories, beliefs and practices that rank humanity according to colour and race. Valuing people of all races and colour equally is a much wider, and infinitely more difficult, project than multiculturalism. Until this is accomplished, Canadians will not be able to derive the full benefits of multiculturalism—even in the limited sense in which this is ever possible.

Jacqueline Dumas

Jacqueline Dumas has been part of the book industry for 35 years—as writer, publisher, and bookseller. She is the award-winning author of two novels: *Madeleine and the Angel* [Fifth House, 1989] and *The Last Sigh* [Fifth House, 1993]; and one book for children: *And I'm Never Coming Back* [Annick, 1986]. She is also the owner/operator of Orlando Books in Edmonton.

Her ethical stance and concern for the well-being of the world, in all its manifestations, shines through her work and her writing.

"V Day" first appeared in *Other Voices*, II.1.

V Day

On the morning of April 3, I crawled out of bed and wondered exactly what had changed now that the Supreme Court of Canada had ruled that lesbian and gay people are … people. In other words, despite the opposition of our provincial government, we can no longer be denied a job, an apartment or services, solely on the basis of our sexual orientation. But what about more subtle implications? For example, can my female lover and I now walk down the street with our arms around each other just like heterosexual couples do [forget the kiss!], and can we do it without drawing unwelcome attention?

In Alberta, the lesson learned by most gay and lesbian people has been: Don't draw attention to yourself. In other words: Don't flaunt it, don't be too political, and everything will be okay. As a result, many in the gay community would prefer that an obvious queen [male] or hutch [female] not speak for us, and are more comfortable when the spokesperson is someone mainstream attractive who looks just like everybody else: i.e.: someone who can pass as heterosexual. Even gay-owned businesses tend to be discreet, relying on word-of-mouth to advertise their gayness.

On the other hand, flaunting one's heterosexuality, is encouraged. [Note Whyte Avenue on a Saturday afternoon, filled with boasting honking cars smothered in paper flowers and swaggering pedestrians flagrantly displaying wedding bands.] Also acceptable is the flaunting of one's wealth.

Earlier this year, 100 people, some in Abouhassan suits, paid $1,000 each to meet Gerald Ford at a private reception, and another 1,100 paid $225 to listen to him talk about "family values." About the same time, almost the same number of people, many in tuxedos and evening gowns, attended the annual Black & White Affair which benefits the AIDS Network. Probably the people who attended these events felt pretty good about themselves, and possibly those who spent the most felt the best.

Also about this time, a few weeks before the Vriend Decision, hospital support workers and licensed practical nurses went on the picket line and public school teachers were threatening to walk out. And five years before the occurrence of any of these events, I accepted the fact that I was lesbian and left my common-law husband of 18 years, and, a year after that, opened a bookstore, fell in love with a woman, and moved in with her.

Are the above events related? Shouldn't people attending charity benefits feel good about themselves? And what does becoming lesbian and opening a bookstore have to do with anything?

My lover and I attended the AIDS benefit this year, which was held at the fashionable Winspear Centre. We were surrounded by hundreds of beautiful people, straight and queer, some in drag: a glamorous event at which to gaze about and be seen. In some ways it was a replication of a heterosexual graduation ball, except with better clothes and lots more men. What was absent was any sense of the reality of AIDS, or of anything discomforting enough to remind us of why we were there in the first place—because one of the unspoken rules of such fundraisers is that there be no visible signs of the underlying causes of the benefit, be it poverty, children in distress, violence against women, or illness.

Some of the underpaid, undervalued hospital workers and teachers attended the AIDS benefit, and perhaps a few even scrimped together $225 for the Ford function. But these glitzy affairs cater to the rich, encouraging them to drop a few thousand tax-deductible dollars out of the millions they've sucked from the system. I wonder how many of the people who attended these two events favour an equitable tax system that would render such benefits obsolete. Which brings us to the matter of my leaving my husband.

Heterosexual women my age don't usually leave men, so perhaps I shouldn't have been surprised when some of my friends reacted as if they were the ones being left. A few friends and the two people most affected—my former partner and our fifteen-year-old daughter—respected and supported my decision. But others were aghast: It must be your menopause, they said, or, Are you crazy, sneering at financial security? and, finally, It's probably not too late to go back. More than one person suggested counselling. Those with the most to say were married women who, as far as I could tell, had made decisions to remain in bad relationships. One friend I hadn't seen in a year called long distance to tell me, You're being selfish, Think of your child, and When you reach a certain age, it's time to grow up and let go of your dreams. The first months were difficult, lonely ones, but what did I expect! It was my own damn fault.

Now when I made my decision, I did not get on the phone and tell all my married friends that they too should leave their husbands and become lesbians. I thought I was making a choice that would have consequences for my private life only, and didn't think that my being lesbian would concern anyone who didn't want to ask me out on a date.

So what was it I had done? Most of the remonstrating women had either slept with me [the one who phoned] or knew that I had had women lovers. Having women lovers seemed okay as long as they were kept under the covers. The sin was to make myself visible.

It may or may not be a choice to be lesbian, but it is a choice to be a visible one.

In the year that followed, I discovered that this choice is a deeply political one. To say, in our society, I am lesbian, is a political act. It is to choose to have less power than other adults, even heterosexual women, and to be subjected to the extremes of misogyny. It means being sexualized, being defined by virtue of what one's most private moments are imagined to be, and nothing else. It's true, heterosexual women are also sexualized. But before I left my husband, I was also allowed to be a good teacher, a good mother, and presumably an acceptable foster parent [had that been my wish]. Now, overnight, foster children were better off watching TV sit-coms in a motel room than they would be chatting and munching cookies at my now sexualized kitchen table. I could be denied accommodation or be fired from my job no matter how competent I might be. But acknowledging my lesbianism was also to free myself. I no longer felt a need to placate men, to make myself think a particular way, to be complicit in the patriarchy. To say, I am lesbian, was to empower myself.

I've come to love dykes who look like dykes; I admire butches, whose appearance asserts: This is who I am; I don't care what you think. Had I looked more butch when I was growing up, been taunted and called names, perhaps I wouldn't have assumed so readily the mantle of heterosexuality. My appearance leads others to assume that I'm heterosexual. To be truly authentic, I realized I would have to come out a hundred times a day—a tedious, exhausting process at best. And I no longer wanted to "pass." I wanted to meet others like me, to talk about this coming-out process with someone who'd been through it.

But where was everybody? Where did they hang out? Had they all moved to Vancouver? So much for the so-called homosexual lifestyle.

One way of coming out, and of creating the kind of inclusive environment I was looking for, was to open a bookstore. Focussing on the kinds of books I was interested in—by feminists and other traditionally marginalized writers—would assist me in my search for authenticity. And as a bonus, perhaps I would finally meet some of those people I was looking for.

Not long after opening, I was told that the store was getting a reputation for being too extreme, that some people weren't shopping at my store because although I had a diverse selection of literature, music, history, philosophy and everything else a good bookstore has, the words Women, Lesbian and Gay on the sign above the door were scaring them off. I wondered who were these scared-off people who thought that books on science, nature, poetry and queer theory were mutually exclusive. When my window got kicked in during Freedom to Read Week, I was told that the books in the window display were the problem. If I were more discrete in my advertising, if I toned down the store [papered over the windows?], probably I wouldn't get attacked. In other words, once again it was my own damn fault.

One day students from a local high school approached me to place an ad in their newspaper. I gave them one that said, Books for lesbian and gay youth and their friends. But the principal refused the ad unless the words gay and lesbian were removed [in which case the ad would be printed for free]. He must have thought that the stories about gays in the school library's copies of Alberta Report provided sufficient information for his students. We don't make distinctions between students here, he told me [another call to enforced invisibility]. But I suspect that the principal would have allowed the students to run an ad addressed to Christian students, or to French or Chinese students, or to those who play chess.

The principal might even have accepted an ad from an oil company like Shell, with its dismal record on human rights [remember Nigeria and Ken Saro Wiwa?]. And what about welcoming corporate leaders to his school? Some of the proceeds from the Gerald Ford benefit went to an organization of volunteer business consultants who work to promote "business ideals" [like Shell's?] in schools. Would the principal have allowed a volunteer from this group to come into the school to talk to the students?

Does it give you pause to think that a school might give students

access to the homophobic rants and monolithic corporatist notions
such as those printed in *Alberta Report*, but censor an ad which indicates where these same students might find an alternate view of the
world? Keeping positive gay images out of the school encourages
the silencing of lesbian and gay teachers and students. And how does
the school benefit anyway by first telling them that they must
remain invisible, and then, because they're invisible, denying that
they exist?

When the hospital support workers were set to walk out, *The
Edmonton Journal* printed a photograph of nine people—one supervisor with his eight support staff. Statistically, one of the nine people
in this picture could be expected to be gay or lesbian. But what matters in the photograph is gender and race: the supervisor is a white
male, and the eight workers are women, a few of them members of
visible minorities.

Most workers in the helping professions are women, and some of
them are lesbian. My lover is a hospital worker who helps sick people every day, even those who would deny her the right to her job.
Some of these thank her when they leave the hospital, and even send
her gifts. But they don't know she is lesbian; she is part of an invisible
minority.

This point was hammered home to me one day when I invited my
lover to coffee with a group of other women, most of whom she was
meeting for the first time. Months back one of these women had
introduced a group of us to her new lover, a man, and the other
women had gone to absurd lengths to make him feel comfortable,
directing much of the conversation his way, laughing at his jokes. But
here, at this table in this restaurant, the conversation developed as if
my lover were not present. These same women talked around her,
making no effort to include her. My lover sat invisible as they continued to ignore her and implicitly deny the reality of our relationship.

Which brings us to April 2, 1998, when the Supreme Court
announced that Delwin Vriend had won the right to appeal his dis-
missal from King's College to the Alberta Human Rights Commission,
and went on to "read in" sexual orientation into our human rights
legislation. Well-meaning people said, What a wonderful day! as if
the fight were over. But we knew the fight was just beginning.

A decision favourable to Vriend had been expected since the
Alberta lawyers and intervenors from various evangelical groups had
made buffoons of themselves at the Supreme Court. The government
had had months to prepare its response to the decision. Instead,

it chose to act as if it had been caught unaware. Ralph Klein announced that he needed a week to consider options, and cynically appointed a four-member committee which included two anti-gay members of his cabinet. Then he called on the people of Alberta to phone in and express their opinions about the decision, thereby validating public expressions of hatred. We were subjected to a stream of vitriol in the newspapers, on radio talk shows, and on television by people who must find homosexuality so irresistibly attractive that they must deny its existence lest they fall prey to its temptation.

Yet I heard none of us telling these so-called Christians, many of whom flaunt their wealth in ostentatious churches, that they must give up their families because their brand of heterosexuality promotes licentious breeding and the preaching of hate rather than love. None of us suggested that they must hide their religion, or lose their jobs, or be denied a place to live, or even lose their schools based on their limited lifestyles. Yet they tried to frame the issue in such a way that it was their rights which were at stake, and not an attempt to legalize their discrimination.

Klein tried to create the impression that he was caught between two extreme points of view, and managed to orchestrate a spectacle which was like a boxing match with himself as the beleaguered referee in the middle. What would be the outcome? Would the government invoke the notwithstanding clause? Would the group that got the most people to push the redial button the most often win? If it came to a popularity contest, we couldn't possibly win. We are a minority: it's why we need legal protection. My lover and I were stressed to the limit, especially her, who has been experiencing homophobia since she was a teenager. We had a right.

Finally, on April 7, after a closed-door meeting with his caucus [this is how decisions are made in Alberta], Klein made his pronouncement: the government would accept the court's ruling in its narrowest sense: that is to say, as it pertained to employment, housing and services. But wasn't that what the court case was about all along? There was talk of fences [not bridges] as he stressed that the government would keep the floodgates closed by ensuring that the court decision had no bearing on same-sex marriages, adoptions, schools, and pedophilia.

Wait a minute—pedophilia?

Klein had done it again. Opposing politicians and members of the gay community praised him for having done the right thing. Just as the hospitals were expected to be grateful when some of their budget cuts were partially reversed, we were to be grateful for having had returned to us that which we had a week ago.

In Alberta, gays and lesbians are often told that we form a special interest group, which is to say, we can be identified and denied equality. Straight white guys with money, banks and multinational corporations, right-wing Christians—none of these form special interest groups. When the government takes money out of the public school system, which all children can attend, and puts it into private charter schools, which only some children can attend, it is not catering to a special interest group.

But special interest groups have ruled our province since the arrival of the Europeans. And what these groups have had in common is a special interest in money—be they fur trade companies, the CPR, or modern friends of the government. To create our province, special interest groups recruited large numbers of immigrants from white Europe to overwhelm the Native and Métis population, and manipulated these immigrants into thinking they must be smarter and better than those who were already here. But we like to forget these racist, predatory, corporatist beginnings, and like to preserve the myth of the hardworking, deserving, God-fearing individual as the builder and keeper of our province.

A government that suspends a sitting of the Assembly "to save money" [as this government has done], and then proceeds to rule by decree, keeping us "informed" through statements to the media, is in keeping with our undemocratic origins as a province. A government that uses our taxpayer money like a discretionary slush fund is keeping up tradition: that of kowtowing to the real special interest groups.

A couple of weeks after the Vriend Decision, two young women walking hand-in-hand along Whyte Avenue were verbally assaulted and spat upon by two men, perhaps underlining the fact that for some Albertans, at least, it's okay to be lesbian or gay as long as we're not too visible. Likewise, some businesses on Whyte Avenue would like the beggars—another sort of undesirable to be rounded up and, what? moved to a different part of the city? where we can't see them. Hide poverty, illness, people who aren't like us—in fact anything that makes us uncomfortable, and maybe we can pretend none of it exists.

CHAPTER SIX: COMPARISON ESSAYS

It is human nature to compare things. We make value judgments all the time in our everyday lives. It is the way we determine which stereo to buy, which apple to put in the grocery basket, which puppy to take home, which person to marry. Comparing is an innate, useful way to learn, to determine our own position about things, and to arrive at conclusions based on weighing and examining common factors.

You will hear this type of essay described as various things: comparison essay, contrast essay, compare and contrast essay. They are all the same beast. The writer has taken two things (or two concepts, or two people) and set them up against each other to show their similarities and, moreover, their differences. You may decide that one is superior to the other; or your conclusion may be that although they seem different, they are in fact much alike (or the reverse, that although they appear similar, they are truly very different). In a shorter essay, it is always most useful to compare only two things, otherwise you begin to juggle. When introducing difference, there must be an equal balance in place.

When you choose two things to compare, make sure they have enough in common to make an interesting and valid comparison. There is nothing to be gained by comparing elephants to watermelons. On the other hand, comparing wildflowers to grass as a groundcover, or dogs to cats as house pets, makes for an interesting discussion. Try to make the two things you are intending to compare balanced in terms of being a valid comparison. While your opinion and conclusion can come to the foreground, and you indeed can attempt to lead your reader to your way of thinking, there is nothing worse than setting up a "straw man" to knock down in an argument.

It would be a valid comparison to look at the distinctions in skating styles between Kurt Browning and Elvis Stojko, in that they are both Canadian champions. It would be less satisfying to compare Kurt Browning to Wayne Gretzky, for although they are both stars on ice, there is less to be gained from the exercise. Suppose you are the president of the Kurt Browning fan club, and you want to prove that

Kurt is the greatest athlete in the entire world. While it would be very easy to make this contention if comparing him to Preston Manning, it would be setting up Mr. Manning as a straw man, to blow down in your argument. Your reader will cry foul, and then nothing is accomplished.

There are two basic methods for ordering a comparison essay. While either is an acceptable approach, depending upon your topic, one or the other may appear superior as an organizing principle. The first is called the *point-by-point* method, where you compare each item immediately, back to back, as you work your way through the points of your argument. In other words, the first paragraph of the body of your essay would consider both items, in the context of the argument. This format is easily recognizable because of all the *howevers, althoughs, in contrasts,* and *converselys* you'll see dotted throughout the text.

The other organizing method is prosaically called the *block* method, in which you delineate all the characteristics of Item A, then turn to Item B and do the same for it. In the next part of your essay, you draw your reader to the obvious comparisons you wish to underline, and your conclusion becomes the comparison itself. This has advantages to it, in terms of letting your reader enjoy some part of the thought process behind the argument. While you are still controlling the information that goes into the comparison, your reader is making the connections as he reads between the lines, having it reinforced by you as you near your conclusions. It is also useful to keep the argument from feeling like a tennis match between Item A and Item B, which can sometimes occur in the point-by-point method, especially if they are sharply drawn contrasts that require little more when being stated.

As a rule of thumb, if your argument is driven by the points you intend to make, then the point-by-point method might be the more useful to your organization. If, on the other hand, your material is stronger when considering each item in its entirety, then the block method would likely be your better bet.

You will note, by studying essays of this type, that sometimes the writer will alternate between the point-by-point and the block methods. This is fine as well. It is often helpful to the argument to bring the two items together in sharp relief, and then at other times to draw back and concentrate on first one item and then the other.

In fact, in all of the professionally written essays, you may note places where the writer strays from some of the rules your instructor is setting down as carved in stone. Sometimes you will find a sentence fragment. You may see block comparisons interspersed with point-by-point contrasts. Some narratives may lack a chronological cohesion. Rules will be broken and you will point to them plaintively when you see the same things underlined malevolently in red on your essays.

The simple answer is that, to paraphrase George Orwell from his essay *Politics and the English Language*, any rule should be broken before you write an inelegant or boring sentence. However, it must also be said that the writers you are reading in this volume have all paid their dues and earned their stripes. They know when they're breaking the rules. They know why they're breaking the rules.

Now is the time for you to be learning and practising, sketching the Mona Lisa over and over again, apprenticing. At this stage, style is secondary to a firm grasp of the basic rules. Essay assignments are given to stretch your capacities for formulating arguments, developing rhetorical strategies, and cleaning up your grammar and punctuation.

Given time and effort, you too can arrive at the apex of life, where you can pen a sentence fragment unchastised. You, like the professional writer, will know, unerringly, when to stick to formal prose, and when to push ahead and create emotional magic by breaking a rule or two. Now, isn't that a goal worth striving for?

The last two paragraphs are not merely a justification for all your instructors' admonishments, or the aberrations you may find within the rest of the essays herein. They are also an example of a block method of comparison. In the last passage, I compared a professional essay with an assigned class essay, and gave various reasons for why certain things were expected of student essays that may or may not be found in all writing. It was better to deal with it as a block structure, given the need to highlight the reasons and expectations for each type of essay.

A final word on comparative essays is to remember to arrange your material to its best advantage. This usually means that you will want to place the most significant similarities or differences either at the very beginning or the very end of your discussion, so they are not lost on the reader. Aside from the points of similarity or difference themselves, the arrangement is the most important aspect of this type of essay, and you cannot go wrong spending a decent amount of time in the outline and organizational phase of a comparative essay.

There is a great joy to be had from reading a particularly well-argued comparison essay. Either your reader will discover essential distinctions between things she previously thought virtually identical, or will suddenly see links to things she never before associated as similar. You will be making a difference, in all senses of the word.

Marni Stanley

Marni Stanley earned her Doctorate of Philosophy at Oxford University, in England. She has lectured on Women's Studies and English Literature and Communications at the University of British Columbia, Simon Fraser University, and Malaspina College.

This essay first appeared in *Pacific Encounters: The Production of Self and Others*, edited by Kroller, Smith, Mostow, and Kramer.

Wasp Waists and Lotus Buds: The Corset Looks at Footbinding

In Lucy Fitch Perkins' primer *The Chinese Twins*, published in 1932 and targeted at grade three and four readers, a little village girl named Moon Flower is threatened with footbinding, though the practice was then out of style in the cities. "[T]he thought of never again being free to run about as she pleased made her feel like a bird beating its wings against the bars of its cage" (Perkins 19). She tries to run away to escape her fate: "'I can't do it, I can't *do* it! I can't stay shut up forever! ... I'll ... I'll ...' The rest was lost in a storm of tears" (21). Fitch Perkins wrote a series of seventeen of these geographical primers, including *The Dutch Twins, The Pickaninny Twins,* and *The Scotch Twins. The Chinese Twins,* a copy of which was in my elementary school library, was my introduction to footbinding. Perkins' series was designed to make travellers of us all, if only in our imaginations.

By the time of Fitch Perkins' geographical primers, travel writing was an established field. Throughout the great period of European empire building, from the 1870's to 1914, western travellers catalogued and commented upon the rest of the world in annually increasing numbers, thereby feeding the public curiosity about colonies and potential colonies that had been aroused by Imperialism. The establishment of military and commercial bases all over the world made for safe enclaves for the weary traveller and provided interesting plot material about suffering or successful exiles. The opening of the Suez canal in 1869 made the journey to the East both safer and quicker, and China was opened up by the forced treaties with Britain, France, America, and Russia of 1858 and 1862. Women travellers began to make their presence felt among the previously male dominated genre of travel writing.

During the age of empire, wives of civil servants, soldiers, and viceroys, and single women like missionaries, tourists, and adventurers paused to comment on newly acquired territories. Most European travel writers spoke with the confidence of an unwavering belief in their moral and cultural superiority. In the past, as Susan Sontag notes:

> To speak in the persona of the traveller, a professional (or even amateur) observer, was to speak for civilization; no premodern travellers thought of themselves as the barbarians. (699)

Instead, travellers thought of themselves as the apogee of human-kind, born to wield power with inherent or even natural justice. They criticised and interfered with cultural practices all with the goal of civilizing the barbarians. In a similar matter, a favourite cause of the British women travellers of the late 1900's was the plight of their crippled Chinese sisters. While they campaigned hard to stop the mutilation caused by footbinding, they simultaneously denied any connection between it and the practices in their own culture—such as tight-lacing—which could also injure women in the name of beauty and marriage-marketability.

The practices of footbinding and corsetry both have long histories. Corsets have been found in Minoan Bronze Age sites dating to the second millennium B.C. when they were worn by both sexes, but by the middle ages they had become primarily female garments. While the corset went out of style after the French revolution for a period of about twenty years, it was an essential part of a well-dressed woman's costume up until fairly recently. Functional and decorative versions of the garment are still available today although modern corsets are no longer stiffened with whale bone or steel. While the origins of the corset are buried in antiquity, footbinding originated at the Chinese court in the 10th century and moved out into the population at large by the 14th century. It remained a common practice until the first decade of this century. Girls' feet were wrapped from one year of age and were bound at about five years of age. The toes, except for the big toe, were bent under the foot and the front and back of the foot were bound tightly together in order to break the arch of the foot. The women walked on the heel and big toe of the foot. Walking was painful and difficult; the ankles were deformed and ulcers and infections were common. Gangrene was not exceptional, and the practice may have been fatal to as many as one in ten girls. The Sung philosopher Chu Hsi (1130-1200) argued that footbinding preserved women's chastity and taught "the separation of men and women" (Qtd in Levy 44).

Although many classes took up the practice it was primarily the upper class women who strove for "golden lotuses," or four-inch long feet.

English women, who were to have such a profound effect on the practice of footbinding, began to go to China with more frequency from 1870 onwards. During the period of increased contact with the east which followed, fashionable English dress demanded a well-boned waist with an ideal of twenty-two inches. Long hip-length corsets restricted the stride and, if combined with the very tight sleeves and tight skirts of the early 1880's, resulted in styles nearly as disabling for women—albeit temporarily—as their Chinese contemporaries' bound feet. Many historians argue that the corset disabled women and caused, or at the very least contributed to, the Victorian ideal of the delicate, sick, or fainting woman. While stories of women cutting their livers in half by tight-lacing have never been substantiated, over-rigorous lacing could produce serious discomfort and was especially dangerous for pregnant women. The obvious question remains: Why do such obviously undesirable practices get established in the first place? Both footbinding and tight-lacing clearly had their erotic component. The corset produced an hourglass figure and the emphasis on the breasts and hips highlighted the woman's sexual role. Constriction also affected breathing. Havelock Ellis argued that corsets make breathing thoracic instead of abdominal, thereby keeping the bosom in a constant, and presumably sexually attractive, state of movement (Ellis 172). Like other hidden or forbidden garments, like the little Chinese shoes themselves, the corset also attracted a lot of attention from fetishists and pornographers. From 1867 to 1874 *The Englishwoman's Domestic Magazine* published a controversial and frequently bizarre series of letters on tight-lacing. While the letters appear to be fantastic, they raise many issues about such things as the use of tight-lacing as punishment or as a control over women, indicating that these ideas were being considered by some part of the population. The number of letter writers was not large, of course, but the magazine was not a fringe underground publication and had a very mainstream and establishment readership. The evidence for the erotic function of footbinding is well established. One of the theories behind footbinding, which like the name lotus foot was taken from horticulture, was the notion that pruning would accentuate development in other areas. So in women the hobbling was thought, partly because of the way it altered the walk, to produce changes in the vagina. Ku Hung-Ming, a proponent of footbinding, argued:

> The smaller the woman's foot, the more wondrous become the folds of the vagina ... [F]ootbinding ... concentrates development in this one place. There consequently develop layer after layer [of folds within the vagina]; those who have personally experienced this [in sexual intercourse] feel a supernatural exaltation. So the system of footbinding was not really oppressive. (Qtd in Levy 141)

He speaks here only of male pleasure, not of female pain, and the theory has no scientific validity. This "theory became a self-fulfilling prophesy," Stuart and Elizabeth Ewen write in *Channels of Desire*. "By limiting the ability of women to function in the broad range of human activities, foot-binding did—in effect—accentuate the primacy of their sexual function" (Ewen 139).

The Ewens understate the problem. Footbinding doesn't merely accentuate the primacy of the sexual function of women, it creates that primacy. As Andrea Dworkin argues in *Woman Hating*:

> *Footbinding did not emphasize the differences between men and women—it created them*, and they were then perpetuated in the name of morality. Footbinding functioned as the cerberus of morality and ensured female chastity in a nation of women who literally could not "run around." Fidelity, and the legitimacy of children, could be reckoned on. (103)

The arbitrariness of this gender distinction did not escape the attention of Chinese writers. Lii Ruszhen's nineteenth-century novel *Jihng hua yuarn*[1] *(Destinies of the Flowers in the Mirror)* is best known for the passage in which the social roles of gender are switched. In the land of Women, women govern and men became servants and harem members. The character Lirn finds himself fancied by the ruler who has him transformed into a sex object. In the process he loses control over his body as the ruler's maids prepare him for the harem. His feet are bound and when he unbinds them he is flogged and tortured. His ears are pierced and his eyebrows are plucked and he is painted and perfumed and transformed into a suitable object for the "king's" desire. He attempts suicide but is interrupted. As Mark Elvin has

---

[1]Lii Rurzhen is sometimes written Li Ju-chen and the novel's title *Jihng hua yuarn* is also written *Ching-hua yuan*.

pointed out in his article, "Tales of *Shen* and *Xin:* Body-Person and Heart-Mind in China during the last 150 Years," the novel deals with

> the way in which the heart-mind could be reconditioned by the breaking-in and domesticating of the body, especially in the case of women; and the uneasy sense that was abroad during this period, at least among the more perceptive members of society (for Lii was not alone in this), that the roles assigned by social convention on the basis of bodily differences were, to a large extent, arbitrary. (281)

As Lirn the sailor is transformed into Lirn the concubine he feels his spirit being destroyed along with his free will as he becomes, both literally and figuratively, a prisoner of someone else's desire.

While there was some internal opposition to footbinding in China, western women began an organized and aggressive assault on the practice. Alicia Little moved to Shanghai with her merchant husband Archibald in the 1880's and remained in China for nearly two decades. She travelled widely and began to publish on China in 1898 with her book *My Diary on a Chinese Farm*. In the mid 1890's a group of western women in China founded the Natural Foot Society (*T'ien tsu hui*) with Little as president. They submitted a petition with the names of most of the European and American women in China to the foreign ministry, and began a letter campaign and a series of public meetings. In *The Land of the Blue Gown* (1901), Little recounts her lecture tour in China. She used her husband's business connections to obtain the sponsorship of the China Merchant's Company who provided her with passage on their ships. She attracted large crowds and had a good deal of success in attracting support. She handed out tracts, gathered signatures and met with leading figures in both the Chinese and foreign communities. She was probably the first woman in Chinese history to travel the country on what was essentially a political campaign. It is clear from her success that the Chinese, and especially Chinese women, were ready for the change. Previous attempts to mobilize an anti-binding movement had concentrated on Christian converts, but the Natural Foot Society was purposefully nondenominational. This decision probably allowed its survival throughout the anti-foreign Boxer Rebellion of 1898-1902. Some of the society's ideas for ways of eliminating binding were rather extreme. At one point it suggested to the government that foot-bound daughters should not be recognized as

legitimate under the law. In 1897 a Chinese doctor (male) joined the
society and in 1908 the society turned over its operation to a group
of Chinese women.

Meanwhile, back in Europe, corsets attracted opposition parties
of their own. The Dress Reform Society, the Aesthetic Dress movement and the Rational Dress movement all campaigned against the
corset, but with differing motives. While the Aesthetic movement
argued for the beauty of the natural form against the ugly and artificially distorted corseted form, the other two groups opposed the
corset on health and moral grounds. Rational Dress promoted
Amelia Bloomer's eponymous invention, as well as shirt-waist
blouses and practical suits that allowed greater freedom of movement for women. These movements were favourite targets of car-
toonists and satirists. The dress reformers argued that, because the
corset's role in fashion was to highlight the sexual attractiveness of
women, it was immoral. Their opponents argued that it was moral,
that the woman with a bound torso was not a loose woman either
physically or sexually. Some even defended the corset as part of a
woman's self-defense—an inner fortification in the seduction battle. Doctors warned that the corseted woman might damage her
reproductive organs. While the proponent of Aesthetic Dress,
Henry Holiday, accused corset wearers of prudery, others saw them
as sexually assertive women. In 1899 Dr. Coleman, a American
physician, wrote:

> Women beware. You are on the brink of destruction: You have
> hitherto been engaged in crushing your waists; now you are
> attempting to cultivate your mind: You have been merely danc-
> ing all night in the foul air of the ball-room; now you are begin-
> ning to spend all your mornings in study. ... Beware!! Science
> pronounces that the woman who studies is lost. (Qtd in Steele
> 165)

The good doctor clearly equated corset-wearing and book-learning
as the equally insidious and revolutionary practices of woman with
liberation on their (now dangerously over-cultivated) minds.

Some of the western women in China studied and some did not.
Some opposed the wearing of corsets while others, like Isabella Bird
and Alicia Little, are obviously wearing them in many of the photographs we have of them. Almost all the women travellers to China
viewed the practice of footbinding with horror and contempt. Some

were even willing to speculate delicately about parallels between foot and torso binding although all who did so accurately acknowledged that footbinding was far and away the greater danger to the lives and health of women. Alicia Little, president of the Natural foot Society, felt that the Chinese women had somehow managed to revenge themselves on the culture:

> Confucius and Mencius are both said to have had remarkable mothers; and it is at least noteworthy that, since the Chinese have taken to mutilating the feet of their women, there has not been one man whom they reckon great born among them: so true it is that any injury to the woman of a nation always reacts upon the men with redoubled force. (*China* 183)

In *Land of the Blue Gown* Little has two chapters describing her anti-footbinding tour through China. She hopes that soon "golden lily" shoes will only be found in the shape of Liberty pincushions. While she understands that women footbind in order to be marriageable, she constructs this compliance as an indication of the female desire to captivate:

> For though it is to please men and win husbands of good social position for their daughters that women bind their little girls' feet, it is again and again the case that the elder men, especially amongst the learned classes, object to the practice as barbarous; just as men of a certain age in Europe denounce ear-piercing, tight-lacing, high heels, whilst yet women know but too well that the eyes and inclinations of the younger and marriageable part of the male community are attracted by these or any other follies plainly done to please, and thus serving to a certain extent as an announcement of the desire to captivate. (*Land* 256-7)

When a young woman with bound feet opposes Little's contention that binding disables women, and refutes it by jumping, Little expresses her shock at what such energy implies:

> But we trembled to think what must come of so much suppressed energy in a girl evidently brimming over with vitality yet cut off from almost all natural outlet [sic]. As she is very rich possibly the bicycle will come to her relief. (*Land* 296)

While avoiding any indelicacy, Little conveys the notion that when women's choices of cultural and physical activities are so closely prescribed, sexuality becomes the only remaining definition of womanhood. Of course there was a whole other argument going on back in Europe about whether or not the bicycle was really an appropriate—and not too sexually stimulating—mode of exercise for women. ...

Much more mild in her approbation was Isabella Bird who felt that women were otherwise compensated in matters of dress:

> As a set-off against the miseries of foot-binding is the extreme comfort of a Chinese woman's dress in all classes, no corsets or waist-bands, or constraints of any kind, and possibly the full development of the figure which it allows mitigates or obviates the evils which we should think would result from altering its position on the lower limbs. So comfortable is Chinese costume, and such freedom does it give, that since I wore it in Manchuria and on this journey, I have not been able to take kindly to European dress. (238)

Of course Bird is combining comfortable dress with equally comfortable shoes—although she is careful to point out that her shoes are "only threes" (236). While she, like Little, recognizes that "a girl with unbound feet would have no chance of marriage" (236), she nevertheless argues, also like Little, that "the weak feminine nature desires to secure the admiration which in poetry, prose, and common speech is bestowed on the 'golden lilies'" (237).

In *A Broken Journey* (1919), Mary Gaunt openly concedes that the motivation for footbinding is sexual, but she denies any understanding of how it might be so. She is quick to make clear that there is absolutely no connection between footbinding and tight-lacing:

> ... the reason for footbinding is not very clear. There is something sexual at the bottom of it, I believe, but why a sick and ailing woman should be supposed to welcome the embraces of her lord more readily than one abounding in health passes my understanding. Of course we remember that not so very long ago, in the reign of Victoria, practically the delicate woman who was always ailing was held up to universal admiration. Look at the swooning heroines of Dickens and Thackeray. But let no man put the compressed waist on the same plane as foot-binding. I have heard more than one man do so, but I unhesitatingly

affirm that they are wrong. Foot-binding is infinitely the worse crime. The pinched-in waist did not begin until the girl was at least well on in her teens, and it was only the extreme cases— and they did it of their own free will I presume—who kept up the pressure always. There was always the night for rest, whereas the Chinese women get no rest from torture. (*Broken* 82)

Gaunt distinguished between corseting, which she sees as woman's choice and footbinding, which is imposed. In *A Woman in China* (1914) she refers to "the usual agonies that custom has ordained a woman shall suffer before she is considered a meet plaything and slave for a man" (*A Woman* 170-1). For Gaunt the sexually perverse must needs be foreign. She raises, but then immediately suppresses, the idea that women's suffering for marriage-marketability, even at a time when marriage was their most common means of support, is virtually universal. To repeat Elwin's phrase, "the heart-mind could be reconditioned by the breaking-in and domesticating of the body, especially in the case of women." By refusing to acknowledge that men might also be—in some way—responsible for tight-lacing, Gaunt suppresses any notion of the sexual motivation for the practice.

As part of the campaign to convince their readers of the barbarity and uncivilized nature of footbinding women travellers sometimes used animal metaphors in their descriptions of the victims of this practice. For example, the American journalist Agnes Smedley describes her revulsion with footbinding thus:

rows of foot-bound women sit along the streets all day long sewing inlay soles for shoes and stockings. They laugh at my big feet. I shiver when I look at theirs, so crippled that they look like the hoofs of goats. (*China* 205)

Ida Pfeiffer, a Viennese traveller of the 1840's and 1850's, writes:

Although I had heard so much of the little feet of the Chinese women, the first sight of one excited my highest astonishment. The sight of these feet *in natura* was procured for me by a missionary's wife, Madame Balt. The four smaller toes seemed to me grown into the feet; the great toe was left in its natural position. The fore part of the foot was so tightly bound with strong broad ligatures that all the growth is forced into height instead of length and breadth, and formed a thick lump at the ancle

> [sic]; the under part measured scarcely four inches long and an inch and a half wide. The foot is constantly bound up in white linen or silk and strong broad ribbons, and stuck in a very high-heeled shoe.
>
> To my surprise these crippled fair ones tripped about with tolerable quickness; to be sure they waddled like geese. ... (50)

Pfeiffer seems not to understand that the foot is broken to achieve this shape and that the shoes are not high-heeled but rather the woman walks on her heel and big toe folded together. Her desire to procure a view of a naked bound foot (an extraordinary request when you consider that the feet were never seen unbound, even by the woman's husband) illustrates the degree of fascination the practice aroused in the western mind.

The Canadian traveller Margaret MacLean was also fascinated by the bound foot, although against her own better judgement. She describes "little girls with cheeks painted pink to represent the flush of youth, but the windows of the soul showed what suffering they were enduring with their bound feet" (MacLean 79). She wants to acquire one of their exotic little shoes for her drawing room table. In China in 1905, MacLean is well aware that the practice is on the wane making it even more important for her to acquire such a soon-to-be-rare item for her collection. She asks for a pair of shoes on a visit to a Chinese home:

> I asked one of the ladies of this home if she would give me a pair of her shoes. She had "golden lilies." She regretted she did not have a new pair and could not understand why I should prefer one showing evidence of wear. They are four and half inches long, so are not considered very small. In the flip of one, a "cash" piece for luck. These small shoes will in time be curiosities in China, so rapidly is the anti-footbinding movement spreading. (82)

Later she has a chance to reflect on her new acquisition:

> When I returned to my residence, I studied the gift of little shoes I had been given and thought about this hateful custom.
>
> What is a bound foot like? Place the thumb on the table, then curl the fingers underneath and you have some idea what the position of the bound foot is—the big toe taking the place

of the thumb, and the little toes the fingers—the part of the foot corresponding to the palm of the hand is a very tender place and very susceptible to decay, or gangrene, and must be kept very clean. The foot is humped so that only the big toe and the heel really go into the shoe. This hump is much admired and is called the "Golden Hook."

I did not see a bound foot uncovered. I might have, but shrank from the painful sight, as photographs and description gave one a fair idea of this barbarous custom inflicting lifelong suffering on millions, no matter how gradually and carefully it is performed.

The crowding of all the toes under the foot, save the big toe, the arching of the foot, the gradual snapping of the instep, all cause a life of misery from about the age of seven. This is when the binding is carefully done: what if it be carelessly done? In that case, the feet often rot, blood poisoning sets in, and death becomes a happy release. (83-4)

MacLean is reminded of the pain these women suffer by her western guide. This woman reminds MacLean that one should never keep Chinese women standing for long when calling upon them as this may cause their feet to bleed. MacLean has trouble reconciling her disgust with the practice of footbinding with her fascination with the aesthetic effect:

I am, of course, no advocate of foot-binding, but I confess that the tiny red shoes, exquisitely embroidered, peeping from under the short skirts of a Chinese lady, look very dainty and attractive. I can quite understand the men admiring the small foot when they do not have to suffer for it. (84)

MacLean concludes that both tight-lacing and footbinding are merely fashionable practices that women inflict upon themselves. Her critique of the practise is no more sophisticated than were Little's or Bird's before her:

Dame Fashion, although called by another name in the Orient, is the same firm, cruel despot here as where you are. Western women are pulled tight in corsets; Eastern women bind their feet, as mentioned earlier, and bind also their bosoms. A band is tightened across the breasts to produce a flat appearance that

> is highly beautiful in their eyes. I am told this causes great pain;
> but it being a mark of beauty, women will suffer and smile. (86)

To whom does that third "their" refer? The first two are gender-specific; it is only women's feet and breasts that are bound, but surely the third occurrence of the pronoun, the "their" that finds these practices beautiful, includes men or even refers to them exclusively. This erasure of male responsibility is one of the seven elements of what Mary Daly in *Gyn/Ecology* calls the "Sado-Ritual Syndrome" (130). Daly argues that most of the "atrocities of androcracy" (131) follow the same pattern sharing an obsession with purity, compulsive repetitiveness, the use of women as scapegoats, and so on. Daly argues that:

> No one was guilty except the girls and women who attempted to disobey or escape. No one was to blame for the evil of maiming women, since the reality of evil and maiming was not acknowledged. There were only "beauty" and "the extremes of pleasure." Among the Chinese, footbinding was universally legitimated. Its apologists included philosophers, poets, authors of erotic literature, diplomats, and ordinary "honourable men." (138-9)

Unlike her Victorian predecessors, Daly does not hesitate to name the real agents of women's mutilation.

Western women found it relatively easy to recognize and describe the physical or sexual oppression of their eastern sisters, but much harder to confront that which awaited them at home. For many their own impractical, uncomfortable, or even hazardous clothes represented an investment in cultural and racial identity. And, as Valerie Steele has argued in *Fashion and Eroticism* "[a] woman who went out without a corset was generally thought to show an indecent state of undress and to lack 'tenue' (correct manners, bearing, and deportment)" (161).

Rigid adherence to a dress code was part of the duty of an imperialist. Mary Kingsley argued that "you have no right to go about in Africa in things you would be ashamed to be seen in at home" (19), and when she broke her corset lace she took a lace out of her boot rather than go without. Mary Billington wrote of the lax dress she encountered in India:

The first sign of deterioration is when a woman omits her corsets from her toilette, and begins lolling about in a sloppy and tumbled tea-gown in the mornings. Then the downward course is rapid, and she soon joins that large army of her sisters in the East, who, save "for company," or in calling hours, or when she goes out, is never to be found trim and neat. If the habit is once permitted to begin, it will develop other forms of laxity, and the slackness and indolence that characterizes so many Anglo-Indian women will become a second nature, requiring all the awakening that busy English folk can give it. (291)

Slackness and indolence are two of the characteristics associated in the Orientalist's imagination with harem women—Billington could not have made more clear the degree to which she loathes and fears this corrupt custom. She calls the attention of her readers to the trap that may await the European woman who lacks her own intelligence and discipline. She suggests a kind of community policing to guard against any backsliding in the hierarchy of civilizations. A constantly refreshed supply of busy English folk—visitors like herself—is required to sustain the discipline of home, however unsuited the new clime.

Tight-lacing gradually went out of style with the fashion ascendancy of artistic clothes and the gown and with the popularity of 1920's dances that could not be performed in a whale-boned corset. China did give up footbinding when the natural foot movement convinced Chinese leaders that the country could not afford the bad public relations that the practise caused. The argument for sex equality also played a part. The anti-footbinding advocate Liang Ch'i-Ch'ao concentrated his arguments on the idea that women were created equal and men had altered that balance:

> Men and women share equally. Heaven gives them life and parents give them love, treating them equally. ... But the difference between strong and weak is most clearly marked in the difference between man and woman. Over the vast universe and throughout the ages, political edification from the sage and virtuous was diffused like the vast seas, but not a word was said or a deed committed for the sake of woman. Women were treated in one of two ways; they either fulfilled a series of duties or served as playthings. They were reared like horses or dogs to satisfy the first need and adorned like flowers or birds to satisfy

the second. These two methods of oppression gave rise to three types of punishment. In Africa and India they pressed a stone against a woman's head to make it level ...; in Europe they wanted the woman to have a slender waist, and to accomplish this they punished her by pressing wood against her waist; in China the woman had to have her feet bound, a punishment like cutting off the lower legs. (Qtd in Drucker 193-4)

While Liang used his cosmopolitan argument to condemn the oppression of women across the map other men, defenders of footbinding, were quick to point out the hypocrisy of the European protests. For example, according to Howard Levy in *Chinese Footbinding: The History of a Curious Erotic Custom*, Ku Hung-Ming

> ... contrasted the European practice of confining a woman's waist with the Chinese one of footbinding, stating that a woman's gracefulness resulted from the way in which her figure impressed the observer. Foreign women emphasized small waists to make their hips protrude and accentuate the beauty of their curves. But pressure on the waist injured the internal organs. Footbinding, however, did not interfere with well-being, but naturally broadened a woman's hips and enhanced her femininity. Rather than imitate Westerners and tamper with the waist, a region which contained the source of future generations, Ku asserted that it was much better to bind the feet instead. (140)

The possibility of not tampering with women's bodies is not even mentioned. In *Sexual Life in Ancient China* R.H. Van Gulik criticizes a western writer for denouncing footbinding by reminding him of tight-lacing and the contented, and international, masochism of women:

> at about the same time his wife and female relatives at home were bringing upon themselves cardiac, pulmonar and other serious afflictions by the excessive tight-lacing of their waists. Footbinding caused much pain and acute suffering, but women of all times and races have as a rule gladly borne those if fashion demanded it. (222)

While men of both east and west reminded each other of women's tendency to self-mutilation, western women confronting their eastern counterparts, whose oppression reflected and enlarged upon their own, often revealed only the extent of their own prejudices and their acceptance of the dominant discourse. Few escaped the conventions of patriarchal Orientalism in order to seek out the similarities, rather than the differences, between an Englishwoman and a Chinese woman.

Marian Engel

Marian Engel, who died in 1985, was a thought-provoking novelist who wrote *Bear*, *The Glassy Sea*, *Lunatic Villas*, and *Sarah Bastard's Notebook*. She was at all times marvellously helpful to aspiring writers, and pragmatic about the craft and business of writing.

This comparative essay (taken from the anthology, *Women and Words*), which tackles the metaphor of writing as giving birth, should be read by all would-be writers, not just the female of the species.

Twins and a Typewriter

Basically, we're talking about motherhood and child-bearing and child-rearing as it affects writing, and writing as it affects child-bearing and child-rearing. I personally don't see that the two are perfectly connected. Furthermore, I get annoyed when people compare producing a book with producing a baby. The processes are completely reversed. Producing a book is an act of the will and, when a book is out, it's out, it's finished. You don't have to tie its shoelaces, change its pants, or send it to school and then wrestle with its teacher. Having a baby isn't necessarily an act of the will, though sometimes it is. Your body can have a baby when you don't want it to. You can't write a book without wanting to. So, although the two acts are used as metaphors for each other, I discourage in young women romantic attitudes toward childbearing. I think we ought to keep the processes distinctly separate.

I have a hard time being a realist, but I prefer to look things in the face because it's more interesting than fantasizing. Child-rearing can be a creative act. Certainly, many of the things that go with domestic life are creatively very satisfying. Mothering takes a lot of energy but it doesn't necessarily sop up your creative energy. Giving birth is, I think, a privilege. Because it is, in fundamental human experience, one of the great experiences. It isn't always pleasant, but nevertheless, it's extremely important. I always felt that since I was put on earth with that equipment, I wanted to use it and know what it was like to use it. I found it to be a fabulous experience.

I had fantasized that I would have one very academic, scholarly child that sat under the table and read through its large glasses while I typed. I had a pair of twins, one of whom was hyperactive. If there's a certain sort of squeal in my work, it's related to the fact that it was an enervating kind of situation. It continues to have its strange aspects, so I am probably not as glowing and cozy about motherhood as some who have had it easier.

My own feeling about motherhood and writing is that it's completely possible to do as long as you can figure out where to get the money for the shoes. It is very, very hard to support children from writing. I've been trying to do it for years and I still don't completely support my family by myself. I was always getting bits of income from the family or from my ex-husband (although that is no longer the case). I never have done it all by myself. I expected, of course, to write best-sellers and make millions, but there's only so much money to go around and I think I earn a lot more than other writers. I would worry about anyone who is saying to herself, I would like to have a child and I will support this child by writing.

Now writing has been a traditional female occupation because pencil, paper, and typewriter (you can still get a typewriter for twenty-five dollars) don't cost much and children do sleep at night. They go to bed and you have some time, peaceful time, in which to write. I never did write well when they were up. Sometimes I did some typing or business letters, but I found that if they interrupted me, I got wildly angry. I thought that was really bad for them, so I worked while they were in school and while they slept. This gave them the firm opinion that I do nothing. What I learned from that time was how to keep a sentence in my head for two weeks.

They open up your feelings. I've never loved anyone the way I love my children. That is important to me. The other thing is that I can't help avoiding their culture. I don't know all the words to the Police songs, but I really should. They give you a chance to live in more than one generation at once. This material is hard to write about (if you are going to use your mothering material in your work). There is a strong women's magazine tradition of writing stories about domesticity, but sometimes it distorts reality. There's also a strong tendency for male critics, and some female critics, to think of domestic material as inferior. Therefore, you become a "women's writer."

Having to earn our living (after I divorced) did cause me to make some commercial compromises. I write anything. I'm going to spend July writing yet another Christmas story for yet another magazine. That's just fine; it'll pay the mortgage. I'm not the idealist I was at twenty. I'm not the precious, pie-in-the-sky writer I wanted to be; not the artist I wanted to be. But I'm tied down to reality in a way I like very much and I shall continue to operate that way. Write Christmas stories, keep the artistic side of my writing for my novels, and continue to care about the children.

Don't be superstitious: children won't sap your creative powers. But they will take time, money, and attention: they are needier than a novel or a poem. Be fair to them if you decide to have them.

Peter C. Newman

Peter C. Newman is the senior contributing editor and regular columnist to Canada's news magazine, *Maclean's*. His books have sold over 2 million copies and his most recent volume, *Titans,* has earned him #1 best-seller status once again. His anecdote-filled, yet hardhitting speeches describe how this country got into its current mess, emphasizing how and why Canada will survive.

"Slouching Toward the Millennium" comes from another of his best-sellers, *The Canadian Revolution.*

Slouching Toward the Millennium

If there is one safe generalization in human affairs, it is that revolutions always destroy themselves. How often have fanatics proclaimed: 'The Year One!'

Essayist William Ralph Inge

Ten years after the journey that began this book [*The Canadian Revolution*], I was in the air flying back to Vancouver from Toronto. As the Pearson International Airport runway lights fell away and we began the arched passage across the plains to the Pacific and home, it hit me yet again: this is not a country; this Canada we call home is a continent. How in heaven's name can anyone govern a continent? Or even pretend to? How can anybody fashion policies that will meet the divergent imperatives of an unemployed Newfoundland fisherman, an upwardly mobile Markham broker, an oil-patch roughneck and a Vancouver craniosacral therapist? As Samuel Goldwyn used to say: "In two words: *im-possible.*"

Viewed from my 30,000-foot aerial platform all that piss and vinegar spent bickering over constitutional crumbs seemed about as relevant to Canadian daily life as the mating habits of Brazilian killer bees. What mattered was that, unlike most industrialized countries, the glorious hunk of geography which we claim remained authentic—and ours. Sure, the idea of drawing our national identity from the land had become an obsolete concept from the first day we logged on to the Internet. But the land was still our beginning, the source of our spiritual sustenance, whether we worshipped it from the porch of a toy cottage on a crowded lake, the cockpit of a sailboat or at sunset from a bench in a city park still reverberating with the echo of the children's daytime hooting.

The aircraft was sizzling along at cruising altitude with Toronto far behind us, appropriately faded into an indistinct smudge of flickering shadows. Just before the clouds cut off my view, I could see the tapestry of central Ontario's market-garden farms draped over low ridges, marching toward the horizon where I mentally mapped the rivers that had first brought the voyageurs inland in their quest for adventure and fur. I visualized the back roads that twisted away from the country of the mind into the real Canada—brooding, silent and inaccessible, an empty land filled with wonders.

Below me, one belief system had given way to another. Despite appearances, the country was more than a collection of Potemkin city-states on the tremulous edge of an uncertain millennium. During the previous ten years Canadians had reinvented themselves, from deferential nerds living in a quiescent and faintly colonial society to articulate and astonishingly defiant arbiters of a sophisticated nation-state. The Protestant ethic had become as rare as the Sunday suits and crinoline skirts that had symbolized it. In its place Canadians had substituted an ethic which was more suited to the reality of their lives. People had moved from a preoccupation with values as the source of experience, to experience as the source of values.

Great institutions can only be reformed by stealth or by revolution. Canadians had tried both and it was difficult to judge exactly when, or if, the Revolution had run its course. Canada takes a lot of killing and its historic cycles have a way of coming most sharply into focus at a distance. Canadians feel outrage most acutely when they conceive the gap between possibility and reform.

To authenticate the Revolution's final outcome will take another decade or more. As Mohandas Gandhi wisely observed: "A non-violent revolution is not a program of seizure of power. It is a program of transformation of relationships, ending in a peaceful *transfer* of power."

That had been very much the process of the Canadian Revolution, 1985–1995.

Just about every faith and tradition we had held sacred was in play. The *status quo* had fallen to its demise through the chasm that separated illusion from reality. Gone was certainty, the idea of being able to depend on the past as a guide to the future. Gone also were the dated notions of deferring to authority and allowing representatives—even elected ones—to make the significant decisions. Experience had made it impossible to believe any longer in responsible politicians, pious priests, sensible Royals, trustworthy lawyers, peace-loving peacekeepers, reliable bankers, principled businessmen or honest diplomats. As they sank in the quicksand of 1980s greed, they dragged down with them much of the corresponding faith in politics, religion, monarchy, government, business or the law. Like it or not, Canadians had no choice but to accept the dictum of University of Toronto political economist Abraham Rotstein, who had written that "much will have to change in Canada, if the country is to stay the same."

The only thing left unchanged by the Revolutionary Decade, it seemed to me as I flew west, was airline food—an oxymoron if there ever was one. I was aboard a privatized aircraft bound for a privatized airport. The gap between business class and steerage had widened, as had every other social and economic dividing line in the country, especially the distance between the governors and the governed. The cities, towns and villages I was passing over had been deconstructed. The train stations had been mostly closed or turned into museums, the bank branches were no longer places of fiscal worship, the churches found their most faithful flock among the hungry who crowded their basement food banks, the army drill halls were shuttered, the local MP's office was just another franchise, no more worth visiting than the Tim Horton doughnut shop next door.

To dare and dare again is the secret of revolutions, but Canadians had no tradition of being either daring or revolutionary, so they had improvised. Instead of the endless search for a national identity, they opted to assert their own identities. Not since frontier days had there been such a surge of self-reliance, such determination by a people to exercise more control over their lives.

It was a giddy feeling, to be alive in the interval between casting off obligation and taking on responsibility. Instead of feeling as if they were carrying the Precambrian Shield on their shoulders, Canadians took a break from lugging around the cumbersome baggage of their national virtues and became most untypically Latin, finding strict morality tedious, tidy living boring, frivolity endearing and passion inviting. Personal identities were up for grabs as people yearned to transcend their birthright. They tended to agree with Woody Allen, who equipped: "I don't want to achieve immortality through my work. I want to achieve it by not dying." In practical terms, this meant having some fun on the way through, cramming into a lifetime as many experiences as one could and letting the after-life take care of itself. "Deference is absolutely at odds with these transformational tendencies slowly establishing themselves in

Canada's culture," noted Michael Adams, head of the Environics polling firm. "Suddenly, we can give ourselves to the future by divorcing ourselves from the past—jettisoning the old-fashioned reflexes of deference and blind loyalty."

The problem with Canadians' new-found liberation was that, left untended, it could easily turn into anarchy: collective conscience finds few outlets in the mere defiance of authority. Selfish bedlam was not what most Canadians had in mind. The aspect of deference worth preserving was the civility that usually accompanied it. While they were firmly set against the old style of leadership, Canadians were determined not to abandon the mutual respect that had always separated them from Americans. They longed to recapture the feeling of community that had animated such events as the Grey Cup, the Stanley Cup, Montreal's Expo '67 and Vancouver's Expo '86, which had turned collections of strangers into tribes. The achievement which most lent itself to unity and common purpose during the decade had been the 1992 World Series win by the two dozen Latinos under contract to the Toronto Blue Jays. It was a great victory, but not quite the moral equivalent of building the CPR—though, as Grant McCracken, an ardent Jays fan and cultural anthropologist at the Royal Ontario Museum, pointed out: "If we Canadians can identify with twenty-five ball-players who are not obviously Canadian, then we can identify with anybody—even each other."

While I fear for our common future in a culture of self-interest, I take heart in the conviction that a collective purpose is bound to emerge at some indeterminate point in the future, when more Canadians learn to encompass within their daily striving the quest for a more spiritual outlook. A longing for this was documented in a survey published by *Maclean's* on Canada Day in 1995. Allan Gregg, last seen throwing himself under the Kim Campbell campaign bus, was back in business reporting the startling notion that "given a choice, many Canadians appear to place spirituality on a higher level than they do having sex on a regular basis." While I do not personally subscribe to this dictum, two thirds of Canadians surveyed said the notion of being "a good person and finding spiritual fulfilment was 'more and more on their minds lately.'" It was natural for Canadians to want to tend to their own spirits in the absence of a national soul, I reflected, and perhaps it was about time the values that Canadians really cared about—co-operation, tolerance, genuine gender equality and civility—sprang from the people's hearts, instead of their crumbling institutions.

Jetting over the Rockies, a thrill no matter how frequently that route is flown, I thought how often we fail to appreciate the value of a relationship, an event or an experience—until it's over. The time had come, it seemed to me, to take better care of our patrimony. My mind, as always, floated to my favourite jazz metaphors. I thought the best advice for Canada had been rendered by Eubie Blake, who had played ragtime piano at most of the New Orleans cathouses. When Eubie was celebrating his one hundredth birthday, he told a friend: "You know, if I'd realized I was going to live this long, I'd have taken better care of myself."

Blake died the next day. Still, it seemed like wise counsel. Being a Canadian isn't a nationality, it's a condition. When citizens of Japan or Sweden declare their nationality, it's a self-defining statement. Citizenship in Canada is an act of faith, a promise of potentials that will take generations to realize. Canada was built from the beginning on dreams as well as appetites. Too often—as a nation and as individuals—we have decried what we lack instead of celebrating what we have. Revolution or not, to most of the world's troubled citizens, Canada still appears to be blessed with the mandate of heaven.

Sally Armstrong

Sally Armstrong is the Editor-in-Chief of *Homemaker's Magazine*, which is one of Canada's best little magazines, and "little" is the operative word. Amid the recipes and gardening hints, there are essays that make us question some of the parameters of our world.

This essay, written as a result of Armstrong's visit to Afghanistan, shocks and provokes, as it was intended. Reportage is openly filtered through the eyes of a North American woman, but the force of the essay comes with the realization that this spectacularly barbaric practice is happening today, in a country that formerly allowed women in universities and professional positions. It first appeared in *Homemaker's Magazine*, Vol 32, Issue 5, in the summer of 1997, (pp. 16-30)

Veiled Threat: The Women of Afghanistan

It's hot in here. Shrouded in this body bag, I feel claustrophobic. It's smelly too. The cloth in front of my mouth is damp from my breathing. Dust from the filthy street swirls up under the billowing burqa and sticks to the moisture from my covered mouth. I feel like I'm suffocating in stale air.

It also feels like I'm invisible. No one can see me. No one knows whether I'm smiling or crying. My view isn't much better. The mesh opening in front of my eyes isn't enough to see where I'm going. It's like wearing horse blinders. I can see only straight in front of me. Not above or below or on either side of the path I take. Suddenly the road changes. I step on the front of the hideous bag that covers my body and tumble to the ground. No one helps me. It feels like no one in the world wants to help.

—Fatana, 28

Who "in the name of Allah" has decreed this wretched fate on the women of Afghanistan? A ragtag band of bandits called the Taliban, who are mostly illiterate and mostly in their 20s, thundered into the capital city of Kabul on September 27 of last year, and overnight the lives of women and girls were catapulted back to the dark ages. After hanging the government leaders in the public square, the Taliban announced their draconian decrees on the radio: schools for girls were immediately closed. Women could no longer work. They had to be completely covered by the head-to-foot wrap called a burqa and kept in purdah (secluded from the public) because, according to the Taliban's leader, Mullah Mohammad Omar, "A woman's face corrupts men." Afghanistan has become a place where mothers and wives, sisters and daughters, are seen as a holy threat. Today, a woman can only leave her home in the company of her husband, brother or son, and only if she is shrouded in the hated burqa and carries a permit that gives her reason to be outside.

To disobey is to die. Soon after the takeover, a group of women in the city of Herat marched in protest. According to eyewitnesses, the Taliban surrounded the women, seized their leader, doused her in kerosene and burned her alive. Women have been sprayed with acid, beaten with twisted wires and shot for crimes such as showing their ankles, letting a hand slip out from under the burqa while paying for food, allowing their children to play with toys. For being outside with anyone who is not a male relative, the sentence is death by stoning. The hooligans in power dig a pit and bury the woman to her shoulders. Then they form a circle around her and throw rocks at her head until she is dead.

They say they do it for Islam. But Muslim scholars all over the world say this has nothing to do with Islam. It's a grab for power and control in a country that's been struggling with unrest for 18 years. It is also misogyny, a contempt for women that goes hand in hand with the disturbing rise in extremism in Muslim countries. In Bangladesh, a woman can receive 50 lashes for speaking her mind. In Pakistan, a rape victim can be jailed for fornication. In Saudi Arabia, women are forced to cloak themselves in black chadors that absorb the stifling heat while men walk about in white robes that deflect it. Afghanistan is a human rights catastrophe.

Astonishingly, this throwback to a medieval era has created a strange wall of silence. The United Nations is wringing its hands. Government leaders are looking the other way and the women of Afghanistan are asking what in the world is going to become of them.

I met Fatana, 28, a psychiatrist, Farahnaz, 26, a civil engineer, and Mina, 28, a pharmacist, six months after the beginning of the darkest days this country has ever known. [We agreed that their last names, the towns where they have found shelter and their former employers would not be named to protect them from the terrible retribution of the Taliban.] For them, life under the Taliban is nature thrown into reverse. They're like spring blossoms that were forced to fold their beautiful petals back into their casings. With downcast eyes and sagging shoulders these young women describe their grievances in words that make me think of a line from the poem *In Flanders Fields*. "Short days ago we lived." They went to university in Kabul, wore jeans, short skirts, met at the restaurants on Da Afghanan street and went to discos on Froshga. Like other young people, they walked along the river and through Pul bagh Vuumi park with their boyfriends. Their lives were full, their futures hopeful.

But the convulsions that shook the country out of communism in 1992 threw the formerly cosmopolitan city of Kabul into utter calamity. Extremist factions fought each other for control for four deadly years. Last autumn, the ultra-extremist Taliban won the spoils of war. And women like Fatana, Farahnaz and Mina became invisible. Their jobs, social lives and self-esteem disappeared overnight.

"On September 26, we were at work," says Fatana. "Everyone was anxious. The Taliban were near the city. We were waiting for something bad. At noon most people went home because we could hear the shelling. We'd heard about Taliban policies and we were afraid for our futures."

The next morning they heard about the fate of the government leaders on the radio. And they heard the Taliban's misogynist manifesto for women. "I'd never owned a burqa in my life," says Fatana. "Most women in Kabul had never even worn a scarf over their heads." When I ask her what effect this will have on the mental health of the women, Farahnaz speaks up. "I can answer that question for you. I've lost my mental health. I don't want to leave my house. I start to laugh or cry and I don't know why I feel sad all the time. And I cannot concentrate. The other day I was helping someone with accounting and I realized I'd entered the same number over and over again. I have no hope for my future and, what's worse, I have no hope for the future of my two children."

Today the streets they walked on as students are like a moonscape. The shops are closed. So are the restaurants. Sixty per cent of the city has been destroyed. The roads are full of holes. There's garbage all over the place, there's no electricity in most parts of the city and few people have running water. The university has reopened for boys only. Women doctors have been allowed to return to work but only to treat women patients. And if women and girls can't find a woman doctor, tough luck. "Let them die," say the Taliban.

In the absence of any real protest from the international community, a litany of new regulations is visited upon the people on an almost daily basis. Radio and television are forbidden. So is music, clapping, singing and dancing. Photographs, even at weddings, are considered unIslamic. So are sports for women. Makeup, nail polish, high-heeled shoes and white socks—the only item of clothing that shows beneath the burqa—are also forbidden (white is the color of the Taliban flag). There's to be no noise made by women's feet when they struggle to the bazaar to find food and water for their families. Windows must be painted black to prevent anyone from seeing a woman inside the house. New houses can have no windows on the second floor. In a stupefying rationale, Omar explains the Taliban's actions against women by saying, "Otherwise, they'll be like Princess Diana."

There are 30,000 widows in Kabul who are virtually destitute. When asked how they should cope, the Taliban reply again, "Let them die." In a particularly hateful response to the handicapped, some men have told their disabled wives that they'll no longer require prostheses as they no longer need to be seen outside.

Afghanistan is a country about the size of Manitoba. It has five major tribes that have warred endlessly throughout the centuries. It was a monarchy until 1972 and a republic until 1978 when the Soviets invaded. Then it became one of the last violent crucibles of the Cold War. The detested boot camp rule of the Soviets spawned the Mujahideen (Freedom Fighter) camps across the border in Northern Pakistan. Funded by the United States, Saudi Arabia and Pakistan itself, the Mujahideen were like folk heroes who represented a spiritual return to pre-communist Afghanistan. But within the camps, several factions jockeyed for power, each pretending to be more religious than the next to win the support of the people. In the process they planted the seeds for a fratricidal bloodbath that began with the defeat of the Communists. Life under the victorious Mujahideen proved to be as violent as it had been under the Communists and more religiously strict than the people had ever imagined. Enter the Taliban, young hoodlums who had never been to school and never known anything but war. Presently they control two-thirds of the country.

While the world has clearly grown weary of Afghanistan and its 18 years of war, the people trapped in that country and the 500,000 refugees who escaped to border towns in Northern Pakistan are hoping someone will "take up our quarrel with the foe." Although the Taliban have no official role in the Islamic Republic of Pakistan, their presence throughout the north is threatening. The steady rise in fundamentalism in Pakistan leaves many Afghan refugees and native Pakistanis in this northern region wary. Many women continue to wear burqas out of fear. Others are careful to cover up just to avoid attention from the extremists. There's an uneasy calm. It's like waiting for an intruder.

At the northwest corner of a Pakistan border town called Quetta, the Afghan diaspora is burgeoning. The dusty, rock-strewn landscape that unfolds from the huge mountains here at the west end of the Himalayas is similar to the refugees' native land. The miniature yellow wildflowers that push defiantly out of the scrubby soil grow like symbols of their struggle. The diorama of contrasts—mud houses and rented two-story homes, the delicious scent of fresh-baked naan bread from the bakeries and the putrid stench from the latrines in the street, the fear and longing of the people—is the quintessence of life in a refugee centre. It was here in Quetta that the Mujahideen assassinated the leader of the Afghan women's movement a decade ago. It is here that I meet Dr. Sima Samar, a precious bead on the world's scanty string of humanitarians.

"I have three strikes against me," she says by way of introduction. "I'm a woman, I speak out for women and I'm a Hazara, one of the minority tribes." The road she travelled from Helmand, the Afghan province where she grew up, to this refugee centre in Quetta, is strewn with the history and customs of her beloved Afghanistan. Her father had two wives (a usual practice for many Islamic men and one she doesn't approve of). She won a scholarship to go to medical school but her father told her she couldn't leave the family because she wasn't married. So a marriage was arranged (another usual custom) and she went to Kabul University. But during the upheaval that finally rousted the Communists, and soon after she'd given birth to their son, her husband was arrested, never to be seen again. Samar managed to finish medical school and wound up practising medicine in a rural district. Her experiences there brutally demonstrated that the lives of women were nearly unbearable and that lack of education was a direct cause of the turmoil her country was in. She decided to do something about both conditions.

Today she runs medical clinics in Quetta as well as Kabul. And she has clandestine schools in rural Afghanistan for more than 4,500 girls, as well as a school for refugee girls here in Quetta. Her steadfast refusal to observe purdah and the stand she takes on equality for women have made her anathema to the fundamentalists and a hero to the women she serves.

When asked how she gets around the paralysing rules of the extremists' interpretation of the Koran, she shakes her head in astonishment at her own audacity. "Let me tell you a story," she begins.

"A 16-year-old girl came with her parents to my clinic. A quick urine test and cursory examination told me what I suspected. She was six months pregnant and terrified. She had been raped. The law according to the extremists is that a woman who is raped must have four male witnesses to prove that she didn't cause the rape. Naturally no such witnesses are ever available. Without them the family is obliged to kill the girl to protect the family honor. This kid had kept her terrible secret until she could hide it no longer. I had to decide what to do. I don't approve of abortions unless there is absolutely no other way. But if I didn't do something for this girl, she would be killed. I chose life.

"Remember, most people here don't have any education, so I can get away with saying things they may not question. I told them their daughter had a tumor and needed surgery. I said she was too sick to have it now and she would have to stay at my clinic. I kept that girl for three months. When the baby was due, I did a Caesarean section. The family waited outside the operating room because it is the custom here to show them what was found in the surgery. I put the placenta in the surgical basin, showed them the so-called tumor and told them their daughter would be fine. Then I gave the baby to a woman who was also in trouble because she is married and infertile."

Dr. Samar can't change the law by herself but she's part of a group that hopes it can. It's an international network called Women Living Under Muslim Laws and it presently has links to 40 countries and an increasingly powerful voice at the United Nations. Farida Shaheed, the Asian coordinator of the association in Lahore, Pakistan, won't even use the word fundamentalist. "It suggests a return to cherished fundamentals of Islam, which it certainly is not," she says. "Extremists aren't religious at all. This is political opportunism. Their strength is in disrupting the political process and using that to blackmail those in political power."

It worries her that such groups are gaining momentum because of what she calls "a refusal of mainstream political parties in Muslim countries to produce democratic rule. But women are gaining as well. There's an unprecedented number of women coming into the workforce [in Pakistan] at the same time that the extremist groups are saying, 'Stay home.'"

They fight back at their peril. Members of the association have been harassed on the street and had firebombs thrown at their houses. And Sima Samar receives so many death threats from the Taliban, she simply replies, "You know where I am. I won't stop what I'm doing."

The rhythms of life rock uncomfortably at Samar's clinic. Her patients, who pay about 30 rupees ($1 Canadian) per visit, come with their full wombs and fears of infertility. They suffer all the ills that refugee camps are heir to: malnutrition, anemia, typhoid fever, malaria. In the lineups at the door, they whisper news of the latest atrocities and decrees of the Taliban. Today, there's a terrible message from Jalalabad, a city across the border in Afghanistan. Yesterday a woman tried to leave. She was wearing her burqa but walking with a man who was not a relative. She was arrested by the Taliban and stoned to death. The man she was with was sentenced to seven years in prison. There's still a hush in the clinic, when suddenly the curtain is pushed aside and a woman appears with her Taliban husband. He tells Samar that his wife bleeds from her nose whenever she works hard in the fields. Samar raises her voice: "She's full-term pregnant, she shouldn't be working so hard." The man replies, "She has to work. Fix her nose." Another young woman has been menstruating for 11 months. Her blood pressure is dangerously low. She's as weak as a sparrow. The doctor says she needs a simple D and C (dilatation and curettage) but culture interferes again. She's a virgin. The simple operation would destroy her virginity, which in turn would destroy her life. So abdominal surgery is scheduled.

As the war against women rages on, a new and menacing problem is turning up at the clinic. "Almost every woman I see has osteomalacia," Samar says. "Their bones are softening due to a lack of vitamin D. They survive on a diet of tea and naan because they can't afford eggs and milk and, to complicate matters, their burqas and veils deprive them of sunshine. On top of that, depression is endemic here because the future is so dark."

Samar is angry with what she sees as all talk and no action on the part of world organizations that claim to be pressing ahead with issues for women. "Recently the UN held a meeting in Quetta for all the various factions to discuss Afghanistan," she says. "They met at a hotel for three days. Can you imagine what that cost? Well, the meeting was for men only. The women were invited to meet for one hour on a different day." There's more. She was invited to attend a meeting in Washington, also held to discuss the situation in Afghanistan. Each delegate was allowed six minutes to speak. Samar was the only woman. She told the gathering, "I represent more than half the people in Afghanistan. How come I only get the same six minutes as all these men?"

When the phone rings in her small office she speaks English to the caller, wanting to know, "Where's my wheat?" The caller explains that her wheat is in Kabul but the priority delivery is to women and girls. "My wheat is going to a school for girls in Ghazni. It's the only school still operating for girls. Why aren't my girls part of that priority?"

Amid the international sound of silence, a lone voice in London is sounding a clarion call for the women. Fatima Gailani, who holds a master's degree in Islamic jurisprudence, is the daughter of Pir Sayyid Ahmad Gailani, the spiritual leader of the Sunni Afghans. He is also a descendant of the prophet Mohammed, which means they both carry a lot of clout. Gailani is outraged with the Taliban's interpretation of Islam. "A woman with a covered head is not more honorable than a woman without a covered head. I can prove that any action of the prophet has nothing to do with this. It goes against the Koran, in fact. The Taliban are against Afghan tradition, against Islam. They only continue because presently there is no alternative." With that in mind, she and her father recently travelled to Rome to meet with the exiled monarch. "My hope is that an Afghan element—the king, the leaders of the tribes, my father—can do something. The Taliban need aid of every description. They need money. They'd respond to pressure." So far there hasn't been any.

Meanwhile, the lineup at Dr. Samar's clinic grows longer. Her schools for girls are working in shifts, since she doesn't have the money to rent more space. The women in Kabul have given up a resistance movement. And some international agencies are caving in to the classic consequences of gender abuse and saying, "At least there's peace under the Taliban." For the women, living in prison isn't peace. The threat of being stoned to death isn't peace. Painting your windows black isn't peace. Being without music isn't peace. And so they wait, for peace.

Gail de Vos

Gail de Vos draws on a wealth of background in storytelling. In addition to teaching storytelling at the School of Library and Information Studies (University of Alberta), she is a resident storyteller at Fort Edmonton Park and performs and conducts workshops across Canada and the United States. She has published three widely acclaimed books: *Storytelling for Young Adults: Techniques and Treasury*; *Telling Tales: Storytelling in the Family*, co-authored with Merle Harris; and *Tales, Rumors, and Gossip: Exploring Contemporary Folk Literature in Grades 7-12*. Her new book, co-authored with Anna Altman, is *New Tales for Old*, which explores modern reworkings of traditional folktales.

In this essay, modified from her book *Tales, Rumors, and Gossip*, Gail compares those fantastical tales we sneak a peak at in the grocery store cash lines to the legends of old once told by travelling storytellers.

Once Upon a Tabloid

Tabloids have, in part, taken on the role of the travelling storyteller, who would set up in the marketplace and tell of other places and people far removed from the home and friends of the audience. Referring to tabloids, Harold Schecter states that "these publications are virtual anthologies of age-old folk themes reincarnated in contemporary terms" (1988, 14). Elizabeth Bird, in her examination of the role of the supermarket tabloids in modern Western society, concludes that they continue the tradition, although obviously dependent on print, of oral folk narratives (1992, 3). Supermarket tabloids are, in fact, one of our main venues for tracking the contemporary legends today.

The tabloids cannot be dismissed lightly, as they, like film, television programs, newspapers, and the oral tradition, "reflect and feed into each other" (Bird 1992, 2). To even a casual observer, the circular dynamic of tabloids becomes obvious. Tabloids and other news media report "hot" contemporary legends as pseudo-news items, which in turn become the vehicle for introducing the legends to readers who haven't heard them before (Grider 1992, 26). Contemporary legends told as fact often grace the page of the tabloids. Tabloids are important for more than just their role in publishing contemporary legends as fact; tabloids, themselves, bear a striking resemblance to contemporary legends.

The place names in contemporary legends are constantly being adapted to the needs of the teller and audience. Legends, regardless of where they are told, usually cite local neighbourhoods as the setting. This device aides in creating verisimilitude for the legend. Similarly, references to place serve to establish authority in news reports and to make the event concrete in the minds of the readers (Manoff and Schudson 1987, 111). Tabloid journalism adopts the legends and sets them in the most "effective" settings.

To satisfy the enormous demands of their readers for new stories, tabloids often recycled old tales with new dates and locations; undoubtedly they did much of this recycling unintentionally, publishing and republishing the apocryphal tales that later became known as "urban legends" (Bird 1992, 10).

> Not only does the content of the tabloids resemble oral tales, but it also works like contemporary legends in validating beliefs, uncertainties, and stereotypes (Bird 1992, 165). The readers gather these stories and use them in their own conversation and gossip. "The tabloids appear to pick up on existing ideas and beliefs, restating them in narrative form, performing much the same function as the teller of an urban legend" (Bird 1992, 188). The readers of the tabloids interact with the stories they read by taking a stand on the plausibility of the tale and, as soon as they have done so, passing on both the tale and their own interpretation of it. As with listening to stories, the reading audience fully participates in "making meaning" of the tabloids, some read for information while others read for gossip and entertainment.

Tabloid readers prize familiar themes and stories "dressed" as original material. To help satisfy this desire for the familiar, the stories in the tabloids incorporate traditional motifs from folklore (Bird 1992, 168). An article in The Weekly World News (March 6, 1990) read "Poodle Squashed Flatter Than a Pancake—In Trash Compactor," telling about an unfortunate incident with a family pet and a toddler in Atlanta. The mother was quoted as saying, "He was no bigger than a cigarette pack and just as flat. ... That could have been Benjamin [her son] in there." This example, along with many of the human interest stories in the tabloids, are reminiscent of contemporary legends about other unfortunate pets and modern technology (Bird 1992, 167). There are also curious parallels to other themes in contemporary legends. A second example, from the same issue of the News, relates one of the legends about foreign cultures and their eating habits:

> **Shocking Reason Why Stew Tasted so Bad: This isn't Rabbit—
> It's DOG Meat** A wife and husband were hospitalized in shock
> after they found out that the rabbit they bought from a butch-
> er and stewed for dinner was actually a dog! The victims, Paul
> and Melissa Gilbert, originally from Chicago, were living in
> Mexico City at the time of this outrage. (Bird 1992, 167)

This tale of "unfood" eaten by "alien cultures" is a familiar theme of
contemporary legends canon. In the majority of the tales, the "victims" either die of shock or are deathly ill and sue for damages. The
horror of these tales is that they could so easily be true! When I was
living in Southeast Asia in the early 1970s, our neighbours planned
a celebration feast. They purchased two live dogs and knowing how
fond Westerners are of pets, they gave me one. The other dog was
slaughtered and prepared for the feast. Needless to say, I lost my
appetite! The second dog was considered "sacred" because it was a
pet. Unlike the legends, however, no one died of shock or was ill from
the experience.

Attribution of the source to a "friend-of-a-friend" or an "authority" in the field is important in both contemporary legends and
tabloid articles. The reference to a source adds to the verisimilitude
of each. Since the 17th century, much of the material in the tabloids
and news sheets has been "drawn from oral tradition or relied on
word-of-mouth reports, often stressing that sources were eyewitnesses or, at the very least, credible—the "insiders" of their day"
(Bird 1992, 10). This is still particularly true of the gossip columnists
in the tabloids today. Though some of the anecdotes printed in
tabloids may actually have been witnessed by a columnist, or have
some other truly reliable source, it becomes clear upon study of the
tabloids that the stories are often essentially folkloric some incident
may have occurred, but in the course of the telling, details are
changed or merged (Bird 1992, 171).

However, as Bird points out, the more respectable tabloids
(Enquirer and the Star), which print human interest and celebrity
stories that are somewhat less bizarre than stories in the Sun or the
News, are also less obviously folkloric. The former tabloids do not
invent sources and events, although their sources and stories still
conform to traditional narratives and motifs (1992, 170).

Like fairy tales and legends, popular fiction is distinguished by a
special kind of immortality: what remains alive is not the language
of the original text or even the name of the creator but simply the

story itself (Schecter 1988, 9). While reporters and writers strive to pit their own unique stamp on their creations, tabloids journalists make little attempt to do so. The mark of a successful tabloids journalist is that story after story flows and fits into the appropriate mold (Bird 1992, 169). Like contemporary legends, the content of the story is what is remembered and transmitted, not the identity of the author.

Tabloids preach that there is little anyone can do to change the world, except of course, to hope for a miracle. This lesson is similar to that of folklore. "Most folk narratives help people cope with daily existence and their position in the pecking order by telling tales that dramatize values that are essentially conservative" (Bird 1992, 207). Wish fulfillment is a large part of both the tabloid worldview and that of the contemporary legend, but it is a wish-fulfillment tempered by reality.

References

Bird, Elizabeth. 1992. *For enquiring minds: A cultural study of supermarket tabloids*. Knoxville: University of Tennessee Press.

Grider, Sylvia. 1992. Tie a yellow ribbon around Elvis: Contemporary legend, popular culture and the media. *Louisiana Folklore Miscellany* 7:22-32.

Manoff, Robert Karl and Michael Schudson, eds. 1987. *Reading the news: A Pantheon guide to popular culture*. New York: Pantheon.

Schecter, Harold. 1988. *The bosom serpent: Folklore and popular art*. Iowa City: University of Iowa Press.

CHAPTER SEVEN: CREATIVE NON-FICTION

Many people balk at "creative non-fiction," claiming it to be nothing more than a term coined by non-fiction writers attempting to give themselves artistic airs. It is an odd term, but it can be useful to create an area within the genre of the essay that allows the writer to come fully into the work in the way more formal essays cannot.

Perhaps a good way of thinking about it would be to see this mode as consciously subjective non-fiction. The writer is never omitting the truth. He is, on the other hand, giving the truth as he sees it, making sure that his reader is aware of the filter he is placing on the situation.

By putting yourself into your essay, you allow your reader to meet you within the world you have decided to show him. This can be as varied as straight autobiography, to arguments shored up completely by anecdotal evidence alone.

Think about television documentaries you have seen. In some of them, the narrator or interviewer is off screen, behind the camera at all times, and the focus is always on the subject of the documentary. There may be a narrator's voice, or questions asked off camera, but they never interfere with what the camera is showing you. In other documentaries (think of Adrienne Clarkson Presents or Wayne Rostad's On the Road series), the narrator/interviewer/host becomes one of the characters within the documentary. Not only do we receive the subject matter, we are also allowed to see the reaction of the interviewer, and can decide whether or not to filter our reactions through hers.

While this might seem intrusive to some, it appeals to other people for just that intrusiveness, which they see as a more honest approach to revealing a non-fiction subject. After all, as we have seen elsewhere in this book, all essays possess various manipulative rhetorical strategies. To have the writer up front and obvious about his biases and reactions is oftentimes more honest, so we as readers can judge for ourselves how much is objective reportage and how much is indeed filtered through the writer's consciousness, deliberately or not.

There have been various arguments in modern and contemporary critical theory, which claim that there has been a "canonization" of literature, where only a certain set of hand-picked pieces of literature have been deemed worthy of study, while thousands of others have been pushed to the margins of history. This has, in the past, been done with no personal rationale, but merely announced, as if carved into tablets on some mountain top. The reaction against this list, mainly consisting, as many have claimed, of "dead white men," created a need to move toward a more inclusive literature, and also toward a critical stance which required the critic to announce his or her own background and stance before making a qualitative judgment.

Another critical position that has been bandied about for quite awhile has been the concept of "private language," which can be an enormously frustrating argument, especially for people devoted to communication. Within this argument, there is a supposition that no one speaks exactly the same language, and therefore accurate communication is very nearly impossible, except between identical twins. If I was to look out the window as I type this and report to you that the sky is blue, what do each of us picture? After all, your concept of blue might be a deep teal, or you may be colourblind. If I were to say that the sky was a pale baby blanket blue, with its softness blurring on the horizon into a wash of near white, I might convey more to a reader, but even so, there may never be a true connection. I can never be sure that what I am saying is truly being understood. If, however, I offer up something about what has determined how I perceive, it is possible that you as the reader may know someone similar, or can cobble together an idea of what an over-educated western Canadian woman in her late thirties might be meaning when I refer to something as spectacular, or visually stunning, or tragic. For instance, having been raised with the Rocky Mountains, I am likelier to have different ideas of what constitutes "wilderness" than someone who was raised on the moors of England. Likewise, my reactions to gratuitous violence and needless suffering may be more acute than someone who was raised in a more fatalistic, less sheltered environment than the Canadian middle-class. These factors have a bearing on the weight the writer gives to an argument. Knowing this much background will enable you, as a reader, to make a more objective conclusion on what it is you are reading, than a less intrusive, more seemingly "objective" reporting could give you.

Creative non-fiction is possibly the most difficult strategy to conquer for the novice writer, as sometimes it takes quite a bit of practice to erase yourself from your writing. To be allowed to throw your self into your essay can create serious imblanace, rather than a carefully conceived subjective perspective. It is not enough to merely have a first person narration, nor a completely subjective opinion-fueled paper. Remember, that although people like to drag out the adage that "everyone is entitled to their opinion," it is perfectly possible to counter with, "Yes, but your opinion is wrong." Creative non-fiction is not a licence to spew forth undocumented and specious arguments. For want of a better term, it is more than objectivity, it is a form of "hyper-objectivity," wherein the writer has to give not only the truth, but also his own reaction to the truth at the same time. Think of it as reportage done with SONAR, where the facts are ascertained as they are bounced off the reaction of the narrator.

Canadians have long excelled at this new entry into the non-fiction sweepstakes. It may have something to do with our constant examination of ourselves in relation to our more powerful cousins to the south, or our attempts to define ourselves culturally within the proliferation of backgrounds and vistas that make up this country. Whatever it may be, writers like Sharon Butala, Myrna Kostash, Caterina Loverso Edwards, Paul Quarrington, David Layton, and Sheldon Oberman all exemplify this gloriously personal form of expression.

When attempting to write creative non-fiction, try not to use narrative as a rhetorical strategy. This may create an urge to concentrate on the personal; rather begin with a thesis as in a persuasive essay. When outlining and plotting your argument, examine if there are points where your own observations and experience bisect the information on your subject. Those are the windows for moving yourself into the topic.

Foremost will be your need to inform your reader about the topic. Secondary will be the connection you deliver between your own personal experience and the topic. In a way, this personalization can often help your reader come into the topic as well. It is an invitation to the reader to discover the subject matter at a personal level, not merely as dry information.

At its best, creative non-fiction is a valuable method for disseminating information. It can be seen as the artistic arm of the critical school which insists on identifying the narrative voice, in order to identify and authenticate the parameters of the argument. More than any other genre of writing, it counters the arguments of private language by defusing and blurring the separation between writer and reader.

A friend of mine recently said that it seemed to him that the only writing one could depend on was fiction, because it was distinctly unreal, but came with its own rules for understanding the contents. Non-fiction had too many hidden "strings" for him; it was impossible to know if he was getting all the facts, or only the facts the writer wished him to have. Creative non-fiction goes a long way to alleviate this problem. Even if the writer is still offering only what she thinks pertinent, the reader can begin to determine what sorts of parameters the writer has used, based on what she allows of herself into the text. In other words, creative non-fiction allows its strings to be seen; it is non-fiction that comes complete with its own special decoder ring.

Myrna Kostash

Myrna Kostash is a fulltime non-fiction writer and author of four books, notably the classic *All of Baba's Children* and most recently the critically acclaimed *Bloodlines: A Journey Into Eastern Europe*. Besides writing for diverse magazines (from *Border Crossings* to *Chatelaine*), Kostash has written for theatre cabaret, radio drama, and television documentary. As one of Canada's best-known writer-exponents of creative non-fiction, she has been writer-in-residence in Minneapolis, Minnesota; at the Whyte Museum, Banff; Ashley Fellow at Trent University; and has lectured throughout western Canada.

She is a member of the Writers' Guild of Alberta, The Writers' Union of Canada, and PEN. In 1993-94 she served as Chair of The Writers' Union of Canada. She is the Alberta representative to the Board of Canadian Conference of the Arts.

"Creative Non-Fiction and Me" first appeared in the fall '94 *Arts Bridge*.

Creative Non-Fiction and Me

Last March I spent a month in Minneapolis as the Creative Non-Fiction Writer-in-Residence at The Loft, an astonishing emporium of literature that offers everything from how-to workshops, works-in-progress readings, mentorship programs for gay and lesbian writers, tutoring by mail and year-round classes in topics ranging from "Intermediate Fiction" and "Songwriting" to "Reading the Landscape" and "I Have All This Stuff But I Don't Know What It Is."

The Loft does not shy away from non-fiction as a literary genre, unlike the practice of most of Canada's schools and programs of creative writing. In fact, the argument for creative non-fiction (aka literary journalism, creative documentary) as literature was won ages ago in the United States.

Last summer, while holidaying in Montana, I dropped in on Bill Kittredge in Missoula. Since 1969 Kittredge has been teaching creative writing at the University of Montana and we had a chat about that, about how his best students were writing non-fiction and were not even "vaguely interested" in writing fiction. I wondered why that was the case.

"They have a political agenda," he said, meaning a subject, "and if you're a writer who doesn't, then you're all wrong, or lying." Still, I argued, you could write fiction-with-a-subject.

"For a long time now, fiction hasn't been about anything important," he rejoined. "It's never about work or money, which is what non-fiction is about. Everyone's tired of the smaller-than-life, ironic, low-mimetic narrator in fiction. In non-fiction it's fun to be able to write as a narrator who is as smart as you can be. But I always tell my students that the most important thing to figure out is *what your subject is going to be.*"

Tom Wolfe, the Grand Wizard of New Journalism (see, most famously, his The *Electric Kool-Aid Acid Test* that spawned a generation of gonzo journalists) would not disagree. In 1989 in *Harper's*, he issued a literary manifesto, "for the new social novel." In it he deplored the belief of the young fiction writers that the act of writing words on the page was the "real thing" while the real world beyond the creative ego is merely "so-called." It has fallen on non-fiction and New journalism, he argued, to exploit the "most valuable and least understood resource" available to a writer: documentation, or what Wolfe calls "reporting."

Thanks mainly to the ruminations of American writers on this battle of the genres, I have come to think of creative non-fiction as a kind of *bridging* genre that shamelessly ransacks the toolkits of fiction *and* journalism to tell its tale. Think of it as linking the Documented with the Imagined, the Fact with the Experience, the observer with the observed, the public not-I with the private I. Think of it as the genre that leaps the gap between the "news from far off" with the "lives of our neighbours."

How does it do this? Unlike traditional journalism with its fetishistic insistence on "objectivity," creative non-fiction accepts a narrator with a point of view—the device by which the writer *takes a position* on what s/he is reporting, an act of citizenship, as it were, as well as of writing.

I have always been moved by the American poet Terrence Des Pres's encouragement to us all that we are *right* to expect a connection between the external events we witness and record the "interior drama" of our own feelings and memories. From another angle, Paul Chamberland, the Québécois poet, analyzes what he calls "civil poetry" as a "passion for the human" that he senses within the "quivering and vibration" of language. This humanization, this *civility*, connects "jubilation and play" with "responsibility to the Other."

The Canadian/American writer, Bonnie Kreps, hanging out with physicists, was fascinated to learn that atomic physics has shattered the old division between the Observer and the Observed and has reconfigured the universe in a "participatory universe." The British writer James Fenton discovered this for himself while travelling in Korea and Vietnam; he was astonished to see how the constrictions of "objective" journalism meant that most journalists were jettisoning their best material "because they know they will not be able to write it up, *because to do so would imply they had been present at the events they had been describing.* And not only present—alive, conscious, and with a point of view."

Well, anyone working in creative nonfiction today doesn't need to be encouraged to be conscious and with a point of view. But I want to re-emphasize the bridging task of the genre which creates a *context* for the personal, underscores the authority and urgency of actual, lived lives, by situating them in the real world.

And to do this, creative non-fiction goes forth and ... reports. At the heart of the genre lies the document—the artifact of actuality. The Out There and the Other Person is where we always begin, curious and enquiring, driven by compassionate concern about our communities, where we've been and where we're headed.

It is this documentary aspect of creative non-fiction from which I emerge, as a Canadian writer. Much more than in the case of American creative non-fiction which has roots in the nineteenth-century personal essay, the Canadian variety is rooted in journalism. Like other young or small countries, Canada has always felt anxious about the viability of its culture and even the reality of its own experience. This perpetual identity crisis has fuelled a very rich documentary tradition in the arts, as artists assume again and again the responsibility to "tell our stories, to name the truth and to possess our history," in the words of non-fiction writer, Susan Crean.

This passion for the actual world beyond the self (beyond the autobiographical, the memoiristic) became a *liet-motif* of my lectures in Minneapolis. I was deluged by manuscripts purporting to be creative non-fiction that were in fact memoirs: songs of the self. It became my mission as a Canadian among Americans to remind workshop participants of the connectedness of their lives and memories and perceptions to the equal authenticity of the Other. *Kapow!*

So I go back to where I began, with the idea of creative non-fiction as the bridging genre between the Private and Public.

It's true that we who write it are stretching the form so we can be more speculative, less linear, more suggestive and less argumentative, less reportorial perhaps and, yes, more memoiristic than in traditional non-fiction writing. But if we retreat from our central concern and passion—bringing back the news from "out there"—then we may as well write fiction.

Sharon Butala

Sharon Butala has been called "one of this country's true visionaries." She is the author of several novels and short story collections as well as two best-selling works of non-fiction, *The Perfection of the Morning* (from which "Belonging" is taken), nominated for a Governor General's Award in 1994, and *Coyote's Morning Cry*. *Country of the Heart*, her first novel, was nominated for the *Books in Canada* Best First Novel Award. Butala lives with her husband near Eastend, Saskatchewan.

Belonging

Often at the ranch Peter would get up at dawn, catch one of the saddle horses in the corral, groom it, give it hay, and come in for breakfast while his horse fed. Then he'd saddle it and ride off into the fields for a day of looking for calves which had lost their mothers or vice versa, for mix-ups of various kinds, for illness or accidents, and inspecting fences and water-holes and the state of the grass in each field. It was not unusual, during those summer days of seemingly endless light, for me not to see him again till darkness had crept up the hillsides, turning them black against the luminous night sky. His father and mother had told me, each in their own way, not to worry when he didn't return: his father sagaciously, "This is the way of cattlemen, of cowboys"; his mother wryly, "They always come back eventually, none the worse for wear."

When the other women of the community were visiting each other, I knew nobody; while they were raising children, I had no young children left at home; while they were growing gardens and preserving food, I had few people to cook for, no garden yet, and the tiniest of houses which took no time to look after; while they were sometimes driving to part-time jobs, there was no real need for me to get a job and we lived so far from the nearest town that any full-time work was impracticable; while they were driving tractors and farm trucks and occasionally running to town for parts, Peter, used to doing everything himself or with hired help, didn't ask me to help, at least partly because I didn't know how. At the advanced age of thirty-six I was just learning to ride a horse.

I began to go for walks. Sometimes I would carry a lunch out to where I knew I would find Peter and the hired man fencing, or I would walk the fenceline to where the herd of horses were grazing and spend half an hour talking to them across the fence till they grew bored with my company and wandered away. I would walk to the places I had seen from the truck where the view was especially distant or beautiful and sit on the stiff, dry, prairie grass and try to assimilate the stunning, bare sweep of land.

East of the house about a mile was one of the highest hills on the ranch—you can see its silhouette blue against the horizon from miles away—and in those early days before I dared to venture too far from the house and yard I sometimes chose it for my destination. More than once from the crown of that hill I'd spotted Peter on horseback, a black stroke against the yellow grass a mile or two away, moving slowly among the cattle, disappearing almost at once between hills. If I felt lonely I'd sometimes walk out and climb that hill in hopes of catching a reassuring glimpse of him.

On a hot summer afternoon, having been alone since dawn and bored with the pursuits I'd been toying with for the last few hours, I wandered out to that hilltop, my head down, thinking. In those early days, as my old life began to waver and dissolve and the new one still had no firm shape, I was always deep in thought.

The side I was approaching the hill from slopes gradually up to the crest; on the other side it drops off abruptly a hundred or so feet to the prairie below where the spring run-off sometimes pools to form a shallow slough. By this time of the year, July, the water had long since evaporated, but it had left behind a stand of grass richer than the surrounding prairie, where there were always a few animals to be found.

On that day, on the far side of the hill in that slough-bottom, twenty or so cows stood grazing or lay with their calves beside them peacefully chewing their cuds. In their midst Peter's saddle horse, reins dragging, browsed lazily too. And far off at the edge of the cluster of cattle, a couple of antelope stood, noses down in the grass. All of them were oblivious to my presence and paying no attention to each other, as if they were all members of the same contented tribe on that still, hot afternoon, under that magnificent dome of sky, and in the midst of those thousands of acres of short, pale grass. About a hundred feet out from the foot of the hill, in the midst of his animals, lying facedown in the grass, head on one bent arm, hat shielding his eyes, Peter lay sound asleep.

I stopped dead in my tracks, overcome with an emotion I couldn't identify: that I had caught him in a moment so private I felt I had no right to be there; that something was happening here that was beyond my experience and my understanding, but that meant something—something significant; I could feel it in my heart and in my gut—which my brain couldn't grasp, couldn't name or classify.

I backed away quickly before I was seen; I hurried down the long slope of the hill and full of silent wonder walked back across the fields to the house. I never breathed a word of what I had seen to anyone.

On her deathbed our mother had dreamt, she told us, that she was back on the farm in Manitoba and the five of us were little girls again. We were in the summer kitchen, she said, and outside it was raining. A tent was pitched in the yard and a family of children were in it. The five of us were begging her to let them into the house with us, but she wouldn't because, she said, they'd track in mud and she had just washed the floor. "I should have let them in," she said, terribly upset, as if it had really happened and wasn't just a dream. "I should have let them in. I shouldn't have worried about the mud."

I knew at once it was a dream about how she had watched us too closely, how she had held firm in her determination to protect us from a world she was herself afraid of, and how she now saw she had been wrong. I grew up timid and afraid of the world as a result of this watchfulness, and any need I had for adventure I had always stifled or fulfilled vicariously. Now, in my only act of real daring, I had turned away from the world I'd been raised for and understood, had thrown away everything I had worked for, in favor of a world about which I knew nothing and the promise of which I couldn't even read.

If I had had stirrings of memories powerful enough to draw me back into the natural world in which I had spent my first years, I was mistaken if I thought I knew anything factual about how to make a living in it, or even how to live in it as my husband did. Whatever it was or would be, I had not imagined beforehand, and even though I was now living in it, it was an uneasy kind of living, laden with a sense of waiting, of discovery and possibility, but without any firm shape or structure. In the back of my mind I must have thought that only the form and the daily activities would be different than my old life, that the mental and emotional texture, the fabric of it, would be just the same. Not having any experience as an adult of any other way of apprehending and of being in life, how could I imagine it in advance? Or expect it? Or prepare for it?

In the city I had had an identity, or rather several identities: divorcée, single parent, career woman, graduate student, future academic. If the day-to-day living of it was hard, and it was sometimes terribly so, as any single working mother will tell you, it had had its rewards, chiefly that, having gone from the daughter of a rather strict and formidable mother (at least I found her so although my sisters, I think, would describe her otherwise) to the wife of a man I had somehow wound up trying to please but never could, I had had for the first time in my life a degree of personal autonomy. I earned my own money and could do with it as I chose; I could paint the walls of my house any color I liked; I could cook food I wanted to eat; I could invite over whomever I chose.

At first after my divorce I realized that I had been so demoralized over the years that I didn't even know what color I might want for my walls, or what I liked best to eat, or whom I wanted for friends, or even what kind of a person I was. But as I slowly recovered from the wounds of my marriage and the trauma of its end, these matters gradually began to fall into place. I had begun to remember the person I'd once been, or was becoming, since I was only twenty-one the day I married. I had begun to remember myself as competent, with certain gifts: I had been a visual artist, a good student, a woman who loved to dance. I had been someone who was capable and who had certain dreams of her own of what her life might one day become.

I had, too, a community I knew well and a place in it. I had lived altogether seventeen years in Saskatoon and I knew its corners, its ins and outs thoroughly. Everywhere I looked I saw familiar faces, people I saw on the street every day, even when I had no names for them. I had spent a total of nine years on the university campus and could remember when it had had only two thousand students and half the buildings it had when I left. I was a member of a large family, with cousins in the city, and nieces and nephews, and not far away aunts and uncles on both my mother's and father's sides, and until their deaths, grandparents too. I had never been without that sense of being part of a family, not even when I'd lived in other provinces; it was not something I'd ever given a thought to.

It's true, though, that I often found the day-to-day living of this life of freedom in many ways terribly hard. I had been raised expecting to be supported by a man and had been trained to be a good wife and mother. Although I'd always worked, I'd never before felt the real burden to succeed in order to support my family in quite the way men do, as a burden they are raised to shoulder, even do with some pride and eagerness. In my career I had to learn all the skills men are so good at, like taking full responsibility, standing up for myself, expecting without thought to take care of myself and my child.

Still, the benefits seemed to me to outweigh the problems, and the most wonderful benefit of all was my women friends. I'd been one of a group, some of whom I'd known for twenty years and others whom I'd just met, who were companions, confidantes, intellectual peers, colleagues, people to go to parties with and plays, concerts, movies and for walks in the park, to eat lunch with, to have over for dinner and who had me to their houses, women to whom I could go, and they to me, when we had to talk to someone, with whom we would trust our deepest secrets. My dearest friends from those days are still my dearest friends, even though they are scattered across the country now, and I see each of them perhaps once a year. Together we were inventing a new world, and that resulted in ties so deep to each other that they'll never be broken in this life.

We were part of the ferment of the new wave of feminism that had risen in the sixties and peaked in the seventies. We were meeting in consciousness-raising groups, whether formally constituted as such or not; we were speaking to each other, for most of us for the first time, as sisters, even though we were not blood relatives and often not even intimate friends. We were breaking down some of the barriers that had existed between individual women as far back as we could remember or had heard about from our mothers, and were seeing that we were a race, a tribe, a nation of people, when we had thought each of us belonged to our mothers and to men.

We were exploring womanhood too, well beyond the stereotypes we'd been raised in: what it is to be female, to be wives and mothers, to approach the world as female beings. We were searching for and finding our power through deliberately trying to tear down the walls of fear society, we had believed, had forced us to erect between us.

So our friendships were wider, deeper, and there were more of them than most of us, at least of my age, had had since we'd graduated from high school and left childhood behind. They also held a more important place in the lives of each one of us. We supported each other at work and in our private lives; it sometimes seems to me that we lived in a sense collectively. It was, I see now, a wonderful time to be a woman, even though what united us primarily, beyond our femaleness, were our common struggles and suffering in a time when, on the one hand, we were being told and telling each other that women could do and be anything we wanted, and on the other, nobody was admitting how very hard that was turning out to be.

But we were also having a lot of fun; it seemed every weekend one of us gave a party where we danced and talked and ate and danced some more, not going home till the sun was rising. We were nearly all divorced, separated or otherwise unmarried, many of us products of the fifties with our overdeveloped superegos, and in our newfound feminism we were experiencing for the first time in our lives a sense that there were endless possibilities to our own lives, not just the single, precise picture we'd been raised to believe was the only possibility: a husband, several children, a house, a car, a lawn to mow, rugs to vacuum, dishes to wash. Although men were also present, it was understood that their presence was great but not necessary, and that we were a gang, not a group of couples, for we were realizing that—oh, most amazing fact of all—we could have fun with each other and as a group, we didn't have to wait around till an individual man invited us. And that realization alone gave us back some of the power we'd lost.

All of this is to say that my women friends had become so firmly woven into the fabric of my life that they were as vital to me as breathing, that I knew I would miss them as much as I would miss the blood sisters I was leaving behind. It also meant that I took it for granted that in time I'd find a new set of women friends with whom I could share my life in the same way I had with my friends in the city, and so I approached the women I was meeting in my new community blithely, eagerly, wholly unaware that things worked differently in the country.

One of the things which I am constantly having to correct people about is the urban perception that rural life is the same whether it's small-town life, or farm or ranch life. Farm life is very different from ranch life although there are similarities, especially for people who do mixed farming. But on a true ranch the primary business is the care and feeding of cattle, big herds of them, who lead a semi-wild life out on the range and whose care necessitates for the ranchers a life lived out in the wilderness in all kinds of weather, and it is true, the worse the weather, the more the cattle need you. Farming means growing grain and that is a spring-to-fall job with a free winter, and it takes place on land that, by definition, is no longer wilderness.

Also, when urban people want to describe me as living in Eastend I always correct them, pointing out that I live out in the country. This distinction appears to seem to them irritatingly trivial, as if I am merely nitpicking. But town life, too, is a different kettle of fish than true country life.

Because I'd never lived on a farm before, and because Peter's main interest and daily work wasn't farming, often I didn't understand even the simplest remarks about what everybody's husband was up to at the moment, much less could I contribute any of my own. Not that it would have been any easier if the women were all married to ranchers, since ranch women tend to be horsewomen, real outdoorswomen, with the same practised eye for cattle as the men, and many of the same hard-earned skills, none of which I had or, to be truthful, wanted very badly.

How the women worked! I'd never seen anything like it. They kept enormous gardens and canned or pickled or froze everything in them, often at the same time as harvest when they had a crew of men, albeit a tiny one compared to the days of threshing crews, to cook for; they knew how to handle every piece of meat from a side of beef, even how to can it, as well as lamb and pork, and how each had to be butchered although the men did the butchering. They understood the mysteries of keeping a milk cow, milking her and using the separator and cleaning it, and raising chicks up to chickens without the coyotes getting them, and of gathering the eggs without being pecked; they could make cottage cheese and headcheese and it wasn't uncommon to make an angel food cake from scratch. In a country where bakeries were either too far away or not much good they made all their own bread; they could and did run the farm machinery and haying equipment, and did all this while driving the boys to hockey practice and the girls to skating lessons and music lessons and a thousand and one extracurricular activities at the school; they nearly all had their hobbies, chiefly handicrafts, and they all did community work besides, in fact, were the organizing force that kept rural communities alive. Beside them I felt like an incompetent idiot, and the longer I knew them, the less I thought that traditional women had it easier than the new breed of urban career mothers. They had husbands, that was all, who presumably, if they did not share the work, then at least provided moral support and companionship.

My own growing sense of inferiority to these marvelous women, combined with a lack of desire to be like them, since I knew I would drop down dead at the end of one day like every one of theirs, and also because I believed something was missing from their lives that I had myself and didn't want to lose (even though, if asked, I wouldn't have been able to say what it was) also got in the way of friendships. Well, I told myself, true friendship takes time to build; I can wait.

That some of the difficulty had nothing to do with me as a person was brought home to me when I asked a woman my own age, who seemed to me subtly different from the others in the room at the time, how long she'd lived in the district. "Twenty years," she said, and sighed. I had been in the community a dozen years when a woman, listing members of the community for some reason I've forgotten now, remarked to me that she'd left out a certain family. "They didn't move here till the forties," she said, "so I never think of them." She meant that even though that family had lived here for almost fifty years, in her estimation, they would never be truly local people. By that time I was the one to sigh.

When I first came here to live, country people were country people to me; big farmers, small farmers, it was all the same to me. I didn't know the basic fact that there's a social hierarchy out here, too, or of what it consisted. Although in a strange way the class system I was familiar with—based on income, visible affluence, education, job type, whether manual labor, blue collar or professional, and to a small degree, family background, as well as whatever else urban sociologists are arguing about these days—didn't entirely hold, there was indubitably a class system at work.

This was a world which at first appeared to me to be nearly all working class, where education wasn't particularly valued since you could be a well-educated bad farmer or a poorly educated top-notch farmer, where differences in jobs were minimal, and where having leisure time wasn't especially desirable—too many farmers lost interest in life when they retired, sometimes turning to alcohol for consolation, or suffering a heart attack suddenly and dying. Yet there were still the aristocrats, plebeians and untouchables, and the trick was to figure out which was which and why.

Land springs to mind at once, for with land comes money, and wealth is certainly a measure of class in both town and country. Yet, when people began to buy more land regardless of the escalating prices, Peter, who had no shortage of land, would quote to me the old Russian dictum, "How much land does a man need?" which his Slovakian father, who'd arrived penniless in this country in 1913, used to quote to him, and the answer to which is, "Six feet to bury him."

But to say land is the basis of the class system is to give an inadequate description of the situation. At least as important is the length of residence of a family in the country. "In the country" means in any particular district. Such is the degree of pride in this that I'm told there is in Maple Creek an organization which holds an annual dinner which may be attended only by those whose families have been in the country a hundred years or more. And even I, I confess, am proud of being able to say that my Manitoba relatives still live on farms established by their families in 1884 and 1885. That my Québécois and Acadian relatives have been in Canada since the mid-seventeenth century counts for less out here than the other.

But as a caveat to the above, to earn respect within this system of landownership and length of residence, a holdover, I think, from pioneering days when all the work was manual, it is also essential to have a reputation for being a hard worker. A man could be a drunk, a wife-abuser, a fighter, I used to tell Peter indignantly, but if he worked hard every day, nonetheless, other men respected him. In fact, it seems to me that that ethic, basic to the besieged rural value system, was the one most in need of revamping to meet a modern agricultural society, and yet was one of the most basic strands to its unraveling fabric.

I learned to be constantly aware of the amount of work accomplished by others. If I felt that in this something was puzzlingly out of sync with reality as I knew it, I still couldn't help but notice that if the men worked hard, it was evident to me that they hadn't a patch on the women, whose work never ended. As an extreme example, one woman told me angrily after she'd—temporarily, it turned out—left her husband: "I work all day out in the field with him and when it's mealtime I come in and cook it while he sits with his feet up and reads the paper."

Eventually, after more than a dozen years, I could see that the reasons for the way people were treated by other community members were frequently things I would never know because they had happened two generations back, or in childhood, or had nothing to do with anybody living today. They were so embedded in the fabric of the community that they could never be teased out, and the people who were responding to them didn't even notice anymore, or never had noticed, that they were. And I, a stranger, would be years in learning what they were, if I ever did at all.

Truly belonging to the community of women in the way I'd belonged to my community in the city was going to be much harder than I'd thought. I still didn't understand that I would never have the conversations with my rural women friends that I had had with my urban friends. I would never have them because not just the daily round of activity but the approach to life, the view of it, was utterly different.

In time I was invited to join clubs whose work, unfortunately, I wasn't interested in, so that after debating with myself, and much as I wanted to belong, I declined. To this day, no matter how it has been here or how lonely I have been at times, I don't regret declining. I longed to belong, but without realizing it I was resisting. Although I hadn't yet figured it out rationally and was acting strictly from the gut, I had enough presence of mind in this case to follow my intuition which said that there was no choice involved; belonging would have to be on my own terms, whatever I might finally discover those terms to be.

Many of us have childhood dreams that are unfulfilled and that we carry with us for life. Mine was to be a visual artist. Despite the fact that my two undergraduate majors were art and English literature, so complete was my rejection of what I now know to be my true nature that when I returned to the university after ten years away in the work force I had deliberately chosen to do a master's degree in the Education of Exceptional Children. This was how I had made my living for the previous seven or eight years, and when I had decided to go back to university, I'd rejected doing a master's degree in art because—it was the early seventies—it seemed to me that fine arts departments had fallen into such chaos that a Virgoish person like myself would be driven crazy in one. I rejected doing a master's degree in English because I thought after all those years of working first with street kids in Halifax and then developmentally delayed teenagers in Saskatoon the sheer boredom of nitpicking over words would be the death of me. At the time I really believed these were the true reasons, and looking back now, I can only add that it is just possible that I refused both courses not only because making a living would be so precarious after but, more than that, because I so loved both fields that I was deeply afraid of failure in them.

From the time I started school as a six-year-old, I'd known I could draw and that drawing and painting gave me great pleasure. As the years of my life as a schoolchild passed, this skill or talent was reinforced over and over again by both my classmates and my teachers, and was cherished at home by our mother. (My sisters were also gifted in this way, my older sister much more than I.) Often I could draw better than anyone else in my class, and I loved art more—though I loathed crafts, which were what art classes more often consisted of and at which I was very bad. I had begun to imagine a life as an artist for myself.

I reached high school and although I attended the high school where the children of the working class and the immigrants went, from which you could graduate already a secretary or a mechanic, by some fluke I've never understood, it was at the time the only school in the city with a full-fledged art program and a genuine artist as department head and the only teacher. I was able to major in art, and to have my thirst for it constantly tended to by my daily classes with him through most of my four years there.

My art teacher (and also my older sister's) was the well-known Saskatchewan artist Ernest Lindner, and as an immigrant himself he understood that those of us who faced the future without financial security or useful contacts needed to be given confidence, needed to be told that even working-class kids had a right to a fulfilling life, that even I might go to university and take a degree in art, which, armed with his certainty that I could, I eventually did.

I had finished the first year of my B.A. majoring in art when I began to worry about making a living. I had had no other plans, no other alternatives in mind but becoming an artist. Now I began to face the fact of the struggle artists' lives are for mere survival, and I knew I did not want to spend the rest of my life in poverty. I had had enough of that—or so I told myself. Now I think that I was simply afraid that I wasn't talented enough, that I simply hadn't the guts to strike out in the world without a sure way of making a living.

At the end of my first year I switched into education, received my B.Ed. at the end of four years—I'd already been married for a year—and stayed on for one more year to finish my B.A., still majoring in art. I would be a teacher of high school English, and if anybody would let me, I'd teach art, as a rather pitiful substitute for a life as a genuine artist.

After that the inevitable happened—nobody wanted an art teacher. I was so busy working and, by then, being a mother that I had no time anymore to paint, and before I knew it, my self-identification as an artist hid faded away to a pale and almost forgotten shadow of its former self. I barely had time to mourn it. Except for my paintings hanging on the walls of our various apartments, no one would ever have known that was who I had once been. Deeply buried though, deeper and deeper with each passing year, was that budding artist inside me. I always believed, without ever really thinking about it, that one day I would return to my art.

Six or so years into our marriage which, although I didn't fully comprehend this at the time, wasn't going very well, during one of our many moves from one apartment to another, my husband threw in the city dump the dozen or so paintings I had kept as proof I'd once been an artist. It was several weeks before I even knew about it; there was then no hope of ever getting them back. I didn't even look for them.

I was too stunned by this act even to express to him my shock. I'd expressed more anger to him for losing my place in a book. I said virtually nothing; not then, not since. And I didn't mean to let it matter; I thought if I didn't let it, it wouldn't. I didn't know that there is a place deep inside where one's real life goes on, much like an underground river in parched, dry country, which flows whether one knows about it or not. Although it was such a blow I couldn't even respond, having been knocked to my knees metaphorically, it was a blow that I would eventually find had nonetheless left a lasting wound.

It is worth mentioning, I think, that I long ago forgave my young husband for this act, not because I am a saint, but because neither one of us understood our own lives then, and had he understood its significance to me, I know he would not have done it. To this day I'm not sure how I repaid this wound, but I know it had to have been something just as terrible, and in just as uncomprehending a way.

During the last year of my city life, after Peter and I decided to marry, but before the ceremony, the way I spent my leisure time had begun to change. For years I had read only in my field, trying desperately to keep up. Now I went back to reading novels, something I hadn't had time to do for years, even though reading had been, from the moment I learned how in the convent on the banks of the Saskatchewan River so long ago, the single most important activity in my life. It was as if, knowing that the end of my long travail at the university was in sight, I was slowly rediscovering the interests I'd abandoned one by one, mostly out of sheer exhaustion, over the previous years.

I took up needlework and made a couple of extremely ugly appliquéd cushion covers. I did some crewelwork and considered, but didn't get around to doing, batik, which I'd learned during a couple of years when I'd taught some elementary school classes in art. I began to realize slowly and with increasing eagerness that the long-awaited day had finally arrived: after the wedding and my move to the ranch, I would once again take up painting.

I arrived in my new life equipped with soft-leaded pencils and thick, rough paper, intending to find my way slowly by honing my drawing skills first. Of course, there were the inevitable physical hardships that initially took much of my energy, but eventually even those became, if not routine, at least manageable. Afternoons, when Peter was off riding by himself or working with other men, or doing business on occasions when I couldn't accompany him, I planned to take out my drawing pad and pencils and go looking for subjects. And I tried to.

I carried my equipment out to the corral and made a few desultory attempts at rendering the barn with its interesting, half-broken cupola full of swallows. I tried the weeds growing up around the weathered bottom rail of the corral, and the rough shacks that had once been bunkhouses or settlers' cabins and now held the detritus of settlers' lives such as worn, stiffened buffalo coats, broken kerosene lamps, nicked and crushed blue granite pots, rickety tables and rusty iron bedframes; I struggled to render the old hand water-pump on its cracked wooden platform. At the stockyards in a nearby town, while Peter attended a cattle sale, I sat in the truck and drew the town's huge grain elevator and its annex. It is the only drawing I completed.

Something was missing. The first few pencil strokes had taught me that I'd lost nearly all my craft in the last twenty or so years. I was not really worried about that; I knew I could get that back. What was missing was something more essential than mere learned technique. Drawing takes intense concentration, a complete absorption in the subject and in the materials one is working with. This is usually a fully joyous kind of concentration—at least it had always been for me.

Now I found I couldn't concentrate at all, couldn't find that level of absorption, could not for the life of me dredge up desire anymore. I had thought naively in my new life I would go back to being a painter, and now I had to accept that that dream was over, that I would never paint again. I had lost the heart for it. I was devastated.

I was still an urban person; I came from a world where everyone was defined precisely by what he or she did. With no job, no friends, no family, *nothing to do*, I began to search for an anchor, or a framework, a shape, in which to live out my days in this strange, new world which unexpectedly was, at least on a day-to-day level, as alien to me as if I'd married an Arab or an Inuit and gone to live in his culture.

The afternoon I walked out into the field, climbed the hill and saw Peter asleep on the ground with his animals was a deeply significant moment for me, a benchmark against which I measured each of my new experiences. It seemed to me that something had been revealed to me about my new husband that I had never guessed at, that I had seen a glimmer of something about my new life that would inform and instruct me if I could just understand it. The moment was like my dream-visions in that whatever its significance was, I *felt* it rather than verbalized it or assimilated it intellectually. Like the childhood morning when my chest had filled with light, my entire body felt what I was seeing not like a blow but more like opening the door of a dark, gloomy house onto the outdoor world of light and warmth and color. I filed this experience away, too, as I had the visions of the spirit coyote, and of the wonder and beauty of the universe. I didn't speak of them, but this did not mean I'd forgotten them.

In secrecy I pondered and pondered over Peter asleep on the grass among the animals, wondering what it meant, feeling that there was, just out of my grasp, a message that once deciphered would be the key to understanding my new world which in turn would provide the foundation I was missing, that would show me what to do with the long hours of my days, the ways in which I might begin to think about this new world and how to live in it. For I was beginning to see that this new world I'd come to live in was different from my old one, not because of education, class or social structure, but because of whatever it was I had seen that so moved and troubled me the day I'd found Peter asleep in the grass among his animals.

Caterina Edwards

Caterina Edwards has published two novellas, *Whiter Shade of Pale* and *Becoming Emma*, and one novel, *The Lion's Mouth*. A play, *HomeGround*, that was performed professionally in Edmonton, was published by Guernica Editions in 1990 as part of their drama series. Moreover, she has published many short stories in literary magazines and anthologies such as Macmillan's *More Stories From Western Canada, Getting Here, The Story So Far, Double Bond, The Best of Alberta, Alberta Bound, Rebound*, and *Boundless Alberta*. Two of her stories were also broadcast on *Alberta Anthology* on CBC Radio. With Kay Stewart, she has edited two collections of autobiographical writing by women: *Eating Apples: Knowing Women's Lives* and *The Second Bite*.

Caterina was born in England of an English father and an Italian mother. She moved to Alberta as a child and grew up in Calgary. She received a Master of Arts degree from the University of Alberta and has lived for many years in Edmonton with her husband and two daughters.

Where the Heart Is

Everyone has been there, and everyone has brought back a collection of photographs.

Henry James on Venice

For years I had a recurring dream. I was about to arrive in Venice. I could see the city shimmering before me. I was almost there. But at the moment of arrival, it vanished. I found myself instead on an empty, windswept street. I could never arrive, never return. Sometimes, I had made a mistake: taken the wrong direction or miscalculated the distance. But usually, there was no reason for what happened. At the moment of arrival, the city vanished. And I was suspended in a cycle of longing and loss.

To arrive was to be safe, to reach refuge, to be home.

As James said, everyone, it seems, has been to Venice. The number of tourists who visit annually is in the millions. On a summer day, they are a horde, a swarm, that invades the city, clogging the narrow streets, overloading the *vaporetti*, funneling into St. Mark's Square as if it were a football stadium. Push, push, must be room for one more, though they stand practically shoulder to shoulder. They have come to see the palaces of marble, the streets of water, to experience the unreality of it all. And too often, they find it reduced to an attraction, a painted backdrop, assembled for their viewing. "Amazing," they say one to the other. "But wouldn't want to live here."

The city becomes a packed raft about to capsize, to sink under the weight of the bodies and the volume of the human wastes. In the evening, the tourists retreat to the mainland, abandoning their debris: plastic bottles and bags, sandwich wrappers, papers scattered over the ancient stones. At night, the cleaners sweep up the mountains of garbage and carry it off in barges. Morning, and again, the tour buses pour over the causeway, disgorging the groups— French school children, American seniors, German honeymooners, the entire first world, it seems. Most of the eastern Europeans arrive dazed; they have travelled a day or more on their buses to arrive in this fabled city, this wonder of the world, once beyond their reach. It seems they cannot afford even the coffee and shade of a cafe. But the sights are free, and they are free to gaze upon them and litter.

The last time I visited Venice, we (husband, two daughters and I) avoided the tourists, renting an apartment in Castello, a working class neighborhood. The stone stairs to the attic apartment were cracked or tilted alarmingly. We sweated at each step. The air was heavy with humidity and heat. At night, since we didn't have a fan, we closed the shutters, but not the windows. There was a *pizzeria* a few doors down, the equivalent of a neighborhood pub. The patrons' laughter, the buzz of their conversations, the sudden shouts of a fight, crockery smashing, chairs splintering, kept us awake late into the night. At dawn, the neighbours began hailing each other in the street, calling from window to window; the woman opposite screeched at her three-year-old son. In Edmonton, we were buffered by trees and lawns, protected by space. Here, everything and everyone was closer, louder, brighter.

I was happy, comfortable, connected to the city by history and family. Two elderly aunts, a multitude of first and second cousins lived here: the conductor on the *vaporetto*, the girl behind the bar, the manager of a leather store, the seamstress, the fish farmer, the bank clerk, sprinkled from one end of the lagoon to the other. I knew the city, not as a tourist does, as a series of 'sights'; I knew its daily rhythms, its hidden life. In those labyrinthian streets, I was at home.

Yet—I am not Venetian.

Despite the many summers I spent there, despite my affectionate, extended family, despite everything I know and feel about the city, I am an outsider. Although my mother has spoken Venetian to me since I was born, when I open my mouth to speak *Venexiane*, I expose myself as a foreigner. My words are correct, but my intonation lacks the melody. I can hear, but not reproduce, the local rhythm. Likewise, although I look stereotypically Venetian with my red hair, long face, and heavy-lidded eyes; the way I dress and move (hesitantly, unobtrusively) is Canadian.

At home and not at home.

Another year, we rented a *capanna*, a hut on the Lido beach. At first, the Venetian families, who had rented their *capanne* for three generations, ignored us, branding us tourists. But after a visit from a cousin, our position changed. "So, you're related to Michele," one mother said, taking us up and in. The Venetians offered food, advice, and conviviality. They also observed and criticized. We were expected to dress with a certain taste, to perform ritual courtesies, including shaking hands on arrival and departure each day, to eat three course lunches on proper dishes, not sandwiches cupped in napkins, to rest quietly for two hours after lunch: in general, to follow all the unwritten rules. "*Signora.*," a voice would intrude. "Haven't your daughters been in the sea far too long?" Or, "Shouldn't the girls change out of those wet bathing suits?"

At home and not at home.

HOME IS WHERE WE START FROM

The Venetian lagoon was first settled in the fifth century by Roman citizens of nearby towns seeking refuge from Attila and his Huns. With each new barbarian invasion, more refugees fled to this delta of three rivers, this swamp of shifting sands. Searching for the safest, most protected spot, the settlers moved from island to island. Heraclea, Mazzorbo, and Torcello took their turns as the major centre. In 810, when Pepin and his army invaded the lagoon, the inhabitants retreated to Rivalto, or Rialto, the core of the present city. And for a thousand years, until Napoleon, Venice was unconquerable. A thousand years of a great Republic. The series of sights the tourists come to see exist because the city was never assailed. Venice needed no thick walls, no fortifications; she could flaunt her splendours.

Venice remains a contradiction: a city built on water, stone that floats in air. Ambiguous, Venice has long inspired its visitors to fantasize, rhapsodize and create bloated metaphors. Centuries pass, yet both the Romantic poet and the latest tourist off the vaporetto call Venice a ship, a haven, a museum, a backdrop, a raft, and the bride of the sea. Venice is compared to a seraglio, a freak, a fairy tale, and a mausoleum. Since Venice's decline in the eighteenth century, the city has been a symbol of decadence, death, and dissolution. *Dust and ashes, dead and done with*, Napoleon said as he handed the city to the Austrians: *Venice spent what Venice earned.*

It is the strangeness, the sheer otherness, of this slippery city that causes it to be classified as a place of reversals, of transgressions. I played with the notion in my first novel. The wicked carnival city, where nothing and no one is what it seems. But with age and experience I am more skeptical of received ideas and literary conceits. Visiting Venice is such a sensual delight that I wonder if her reputation for wickedness sprang from an Anglo or Nordic puritanism. A place so dedicated to pleasure must be evil.

If Venice is sinking, her doom is recent and comes from ignoring ecological, rather than moral, truths. Her survival is threatened by a loss of the delicate balance between sea and city, by the pollution and the tourists, and by her transformation into not the city of the dead, but the city of the near dead, the old. The younger generation is exiled to *terra ferma* or solid land. "Very few of my old classmates live in the city anymore," says Tony, a younger cousin who has managed to stay by buying a tiny wreck of a place and, doing all the work himself, rebuilding from the foundation up. "None of the boys I played basketball with at the parish hall. All gone." They cannot afford the price of apartments in the city, driven up by the international rich, who can pay an exorbitant sum for a second home. Venice has been reduced to a holiday resort, the majority of houses (especially in the better neighborhoods) uninhabited for most of the year.

I bemoan the trend, loudly and sincerely. But if I had the chance—say I won the lottery—I would buy an apartment in a minute. On the last visit, we contacted a real estate agent and toured various renovated flats. All four of us found ourselves fantasizing yearly visits, then a home. Having breakfast on that terrace, setting a computer up in front of that window. *Isn't that all it takes? Cash? You buy a home, and it is yours.*

You wish. Home is not simply the place where you live. Home is a feeling, a haven, a cage, a heaven, a trap, a direction, an end, and the generator of more metaphors than Venice. If I claim that I am both not at home and at home in Venice, it is longing that keeps the contradictory states from cancelling each other out.

On Via Garibaldi where we went to buy sweet peaches and melons, arugula and tomatoes from an open stall, and yogurt, mineral water, and toilet paper from what was called the supermarket but was not much more than a hole in the wall, goods piled to the ceiling, aisles where you had to turn sideways to pass; on Via Garibaldi, the widest and some said the ugliest street in Venice, though the buildings were deep red, sand and buff and geraniums bloomed at the window; on Via Garibaldi, where we sat out in the early evening and sipped *aper-tifs* and watched the parade of young and old; on Via Garibaldi where each time I passed the last house, the one that faced out to the lagoon, I paused and read the plaque: *In this house lived Giovanni Caboto, explorer and discoverer of Newfoundland.* Almost super-stitiously, I paused and felt the glimmer of that other place, where I lived and which I should have called home.

Edmonton in Venice and Venice in Edmonton: in each place, I feel the presence of the other. (Nostalgia is always double, double presence and double absence.)

Who belongs? And where?

When I was growing up in Alberta, going to twelve schools in seven years, when I was at university, I felt different, out of place. I thought I would never belong. Like the dream, I would never arrive. With the years, my attitude has changed, partly because most of the people in my life do not have a specific place they call home. They are hybrids —different in complicated and interesting ways.

My husband grew up in California and though he feels an affection for the climate, the dry, fierce heat, and for the fecundity of that inner valley land, he insists he never felt American. Or rather, he never felt *only* American. It is entirely appropriate, he thinks, that he has three nationalities (Italian, American and Canadian). My adopted sister was born in Yugoslavia, spent her childhood in a refugee camp in Genova, her adolescence in Calgary, her working girl years in New York city, and the last twenty-five years in Puerto Rico, married to an ex-Cuban, who also spent his early years journeying from country to country. These are the lives we lead now—in transit and flux.

HOME IS WHERE THEY HAVE TO TAKE YOU IN.

Since the beginning, for century after century, Venice was a haven for refugees: Byzantine Greeks, Sephardic Jews, Armenians, and Slavs. They were not given citizenship; they had their own neighborhoods and churches or synagogues, but the cultures they brought influenced and altered Venice.

The aesthetic principles seem more eastern than western—gold mosaics and onion domes.

To arrive was to be safe.

In the last few years, the new migrants have come looking for refuge. In the Mercerie, between Piazza San Marco and the Rialto, the Somalis and Sengalese alight on vacant squares of pavement and spread out their wares: fake designer bags and sunglasses. The newspaper complains of the Albanians squatting in an empty palace while I notice more beggars planted at the foot of bridges. A gypsy woman stretches her hand out to me. "Need," I think she says. "The war." Others have their cardboard signs, "BOSNIAN REFUGEE" written in pencil. They look—wretched, hungry, desperate. Yet there is a system of refugee aid, with offices in the neighborhood police stations, jobs and housing provided by the city council. *Extra communitari*, the Italians call them, those from outside the community, and despite Venice's traditional role, now the citizens debate their responsibility. Many of the Venetians complain: what about us, what about that homeless family camping in the middle of Campo Santa Margherita, what about our sons and daughters who are forced to move away.

Venice for the Venetians.

(France for the French. Germany for the Germans. Serbia for the Serbians. And so it goes.)

HOME: WHERE THEY HAVE TO TAKE YOU IN

My grandfather, Renato Pagan, was born in a house on the Calle delle Rasse, a narrow street that runs behind St. Mark's Basilica. According to family lore, the Pagans, like the rest of the Venetian upper class, had lost their fortune years before to the gaming tables.

Renato went to sea to win a new fortune, or at least, a more comfortable living. He found land and a wife in Dalmatia, for centuries a part of the Venetian empire. And he prospered, a pretty house and eight healthy children, he prospered until the first World War. Although Dalmatia was a part of the Austrian-Hungarian empire, he could not imagine himself fighting on the side of the Austrians. He was a Venetian and an Italian. Like many men in the towns of Dalmatia, he joined the Italian navy, sailing under the command of Nazario Sauro.

But the family and the historical stories divide when explaining how he died. My mother claimed that he drowned in a submarine; one cousin insisted he died of hunger, of want, "that's our history," he says. Meanwhile, the history book states that Sauro did command a submarine that ran aground. The patriots were captured by the Austrians and tried for treason. Your ethnic background makes no difference, they were told. You live under our empire. *You owe your allegiance to us.* They were executed.

My grandmother, Caterina Letich (a Croatian), and her children were forced out of their house. Soldiers confiscated their belongings, transported them to Fiume, and loaded them onto cattle cars. (With other wives, and other children of Sauro's troops.) *Go back to where you came from.* Though she and all the children were born in VeliLosinj. Still, they were not sorry to be going to Italy. They thought in Venice, with grandfather's family, they would be safe. Instead, when the train reached the Italian border, the Italians declared them foreigners. The doors of the cattlecars were closed. And they were shunted from place to place. In the dark, without food and with little water. They were all ill; one aunt, Antonietta, nine years old, died. They were locked in with their body wastes and her corpse. And when finally the doors were opened, when they were let out, my grandmother and her children found themselves in a camp in Sicily, a camp for *enemy aliens*. I know little of their experience there. My Aunt Maricci, who was the oldest, told me that they were given nothing to eat. Since my grandmother spoke Italian with an accent, it was she, Maricci, who had to beg the guards to be allowed to take potato peels from the garbage.

Who belongs? (And where?)

At the end of the war, they were allowed to settle in Venice. Twenty-five years later, my grandmother was dead; the seven siblings had dispersed to jobs in the greater Veneto area. One aunt had married a fisherman and lived in Chioggia, a fishing village on the Southwest end of the lagoon. By 1944, the Veneto had become one of the focal points of the war. A German soldier warned my aunt: *Take your children to Venice.* They'll be safe there. And she did, leaving just before part of her street was destroyed.

My mother, working for a bakery in Padova, was in a bomb shelter when it was hit. Since she was claustrophobic, she found the crowded shelter almost unbearable. She stayed by the entrance, and her position saved her. In the centre, everyone was killed. Body parts, she told me, shattered flesh. Nothing else, she said. My mother moved back to Venice. She knew neither side would ever bomb that city. It meant too much to both sides, beloved as it was of Goethe and Wagner, of Byron and Ruskin. In fact, Venice was not touched.

A safe haven.

My father was a Royal Engineer in the British army. My parents met in Venice, when my father's company requisitioned the house where my mother and two aunts were living. (Which is why I am Welsh/English/Italian and Croatian.)

Who belongs? And where?

My sister, the Yugoslavian/Italian/Canadian/Puerto Rican, visited Venice as a child. Thirty years later, arriving again at St. Mark's Square, she burst into tears. "I felt like I had come home," she said. "Though it didn't make sense." She reminds me that my longing for the city is commonplace, rather than unique. The city is both strange and familiar to all its visitors. For its image is everywhere. As James said: "It is the easiest city to visit without going there." The world claims Venice as its own, and as its home, calling it, in the words of a UNESCO document, "a vital common asset."

An international movement argues the city is too precious for the

242 *Chapter Seven: Creative Non-Fiction*

Italians to continue to mismanage. Venice can be saved, the group argues, only if it does not remain a part of Italy but is made a world city. *It belongs to the world.*

This spring a group calling itself Armata Veneta Serenissima and calling for the separation of the Veneto from Italy unloaded a tank on St. Mark's Square and seized the campanile. In a survey conducted by the city's newspaper, a majority of Venetians named these separatists not terrorists but patriots. *Venice for the Venetians.*

Extra communitaria: one who is outside the community, yet comfortable, at home. When I wrote my first novel, I thought I would be able to exorcize my dream of Venice. But the dream repeats itself. I find myself writing this essay.

Venice again.

In explaining the origin of the name Venezia, Ruskin quotes Sansorvino, who claimed that Venezia came from the latin VENIETIAM, come again, for he said, no matter how often you come, you will always see new things, new beauties.

Return.

David Layton

Born in 1964, David Layton is the son of poet Irving Layton, and godson of poet Leonard Cohen. This essay, in part tribute, in part exorcism, was first published in *Saturday Night*, and then in *Why Are You Telling Me This?*, an anthology of "intimate journalism" published by the Banff Centre Press. A book-length version is coming soon.

Irving Layton, Leonard Cohen and Other Recurring Nightmares

There are two observations I need to make about the week I spent in Los Angeles: first, it rained every day, and second, it was the Tibetan New Year. Neither event was related to the other, except that together they conspired to prevent me from achieving the purpose of my visit—interviewing my godfather, the poet-songwriter Leonard Cohen. I had some notion of doing an article on the performer's capacity for personal relationships, and I think Leonard knew I also wanted him to talk about my father, though I'd written him only that I wanted him to talk about himself.

"He is up in the mountain," was how my mother put it. I was staying at her house in West Hollywood. The mountain in question was Mount Baldy, one of the many snow-capped peaks that glitter in the California sun. I tried to locate it on a map, tracing the rumpled geographical folds northward towards Washington State and British Columbia. That's where I always imagined the Rocky Mountains to be, rising inland of the Pacific rain forest. Despite my many visits I always forget that pristine mountains hover within reach of the crowded Spanish bungalows and car-choked highways of Los Angeles.

It was around the second or third day into my visit that I first heard about the Tibetan New Year and the possible connection between this event and Leonard's absence. He was up on Mount Baldy, meditating. And the rain, it turned out, was keeping him there. The news was full of stories about swollen rivers, collapsing bridges and flooded highways. Leonard would not, could not, come back down.

That, at least, was the comfortable answer. Unfortunately, there was a more disturbing possibility—that Leonard was avoiding me. I wasn't here as his godson, to pay him a friendly visit, but as a journalist, to interview him, and it was conceivable that he'd had second thoughts about the whole idea, much as I was now having.

"He's an intensely private man," my mother said. This statement was meant to describe a general trait of Leonard's but it also encompassed his present absence from LA, which in turn hinted at another of the reasons I wished to interview him. I wanted his speaking voice on tape. Despite my childhood memories and more recent conversations with Leonard, I couldn't for the life of me remember more than three consecutive words he'd strung together. Stranger still, my mother had the same problem and she'd known Leonard since he was twenty. She could remember his then-plump face and awkward smile, and she could remember, in later years, the endless and constant conversations between my father and Leonard, but not a word or phrase in his own accents could she muster. Talking to Leonard was like listening to a melody that you couldn't capture the next day.

After eight days of watching the rain fall, of damp sheets and disturbed sleep, I decided to leave for Toronto. My mother, always anxious to dissipate family-induced anxiety, especially if it's being induced in her son, assured me that she would speak to Leonard when he got down from his mountain. I decided to leave it in her hands. When it came to either my godfather or my father, it was often smarter to leave it in her hands.

My father is the poet Irving Layton. He too is a performer although in his case he performs nonstop. His role is the potent genius. He truly believes that he belongs in the pantheon with Socrates and Homer and Dante and Shakespeare, and he never ceases to live up to his status. Besides me, Irving has an older son and daughter by his second wife, and a small daughter by his fourth. Up in the attic, my father enters the pantheon and out come poems about his wives. And his children. "Be gunners in the Israeli air force," his line goes in a poem titled *For My Sons, Max and David*. Or he stands on the podium and says, "This is for my son, David." People come up afterwards and say, "Your father must love you very much." But I am not—none of us is—as close to him as Leonard Cohen. My father, who first spotted him doing a reading in a Montréal coffee house, calls him the "golden boy."

They're not at all alike. Leonard requires himself to be considerate and polite in all encounters, even if he has to fake it. That doesn't keep him, too, from taking his private dramas and shaping them into poems and songs for public consumption. Long ago, there was Marianne, who wanted to marry him. He wrote her a song saying So Long. But Leonard's style is gentle, even patrician. My father's is not. Leonard's clothes always fitted beautifully, whereas my father dressed like a Romanian factory worker. "You see this shirt!" he'd say proudly, pinching the polyester cloth with his thumb and fore-finger. "It cost me thirty dollars." My earliest recollection of Leonard was being driven around in his brand-new sports car. I must have been about six years old. The first car I remember my father driving was a Datsun with a roof so low that a permanent grease stain marked the spot over his head.

There were other differences, age one of them, since my father was two decades older than Leonard. Their backgrounds were anoth-er. My father had been born into terrible poverty, Leonard into the wealth and privilege of Westmount. But for all that they had one great thing in common—they were artists. And—if my father's opin-ion was anything to go by they were much more—they were among the elect. Their poems and music would never die but would, like the severed head of Orpheus, sing for all eternity.

Leonard is also close to my mother. Not only was Leonard the first of his friends my father introduced to her, for months he was the only one. My mother, Aviva, is the third of Irving's five wives, though they never actually got married. They came close once. A few years before my birth my father announced one morning, a morning seem-ingly no different from any other, that he would marry mother. They called Leonard and all three marched down to a jewelry shop in old Montréal where, incredibly, all Irving did was purchase a silver clasp for his previous wife and head out of the shop. My mother, the dis-inherited bride-to-be, stood over the glass counter and found herself unable to breathe.

Leonard, with that winsome smile of his, bought the ring my mother coveted, slipped it over her finger, and said, "Aviva, now you're married." During the twenty-five years that my mother spent with Irving, she never once took that ring off her finger. You can see from all this why the nature of the artist, and the nature of fame, and the effects of both on human relationships—on the possibility of inti-macy—are subjects that interest me. And also why I can never get personal about my father without bringing in Leonard, or personal about my godfather without bringing in Irving.

In our house the personal went something like this: I have home-work and my mother pretends not to understand grade four math, this from a woman who has a Ph.D. in English literature. "Go ask your father." And up I'd go, to the attic, while my mother, safe in her kitchen, would glow with pride at her little, normal family. I'd knock and wait for the thunderclap. "What!" "I have some math homework,"

I'd say. Then Zeus would heave himself from his throne and admit me into his lair which stank of words and pipe tobacco. His forced benevolence would soon wear thin. "What's wrong with you, man?" His finger would jab at the open textbook.

What was wrong with me? It was a good question. I, the son of a great poet, would sit in the back of the classroom and be admonished for picking my nose. When not in class, I'd try to shove my hand between the legs of pink-cheeked girls. This last habit landed me a two-day suspension from school and a handsome accolade from my father. "That's my boy!" he'd shout. "Stick your hands up the dark mysteries of life." And then he'd thrust his own hand into the air and wiggle his fingers. "You see that?" he'd say to my mother, "He has the hands of an artist."

But now, as I tucked the unwieldy math book under my arm, and fled towards my mother's comforts, I knew that the approval had been withdrawn and forgotten.

"Did it go all right?" my mother would ask. I'd nod my head and tell her that everything was wonderful. "Dad really helped me," I'd say. But as she leaned over to kiss me, I could tell that she knew the truth.

When my father came down from Mount Olympus it was usually for food and an audience. Any audience would do. As I watched the mounds of meat and peas pass from the plate to his belly, my father would rail against the "Philistines" and "ass-lickers" who populated the literary landscape of Canada. If my mother came to the defense of any given writer, it would be dismissed with a wave of his hand and the words "literary tapeworm." Then my father would start to laugh, and he'd laugh until he choked.

The more excited my father became, the less food made it down his throat. It would come exploding out of his mouth, along with his invective, until at last the table would be littered with the organic matter that, in my young imagination, was the decayed remains of all those Philistines my father had chewed out.

He was different when we had real guests. Then my father would strain his head forward and listen. Carefully. And he'd wait until the conversation began to meander and then he'd mount a pointed interrogation. "What do you think the role of the artist is, exactly?" Then he'd fold his arms and wait again until it was time for him to become the Great Summarizer. He would gather in all the half-baked, drunken, confused, fragmented ideas that had eddied around him and begin to tell his audience what they had all been saying. It was a *tour de force*.

My father was eighty-one before I had an insight into his technique.

We were sitting in an outdoor cafe, on a summer's evening in Toronto, when an attractive waitress came to our table.

"You're beautiful!" my father exclaimed. "Do you read books?"

The woman said she did.

"You like reading, then." My father had a way of making the obvious sound ominous. "What do you read?"

The waitress said something like "things," and became embarrassed.

"Have you studied?"

The waitress said she had received her bachelor's degree in English literature.

"English literature! Bravo. Do you read poetry? A.M. Klein, have you read him?"

The waitress looked increasingly uncomfortable as my father rattled off the names of several obscure Canadian poets.

"Irving Layton. Have you read Irving Layton?" Irving Layton asked.

To my extreme discomfort the waitress said she hadn't heard of him. I became nervous, but I didn't yet understand.

My father eyed her suspiciously, then said, "Leonard Cohen, have you heard of him?"

The waitress broke out into a radiant smile. "I love Leonard Cohen," she said.

"Good! Good! He's a wonderful writer." My father ordered another bottle of wine and we watched her walk away. I felt a slap on my arm. It was from my father.

"You see that, my boy, first you pull the rug from under them and then, when you give them a few crumbs, they think it's manna from heaven." My father sighed. "I'm too old for all this beauty."

After I failed grade four, we packed our bags and, with no explanation offered, headed for Asia. At first I thought it was a summer vacation but after six months of travelling I became suspicious. Where the hell were we? A place called India, my mother would tell me. But I kept on asking. "Where are we?" India. The word held no meaning, explained nothing, couldn't possibly make me understand why we'd go off every night to a park in New Delhi and meet my "friend," the one whom I initially mistook for a dog. We'd call out his name and he'd come running towards us. On all fours. The crippled dog-boy, the one with the magnificent smile, the one we'd feed. Dog-boy and I would run toward the Red Fort and when I'd look back there would be my father, sitting on a bench, writing.

My father wouldn't hear of any "luxuries." This apparently included sheets for our beds, light bulbs and clean food. I became sick. Every half-hour what felt like a knife would rip through my belly. After several weeks, I was shitting on street corners. There would be my father, with an iron constitution, impatient with child and wife. He'd stride into the crowds, with a book in his armpit, and a sea of humanity would close behind him. In my pocket was a small note that became smudged with perspiration. It said: My name is David Layton. If I'm lost please take me to the Canadian Embassy at —. Attached to the note were a few rupees my mother had added.

Calcutta, Kuala Lumpur, Lahore, Jakarta. Names to be sick by. Names to fear. My father would be there one minute and disappear the next. When I was alone with my mother we would go to Western restaurants and gorge on fruits and vegetables.

We finally came to rest at some beach resort in some country that wasn't India. I spent an entire day building a giant castle with a moat and a pop-drink label for a flag. Towards the end of the day, some dark-skinned, menacing boys with rags for clothes came by and began to kick my walls down. They grabbed stones and swooped by, making artillery sounds as they released their ammunition. My father, sitting farther up the beach, merely watched. With a sense of resignation I walked over towards him as he cleared a space beside himself and patted the spot where I was to sit. Together we watched as a day's worth of labour was destroyed. The sun was setting in front of us and behind the boys who came, one by one, to kick my castle down.

"Look carefully, son, and learn. What you create men will come and destroy."

A year went by before we returned to where our "vacation" had begun: Greece. Our first port of call was Leonard Cohen's house on the island of Hydra. I'd been to Greece before, and had spent time in this very house. I felt safe, and desperately relieved to be back in a country whose name had a meaning that I could understand. Part of my relief was also attached to Leonard himself. He was like a calm sea where my father's boat could rest. With Leonard, my father ceased to be the Great Summarizer. He still made speeches, but he never prefaced those speeches with an interrogation.

As I played with my toys in Leonard's courtyard, I'd watch the two of them, their Greek sailors' hats perched rakishly on their heads, their drinks in hand, their bare chests exposed to the sun. I was just old enough to recognize a strange anomaly in the way they spoke to one another. If, as would sometimes happen, Leonard talked about his latest romantic failure my father would laugh and say, "Leonard, are you sure you're doing the wrong thing?" But right after that the conversation would switch to the third person, for Irving would then launch into a discussion about the poet. He'd speak about the poet as being conflicted. They'd examine the poet as archetype—albeit a vanishing one, along with the priest and the warrior—and about the poet as Lover. The poet, I'd hear my father say, "makes love to the world."

This last concept held a particular significance for me. Whenever my father roared this one out to my mother, I knew there was big trouble brewing. "Goddammit, woman, I'm a poet!" Which meant ipso facto that he was a Lover. This, my mother would point out, was precisely the issue: whose scent was on his shirt this time? My father would become infuriated. "I'm not a lover to a woman but a lover of Women," he'd say, as often as not launching into a speech about breasts as mounds of earth, vaginas as forests. He had no time for a petty mind, he'd say, meaning that he had no time for an unpoetical mind. I began at an early age to connect the word "lover" with my father's wrath.

Unlike my father, Leonard was a man who never seemed to raise his voice. He merely ... disappeared. It was just off this very court-yard in Hydra, my father used to tell me, that Leonard had dropped himself and his typewriter into a pit and refused to come out. Marianne, who was living with him at the time, would implore him to come back inside but he continued to work on his second novel, *Beautiful Losers*. With tears in her eyes Marianne would drop food baskets into his hole. Leonard kept on writing until his fingers seized up. Now Marianne was gone.

For my father, this was as it should be. "Leonard happy?" I can hear him saying. "How can he be happy?" Leonard's destiny was to be more than a poet but a poet first. Let Leonard have everything, be anything: as a poet he wouldn't be able to enjoy it. My father always seemed quite delighted by Leonard's predicament, but his delight was never vindictive. Far from it—in my father's eyes it was the fulfillment of all that Leonard was fated to be.

Thus it only stood to reason that Leonard should lose his interest in sex at the very height of his fame. Women in elevators would throw themselves at him, would arrive at his hotel door with nothing on but a mink coat, but Leonard could give only an affirmative answer to my father's mirthful question, "Leonard, are you sure you're doing the wrong thing?"

It seems it was my father who, one evening in Montréal, hit on a ribald solution to Leonard's predicament. A little healthy competition between two great Lovers would spur Leonard's prick to life. Niema Ash, a woman who dressed only in purple, leapt in and offered to sit between the two men and, with their poetic members in her hand, stir the creative juices. "We need some inspiration," my father commanded. And so my mother, the erotic figurehead, balanced herself on the edge of the couch and thrust her bare breasts into the air.

Leonard won the competition.

It was my father's reported delight in his own defeat that gave me pause. For the first time, when Niema told me the story, it crossed my mind that for Irving to call Leonard "golden boy" was tantamount to calling him "golden son."

After Marianne there had been Suzanne. Actually I remember Suzanne quite well because I had a crush on her. In our house we had a photo of Suzanne and Leonard taken outside in our front yard. If I looked carefully at the picture, and I did, I could see Leonard's fingers inching their way around the hem of her very short skirt. Leonard, no doubt, had the hands of an artist.

There is another memory I have of Suzanne. One day when we arrived at Leonard's house in Montréal, Suzanne was changing her son's diaper. While bare to the world the child began to pee. I was astonished at the power of his bladder. The yellow liquid shot out of his penis, made a magnificent arc over his head, and landed on Suzanne's cotton blouse. I followed the whole amazing performance with my eyes but, as I looked up at Suzanne's face, I saw what only could have been an expression of acute disgust. My mother hurried over to help her diaper the baby before her disgust turned to rage. As for my father and godfather, if memory serves me, they were huddled in a corner, talking in third-person pronouns.

But where was Suzanne now? Where were Leonard's children? Not here, in his house on Hydra. They had disappeared and while I missed Suzanne I was happy to have the kids out of the way. To my father, who constantly burdened himself with wife, children and mortgage, Leonard's recurrent solitude, even loneliness, must have seemed both appealing and exotic.

That was the autumn the Yom Kippur war broke out. Now the two of them, my father and godfather, would sit on Leonard's patio listening to the somber voice of the BBC World Service, swivelling the aerial whenever the short-wave lost its focus. While I had only a vague notion of what was going on—"There were people hurting one another," was how my mother put it—I couldn't help but be impressed by how my father and Leonard discussed the war as if it were a personal matter. As in fact it was. The Israelis commandeered a Hercules transport plane to fly Leonard and his guitar to the front lines.

Not to be outdone, my father marched my mother and me down to the Israeli embassy in Athens and offered his services as a warrior and poet. They politely asked for a monetary donation.

This had less of an effect on my father than one might imagine. In his mind it was their loss, not his. The Israelis believed that they needed Leonard as much as my father believed that the Israelis needed him. It somehow amounted to the same thing. As famous men, as poets, no event, no matter how enormous, was outside their personal jurisdiction.

While they stretched out their arms to embrace the world, their wives, children and lovers kept slipping through the ever-widening circle.

It was in Greece again, four years later, that my mother finally decided to get a "divorce." There was a new man in our life. He had eyes the colour of coal and a moustache whose ends he'd twirl with his fingers. I'd see him in the village, usually with my mother, sitting in a taverna. My mother introduced him as a "friend" and kept on using this euphemism for three entire months.

The village wrapped itself around the side of a hill and at its top, like a crown, stood the remains of a Byzantine fortress. Those who had money found homes in the lower part of the village, those who didn't found themselves in the shadow of the castle wall. The man with the moustache lived in the shadow. I don't think my mother ever looked better than that summer, what with having to run up the hill every night and run down the hill every morning, always remembering to stop at the bakery for the fresh bread and yogurt that her demanding family expected. That summer my father began to shuffle. He'd shuffle into the kitchen, where my mother would prepare breakfast, and then he'd shuffle back to his room. My mother wanted to pretend that what was happening wasn't really happening, so it was my father who told me, one morning when he'd shuffled into the kitchen and found no breakfast and no wife, only an empty space filled partly by a thirteen-year-old son, that things weren't going well between him and my mother. I had a towel slung over my shoulder and was anxious to meet Dania, the first love of my life, down at the beach. After what I thought an appropriate period of mourning I asked to be excused. As I skipped down the cobblestone streets, my father shuffled back into his room to contemplate his own demise.

My mother thought it right that my father and the man with the moustache, who I later found out was named Leon, have a "meeting." In full view of the artistic cabal that congregated every summer in the village, the two men made their way up the street, arm in arm, to an out-of-the-way taverna. Leon, who was expecting the full fury and pain of a man whose wife had been stolen and family destroyed, waited nervously for the explosion.

My father began to explain about the poet as a conflicted being.

"Poets," said my father, "don't make good husbands." Aviva needed to be set free. She needed a good man and Leon, my father implied, was a good man. Leon moved uneasily in his seat. He knew what he was being told: he might be good enough for Aviva, but he could never make love to Women.

My father moved from a treacherous benevolence—"Take her, she deserves better!"—to a rage that could not find a person but only a concept to attach itself to. "Be careful, Leon, women are castrating bitches. If they see one ounce, one OUNCE, of talent in you they'll rip your balls off."

That summer, my father was left with an audience of one. After the "meeting" he began to barge into my room where, with a fresh page of words in his hand, he'd sit beside my bed and carefully read me his newest poem.

Meanwhile, another picture of Suzanne and Leonard came to my attention. I stared at it for hours. There was Suzanne, looking beautiful and slightly cruel—exactly the same look of distaste on her face as when her son had pissed all over her. Only now the look had been transferred to Leonard.

For some reason it made me think of another story my father used to tell: about how Leonard once innocently tried to place a collect long-distance call through a Montréal operator "From Leonard Cohen to Suzanne, please." The operator was clearly stunned. Before she recovered Leonard asked her out on a date. Once lucky, he decided to try again, this time with another operator. Thinking that he was on to a good thing, he kept on with this game, until the night he found himself alone in a room dialing operator after operator, waiting for the breathless recognition he could move in on. It never came.

Now, in the picture, Suzanne was sitting in a beautiful restaurant with high-backed banquettes and long-stemmed glasses for the red wine. And there was Leonard, sitting beside her, looking miserable. "I've had," Leonard once told me, "that sense most of my life that it isn't working." In the picture, he was like a stain on the white table-cloth, a reminder that an accident had happened. Above the picture were the words, "Death of a Lady's Man." It was the title of his new book and album.

Things, it occurred to me, were falling apart a bit for Leonard. Suzanne had left, and his own music was beginning to be defined as defining an era, something that should be played to remind you of what was and not what is. I hadn't yet learned that performers like Irving and Leonard have nine lives.

At twenty-two I was living alone in a basement apartment in downtown Toronto. My mother and Leon were in Los Angeles. My godfather was just somewhere. Who knew with Leonard? It could have been LA, Paris, or Tahiti, and my father was in Montréal living with a twenty-eight-year-old woman named Anna. I'd see him on television talking about Love and Poetry and wonder if he'd actually been in town and not phoned. Sometimes, a friend would ring to tell me that he'd seen my father walking down the street. "Yes," I'd say, "he's in town for a few days." Which was in fact the case—I did, after all, read the newspaper.

Sometimes my father's face would slip through a crack in the door. He had once received, from an admirer, 1,000 envelopes with his face stamped onto them. His stern, unforgiving face, with hair tousled by the wind, would pop through my mail slot and out would fall a series of press clippings: "Irving Layton, Still Fighting Fire With Fire," "The Passion of Irving Layton." These headlines could denote either a speech made to the honourable members of the University of Chicago or a poetry reading given to the Housewives' Association of Mississauga. If there was a letter, it was always typewritten. "The battle has yet to be won," he'd write, and then, if I owed him fifty dollars, he'd speak of the moral imperative to pay back one's debts. And on the reverse side of the letter I could usually detect the carbon smudge left from the duplicate copy he'd made and then sent to the Irving Layton Collection at Concordia University.

It seemed a normal relationship with my father was impossible. Many years ago, when Leonard had given him two hits of acid, the books in my father's library had come out of their bookcase and bowed to one another. It was a ballet as Baudelaire stepped out and was introduced, by my father, to Ben Jonson and Edgar Allan Poe. "Leonard," he said, "I've been here many, many times." The place he was describing was the pantheon. He was there. With Socrates and Homer. He was breathing that air.

Leonard told me this story. He insisted that it was not something my father was putting on. "These," Leonard added, "are his concerns."

This was what I was afraid of.

Prominently displayed on my father's living-room table, whenever either of his sons came to visit, was an anthology of the writings of Freud. Irving's idea, his myth of fatherhood, was that we had come either to bless him or to kill him. His money was on kill. He was just letting us know. One time, I went there to face him down about it. I watched his fingers start their journey across the table and come to rest upon Freud's stern forehead in the cover photo.

"I hear you've been having some problems," he said.

"I need to talk to you," I answered.

He began to massage Freud's bald pate with a rhythmic drumming of his fingers.

I began to tell him that we needed to find some common ground. Perhaps, I suggested, if we told each other what we wanted and expected from each other, some kind of arrangement could be worked out. After sitting for fifteen minutes with arms folded, my father suddenly brought his open hand down on the table.

"What the hell are you talking about? 'Arrangements,' 'contracts.' Don't use these words with me. I'm very sorry for you, my son, but your father is not a lawyer, he's not a dentist. He's a poet! Men are vipers, villains, jackals, hyenas. If I've taught my children this one thing and this one thing only, then I have done my duty!"

My father leaned back in his chair. There was no point in trying to outperform the performer. I'd lose. But if I wasn't careful he'd start reading his poems to me.

I told him that for his sake I hoped he was one of the immortals but that I myself only wanted to be on some normal footing with my father. "And," I added, "I have another confession to make. I've never read any of your poems."

My father looked at me.

"You've never read any of my poems?"

"Not one."

He started to laugh. He laughed until he choked. "Bravo!" We spent the rest of the day smoking cigars and drinking port.

I moved out of the basement and into a third-floor loft. I enrolled in university as a mature student and used the Christmas breaks to visit my mother and Leon in LA. If Leonard was in town, I'd go and see him for an hour or two and we'd talk about women, Greece and the mysteries of good coffee. I also started making the occasional trip to Montréal to see my father. I'd talk. He'd summarize. On one occasion I told him that a woman had left me. "Son," he said, "the worst thing you can find out about yourself is that you're replaceable." I never failed to come away feeling I'd been party to a historic event.

One day in Toronto I received a call from my half-brother's ex-girlfriend, now a well-known painter, who said that there was a book launch for my father's new "Selected, collected something or other. Would I like to come?" she asked. Hell, why not?

"My boy!" my father bellowed. "Look at you!" The reception was in full swing by the time I arrived. I grabbed a drink and began to talk to Anna, my father's new wife. While we talked, faces would push themselves into the conversation. "David? Is that you?" And I'd say, "Yes, it's me," and then they'd move on. But I'd been invited. Here was the intimate embrace: the invitation. My father, standing on the podium saying, "This is for my son, David."

Halfway through the evening, an awed silence descended. I turned around and saw him. It was Leonard Cohen, who had come from some corner of the globe to surprise my father.

"Leonard, my boy!" my father bellowed, "Look at you." I stood by the entrance, with a drink in my hand, and waited to say hello to my godfather, and thank you to my father. After thirty minutes the two, linked arm in arm, moved towards me, strode on past, and entered the hotel elevator where I watched them ascend to the heights.

This time I booked my appointment with Leonard through his personal assistant. Leonard had a "window" on Saturday, in the late morning. That was three days away.

When I touched down at LAX there was only a thin strip of ozone where thick storm clouds had been on my last visit. I arrived at my mother's house on Friday evening and I thought about phoning Leonard. But then, why tempt fate? I waited until the hour of my appointment.

"Leonard?" The door to his house was slightly ajar. Before I'd even managed to pass the threshold, he was there, moving towards me, with that gorgeous smile of his. I couldn't help feeling that his presence was somehow attributable to my delicate magic. David Layton, the conjurer of shy spirits.

Leonard quickly deduced that we were short of certain materials. We jumped into his Nissan Pathfinder and headed for the liquor store. Leonard's clothes weren't as elegant as I remembered them; he wore a pair of grubby jeans. I noticed this fact as he moved down the liquor aisle. He spent an enormous amount of time looking at the tequila rack and peering into aromatic cigar boxes. He took the kind of time that indicates a man's occupation. No one who has spent a lifetime working nine to five would be able to develop such a luxurious spirit.

There was Leonard, searching for bottles in a deserted liquor store. With his ill-fitting pants and studious interest he reminded me of an aging professor searching for books in an obscure and neglected part of the library. The effect didn't make him appear old, just vulnerable.

Back at his house, Leonard offered me a ginseng-soaked cognac. He also placed a cup of coffee on the kitchen table and handed me a fat, lighted Dominican cigar. Before I'd taken my second puff, Lorca, his daughter with Suzanne, dropped by to see us. I've only known Lorca for a few years but even so I have a strange urge to treat her as my younger sister, which is no doubt partly attributable to my mother's desire to treat her like a long-lost daughter. But our links are tenuous and, as with all things in our family, ill defined.

Time passed. I placed my tape recorder on the table and tried to let it speak for me. I couldn't bring myself to ask Lorca to leave. We were the children of famous men and it was we who were always asked to leave.

Lorca, thankfully, saved me from my predicament by taking the initiative and leaving her father and me to conduct the interview. We were alone.

"I don't have much time," he said.

I pushed the record button.

"The relationship I had with Irving was not personal but it was intimate. We weren't friends in the sense that we knew or cared about each other's lives. We did know and care about each other's lives, but that wasn't what it was about. That's a personal relationship. This relationship was the poet talking to the poet about poetry. It was more intimate than a personal relationship could ever be. That kind of intimacy has sustained me my whole life and anything that is not that has always been troublesome."

On his table is a picture of Roshi, the spiritual leader of Leonard's retreat on Mount Baldy. He looks like an Oriental version of my father; the fleshy face, the truculent expression and, behind it all, the unmistakable hint of mischief. They have the faces of boxers, of men who know about getting in the ring and beating the immortal shit out of each other without hatred.

I couldn't help thinking the connection was more than a passing coincidence. Leonard invited the comparison. Leonard said, "When I study with Roshi, it's consciousness speaking to consciousness about consciousness." And anything else, I thought, is troublesome. A godson is trouble, children are trouble, and wives are the genesis of all trouble.

Speaking of consciousness, I was losing mine. The ginseng was hallucinogenic and the cigar smoke was making me exceptionally sick. "Leonard," I said, "I don't think I can drive home right now." "I know," Leonard answered. "The ginseng has been soaking in the cognac for six months. It's very potent." Leonard smiled. Then, just sitting across the table from me, he began to sing. All by itself Leonard's voice began to make my upper lip quiver. I cupped my hand over my mouth and when he had finished singing I excused myself and ran for the bathroom where, like some hormonally flushed teenager, I splashed cold water over my face.

When I returned to the kitchen Leonard was on his way out. He had to go, he said, but I could stay for as long as I liked.

He'd given me his intimate embrace: the performance. Now I was stoned and alone in his house. I looked for a picture of my father but couldn't find one. I started laughing, and once I started I couldn't stop. "Leonard!" I shouted. "Leonard, you bastard, you've done it again! You've disappeared."

Paul Quarrington

In 1986, at the age of 33, Paul Quarrington was classified as one of the top 10 Canadian writers under the age of 45. He has published seven novels: *The Service*, *Home Game*, *The Life of Hope*, *King Leary*, *Whale Music*, *Logan in Overtime*, and *Civilization*. Quarrington was awarded the Stephen Leacock Memorial Medal for Humour for *King Leary* and won the 1989 Governor General's Award with *Whale Music*.

In addition to his novels, he has written works of non-fiction, *Hometown Heroes: On The Road With Canada's National Hockey Team* and *Fishing With My Old Guy*. He won a Genie for Best Original Screenplay for "Perfectly Normal" while "Whale Music" picked up four Genies, including Best Song for "Claire," which was co-written by Quarrington.

Quarrington recorded an album with Martin Worthy in 1978 that contained the Canadian number one single "Baby, and the Blues." He also was the bass player for "Joe Hall and the Continental Drift" for several years, touring and recording three successful albums. He has participated as both author and musician in PEN benefits for persecuted writers around the world.

Epilogue from *Fishing with My Old Guy*

Last night, I attended the Scarborough Fly and Bait Casting Association's annual Christmas party. I admit, it was a function that I'd half a mind to duck, but I went for a couple of reasons.

One was to get my fishing rod from Paulo. You'll recall that I'd left half of it behind in the bush on Murphy's Island, so when we arrived back from Quebec, I had gone down into Gordon's basement and sorted through the mountain of junk there until I found a suitable rod tip, itself lost beside some river until reclaimed by Gordon. The piece was unfortunately cracked and splintered around the receiving end. Gordon was, of course, full of instruction, explaining how to wrap monofilament around the defect, but at some point he looked up into my eyes and saw that I was not taking this in. He patted the piece of fishing rod gently. "Maybe Paulo will do it for you," Gordon suggested.

Which is what Paulo had done, and he'd called to say that he would bring the rod to the annual Christmas party. So although it had been some time since I'd cast with the men and women of the Scarborough Fly and Bait Casting Association, I drove northward into the heart of Scarborough.

The party was not at Gordon's house, rather at a house a couple of blocks away. I was greeted by a young couple, Dave and Ella, who made me welcome as children of various ages scurried about behind them. The kids didn't all belong to Dave and Ella, mind you; most of the club members were now parents, it seemed. Although all were younger than I, there had been a quantum leap in the maturity of the membership. Still, there was a sameness about them, something recognizable and identifying. It wasn't anything so simple as a shared physicality, although stockiness was the order of the day, tournament casting being a bit like sumo wrestling in its conception of the perfect athlete. No, what I recognized was more ethereal than any of that. There was an attitude of affability, a great deal of locker-room banter and teasing in which everyone, men and women alike, took part. When someone would tell a fishing story, he or she was allowed the floor, and everyone would inch forward on the sofas or hunker down nearby. There was—not that it should have been such a great surprise—a sense of community. And I suppose that was what I had been looking for, ten years earlier, even more than casting skills or fishing acumen.

There was even a sense in which I was the prodigal son. Gordon sat in the middle of the party, looking hale but immobilized somewhat by a recent battle with a huge kidney stone. "Kew!" he yelled, surprised and delighted that I'd come to the party, even though he'd called almost daily for the past week to remind me about it. "Come here and sit down." He meant in the chair immediately beside his own. I took it, but Gordon did not speak to me immediately; instead he surveyed the room and grinned, finding it to be good. He patted my knee, intuiting my restlessness and keeping me still. And there we sat for many long moments. When he did speak, it was about his medical complaints. I listened dutifully, and left to get a soft drink at the first opportunity.

Paulo had—like myself—regained the weight he'd lost on the fishing trip. He stood in the kitchen grinning, his arms folded across his chest. I admired the work he'd done on my rod, which was now whole and complete again. The colours and wrappings were mismatched, but I sensed—and the summer to come would prove this—that it was now a better, more reliable stick. I don't think Nietzsche was thinking about fishing rods when he came up with "What does not destroy me, makes me stronger," but it's no less true.

Paulo had been working very hard in the four months since our return, taking a course that had improved his standing and status at work and, not coincidentally, given him a lot more responsibility and, uh, *work*. He'd not been regular in his club attendance, with the result that he'd lost his title as the club's best caster, a situation that he accepted with good grace and humour.

"Do you know what?" he asked me. "I love to listen to classical music now." I remembered how his eyes had lit up that evening when we were bathed in the aurora, when I'd affixed Beethoven's Seventh over his ears. On the long car ride home, he'd asked if he could hear it again, and he'd sat through the symphony with great concentration, in total serenity. "I listen to this music all the time," Paulo told me. "In the morning, afternoon and night. It's like an obsession."

Gary wasn't at the party, having a gig that night. He regularly sends me little flyers now, announcing when groups that he's part of are playing at Toronto's clubs.

But there was at that party a young man named Rick Matusiak, a quiet and diffident sort who had a remarkable story to tell. Gordon had mentioned this fellow to me once or twice. Matusiak is one of the most obsessed anglers who ever walked the face of the planet, and that is surely going some. Matusiak had, sometime the previous year, sought out Gordon, whose book *Fishin' Hats* Rick carried with him always as a kind of talisman. Matusiak had sent Gordon a video illustrating some of the things he was up to. For example, he was raising a pair of rainbow trout in a large apartment aquarium. He had recorded himself ice fishing, holding up a chunk of ice and showing how it had honeycombed, how the slightest pressure would cause its seeming solidity to explode away into nothingness. He had got this chunk of ice from *just where he was standing* at the time.

I joined a little crowd around Matusiak just as someone related a story of ice-fishing danger, a couple of frigid anglers suddenly separated from the shore by a rift of icy water. Matusiak nodded, citing this as quite common. "The thing to do," he noted calmly, "is to always have a portable spade. Make a boat out of some of the ice you're standing on. Paddle across to the mainland. It takes a few hours but at least you'll be dry. A lot of guys panic and try to swim it."

Now, back to that remarkable story Matusiak had to tell. I should point out, although the details are not known to me, that he'd been plagued the previous year with medical problems. I seem to recall Gordon saying something about a heart attack, but this could well be misremembered. Matusiak was not that old, somewhere in his thirties, and seemed healthy enough, if perhaps a bit high-strung. (He had telephoned Gordon earlier that day, wanting to know what people were wearing to the Christmas party. This is a little akin to wanting to know which plays of Shakespeare might be discussed at a Δ Π Δ keg bash.) He was shy, casting his gaze mostly downwards. Matusiak seemed to know few of the people there, although they all knew who he was.

Because there he had been, you see, sitting in his living room watching television, when his cousin suggested that they go fishing. There was perhaps an hour of daylight left, not much time to go adventuring. Matusiak lives to the east of the city of Toronto, where many fine rivers romp up from the grey lake. He thought initially about hightailing it over to one of these, perhaps the Ganaraska. Then he decided to simply head down to Lake Ontario, to cast from the shore near the hydro station. "It is a place," he told us quietly, "where I'd caught large fish before."

He fired a Little Cleo into the roiling water and almost immediately began to grapple with a large fish. "I was certain I had a big salmon on there," he related at the Christmas party, as members of the Scarborough Fly and Bait Casting Association pressed in upon him. "It took about half an hour to land it. Then I looked at it and I said, 'Hey, that's no salmon. That's a brown trout.'"

As Matusiak's luck would have it, there was a gentleman from the Ministry of Natural Resources not fifty feet away. He came over and looked at the fish. "I think we'd better get that weighed," he said.

Matusiak's fish bested the previous Ontario record by a good two pounds. It is also a world line-class record, although at the point in time when I'm actually typing this sentence, which exact record remains to be seen. The International Game Fish Association, the keepers of such arcana, demanded thirty feet of Matusiak's line to be tested, and the procedure was scheduled to take five months. Apparently the manufacturer's specifications are next to useless. Line labelled eight-pound test is as likely to be nearer six or ten.

The International Game Fish Association was founded in 1939 and became *the* body of record when the magazine *Field & Stream*—which had been recording fresh-water catches for sixty-eight years—turned over its historical data. Ernest Hemingway served as a vice-president from 1940 until his death in 1962. The IGFA publishes a book called *World Record Game Fishes*, and the next edition will include Rick Matusiak's name.

Later that same month Matusiak took a twenty-one-pound rainbow out of the Ganny. "I don't catch many fish," he told me, "but they tend to be large." His reputation in angling circles soaring,

Rick had recently been approached by a magazine to write about his brown trout. He was, at the Christmas party, brimming with scientifical data culled from the library. "Large fish like that are either eunuchs or triploids," he told the gathering, who tilted their heads politely. "Either no sexual organs," he continued dryly, "or an extra set of chromosomes." One assumes this sort of mutation has to do with the poisoning of the Great Lake; it's hard to discount as coincidence the fact that Matusiak was fishing near a nuclear plant. One worries—*I* worry, damn it, this is no time for circumspection—about a world where one catches either nothing or overgrown neon monsters, many-eyed and multi-finned. "Eunuchs and triploids," Matusiak repeated, himself wary of the words, his face wrinkled with distaste. He was actually worried about the nature of the article he was writing. He was so obsessed with the scientific research he was doing that he feared the finished product would be unreadable.

Being a professional writer, I gave him what I considered sage advice. "Myself," I told him, "I don't do *any* research. That way I don't get bogged down in all the details."

"Uh-huh."

"Did you have any sense, when you left for the lake, that something was about to happen?"

Matusiak shrugged. He has a fairly extensive repertoire of shrugs, this one seeming to mean that he knew more than he was saying. "Oh, you know," he began hesitantly. "I had a feeling that something was going to happen."

"Really?"

He shrugged once more. "I suppose, in my mind, I'd caught that fish a thousand times. I'd been through it over and over again."

"At the same place?"

"Yes."

"You knew it was going to happen?"

"It's a place," Matusiak repeated, "where I've caught big fish before."

"I go up north to this place, Wolverine Lodge," I told him. Journalistically speaking, I was trying to put Rick at his ease. Mind you, the volume and pitch of my voice were unprofessionally raised. "And there's this place, by the second set of narrows, where there's a big stone face before the river widens out, you know, and I've *seen* myself catch a *huge* pike there. I even forget when I saw it, how long ago or in waking dream or slumber. But once or twice a year I'll go out on the vision quest, you know, I'll get out the pike stick and go and cast something big off the cliff face. And I never catch anything, but it doesn't matter. One day I will."

Matusiak shrugged but nodded gently. "That's not the sort of thing," he pointed out, "that people like to read."

I imagine that Gordon has had a vision of himself catching a magnificent speckled trout, working it out of the furious dark water of the Broadback watershed. Perhaps a fisherman holds visions even more dear than memories.

The day after our return from Murphy's Island, Gordon started firing off letters to the Quebec government. In effect they read, "Thank you very much, but I have to go back once again. You didn't allow me to get to my spot, the Old Place I love most in my heart, and that is where it must and will happen." We have yet to hear back. I don't know how likely it is that any more expeditions will be mounted. Paulo might return, although I don't think so. He was disappointed, and a young man's disappointment is obdurate. Gary has announced, with finality and certainty, that he won't go back, although the day of the canoe trip to the Falls he did half-bake a scheme to trip through an extreme river or two.

As for myself, I would have to rate the odds as low. There are simply too many places left to fish. I was deeply affected by a brief conversation with Charles Gaines, author and angler. "Where on the globe," I asked him, "haven't you fished?"

"I've heard there's good fishing in Nepal," he replied, "and there are some rivers in Russia I must get to."

That is the sort of answer I would like to give, although I doubt that I'll even make all the continents.

But something within me is drawn back to the extreme, like Gordon, even though its beauty is so austere that many would fail to recognize it as beauty at all. It is unvaried and seemingly endless. It can be brutal. But it is a place where you can see the hand of God, even if He has only torn out a blank page from His notebook and let it flutter to land on top of the world. It is a place where a little man can leave a big mark.

But my conversation with Rick Matusiak reminded me of something, and I took my place again beside Gordon.

"I checked the IGFA record book," I said.

"Hm-mmm?"

"That fish you took thirty years ago, when you went in with your buddy and Maxim Moisim, the eleven-pounder?"

"Yes?"

"That's the largest speckled trout ever taken on a fly. The one the IGFA has listed is ten pounds, seven ounces. You have the world record."

Gordon smiled slightly, and shrugged.

Sheldon Oberman

Sheldon Oberman is a Winnipeg writer, playwright, film-maker, and storyteller. His songs have been recorded by various singers. His children's books include *The Lion in the Lake* and *The Always Prayer Shawl*. He is the editor of *The Mirror of a People*, an anthology of Jewish-Canadian writing. His story-cycle, *This Business with Elijah*, was nominated for The Journey Prize.

Garage Sales Sailing

My partner calls herself a garage sale widow. Sometimes I think I hear the Saturday paper hit the porch and I'm already guessing how many sales are listed under 505-507 in the classifieds. I cajole my son out of bed one more time, (as I've done since he was three months old.) I do my paper-work (red ink for 9 A.M. sales, yellow highliner for 10 A.M.) Pack a snack and head off to pick up whoever is joining us this week (I have a guest list from May until October).

I used to get the same kick going fish but this haul is so much more amazing. For twenty bucks I fill my station wagon with stuff to replace the stuff I filled it with before. Then I'm quite stuffed, thank you very much. I have my consumer fix so I can scoff at flyers and malls and red tag days for a while longer.

Eventually, I join my neighbours (who bought their stuff retail) and we have a sale together, a potlatch to dump the excess of our material success, everything we craved and saved and shopped for. We make a few hundred dollars and all go out to buy some more.

Winnipeg may be the motherlode of that great ritual purging we call garage sales. We are true shoppers—dedicated but canny—a test market for the continent. If it sells in Winnipeg, it will sell anywhere. And garage sales sell. Winnipeggers seem to excel in turning their private reality into public retail. Everything's for sale and everyone becomes Nick Hill for a day.

In high seasons (late spring and early fall) you don't need to check the classified at all—you hardly need to read the signs. Just drive down any lane, look for a jam of cars and parents hurrying their children or loaded down with old track lighting, engraved beer mugs and the past five years of People magazine, a buck a dozen. It's a sale. And if it isn't, make an offer anyway.

A friend of mine was cleaning his garage when his neighbour for a prank put up a sale sign with his address. By the third carload of garage salers, my friend gave in and made $200 in three hours.

If you really want to learn about Winnipeg, take the Garage Sale Tour down our back alleys and into our yards, porches and basements. You'll see more than on any red double-decker tour bus.

I remember what I call the Angst Sale with most everything spray-painted black. It required major burrowing through boxes strewn about the gravelled yard. The sellers were too deeply in despair to do more than raise a palm for payment. "You want change, mister? Ha, don't we all!"

There was the Party Hearty Sale where good old boys were playing all the records before they could be sold. "I don't know the prices. Hey, Frank, do know the prices? Say, how about a beer?"

The Fisher Price Sale had twin sisters pumping me with Koolaid and their little brother howling when they tried to sell his teddy bear. There were Girl Sales of stemware, Avon cosmetics and macrame planters. There were Guy Sales with oily tools, old cameras, a couple rotweiler puppies in a cage. There were Righteous Sales in a church basement with the same battered pots and pans from year to year unto eternity, hovered over by a sweet teetering old woman blessing every purchase.

There was the Family in a Very Tense Estate Sale with kin conspiring in various rooms, teeth clenched in strange smiles. The uncle's death was not the shock, it was seeing how little he was really worth. They'd been eyeing his possessions for so many years and were horrified to see them fetching such small change.

I'll never forget the Grudge Sale. There weren't many items but one was a new exercise bike, without a klik on its odometer. The owner, quite a substantial woman, was working through a box of doughnuts on her front stairs. The price tag read, $10. I said, "seven". She said, "sold". As I paid, I asked why she took so little. She scowled at the bike and muttered, "It was a gift!".

It was the Student Sale where I learned my lesson. I had donated odds and ends to a young woman trying to raise tuition. When I stopped at her sale I bought a set of glasses. It was only afterwards that I realized they were the ones I'd given her. And I didn't even get that good a deal.

Every sale is a stage set for confessions, accusations, crises and resolutions. Every object has its story. Maybe some stories are better forgotten and that's one good secret reason for a sale. But, surely, not all. Being a writer, that's what draws me most, the stories, real or imagined that possess the things that we come to possess. I've picked up some terrific bargains and treasures, too, but my favourite is a battered model car, 1930's style, made of scrap wood and Meccano pieces with windows drawn in pencil. I imagine it was put together by some unemployed father during the Depression. To me it's the best toy that any kid could get.

CHAPTER EIGHT: SPEECHES AND ORAL PRESENTATIONS

For some people, the thought of standing in front of a crowd of more than three people and making a speech is comparable to strolling through a room of cobras and pit vipers. There is the fear of stuttering, the fear of saying something stupid, the fear of having your clothes fall off, the fear of having people laugh. In fact, sometimes, it is the very best writers who are the most fearful of public speaking. It is one thing to order your thoughts on paper and structure your argument to perfection, quite another to stand up and deliver it orally. Or is it?

This section is filled with some of the best speeches this country has ever heard, some of which I've had the honour of hearing firsthand. But this introduction is devoted to pragmatic tips on how to make an oral presentation without dying.

The most common error anyone who flounders when making a speech commits is to under-prepare. For some reason, there is a presumption that an oral presentation requires less work than a written presentation. This is simply untrue. Although there are differences in structure and each has its own separate strengths, speechmaking is just as labour-intensive as formal essay writing.

While there may come a time in your life when you will be called upon to make an impromptu speech, it is likely that you will be given some advance warning if you are being asked to accept the Governor General's Award or the Pulitzer Prize. Aside from that, a simple thank you will suffice. What we are going to consider here are prepared presentations.

One has to understand that there is a difference between the written and the spoken word. A reader has the luxury of rereading a passage that is perplexing. A listener doesn't share this. However, a listener has the extra perceptions that body language, vocal tone, and emphasis allow. These things have to be crafted into your talk, not left to chance. There is no need to have your body language inadvertently working against your presentation.

You've already heard the old saw of "tell them what you're going to tell them, tell them, and then tell them what you told them" as a means of structuring an essay. This is just as true, if not more so, in an oral presentation. Redundancy is never allowed, but sometimes repetition is all right. There has to be a rhythm within your diction when speaking in public more so than on the page (although on the page it is important too). Your listener requires a flow of information, but also requires even more in the way of guidance, given that they will be hearing the material only once.

It is an unfortunate thing to admit, but most people do not listen very well. That is why instructors write things on the board, why marriages break down, and why mothers turn blue in the face. You have to create a very explicit structure and use an inordinate amount of "signpost" language to carry your listener along with you in your presentation. This is not that difficult. The first thing is to organize your argument clearly; give an overview at the beginning that you come back to at the end of the presentation. Pause between the major points in your argument, to allow them to sink in. This device also helps to underline for your listener that what you have just stated is of major importance. Signpost language, such as: "the second crisis point," "the three things we must remember," "from this supposition we naturally move to," must be built into your talk. These work to give the listener explicit transitions from one point to the next.

The final thing to remember in terms of organization is to avoid long, complicated sentences. People don't hear semi-colons. Not only this, you might get tangled up in a run-on sentence. There is nothing worse than looking lost in your own material. Try to stick to concrete examples, even if your ideas are abstract. Analogies work very well in oral presentations, as a result.

When beginning to prepare your presentation there are several things to consider. How long a presentation will you be allowed? Will your material benefit from visual aids or handouts? Who will be your audience? Will they be as informed as yourself on the topic? Or will they be looking to you for background as well as a specific argument? What is the purpose of your presentation? Will you be leading a discussion? Presenting a proposal? Teaching a lesson? Giving a report? Engaging a group in an activity? These will all require slightly different structuring.

While all of your material is vital, work especially on your introduction and conclusion. Listeners hear beginnings and endings. Your introduction should give them an easy overview of the material, and the conclusion should bring back all the salient points you made during your talk.

Now we're going to get to the nuts and bolts of how to survive a speechmaking endeavour. You should give yourself every break possible, and prepare your text for ease of presentation. If you are using cue cards, organize them so that they each hold only one major point. Number them to keep them ordered, in case you drop them in a fit of nerves. If you are using a manuscript form of text, double or triple space it for ease of reading, and use a larger font if necessary. This should allow you to have eye contact with your audience without losing your place in your notes.

Mark the places where you intend to pause with (PAUSE) set into the body of your text. Underline words that should be <u>emphasized</u> when speaking the sentence.

Here, for instance, is a passage from Richard Gwyn's essay on Canadian citizenship:

> Northrop Frye once declared that 'identity is local; unity is national.' Indeed, 'local' now encompasses not just region but the post-modern identities of culture, ethnicity, race, gender. We belong, is the impression created by this dictum, to our own communities rather than to the national community, about which, by extension we care to know little about.
>
> But this impression of a withdrawal from Canadian-ness is largely illusory. In polls, as by Ekos Research, many more Canadians say they identify primarily with Canada than with their province or ethnic group. By far the commonest flag chosen to fly at summer cottages—a crucial political indicator this because the choice is almost always innocent of any political intent—is the Maple Leaf rather than of any provincial standard (expect, in Quebec, for the fleur-de-lis).

Here is that same information, and ostensibly the same presentation, transposed into an oral presentation, complete with speaker cheat-notes:

> The renowned Canadian critic Northrop Frye once said that '<u>identity</u> is local; <u>unity</u> is national'. (PAUSE) By this we have to assume that <u>local</u> now includes more than <u>region</u>. (PAUSE) It now also includes culture, ethnicity, race, and gender. According to Frye, we belong to our <u>own</u> communities rather than to the <u>national</u> community, and we don't care to know much about that national community. (PAUSE)

BUT this impression of a withdrawal from Canadian-ness is largely an illusion. In reality, as shown by various research polls, many more Canadians say they identify primarily with Canada than with their province or ethnic group. (PAUSE) And as a further proof, the commonest flag chosen to fly at summer cottages is the Maple Leaf—this more than anything is a crucial political indicator because the choice is made from pride rather than political in*tent*.

Notice how many complex sentences, which are lovely to read, have been brought down to easy-to-digest aural sound bites. You are leading the listener along with you, defining terms in easy-to-grasp phrases as you go, and pausing for effect. Punching an underlined word helps your listener to shape the sentence in his mind as you speak.

Beyond the research and organization of your presentation there are a couple of other variables to consider. One of these is whether or not you will benefit from visual aids. By this, I mean anything from flip charts to writing on the board. You might even want to bring in a demonstration model of something. I had one student bring in a series of dentures, as her presentation was to show how false teeth were made (this is taking the term "oral" in oral presentation to its limit, in my opinion). Visual aids may be a great boon to your talk, but my advice is to rehearse with them prior to your presentation. Know how the chart flips, make sure you have white board pens on hand, in case there are none in the room, get there early to do a test run on the overhead projector.

Handouts should only be used if necessary. Anything that keeps your listeners from concentrating on your words is to be avoided if at all possible. If you must, hand out notes, or a bibliography, or whatever, at the end of your talk.

The other incidental, which is going to sound rather shallow, but is one of the most important factors to a successful presentation, is your wardrobe. There is a running joke between a friend of mine and myself that whenever we are approached for a speaking engagement, our initial thought is, "What to wear, what to wear, what to wear?" This isn't completely facetious. If you know you are looking your best, that you are dressed in a manner that won't shock or hurt your chances of communicating with your audience, that you are dressed in an outfit which won't fall apart at the seams while you are standing there with nothing to hide behind but a thin podium, you've eliminated a whole passel of worries.

I have a dress. It's the most wonderful dress in the world. It's ten years old, but because it has a designer label, I have convinced myself it is a classic. I wear this dress when I need to feel armoured for any eventuality. When I wear this dress, I am confident that I look as good as I possibly can. As a result, I never have to worry about my appearance. I can concentrate on my presentation, which should be more than enough to worry about.

Now, I am not advocating you go out and buy a designer wardrobe (although, if he were to send me some clothes I would be sure to put "Ms. MacDonald's wardrobe courtesy of Simon Chang" at the bottom of every syllabus). What I am trying to emphasize is that you should pay attention to how you present yourself to your audience. An oral presentation is more than a verbal essay; it is a performance. Wear a tie, sport a blazer. Look professional. It's all part of the body language your listeners will perceive. You respect yourself, and your material; they will too.

Likewise, there are simple strategies for your physical presentation when giving a speech. Place your feet about a foot and a half apart, so that they are directly below your shoulders. Stand straight, and keep your shoulders back. This not only helps you to look more confident, it also helps your voice to project further. Empty your pockets of keys and change. If your hands have a habit of straying about the room as you speak, stick your hands in your pockets while you speak. Put a rubber band in your pocket to keep them happy. While it is occasionally nice to use a gesture for emphasis, it can detract to have your hands moving too much. If you don't normally talk with your hands in motion, to incorporate gestures is dangerous, as you tend to look like your Great-Aunt Jessie orating her party piece.

Try to establish eye contact with your audience as much as possible. If you find that intimidating, aim your eyes slightly over the heads of the middle of the crowd. This gives the appearance of connecting with someone, even though no one will be quite sure who. To keep yourself on track, place a finger along your speech when your eyes move upward, so that you know where to return to.

Before you begin, place all your notes on the podium in front of you, take a couple of deep breaths, and concentrate on the first two sentences of your presentation. Look up, smile, and begin. Don't be afraid to pause. You will likely be speaking much faster than you believe yourself to be going. Pace yourself far slower than you can possibly imagine. It will end up sounding almost to speed.

The most important ingredient of any successful presentation is

274 ⁜ *Chapter Eight: Speeches and Oral Presentations*

to know your material. Once you have mastered your topic, turn to the presentation itself. Practise your speech, in front of a mirror, in front of a roommate, in front of tethered animals. If you can, make an audio tape of yourself. This will help you see if there are sections you stumble over, or if there are gaps in your argument. It will also familiarize you with the rhythms and tempo of your talk. The more it sounds like a spontaneous thought process, the greater your listener's response.

You will likely be given a time frame for any oral presentation you may be asked to give. It is good policy to remain within this, or you will risk glassy-eyed stares from your audience. The general rule of thumb is that an $8\frac{1}{2} \times 11$ sheet of double-spaced manuscript will run about two and a half minutes orally. Time yourself in your rehearsals.

Be prepared, be passionate, and be presentable. Care about your material will be evidenced in your research and your rhetoric. Care about your audience will be reflected in the preparation you have gone through. And remember, there is no great shame in being nervous. Everyone is nervous. The only thing to do is not demonstrate your nervousness. And really, what is there to be nervous about? Although many great people in history have been killed as a result of making inflammatory speeches, no one in history has ever actually died FROM making a speech. To be on the safe side, however, never agree to talk on the 15th of March.

So, straighten your collar, and check your slip. Get your notes in order, and go up there and change the world. Someone's got to do it.

Tommy Douglas

Tommy Douglas is known by many as the little man with a big heart. Throughout his long political career, he built a reputation for a devastating wit and oratory, and universal respect for always standing by what he believed, no matter how unpopular.

Born on October 20, 1904, in Falkirk, Scotland, Douglas (who emigrated to Canada, with his family, at the age of 14) was a printer, and a Baptist minister before undertaking his political career, which would carry him to the premiership of Saskatchewan at the age of 39. As Premier of Saskatchewan, he presided over the birth of public hospitalization and Medicare. Through his five terms as Premier, and later as the leader of the Federal New Democratic Party, Douglas pioneered reforms which made both Saskatchewan and Canadian society both progressive and prosperous.

He was the father-in-law of actor Donald Sutherland and the grandfather of actor Kiefer Sutherland.

The following speech was made in the House of Commons during a debate on capital punishment.

Capital Punishment

There are times, Mr. Speaker, when the House of Commons rises to heights of grandeur and becomes deeply conscious of its great traditions. I think this debate has been one of those rare occasions. There has been a minimum of rancour and there has been no imputation of motives because I think that the abolitionists and retentionists alike have been sincerely searching their consciences to see if we can honestly resolve a moral problem. This problem is, how can we abolish a brutal punishment without endangering the safety of society?

I am in favour of the motion to abolish capital punishment and I am also supporting the amendment to put it on a five-year trial basis. I doubt that there is much new that can be said in this debate. The entire field has been well covered but I should like to put very briefly four reasons for my opposition to capital punishment. The first is that capital punishment is contrary to the highest concepts of the Judaic-Christian ethic. I do not propose to go into theological arguments, but both in this debate and in the discussions which have taken place outside the House many people have been quoting Scripture in support of retaining the death penalty.

It is always a dangerous practice to quote isolated passages of Scripture. The Bible has been quoted in times past to support slavery, child labour, polygamy, the burning of witches, and subservience to dictators. The Scriptures have to be viewed as a whole. The Bible is not one book; it is many books. It does not have a static concept. It represents man's emerging moral concepts as they have grown through the centuries.

It is true that the Mosaic law provided the death penalty for murder. It is equally true, if one looks particularly at the 20th chapter of the book of Leviticus, that the Mosaic law provided the death penalty for 33 crimes including such things as adultery, bestiality, homosexuality, witchcraft and sacrificing to other gods than Jehovah. It seems to me that those who want to pick out isolated texts from the Bible in support of retaining the death penalty for murder have to be equally consistent and ask that the death penalty be retained for all the other crimes listed in the Mosaic law.

Of course, those who take this position overlook several facts. They overlook, first of all, the fact that the Mosaic law was an advanced law for the primitive times in which it was formulated. It was later succeeded by the Hebrew prophets who introduced the idea of justice superseded by mercy, the possible redemption and reestablishment of the individual. They overlook the fact that if any nation in the world ought to feel itself bound by Mosaic law it should be the state of Israel. The state of Israel abolished the death penalty many years ago except for Nazi war criminals and for treason committed in times of war. The religious hierarchy of the state of Israel enthusiastically supported the Knesset in abolishing the death penalty in that country.

But for those of us who belong to the Christian religion it seems to me we have to remember also that the Christian religion went far beyond the Mosaic law. In the days of the founder of Christianity the Mosaic law still obtained. This law decreed that a woman taken in adultery could be stoned to death. We should remember the statement of Jesus of Nazareth when he came upon a group of people preparing to stone such a woman to death. He said, Let him who is without sin among you cast the first stone.

When the crowd has dwindled away so that only the woman was left he said to the woman, "Go and sin no more." It seems to me that this is the ultimate culmination of the Christian concept of the application of mercy and the possible redemption of the individual.

My second reason for opposing capital punishment is that I believe capital punishment brutalizes the society that uses it without providing any effective deterrent that cannot be provided equally well by life imprisonment. I believe that any society that practises capital punishment brutalizes itself. It has an effect upon that society and I do not believe that society can rid itself of murderers by itself becoming a murderer. Surely if brutality would deter the committing of a crime Great Britain should have been a place of law-abiding citizens because a little over 150 years ago there were over 200 crimes for which an individual could be put to death. Instead of making Britain a nation of law-abiders it was a country where crime abounded, where human sensibilities were dulled by the public execution of criminals. It is rather significant that in that day, as in this, it was often the juries who were more humane than the lawmakers. It was only because juries refused to convict, knowing the terrible punishment which would follow, that the lawmakers were forced 150 years ago to remove the death penalty from a great many of the crimes for which it had been prescribed.

All of the evidence which can be gathered seems to indicate that the death penalty is not a unique deterrent and that life imprisonment can be equally effective. ...

I readily agree, Mr. Speaker, that quoting endless statistics is not going to prove either the case for abolition or the case for retention, but there certainly seems to be no convincing volume of evidence which would satisfy any unbiased individual that abolishing the death penalty has resulted in an upsurge of homicide or that those states which have retained the death penalty are any freer of capital crimes than those which have not.

After all, Mr. Speaker, who is it that the death penalty deters? It has certainly not deterred the man who commits murder. Will it deter him in the future? Surely he can be deterred in the future by being incarcerated for the remainder of his life. Who is deterred if this man is hanged? Is he to be hanged as an example to the rest of the community? I can conceive of nothing more immoral than to break a man's neck as an example to other people, but if that is the argument then surely, as the Leader of the Opposition [Mr. Diefenbaker] said yesterday, we ought to have public executions.

The hon. member for Winnipeg South Centre [Mr. Churchill] said that the fear of death will deter men. The fear of death will deter normal men but when a man commits murder, is he normal? Can we understand the motivation that causes a man to take a human life? When a man commits homicide, does he sit down and assess whether he is committing it in a state that has capital punishment or in a state that has abolished capital punishment? I think not. In the main the man who commits homicide is the man who is mentally ill; the man who kills does not make the common, rational judgments that are made by the average individual.

An individual who has become so mentally sick that he will take another life or ravage a child is certainly not a mentally healthy or normal individual.

The third reason I am opposed to capital punishment, Mr. Speaker, is that I believe there are better ways to ensure the safety of society. I completely disagree with the hon. member for Winnipeg South Centre who argued that we must be concerned about the safety of the public. When he asks which is the more important, the life of an innocent person who may be killed or the life of a murderer, there is no doubt that the life of the innocent person is the more important. But is the fact that we break a man's neck any guarantee that innocent people will not be hurt?

We are not suggesting removing the penalty. We are saying that the penalty which ought to be retained is one that will do the two things which are important. First of all, it must be a penalty which will remove the convicted person from human society as long as that person is likely to be a menace to the safety and well-being of his fellow-men. Second, that person should be given an opportunity to receive whatever psychiatric treatment and rehabilitation is possible in the light of his own particular circumstances.

What we have to decide is what we are trying to do, Mr. Speaker. Are we thinking purely of punishing somebody because they have done wrong? Are we thinking purely in punitive terms? Are we thinking purely in terms of vengeance or retribution? Or are we thinking of the two things I have mentioned, first, the safety of society by incarcerating the convicted murderer for life and, second, the possible rehabilitation and redemption of that individual? There is additionally the third great advantage that if society has made a mistake it is possible to rectify the mistake because justice is a human institution and like all human institutions it is liable to error.

I maintain that society has no right to take from a man something which it cannot restore to him. If society makes a mistake and confines a man to prison, depriving him of his freedom, when that mistake is found out society can at least restore to him his freedom and provide him with some compensation for the years he has been incarcerated. But if we hang a man and then find that a mistake has been made there is nothing at all which can be done to make amends.

My quarrel with the death penalty is that it is purely a negative attempt to promote the safety of society. We need to adopt positive measures to promote the safety of society. For instance, we need better law enforcement. In both Canada and the United States every year a great many unsolved crimes are committed. One of the best deterrents is for the criminal to know that if he does commit a crime he will be found out, that he will be incarcerated and put in a place where he can no longer be a menace to the community. We need quicker crime detection methods. For some types of crimes, particularly for those involving psychotics, there ought to be indeterminate sentences.

We all recall a case a few years ago in which a man sexually assaulted a child. He was sentenced to five years in jail. To my mind this was ridiculous because it was based purely on the punitive concept and not out of regard for the safety of the community. It was assumed that at five years less one day, when he was in jail, he was a menace but at five years plus one day he was no longer a menace. Such an individual ought to be sentenced to be kept out of circulation until such time as a panel of judges, psychiatrists and social workers are as certain as a human person can be that the individual is no longer a menace to the safety of the community. I think that in many cases indeterminate sentences to keep out of circulation psychotics who are likely to commit crimes would be of great advantage. In the case I referred to the man got out of jail after five years. Within six months he had not only assaulted another child but had killed the child in the process. Had that individual been sentenced to an indeterminate sentence in the first instance he would not have committed this second heinous crime.

If we want genuine deterrents in this country we need a program of penal reform for the segregation of prisoners and for their rehabilitation so that young first offenders do not go to jail to take what is virtually a postgraduate course in crime.

Let us face the fact that when we talk about retaining capital punishment as a deterrent we are really trying to take the easy way out from solving our problems. In the long run society often gets the criminals it deserves.

Why do we have criminals? What is wrong with the society that produces criminals? Some years ago when I was attending Chicago University I remember that every newspaper in the United States had a heading, "Where Is Crawley?" Crawley was a young gunman who was being hunted across the United States for a series of murders.

A very great columnist in the United States wrote a column which he headed, "Why Is Crawley?" He said that the people of the United States, instead of asking "Where Is Crawley?", ought to take a little time out to ask "Why Is Crawley?" The columnist went over his history. He came from a broken home which the father had deserted and where the mother was out working all day. The boy lived on the streets. He was part of a gang of hoodlums. He was sent to a reformatory and then was back on the streets. He was without proper education and without any counseling. He was sent to jail and associated with hardened criminals. He came out of jail twice as tough as when he went in. By 19 he was a hardened criminal. By the time he was 21 he was a killer. He was finally shot down by the police who were trying to capture him.

I suppose one of the most lamentable murders in our time has been the killing of President John F. Kennedy. Yet, when one reads the story of the man who is believed to have been responsible for his death, we find that when Lee Oswald was a boy in school he was recommended to undergo psychiatric treatment because of the dangerous psychotic tendencies he then displayed. But there were not enough psychiatrists to look after all the children in that particular part of New York city and this boy was not treated. This boy grew up with his psychotic tendencies expanding, and he is believed to have been responsible for extinguishing one of the brightest lights of our generation.

If we really want to tackle the problem of eliminating crime, we must tackle the problem of the slums which breed crime and we must tackle the problem of the lack of psychiatric clinics to take care of psychotics and persons who may become criminally dangerous. We need the kind of penal reform that will make possible the rehabilitation of first offenders with proper probation and parole. We need to go to the roots of the cause of crime and to ask ourselves what it is that produces the murderer in society. ...

My final point is that I am opposed to capital punishment because I believe that the measure of a nation is the manner in which it treats its misfits and its offenders. Capital punishment has already been abolished in most of the advanced nations of the Western world. The abolition of capital punishment has come to be taken as the hallmark of a nation's conscience. I want to see Canada take this great forward step, and I want to make a special appeal to the members of the House to consider how important for Canada and for its future will be the vote we shall take tonight.

I should not want to be in the shoes of the Prime Minister and the members of his cabinet who have to face up to this very difficult problem. Nobody has been hanged in Canada since 1962. If the motion tonight is defeated the government is going to be in an awkward position. Either it will have to commute those sentenced to death to life imprisonment, knowing that the House of Commons has just rejected a motion suggesting the abolition of the death penalty, or it will have to take the defeat of the motion as an expression of opinion and allow the death sentences to be carried out.

I urge the members of the House to consider the predicament which faces the Prime Minister and the cabinet. I want to urge the House to give a five-year trial to the abolition of the death penalty. If the fears that have been expressed prove to be warranted, if there is an upsurge in the rate of homicide, if we are faced with an increase in crime rate, then in five years the members of the House of Commons who are here then can allow the death penalty to become effective again simply by taking no action. But I would urge that we give this a chance, that we step into line with the progressive countries of the world which have already abolished the death penalty.

What I plead for is that we pass this resolution tonight, with the amendment, which will declare in principle that the House is in favour of abolishing capital punishment and replacement with life imprisonment. If we do that then I believe the House of Commons will have won a great victory, not a victory that will be accompanied by the blaring of trumpets or the rolling of drums but a victory in that we will have taken a forward, moral step and left behind one of the last relics of barbarianism. We will be moving forward to a more humane approach in dealing with crime.

Robert Fulford

Robert Fulford is a Toronto author, journalist, broadcaster, and editor. He writes a weekly column for the *Globe and Mail* and is a frequent contributor to *Toronto Life, Canadian Art*, and CBC Radio and television. His books include *Best Seat in the House: Memoirs of a Lucky Man* (1988), *Accidental City: The Transformation of Toronto* (1995), and *Toronto Discovered* (1998).

The following lecture was given at The Hebrew University in Jerusalem on June 5, 1997.

Mary Pickford, Glenn Gould, Anne of Green Gables, and Captain Kirk: Canadians in the World's Imagination

I'm delighted to be here and deeply grateful to the Halbert Centre for Canadian Studies, which invited me to Jerusalem. In Toronto in the 1980s I served on a committee choosing scholars to come to Jerusalem as Halbert Fellows, and at that time the program existed in my mind principally as a fascinating rumour. Now I've had a chance to experience the reality, and learn with pleasure how extensive and valuable it is.

My hope today is to outline certain aspects of Canadian culture and suggest how they fit into, or occasionally impress themselves upon, the culture of the world beyond Canada's borders. My story concerns a diverse people, mainly defined by geography and politics, trying to discover who they are as individuals and as communities within the almost unthinkably large and rich territory they have inherited or embraced. I want to visit several of these issues and also describe certain specific artists and how they have dealt with the opportunities of Canada as well as its limitations.

Canadian artists tend to be easily absorbed into the stream of international culture, so that their national origin quickly becomes obscured or forgotten. Recently an English magazine described Rohinton Mistry as an Indian novelist and an American journal called Michael Ondaatje, the celebrated author of *The English Patient*, a Sri Lankan novelist. In fact Mistry does come from Bombay, but he's been a Canadian and a resident of Ontario for many years. Ondaatje has been eminent in Canadian literary culture since the 1960s, and he's never lived in a country called Sri Lanka; when he spent his boyhood there it was still Ceylon.

In Canada, Mistry and Ondaatje and many like them are enthusiastically claimed as Canadians, and their work as part of Canadian culture. We say this with confidence even though we find it hard to state precisely what makes a work of art Canadian. In English Canada particularly, we have defined ourselves mainly in relation to others. For generations it was Britain that provided the reference point, but since the 1950s Canadians have shaped their vision of themselves by reference to the Americans. To outsiders, we may appear to be near-Americans, or a modified version of Americans, or perhaps a marginalized form of Americans; but we see the distinction more clearly. We may resemble the Americans, we may share a great deal with them, but we are different.

We believe, with only a little evidence to support it, that we are more open and more international in our ideas and connections. After all, most of us exist imaginatively in at least two countries, Canada and the United States, absorbing the culture, politics, and social issues of both. To be a Canadian is to live a two-tiered life. At the same time we are more conservative than the Americans in our hopes, more conscious of our limited powers. Canadians often point out that while the American constitution promises "Life, liberty, and the pursuit of happiness," the constitution of Canada—written in the 1860s in England—sets a more modest goal: "Peace, order, and good government." This difference reaches into every corner of the two nations.

My favourite example is a book of medical advice. It was written by a Canadian, Judylaine Fine, and published in Toronto under an extremely modest title, *Your Guide to Coping with Back Pain*. Later, American rights were acquired by New York publishers; they brought out precisely the same book under a new title, *Conquering Back Pain*.

And there, in a grain of sand, to borrow from William Blake, we can see a world of differing attitudes. Our language reveals how we think, and what we are capable of thinking. Canadians cope. Americans conquer. Canadian readers of that book will assume that back pain will always be with them. Americans will assume that it can be destroyed, annihilated, abolished, conquered. Americans expect life, liberty, happiness, and total freedom from back pain. Canadians can only imagine peace, order, good government, and moderate back pain.

To understand where this attitude is born, imagine Canada, first of all, as in itself an art object, an abstraction—a piece of fiction, perhaps. As a nation Canada was not inevitable. In the Renaissance, at the moment when Europe began to understand the existence of an unknown continent within sailing distance to the West, there was no logical reason to imagine that the northern reaches of it would be one country. Had certain historic events occurred differently, Canada could be three or four or five countries today, each of them probably more populous than many current members of the United Nations. An island republic, Newfoundland, might well exist as its own state off the Atlantic coast, as some Newfoundlanders still believe it should. If we brush away two hundred years of history, the province of British Columbia, between the Pacific ocean and the Rocky mountains, appears perfectly designed for a separate national existence. The results of the 1993 and 1997 federal elections illustrate the persistence of regionalism in Canada. If there *is* a national vision in Canada, it is increasingly obscured by the forces of decentralization and fragmentation.

The greatest of these, of course, is Quebec separatism, which has been advocating a separate state for many years and in the process has traumatized Canadian politics and called into question the very existence of this historical artefact, "Canada." Separatism is an attempt to re-think and re-write the work of imagination by which Canada was created. In the 19th century, when politicians and surveyors imposed a grid of European rationalism on our wilderness, they were sketching the outlines of a narrative of aspiration that was summed up by a historian of this century, Arthur Lower, in the title of his best-known book, *Colony to Nation*. Today many Quebeckers want to tear up that narrative and write their own—a vibrant and heroic story, as they see it, of a French-speaking people who survived both the military defeat of France in the New World and the imposition of British and then Canadian imperialism, eventually emerging triumphant as owners of their own state and their own destiny in the 21st century. I am among those who hope this will not come to pass; I believe that speakers of French, speakers of English, natives, and the many people who have come to Canada from elsewhere can all live freely together within the capacious civilization outlined by Confederation. For generations our academics and occasionally our politicians liked to say that Canadians had learned the arts of compromise and could serve as an example to a fractious world. Perhaps we can reach that happy condition again, but in the meantime the creation of a new state within Canada remains a lively possibility.

This fact demonstrates something essential about Canada, something that those born there and those who immigrate find equally hard to understand and deal with. Canada remains a place without final definition, a place whose inhabitants have not all made a total commitment to its existence, a country that is forever reshaping itself. Even the most passionate beliefs of its citizens change with the generations. When I grew up in Toronto, half a century ago, it was common to say, "This is a *British* country." People said it with confidence, pride, even sometimes anger. Today we remain a part of the British Commonwealth, and of course the Queen of England is also our queen, but I can't imagine anyone calling us a "British country" now. For the most part, British symbols as well as British power have disappeared, and the way we think about Canada has changed fundamentally. Today we speak not of overseas ties to Britain and of a culture dominated by Europe but of discovering, asserting, celebrating, and reconciling the many cultural forces existing among us. But there is no obvious way to organize our society so that every group can feel at home. This means that devising imaginative ways that we can live together, through our constitution or otherwise, is the abiding preoccupation of Canadians involved in public policy.

The feeling of being always on unsound political and constitutional foundations is the direct result of our beginnings. We have no "foundation myth," as the anthropologists say. Canadians did not emerge slowly from the mists of time, far back in unwritten history; nor did we, like the Americans, found our state on Enlightenment principles inscribed in a sacred constitution; nor can we, like the Israelis, look for national legitimation through either ethnic history or a covenant with God. We lack ethnic, religious, and ideological identity. We came slowly together, gathering in sparse settlements on the Atlantic coast and later the Pacific coast, and along the way slowly filling the arable land between. Even today, when Canada is one of the oldest nation-states on earth, it is not "settled" in the way many countries are. A geographer has called western Canada a kind of archipelago of settlements, little islands of people scattered across vast open spaces. You can see this as you fly across the West at night—the towns and cities are bright little dots, isolated in the blackness. Experiencing that, even from far in the air, you can imagine why Canadian literature, more than most, is preoccupied with loneliness.

Geography has always been the central fact of Canadian culture as it is the central fact of Canadian politics. For most of the artists of Canada, geography is inescapable. The pianist Glenn Gould, for instance, begins his musical life as a student of the German musical tradition, absorbs it brilliantly, and becomes a leading artist of his time, within European musical thinking; and yet at the same time, though he lives most of his life in Toronto, he finds himself constantly preoccupied by the Canadian North. He studies the North, writes about it, makes radio documentaries about it.

His involvement with it was beautifully depicted in the biographical film, *32 Short Films About Glenn Gould*, which began with a long shot of Colm Feore, as Gould, walking across a vast lake of snow toward the camera. In his notes to a 1967 radio program, *The Idea of North*, Gould wrote: "Something really does happen to most people who go into the north—they become at least *aware* of the creative opportunity which the physical fact of the country represents and—quite often, I think—come to measure their own work and life against that rather staggering creative possibility: they become, in effect, philosophers." Gould says that despite himself he was affected by the North, even in his thinking about music. He says, "I found myself writing musical critiques ...in which the north—the idea of the north—began to serve as a foil for other ideas and values that seemed to me depressingly urban oriented and spiritually limited. ..." For him, the North became a point of reference and remembrance, a kind of alternate truth to which his life as a Canadian gave him access.

A fundamentally different artist of the same generation, Mordecai Richler, has had a similar experience, equally surprising to him. Richler begins his life in the Montreal Jewish ghetto, and he identifies with urban literary culture, the culture of New York and London as well as Montreal. He seems to be, in his early works, an entirely urban man. And yet at some point Richler finds himself going to the North, first as a journalist, then as an avid student. In the 1970s he begins a book about the North that takes him at least a decade to write. This novel, *Solomon Gursky Was Here*, places the Jews in the North; that is, it imaginatively moves the Jewish people toward the frontier of Canada. Richler rewrites the chronicles of the North, including the story of the tragic Franklin expedition to the Arctic, in terms that connect it to Jewish history. In this gigantic and ambitious book we can see Richler uniting two major strains of his own history and Canada's, the urban life most Canadians live and the power of geography. Gould and Richler are two entirely different Canadian artists whose work—despite their own early intentions—has gone out to the world bearing the marks of its specifically Canadian origin.

Both Gould and Richler exhibit what one Canadian literary critic, John Moss, calls "the geophysical imagination." Both of them attach their work to a myth of distance and purity that has been growing ever since the earliest explorers of Canada.

It was Marshall McLuhan who said that in this era, increasingly, humans live mythically. McLuhan, whose thinking influenced his fellow Torontonian Gould, and vice versa, said the speed of information dissemination "makes inevitable the handling of vast quantities of information in a highly structured and, indeed, 'mythic' way. Under electronic technology today man lives mythically. ..."

McLuhan predicted that in the media age the world would become more tribal and regional rather than less, a prediction certainly confirmed by the history of Canada (as well as the history of many other places) since his death in 1980. His term "global village" has become part of global language, but he did not mean by it that everyone in this global village would necessarily think alike, or live by the same myths. In his view, each region, each tribe, would continue to carve out its own mythology while eavesdropping on (and sometimes borrowing) the mythology of others.

Within Canada it is the landscape to which the myth-seeking artist eternally returns. In each generation Canadian painting goes back obsessively to the wilderness. The Group of Seven, who flourished from around 1915 to 1940, were self-proclaimed nationalist landscape artists, their stated mission being to convey an understanding of the northern wilderness to the Canadian people. In their time they were the only artists of any kind who reached beyond the usual limitations of art audiences and caught the imagination of the Canadian public as a whole. Each generation of Canadian painters since then has consciously set out to reject them, to reject the landscape as well, and to devote itself to the more sophisticated and more urban concerns of international art. Yet each generation has returned not only to the landscape but often to the Group of Seven itself as a subject.

Canada's destiny in this sense is inescapable: geography is our real teacher, the one to which we listen with the greatest care, the force that sets the tone of our lives.

Inside the unconscious of even the most citified Canadian sits the vast and almost unimaginable empire that we govern. Its presence colours all that we do and feel. In 1946 the English novelist and painter Wyndham Lewis wrote, "Canada will always be so infinitely bigger physically than the small nation that lives in it ... that this monstrous, empty habitat must continue to dominate the nation psychologically, and so culturally."

Half of what Lewis calls a monstrous, empty habitat is empty in part because it is rock, the Precambrian Shield, either bare rock or rock that has acquired a thin covering of soil since the last Ice Age scraped it clean seven or eight thousand years ago. This rock and its outcroppings are the major subject of Group of Seven paintings. This is what the explorer Jacques Cartier saw when he came up the St. Lawrence River from the Atlantic in the 16th century—grey towering bluffs of rock. He called it "the land God gave to Cain," and he did not imagine for a moment that anyone would be happy living there. Barbara Moon, in her book *The Canadian Shield*, said this about Canadians and our relationship with all that rock: "Canadians are a shield race ... they live with this permanent reminder of elemental process. They live with bedrock and bush and a million hidden lakes always at their backs. They live with a greedy secret of riches. They live with a vast waste space. They live with terrifying Boreal, god of the cold void." Or, as Margaret Atwood put it:

> "When we face south, as we often do, our conscious mind may be directed down there, towards crowds, bright lights, some Hollywood version of fame and fortune, but the north is at the back of our minds, always. There's something, not someone, looking over our shoulders; there's a chill at the nape of the neck ... The north focuses our anxieties ... Always, in retrospect, the journey north has the quality of dream."

So, understandably, a large part of our culture—literary, visual, musical—deals with the slow, fearful recognition that this piece of real estate is far larger than we can begin to encompass imaginatively, much less subdue physically.

In culture as in economics, the United States remains the most potent external influence. The Americans have created a mass culture so powerful that it envelops not only much of Canada but much of the world; and no matter how much resistance it encounters, this gigantic cultural engine shows no sign of slowing down. In English-speaking Canada, we watch American TV and movies and read American magazines, far more than we attend to equivalent Canadian work.

Given this fact, Canadian artists have developed over the years two quite different strategies.

One is to be willingly absorbed by the Americans, move toward the centre of that culture, and take part in it, perhaps rising to its heights. The other is to create centres or clusters of talent and production within Canada and try to appeal first to fellow Canadians with distinctive forms of expression, *then* perhaps move out to the larger world. In general, French Canada has succeeded much better than English Canada at the creation of its own cultural centre, Montreal: beneath the sheltering umbrella of the French language, it has been able to make its own radio, television, popular songs, magazines, and, during the last thirty years or so, movies. U.S. culture plays a large part within Quebec, but beside it there exists a vibrant Quebec culture.

In English-speaking Canada for a long time, most of our artists took it for granted they would be absorbed somehow into America—if they were lucky. And the U.S. has indeed found places, sometimes places of prominence, for Canadian artists. What's interesting is the role the Americans have assigned to immigrants from the north, in particular the actors. First, the actors are instantly transformed into Americans. Because they speak English with generic North American accents, they are almost never regarded as foreigners. If anyone remarks on their place of birth it is considered a barely relevant biographical detail, even if they received all their training in Canada and spent their first thirty years there. The British actor Michael Caine, no matter how long he works in Hollywood films, will always be marked by his accent as an Englishman. But Michael J. Fox of Vancouver was regarded as an American actor ten minutes after he got off the plane in Los Angeles.

Canada has also produced a generation, or a generation and a half, of comedians who have flourished within the United States—Dan Ackroyd, Martin Short, the late John Candy, Eugene Levy, Mike Myers. They grew up immersed in American culture yet separate from it, uncommitted to it, and they turned this personal history to good effect by making American culture itself, and in particular television, the main subject of their comedy. In an odd way, their talent is deceptive, perhaps even marginally subversive: they are outsiders who satirize America from the inside, while cleverly disguised as Americans.

This easy acceptance of Canadians in the U.S. is not hard to understand. What is more surprising is the particular role Canadian actors play.

Before describing that role, I want to go back to the Group of Seven and its most articulate member, Lawren Harris, whose stylized and eloquent paintings of the Canadian Rockies are among the great achievements of his generation. In 1928, Harris published in a McGill University magazine some thoughts about the North that probably sounded to many of his readers like wishful thinking. They may seem that way even now. This is what he said:

"We [Canadians] live on the fringe of the great North ... its spiritual flow, its clarity, its replenishing power passes through us to the teeming people south of us. It may be that the very glory of our life is in giving expression to this that comes to us *pure* in ideas, thoughts, characters and attitude ... Indeed the continuous movement of Canadians to the States—teachers, doctors, nurses, writers and the like—may ... be one means of the infiltration of a certain clarity and unpretentious devotion, certain intangible elements in the ...Canadian character ... born of the spirit of the North ..."

Lawren Harris, like Glenn Gould, was in love with the idea of the North, and those remarks may sound like a lover's delirious ambitions for his beloved. But the Americans who run mass culture have actually played out Harris's fantasy of Northern purity—in fact, American silent movies were beginning to follow Harris's script even before he wrote it. American producers have again and again chosen Canadian stars who project a certain purity, sometimes a degree of innocence and occasionally even nobility. Americans tend to make their Canadian-born stars into super-Americans, improved versions of the real thing. Consider D.W. Griffith, the film director from Kentucky, who did as much as any other human being to create the mass imagination of our century. He grew up dreaming Old South dreams about the purity and innocence of young womanhood. Those dreams, through Griffith or his imitators, ended up influencing the 20th century's ideas about women; certainly they affected everyone on the planet who entered a movie theatre. To embody those fantasies Griffith chose a young woman from Toronto named Gladys Smith, who under the name Mary Pickford became known as "America's Sweetheart" and established herself as the first movie star of the world. This Canadian woman fleshed out a cherished American dream.

Her national origin would have been only a footnote if Mary Pickford had not been followed by so many other fresh-faced, open, innocent-looking Canadians, all impersonating Americans: Deanna Durbin and Glenn Ford in one generation, William Shatner as Captain Kirk on the starship *Enterprise* in another, then the singer Anne Murray and later the comic actor Michael J. Fox. Perhaps the case of Raymond Massey is most instructive, because he embodied for his time not *an* American but *the* American, Abraham Lincoln.

Massey was born to a famous Canadian industrial family and was the brother of a future governor general of Canada. In the 1930s he played the main role in Robert Sherwood's play, *Abe Lincoln in Illinois*—first in New York, then on a trans-continental tour, and then in the Hollywood film—in which, as someone wrote, he "took the face off the penny and put it into the hearts of millions of Americans."

He was almost perfect for the part, and was brought still closer to perfection with the help of the most popular of American artists, Norman Rockwell. Before the play opened, the producers commissioned Rockwell to make a drawing combining elements from photographs of Lincoln and Massey. Massey then used the drawing as the basis of his make-up: hollowed-out cheeks, built-up nose. Soon Massey and Lincoln were interchangeable.

Aside from his weathered, craggy, Precambrian looks, Massey had a gravity of manner that had been created in Edwardian Methodist Toronto, honed at Upper Canada College and Oxford, and refined in the London theatre. He spoke a precise stage English that the frontiersman Lincoln might have had trouble understanding, much less speaking. His mid-Atlantic Canadian English style was perfect, not for impersonating Lincoln but for establishing the *persona* of Lincoln, solemn and straightforward. Massey spoke as Lincoln *should* have spoken. He was more Lincolnesque than Lincoln.

Toward the end of his career, Raymond Massey played a wise old physician in a TV series, *Dr. Kildare*. About the time that program ended, another series, *Bonanza*, was starting, a western that in the mid-1960s became by far the most popular drama in America. The star of *Bonanza*, Lorne Greene, was another easily absorbed Canadian and another super-American. His stolid honesty and fatherly wisdom dominated the Ponderosa ranch, where the stories were set. Greene's movement across two cultures illustrated the difference between the two. In the Second World War he had been the announcer behind National Film Board propaganda documentaries, in effect the official voice of the government speaking to the people. The patrician manner he developed in that role apparently made him an ideal father figure in America.

These Canadians, while they helped define American mythology, were also swallowed up by it—and when their images re-appeared in Canada they were part of the American mass culture that has swept over the country for most of this century. There has always been a degree of resistance to this tidal wave, sometimes modest, sometimes

292 ■ *Chapter Eight: Speeches and Oral Presentations*

impressive. The late 1960s created in English-speaking Canada a highly organized and self-conscious form of cultural nationalism— book publishing subsidized by government, broadcasting controlled by government in the hope of maintaining Canadian culture, movies subsidized by government. Much of this activity has been reduced as a result of budget reductions in recent years, but the arts in Canada are still subsidized by governments.

The purpose of these policies is to provide the people of Canada with a cultural choice, to make available cultural expression created in our country and reflecting our reality. We remain heavily Americanized, but we insist on providing space in which Canadian culture can flourish as well.

Canadians have been a fortunate people in most ways, but we have often thought ourselves culturally short-changed by history. We've looked with envy at traditional cultures elsewhere, cultures whose sense of identity stretches back for centuries or millennia. We have been internationalists, ready to appreciate American movies, English plays, French painting, German music. But this has often been a one-way internationalism—everything coming in, little going out. The most important change for Canadian artists in the present generation is that internationalism has become a two-way street. Writers such as Ondaatje and Atwood are translated into a dozen or more languages; Robert LePage's Quebec City theatre company has proven itself one of the greatest in the world; Le Cirque du Soleil of Montreal has shown that it's possible to re-invent an ancient art form, the circus, and show it around the world to appreciative audiences. And a few of our filmmakers, notably David Cronenberg, have demonstrated that they can make movies as repulsive as those produced in Hollywood.

These issues are part of everyday discourse in Canada; I myself have been writing about them since 1955. In this context, when I consider how Canadian artists reach out to world culture, I think about two quite dissimilar artists. Both have affected me personally—one as a close friend, and one as a writer I've read over and over. The first is Glenn Gould, the second L.M. Montgomery.

One day in my class at an elementary school in Toronto, fifty-six years ago, the little boy in front of me turned around and told me his name, Glenn Gould. We discovered we were about to become neighbours: my family had just rented the house next door to the Goulds. Soon I learned that Glenn was an exceptional nine-year-old, a pianist of prodigious abilities.

From the beginning no one in Toronto doubted Glenn's genius. Right up to the conductor of the symphony, musical Toronto swiftly understood the size of the talent that had arrived in their midst.

By the time Glenn and I entered high school, we were occasionally arguing, in a friendly way, about music. I liked listening to him play (I still do), but by 14 or so I was a jazz fan—and he was not. To Glenn, jazz was a minor and transitory offshoot of the romantic movement. If he listened to the works of people I regarded as geniuses, such as Duke Ellington, he did so only out of tolerance. We were heading toward radically different views of music—and of culture in general. I was beginning to understand music as an almost physical form of expression, charged with sexuality. Here I think I caught an early glimpse of the form his genius was to take. In Glenn's mind, music was refined, bodiless, separated from the physical world. He seemed to resent the necessity, in music, of fingers and wood and mouths and catgut, the physical limitations placed on an ethereal art. His decision to stop playing concerts and give all his time to records sprang from this view. He knew there were always imperfections in a public appearance, whereas recordings could be edited to eliminate them. More important, recordings circumvented the charisma of personality. Glenn hated the idea of showy, old-fashioned concert-hall stardom, which only got in the way of the music.

His great project was to re-invent musical performance for the electronic age. In his view this approach, though modern, would pay the ultimate tribute to the great composers of history by delivering a clarified, nearly perfect account of their intentions. In doing this he became, as a French critic put it, "the theoretician of a purified humanity."

Glenn once wrote: "The purpose of art is ... the gradual life-long construction of a state of wonder and serenity. ..." The serenity part sounds impossible to me. I can just barely imagine existing in such a state. I've never managed it, and I believe Glenn never did either. But my sense of wonder remains exuberantly healthy, having been nourished by proximity to this amazing figure. Before I was old enough to vote, I had already observed the making of a great artist, who eventually became known through his recordings in every corner of the world. Those recordings, incidentally, gave him a posthumous victory over everyone who said that deserting the concert hall would destroy his career. In fact, his reputation today is larger than it was in 1982 when he died of a stroke, because he put all his energy into recordings rather than spending it on public performances.

The spring after Glenn and I met as little boys, the spring of 1942, L. M. Montgomery died, sixty-seven years old, in a house at the other end of Toronto. I don't believe we heard about this event at the time. Maud Montgomery was no celebrity, then or earlier in her life, and—as I've learned since—the articles about her death were respectful but restrained. Glenn and I knew about *Anne of Green Gables*, however. It would have been hard to find an English-speaking Canadian child who had not heard of Anne Shirley—and already, the book was beginning its long and apparently endless multilingual journey around the world. Anne was a presence in my house before I could read, since I had two older sisters; and I later read her story myself. As a young adult, I imagined retrospectively that the book was slight and sentimental, like many of the books of childhood. I was wrong. When I read it to the first of my children, I discovered there was far more to it than my faulty memory had told me. Since then I have read it to three more children; I can't imagine getting sick of it.

Anne Shirley, unlike any other character made in Canada, is larger than her author, larger than the book she was born in, larger than her time and place. Long ago, Anne rose from the printed page and changed from literary character into phenomenon, joining that exclusive circle of imagined people whose lives become lodged in common memory. Like Lewis Carroll's Alice and Stevenson's Dr. Jekyll, she's known even to people who haven't read the books about her. She keeps coming back, decade after decade, in movies, TV shows, and a long-running musical that has been performed everywhere from Atlantic Canada to Tokyo.

The original book marvellously evokes Prince Edward Island at the start of the 20th century. It establishes this tiniest of the provinces as an intimate Canadian version of Eden, the reverse image of the North—reassuring where the North is threatening, comfortably predictable where the North is unknowable and vast. But there are many idyllic, pre-industrial settings to be found in books, yet few characters like Anne. Clearly, she has something special. She's innocent, but the bookstores are full of innocent, plucky heroines. The tourists who visit Maud Montgomery's home in Prince Edward Island every year, many of them coming from Japan for that purpose, are celebrating something more than an innocent girl in a bucolic setting.

The reason is L.M. Montgomery's treatment of the human imagination, her main subject. Everyone has an imagination, and everyone is encouraged to deny it—or at least fence it in. The world teaches us early that our imaginations are dangerous or frivolous. The world tells us to stop dreaming and be serious. That's the advice Marilla Cuthbert gives Anne, and the advice Anne adamantly rejects.

Dropped into the Cuthbert household by accident, deposited in a narrow, provincial environment, she becomes in her way a revolutionary force. She speaks for the power of dreams. The Cuthberts, who have been boring themselves to death for years, are converted. So are Anne's schoolmates. She offers this tiny world the gift of her imagination, and courageously insists on its value. Her victory retains its freshness after 90 years because it's a victory for everyone who ever dreamed of a large, grander life. This is a book about the saving power of the imagination, and in particular the literary imagination. Anne's unique ability to invest her surroundings with world-shaking, heaven-storming possibilities—this is what gives her story the power of enduring myth. That's also what makes her such a peculiarly Canadian heroine—like the best Canadian artists, she turns an unpromising landscape into a proper home for the imagination.

In Canada, national culture is not taken for granted. Constantly it is examined and analysed by academics, journalists, and government bureaucrats. It was once a matter of almost marginal concern, but in recent times has become the focus for our very idea of nationhood. Like Canadian culture itself, Canadian nationhood remains elusive and shaky. Gould and Montgomery, two artists who were worlds apart in outlook and aspiration, nevertheless both demonstrated a central fact about Canadian culture—that it succeeds and flourishes, at home or abroad, only as it reflects the struggle to come to terms with Canada itself.

Mel Hurtig

Mel Hurtig was born and raised in Edmonton. In 1956 he opened a small bookstore which grew into one of the largest retail book operations in Canada. Hurtig sold the bookstores in 1972 to concentrate on publishing. Hurtig Publishers produced many titles which have won numerous awards and prizes including the Governor General's Award.

In 1980 Hurtig launched the largest and most ambitious project in the history of Canadian publishing, *The Canadian Encyclopedia*, which was published in 1985, with a new and substantially expanded edition in 1988.

Over the past twenty-five years Mel Hurtig has spoken all across Canada about economic, social, political, and cultural matters. A founding member of the Committee for an Independent Canada and the Council of Canadians, Mel Hurtig has been particularly dedicated to preserving Canadian sovereignty against the perceived threat of continentalism. In 1992 Mel Hurtig was elected leader of the National Party of Canada and led it in the 1993 federal election. He was invested with the Order of Canada in 1980.

A Dream of Canada

In the preface to *The Betrayal of Canada,* I wrote:

> The work and the dreams of generations of Canadians are being destroyed. The tragedy of Canada is that this is happening after we have done so very well. Compared with all other nations, we were probably the most fortunate people on earth. Our real standard of living, combined with the quality of life we have had, was unequalled. Our great potential for the future was the envy of the world.

Canada was transformed by the Second World War. We entered the war in 1939 having barely emerged from the Great Depression, badly battered and weakened, lacking confidence as a nation. During the war our transformation to one of the world's leading industrialized powers was truly remarkable. The nation became a beehive of activity while Canadian men and women here and overseas helped defeat the brutal Nazis and the Japanese and helped defend freedom and justice for the good of all mankind.

Almost overnight the depression in Canada was gone; suddenly there were jobs everywhere. With industrialization came new innovation, exciting new products, new lifestyles, and a much higher overall standard of living. From the grinding poverty, bitter frustration and painful agony of the long depression, within a few years

Canadians had, on average, the second highest standard of living in the world. A vital new spirit and a confident new culture reflected our new affluence and a new pride of accomplishment, determination and optimism was found across the country. How well we had done! And the future surely could only be better.

Even though American films, magazines, books and broadcasts largely ignored the fact that once again the U.S. had entered a World War years late, and even though the U.S. media portrayed the Second World War as essentially another glorious battle fought for and won by Americans, we Canadians knew better. We knew about Dieppe and we knew about Dunkirk, just as we had known about Vimy Ridge and Passchendaele. What brave heroes we produced. What terrible tragic losses we suffered. What glory we earned and what grief we endured.

And, how proud we were that we Canadians had asserted our presence in the defence of liberty as a strong, sovereign nation, now firmly in control of our own future. Half way through the century we began to think that Wilfrid Laurier had been right all along; the twentieth century would indeed belong to Canada. After all, look at just how much we had accomplished in such a very short time! And look at all the enormous space and bountiful resources we had to work with, our abundant fresh water, our immense forests, our mines and minerals. And then, in 1947 came Leduc Number One—oil and natural gas in amazing quantities, well beyond our wildest dreams.

Not only had we emerged from the Second World War as an economic powerhouse, but we also had become a truly independent nation, beholden to no one, controlled by no other country, in charge of our own future and a widely respected presence in the world community of nations. From colony to nation, from political and economic dependence, a proud, affluent young giant had emerged.

The tragedy of Canada is that we managed to squander away so much, so quickly. In the face of spectacular opportunity we created truly miserable circumstances for millions of our fellow citizens and dismal prospects for the very existence of our country. With a vital, well educated population and envied resources we allowed inept politicians and greedy businessmen to create a subservient, drastically weakened economic colony.

Only four years after our exuberant centennial celebrations, *The Manchester Guardian* concluded an article entitled *Canada—economic colony*, this way:

Some will recall that in George Orwell's novel "Nineteen Eighty-Four" the hero, Winston Smith, strives hard to maintain his identity and nothing in the novel comes equal to matching this need. But he is already doomed by the actions of past generations in creating the sort of society into which he is born. After a long period of brainwashing he makes the final submission of his own accord. One begins to wonder if Canada is a nation of Winston Smiths.

In the same year, the University of Toronto's great critic, Northrop Frye, wrote in his preface to *The Bush Garden*:

Our country has shown a lack of will to resist its own disintegration ... Canada is practically the only country left in the world which is a pure colony, colonial in psychology as well as in mercantile economics.

Twenty-five years ago, I read these comments with increasing anger, not at the authors, but at the politicians and business elite who had sold our country out and brought us to our knees. It wasn't long before I began to believe that perhaps after all, George Grant, Donald Creighton, and Walter Gordon were right in their pessimistic appraisals of Canada's ability to survive. All three had come to the conclusion that it was already too late to save our beloved country. When I saw the final text of the Free Trade Agreement it was quite clear to me that the dream of Canada would almost certainly disappear once and for all if the agreement were implemented and left in place for very long.

Not long after I entered "public life" I quickly became very tired of endless panel discussions about the Canadian identity. And, I suspect most Canadians shared my annoyance. Most of us knew very well who we were and we had known for many years. Somehow, there developed a preoccupation with asking questions most citizens in most countries wouldn't dream of having to ask. Most of us felt that a key aspect of our identity was straightforward: we Canadians were very fortunate to live in Canada, we could take advantage of our great good fortune and build on it, not squander it; we should value our heritage, be free to choose our own national values, and be free to decide how we developed our economy and our society. *That very freedom was our identity.* It was distinct, it was special, it was real.

Independence? Nationalism? Are these two words even the right

words? I think not. The compradors and continentalists are fond
of quoting Dr. Samuel Johnson's famous line that "Patriotism is the
last refuge of scoundrels." But is it? Johnson, among a long list of
other illnesses, had Tourette's syndrome, one characteristic of which
is uncontrollable vocalizations. In Boswell's *Life of Johnson*, the
following is recorded:

> Patriotism having become one of our topics, Johnson suddenly
> uttered, in a strong determined tone, an apothegm, at which
> many will start: "Patriotism is the last refuse of a scoundrel."
> But let it be considered, that he did not mean a real and gen-
> erous love of our country, but that pretended patriotism, which
> so many, in all ages and countries, have made a cloak for self-
> interest.

Canadians need not fear being patriotic. They do need to fear the
scoundrels who tell them it is evil to do so, and they need be wary of
those who hide their selfish interests in a cloak of globalization.

Is there such thing as "the national interest?" I would certainly
hope so, otherwise what's the use of having a nation? Can there
really be a "national interest" in such a big and diverse country as
Canada? Of course there can and it's easy to define. The national
interest must primarily be the improvement of the welfare of the
nation's citizens. It must encompass fairness and compassion.
What is it that holds a nation together? Surely it must be a body of
commonly-shared moral values and principles based on social and
economic justice.

Ultimately for the survival of Canada there could only be one solution; freedom to choose our own values and our own destiny, and
that freedom could only flow from true democratic decision-making
in our political and economic affairs. If I have learned one thing over
the past three or four decades it is that such democratic decision-
making is sadly lacking in Canada. Behind the facade of democracy lies entrenched, consolidated, dominating economic power.

As the Mulroney government did so often, the Chrétien government repeatedly mentions Canada's number one rating in the United
Nations Human Development Index. But the index is based on a relatively narrow range of out-of-date measurements. Moreover, many of
the qualities measured by the U.N. are a direct result of our benevolent
social programs which are now in the process of being downgraded
and dismantled. The widespread impact of the recent reduction of

federal social transfers will profoundly change Canada and move it increasingly closer to the American model.

The Chrétien government's social policy changes and other plans now under discussion will change Canada in other important ways. In a nation already by far the most decentralized large developed nation in the world, as grasping, parochial provincial premiers and provincial media stridently demand more and more transfers of power from the national government, the Chrétien government, as part of its Quebec strategy, is prepared to further weaken the national government and transfer yet more and more power to the provincial governments. A strong decentralist push has come not only from Chrétien and Paul Martin and the provincial premiers, but also from the right-wing think tanks and the conservative media beholden to a multinational business community that likes nothing better than a weak national government. What was once a national community of dreams is being replaced by an inept, weakened federal government whose vision of Canada seems to be a balkanized collection of decentralized states, a loose association of increasingly foreign-owned fiefdoms that will never survive American manifest destiny.

I have said very little in this book about Quebec. This is not because I am not terribly concerned about what has been happening, but rather because I intend to address the subject in some detail elsewhere in the near future. I will say this: the Quebec Liberals and the Chrétien government grossly mismanaged the referendum campaign in 1995. More of the same shoddy performance will certainly mean a shattered country. And those misguided souls who believe that transferring more power to the province of Quebec will ever placate the separatists are as hopelessly naive as those who believe more powers can be transferred to Quebec without transferring those same powers to other provinces. In 1996 new asymmetrical federalism has about as much chance of succeeding as the reintroduction of Meech Lake or the Charlottetown Accord. (This said, lest anyone think otherwise, I strongly support the protection of French language and culture in Quebec and official bilingualism in Canada.)

During the last federal election I said that I believed that if the Conservatives of the new continentalist Liberals were to win a majority government, then the dream of Canada would likely be over: "Already so close to the precipice, I think another four more years would push us over the edge."

Today, the stark and simple question is quite clear. If we continue to abandon the important differences that have, for so long, distinguished us from the United States, why should there continue to be any demand for a separate country? The reality, of course, is that there will not be such a demand. Moreover, with increasing foreign ownership, balkanization and the abandonment of national standards, at a certain point, even if the spirit and the desire are there, even if the assembled documentation and human misery are overwhelming, even in the face of a new Vietnam or a new Richard Nixon, even if the Canadian standard of living plummets and the anger of betrayal surges across the land, at a certain point the chance to turn things around will have passed us by forever.

Perhaps Canada will not disappear. Perhaps there will still be maps with a different colour on the top half of the North American continent and on our National Geographic globes. There could still even be a Maple Leaf flag. But the nation that we are now in the process of becoming will be a nation essentially in name only—an economic, social, political and cultural colony, a place not a country, a feeble remnant of a once proud nation.

How do Canadians feel about what is happening? The latest polls still show that, by an overwhelming margin, Canadians still love their country, still want to live here and nowhere else, still feel we have a distinct identity worth preserving. But, for the first time in my memory, they also show something else.

Pollster Allan Gregg termed the most recent annual *Maclean's/CBC* poll "... the blackest I have ever examined in twenty years of analyzing poll results ... Canadians believe that virtually everything about Canada not only has got worse than it was in times past—but that we can expect continued deterioration ... the aspects of Canadian life that have given us a common sense of purpose and character will exist—if at all—only as pale imitations of what they were ... As I look at these findings, I see very little cause for optimism that the public opinion fabric of the nation is strong enough to hold Canada together."

Today we are witnessing the tragic shattering of the Canadian dream and the virtual abandonment of the idea of a national community and national public philosophy. Across the country there is a pervasive feeling of helplessness and insecurity. As government increasingly acts as an agent of the large corporations, citizens are at the mercy of powerful interests that they cannot combat. And all across the land it is the unfortunate, the underprivileged, who, in the absence of a sense of community and common good, bear the brunt of an abandonment of standards that would have been unheard of a generation ago. The "War on Poverty" has been transformed into a war against the poor.

Meanwhile, the four horsemen of the national eclipse, somehow ignored by our politicians and most of our journalists, continue to leave their deep imprint on our public policies and our freedom. Foreign ownership, corporate concentration, the FTA and NAFTA, all led by our abysmally outdated, undemocratic electoral system continue to gallop across the national landscape without restraint.

Donald Creighton asked *why*, given their good leaders, their bountiful documentation to back up their positions, plus "a large and vocal following among the Canadian people"—why then have the results for Canadian nationalists been "so tragically disproportionate" and such "a dismal story, full or retreats and defeats and frustrations." Nothing could be clearer in my mind than the failure of Canadian nationalists to engage directly in politics is the overwhelming reason for such dismal results. The nationalists in Canada have been defeated because they spent too much energy on a multitude of skirmishes without engaging in by far the most important battle—the battle for political power. Today, Canadian nationalists are without a political voice. While all across Canada there are millions of proud Canadians who yearn for a confident Canada in control of its own future, the Liberals, Conservatives and Reform parties are all aggressive continentalists and the NDP seems lost and dispirited.

The predominant political philosophy in Canada today is the dismantling of government. And don't the big transnational corporations love it! Instead, what is needed is for citizens to *take control* of government, for government to become a true manifestation of the will of the people.

How far have we strayed from such an ideal? Let us go back over twenty-four hundred years to Pericles's funeral oration recounted in Thucydides' *History of the Peloponnesian War*. Compare the words of *Pericles* with Canada in 1996 and weep:

> Our constitution is called a democracy because power is in the hands not of a minority but of the whole people. When it is a question of settling private disputes, everyone is equal before the law; when it is a question of putting one person before another in positions of public responsibility, what counts is not membership of a particular class, but the actual ability which

the man possesses. No one, so long as he has it in him to be of service to the state, is kept in political obscurity because of poverty.

We give our obedience to those whom we put in positions of authority, and we obey the laws themselves, especially those which are for the protection of the oppressed ...

Some people say that people get the government they deserve. I don't believe this for a moment. I say we get the government the economic elite want us to have and they are victorious because the system is of their design. There is no hope that they will ever want to change a political system based on money, for such a system works directly for their benefit.

Martin Luther King said "We know through painful experience that freedom is never voluntarily given by the oppressor." In Canada, freedom will never voluntarily be given by the economic and political elite. We will have to take it back ourselves.

Time after time the nationalists in Canada won the battles for public opinion whether it was on the questions of foreign investment, cruise missile testing, the Free Trade Agreement, NAFTA, etc., but time after time we lost the only battle that counts, the battle for power, the power to enact legislation.

Is there still hope for our beloved country? Yes, there is; we must never, never ever surrender to the selfish, the greedy, the deceitful who would rob us of our birthright and destroy our nation.

Everything I know tells me that there will soon be a widespread and growing backlash against an undemocratic world controlled by big corporations and a backlash to attacks against the nation-state. Moreover, the neo-conservatives are already finding themselves under increasing unfavorable scrutiny. The pendulum may not be stuck; it could swing back. But it won't swing back by itself. In Canada it will *never* swing back unless many, many more men and women decide that they will become directly involved in federal politics. Every man and every woman *can* make a difference. The history of Canada has always been one of waves of continentalism and nationalism. True, today we are engulfed in an unprecedented massive tidal wave of neo-conservative continentalism, but things *can* change.

Richard Gwyn has put it well:

> Neo-conservatism has just one serious flaw: It's unworkable. It's unworkable because it's inhuman. It's all about 'me, me, me' and to hell with caring and sharing ...

> At some point, in a repeat of the Great Depression, the economy will implode because too few people will have enough money to buy the goods being created by the wealthy. A backlash against neo-conservatism thus is inevitable.

The backlash can and must turn into a political revolt. The public is now beginning to understand that the elite's neo-conservative globalization propaganda represents a massive transfer of power and wealth from citizens and employees to corporations and the already wealthy. As this understanding broadens, the possibility for well-organized political action will increase.

Despite all of our serious problems, more than four out of five Canadians still believe that Canada has the best quality of life of any country in the world. And last year a national poll showed that only three percent of Canadians would like to see Canada join the United States, the lowest such figure that I can *ever* recall. This despite the fact that two out of three Canadians feel our country is in "deep trouble."

Many Canadian politicians and other public figures have been fond of saying that the price of being Canadian is a price worth paying. I always thought that such statements were nonsense. There is no price to pay. On the contrary, there is great good fortune to be had by remaining Canadian instead of dissolving forever into the American melting pot.

In *The Betrayal of Canada* I warned that unless there was a dramatic change in Canada, it would soon be too late for change. Now, five years later, Canada has indeed changed, but it is a dramatic change for the worse. The Americanization of Canada, expanding corporate concentration and foreign ownership, the erosion of our social programs, the evaporating sense of community and absence of a national spirit are now the dominant characteristics of a once-proud nation whose foundations are crumbling as our national character and identity disintegrates.

For some thirty years now I have talked about my dream of Canada—a vision of a free, democratic country in charge of its own affairs and its own destiny, a country where a man or woman who wants a job can find a job. My vision of Canada is of a strong, united, prosperous nation that plays a major role in making the world a better and safer place for all mankind, and a nation that is the most compassionate, tolerant, non-violent place on earth. And my vision of Canada is a country where future generations will have no need to ask if there is a Canadian identity because their own self-knowledge and self-confidence will make such questions completely unnecessary. Canada will be a proud, affluent, sharing nation that fully understands how fortunate we are and how important it is that genuine democracy prevails to protect and to extend that good fortune.

What is the ultimate purpose of a nation? Surely it must be to do whatever it can to improve the standard of living of its citizens, to ensure that justice prevails and that freedom is maximized. Someone has said that you can judge a country by how it treats its underprivileged. Given the widespread poverty we now have in Canada, surely we grievously fail this test. For such a comparatively wealthy country to allow so many of its children to live in poverty is a situation that should never be tolerated. In 1988 fewer than one million Canadians had to rely on food banks. Today that number is approaching four million, and some forty percent of these are children. What can one say about a wealthy society that has produced such misery and not only tolerates it, but whose elite largely ignores it? What can one say of political leaders who never even mention it?

Let me end by returning to Pericles,

> ... the man who can most truly be accounted brave is he who best knows the meaning of what is sweet in life and what is terrible, and then goes out undeterred to meet what is to come.

> ... fix your eyes every day on what was the greatness of our country ... fall in love with her. When you remember her greatness, then reflect that what made her great were men and women with a spirit of adventure who knew their duty, who were ashamed to fall below a certain standard. If they ever failed in an enterprise, they made up their minds that at any rate their nation should not find their courage lacking to her, and they gave to her the best contribution that they could.

And finally

> Make up your minds that happiness depends on being free, and freedom depends on being courageous.

Robert Kroetsch

Robert Kroetsch has taught literature and creative writing at the State University of New York and the University of Manitoba. During his long career he has authored more than twenty books of poetry, fiction, and essays, including *The Studhorse Man* (Governor General's Award, 1969), *Badlands*, *The Words of My Roaring*, *What the Crow Said*, *Excerpts from the Real World*, *The Lovely Treachery of Words*, *The Puppeteer*, *The Man from the Creeks*, and *A Likely Story*.

A longtime friend and colleague of Dr. Mort Ross, who was an acclaimed professor at the University of Alberta, Robert Kroetsch delivered this moving eulogy at Dr. Ross's funeral on December 31, 1995.

Eulogy for Mort Ross

Dear Family and Friends of Mort Ross

I think of Mort Ross as seated at a table.

When I first met Mort, sometime in the 1950s, in Iowa City, he was seated at a table in a famous place called simply, Irene's. Needless to say, he was not there alone. He was, even then, uniquely able to create community. Among the graduate students in English and American Civilization, there at the University of Iowa, he was, by virtue of his generosity and his refusal of any need to compete, the center towards which we gravitated. Mort was the first native-born Iowan I met, there in Iowa, and he came to represent a kind of caring that I credited to the whole Midwest. Most of us were from exotic places—like New York or Alberta. He was from a place I recall as being named Olewein. I can't find it on my atlas. Perhaps the place was created by Mort's ability to tell stories—and Mort told stories.

Sitting in Joe's Restaurant and Bar on a Friday evening, having the luxury of a small steak called half-a-Joe's—since none of us could afford the huge full meal—we, his fellow students, had the pleasure of sharing his talk for hours on end. One time some of us drove all the way to the neighboring state where he was vacationing with his wife, Kettle, in her hometown, Gary, Indiana. We drove for half a day to picnic on the shores of Lake Michigan, and to talk and listen. We were lonesome.

Mort's father was a union leader employed by the Grand Trunk Railroad. Mort's sense of fairness bespoke his connection with and admiration for his father. In a world where we were studying literature, Mort insisted that literature is connected, directly and wonderfully, with life.

He would make his career by reminding us of that connection, insisting that we take seriously the stories we read—and tell. There in that university town just a few miles from the Mississippi River, near Hannibal, Missouri, near the locales of Mark Twain's stories, Mort was a kind of Mark Twain, reminding us with his soft chuckle that in our various obscurities we live important lives.

Mort left Iowa to become a professor. When I met him again, this time at the University of Alberta, he was, again, at a table. At Mort's Table. Home was something that Mort could carry with him. He was its embodiment, and to sit down at his table was to feel at home.

One summer my wife and I were going away from our house in Victoria and we asked Mort and Janis if they'd like to loaf for a few weeks on the West Coast. They agreed.

I returned to find that Mort had coaxed and shaped my rocky garden into the elegance of a poem. I was surprised to think of Mort as a gardener. And yet I should have known—he was a gardener, always, showing the same care for the physical world that he did for people. He had listened to Whitman, and in his own version of the Whitmanesque he cared for the grass, for the varieties of moss on a stone, for the shapes of rosemary.

Mort was a member of the editorial board of NeWest Press. A board is, in one of its definitions, a table. Mort was strangely quiet at that table. He enjoyed being the board's secretary, as if by that act he might collect a new provision of stories. And yet he wasn't quiet at all. Because his presence—his listening presence—reminded us that the books we publish and the immediate world around us must connect.

As a member of that editorial board, Mort was the model of what an editor might be. He had a rare ability to persuade an author to make changes. He could, by the quiet magic of his elegant prose style, persuade writers that the beautiful revisions were their own.

That was one of Mort's precious accomplishments. As a teacher, as a writer, as an editor, as a drinking companion, as a friend—he persuaded us that we had things to say and lives to share—and he persuaded us there must be a deliberate grace in what we do. And by the way—when you saw Mort dancing you realized the absolute grace of his seemingly awkward figure.

During the past few years, Mort was under contract to NeWest Press—to write his literary memoirs—his recollections of a life spent reading and making literature in the United States and Canada—and particularly at the University of Alberta.

How might he ever have accomplished such a project? It seemed impossible. We, his friends, confounded him, always, by sitting down, by filling our glasses, by beginning to talk.

And yet, now, we complete his project by continuing on.

We sit down together, again, and over and over. We remember his gentle grimace that seemed to signal a reluctance to speak. We remember his soft voice, inviting us into the circle of conversation.

Love, in one of its varieties, is a kind of communal discourse that takes place at a table. Mort Ross showed us that. Janis Watkin showed us that. Together, they showed us how to make love grow.

Maude Barlow

Maude Barlow is a political activist, author, policy critic, and outspoken crusader for Canada. She is the National Volunteer Chairperson of The Council of Canadians, a non-profit, non-partisan public interest organization supported by 100,000 members. Maude is the author or co-author of ten books about Canada, including the best-selling *Class Warfare: The Assault on Canada's Schools, Straight Through the Heart: How the Liberals Abandoned the Just Society,* as well as *MAI and the Threat to Canadian Sovereignty.* She is on the planning committee of the International Forum on Globalization, a network of individuals and groups from around the world working to take democratic control of the global economy.

The following is the text of Ms. Barlow's speech in the McLuhan Program's *Canada by Design: Visionary Speaker Series* delivered on January 22, 1998.

Canada by Design: Using New Media and Policy to Build a Knowledge Nation

It is an honour to take part in your exciting new series on Canada's future as a knowledge nation and I thank you for inviting me to share my views. Before I respond to the questions you have asked us to address, namely, where we should be heading, and what practical steps are required to get there, I have to share with you my fears that we are not in a position in Canada to address these questions at present. I will try, but not before I sound an alarm.

I believe that the world's economic and social systems are in the midst of a watershed transformation as great as any in history. This transformation is characterized by the growth of giant transnational corporations, an explosion of global speculative investment unrelated to real production or real jobs, economic globalization based on a western market monoculture, the deregulation environmental protection and the privatization of everything.

At the core of this revolution is a battle between the public and private spheres, with democracy at the losing end. The millennium marks a new breed of stateless corporations and corporate states which effectively allow transnational capital to hide behind the protection of a flag when convenient, and to eschew it when it is not. Nation states have, in fact, been eclipsed by corporations. Let me give you just several examples of why I am now saying we no longer live in a democracy, but in a system of "corporate rule."

All told, transnationals, not governments, hold 90 percent of all technology and product patents world wide and are responsible for 70 percent of the world's trade. While the world economy is growing by 2 or 3 percent every year, the biggest transnationals are growing, as a group, by a rate of 8 to 10 percent. The combined sales of the top 200 transnationals are bigger than the combined GDP of all countries minus the biggest 9; that is, they surpass the combined economies of 182 countries.

Wal-Mart is bigger than 161 countries, including Poland, Israel, and Greece. Mitsubishi is larger than Indonesia. General Motors is bigger than Denmark. Ford is bigger than South Africa. Philip Morris is larger than New Zealand. Toyota is bigger than Norway. Japan's top 6 trading companies are nearly equivalent to the combined GDP of all of South America. The Top 200, with a combined revenue of $7.1 trillion, have almost twice the economic clout of the poorest four-fifths of humanity, whose combined income is only $3.9 trillion. However, in spite of their enormous wealth and clout, the Top 200 are net job destroyers—so-called virtual corporations, all together, they employ less than a third of one percent of the world's people.

These corporations, which have abandoned the nation-states of their birth, are successfully challenging the traditional role of government to make law. A Japanese executive with the powerful Keidanran, Japan's Chamber of Commerce, explains kindly that "the nation-state is not really dead, but it is being quickly retired." Meanwhile, the global institutions running the global economy, from the IMF and the World Bank to the World Trade Organization, have been designed in the image and the interests of the corporation. Citizens are losing the power to maintain their social rights and cultural diversity; meanwhile, no global institution has been mandated to protect the earth as nation-states leave the field.

Says businessman-turned-environmentalist Paul Hawken, "Given current corporate practices, not one wildlife reserve, wilderness, or indigenous culture will survive the global economy. We know that every natural system on the planet is disintegrating. The land, water, air, and sea have been functionally transformed from life-supporting systems into repositories for waste. There is no polite way to say that business is destroying the world."

Transnational corporations and their powerful political alliances are also the leading proponents behind the global trade and investment agreements now formally displacing nation-state governments in the creation of public policy. For instance, the International Chamber of Commerce drafted the original wording for the MAI, or what the president of the World Trade Organization calls "a constitution for a single global economy."

The Multilateral Agreement on Investment is a proposed treaty that would dramatically reduce the capacity of national and sub-national governments to limit the degree and nature of foreign investment (both outgoing and incoming) or to impose standards of behaviour on investors. Its purpose is to remove most of the remaining barriers to, and controls on, the mobility of capital, and its passage would result in the sharp restriction of the ability of governments everywhere to shape investment policy to promote economic, cultural, social or environmental goals.

This treaty is the product of a very long and intense U.S. campaign going back decades to secure a global set of rules to protect American business interests around the world. A version of it was presented to the first WTO ministerial meeting but the nations of the developing world blocked it as a dangerous form of neo-colonialism. The U.S., Europe and Canada changed tactics and decided to have the 29 powerful countries of the OECD—home to 477 of the Fortune 500 companies—ratify it first and then use their collective clout to convince Third World countries to join in or be left out of the global economy.

The MAI is a severely one-sided agreement that will give corporations new rights in law to challenge government policy, and new tools to limit the power of elected officials in all the signatory countries. It will thus subsume accepted principles of open, accountable judicial review. I call it "NAFTA on steroids" because it takes the worst provisions of that agreement, magnifies them, and applies them to a whole new host of countries. The MAI would grant transnational corporations more power than nation states in international law. Essentially, the MAI forbids "discriminating" between domestic and foreign "investors" in any sector. While investors are generally understood to be businesses, the MAI considers any government regulations or practices that interfere with the commercial interests of foreign corporations in every sector of the economy—natural resources, health, education, pensions, agriculture and culture included—to be discriminatory, and open for challenge.

The MAI requires that national and sub-national governments refrain from passing any future law that violates MAI rules. In a clause called "standstill," countries agree first to list all their existing measures that do not conform to the MAI, to impose no new ones, and not to amend existing measures in any way that increases non-conformity to MAI.

Under another, called "rollback," the MAI requires national and sub-national governments to eliminate the listed laws and practices, either immediately or over a period of time, that violate MAI rules. Countries agree to reduce and eventually eliminate non-conforming measures, including those listed as "country-specific reservations." The Canadian government insists that sensitive areas such as jobs and health have been protected by the 49 reservations Canada has put forth, but they are subject to these clauses intended to be sunsetted over time.

The most egregious aspect of the MAI is that foreign-based transnationals would have rights and powers not accorded to domestic companies. If a government brought in regulations to protect the environment or natural resources or upgrade health or safety standards that cost the industry involved some lost profits, domestic companies would have no choice but to abide by the new law. Foreign companies, however, could claim compensation for "expropriation" and sue the government under the "investor-state" dispute system. This is the heart of the MAI. Governments would have to pay transnational corporations for the right to make law.

Now, I have taken this time to sound this warning because I don't think we can address the question of how to build a knowledge nation if we don't first address the question as to whether we are still a nation at all in the traditional sense. Do we in fact, as citizens, hold the policy levers with which to design our future? I have to say no. Our governments have given these powers with abandon.

From the mid-1930s until recently, successive Canadian governments designed and implemented cultural policies to build a strong and dynamic pool of Canadian artistic talent and cultural enterprises and to ensure that Canadians' own stories were told and our values and history preserved. These policies were created first and foremost to serve Canadians, not to serve an international trade agenda. Living next to the biggest superpower in the world, our ancestors knew they had to carve out a space for our unique Canadian perspective. Public support for Canadian culture has been crucial to our survival as a nation.

In the 1990s, however, every cultural institution and sector is in jeopardy. Seismic changes in Canadian society and international relations have created unforeseen challenges to the very existence of Canadian cultural policies in which those very institutions are increasingly forced to balance their responsibility to Canadian audiences against the demands of lucrative foreign buyers.

As well, the free-market ideology that drove the Conservative Party under Brian Mulroney is now firmly rooted in the economic ministers and senior bureaucrats of the federal Liberal government and in the political advisors to Jean Chrétien himself. The approach of both these governments to culture has been a shift away from policies and regulations that promote a vibrant domestic cultural industry to an emphasis on advancing the export potential of individual artists and products.

As a consequence, federal funding for culture has been dramatically reduced in the last decade. The assault has been relentless. Funding to the CBC has declined by 47 per cent in a decade, and its workforce has been cut in half. Funding for the Canada Council, the National Film board and the National Library and Museums were slashed by 30 per cent in the infamous 1995 Martin budget alone. Between 1990 and 1992, most indirect forms of support—tax credits and other incentives to attract investment in publishing, recording and films—dropped from almost $1 billion to zero. Communications analyst Paul Audley reports a 41 per cent reduction in overall federal spending on culture (indirect and direct funding combined) between 1989 and 1996.

Meanwhile, a handful of powerful private corporations are expanding their control over the media. Conrad Black's Hollinger Inc. now owns or controls 60 of Canada's 105 daily newspapers, including 80 per cent of all the papers in Ontario and all the dailies in Saskatchewan, Newfoundland and Prince Edward Island. Black extends his control through his ownership of Canadian Press and CP Broadcast News which owns 425 radio and 76 television stations. Through his holdings, he reaches every newspaper in the country but 4.

Black is clear about the right of the private sector to own and control the media, and, indeed, everything else. "It has always seemed to me that the real establishment in this country should be a handful of owners and a group of extremely capable managers so self-assured as to *behave* like owners, plus a battery of some lawyers and heads of large accounting firms and discreet stockbrokers who serve them well and with whom they are comfortable. The core of the actual establishment ought to be this relatively small numbers of actual proprietors whose companies are on the move."

Well, Conrad Black is getting his way. Just 10 corporations control 55 per cent of revenues in radio, an increase of 50 per cent over the past decade. Three giant cable companies have nearly 70 per cent of the market. This trend in Canada mirrors the global trend in which a handful of players like Ted Turner, Disney, Time-Warner and

Berlusconi control not only the major entertainment outlets, but the news as well. These corporate powerhouses are pressing politicians everywhere to eliminate public broadcasting and remove the civic purpose mandate of this most powerful medium on earth. They also want national foreign ownership rules to come down.

Izzy Asper, president of CanWest Global Communications has proposed that foreign investors should be allowed 49.9 per cent ownership of Canadian broadcasting companies and be allowed to hold unlimited shares. The Canadian Association of Broadcasters is currently seeking to deregulate private radio and have Canadian content rules dropped.

When he was trade minister, Art Eggleton contradicted the public statements of Heritage Minister Sheila Copps when he said, "The trend to open markets and communications is global and irreversible." His position is reminiscent of Mulroney's finance minister, Michael Wilson, who, in 1991, overruled then culture minister, Marcel Masse, on policy intended to Canadianize the book publishing industry. In both cases, it is clear that power over culture resides, not with the minister responsible in name, but with the real power brokers in government—the ministers and bureaucrats responsible for trade and finance.

The Senate's Standing Committee on Transport and Communications recently published a report called *Wired to Win, Canada's International Competitive Position in Communications* in which it calls for the dismantling of Canada's cultural policies in favour of open global competition. The committee approvingly quoted the presentations from big business: "IBM Canada recommended a three-phase transition period that would, within a period of roughly 10 years, see the complete phasing out of all regulations in the area of licensing, foreign ownership, Canadian content, and mandatory contributions to Canadian production ... The final phase would see the lifting of all rules: unconditional exemptions, 100 per cent foreign ownership, no content rules, and no mandatory expenditure on Canadian production."

Distressingly, the forces of privatization are now operating inside the very institutions whose core mandate is the promotion of Canadian culture. James McCoubrey, the new executive vice-president of the CBC, spent most of his career with the huge transnational advertising firm, Young and Rubicam, and is, in the words of the *Globe and Mail*, "pure private sector." Francoise Bertrand, who in 1996 replaced Keith Spicer as chair of the CRTC, openly sees her

role as strengthening the cultural sector before it is fully deregulated
—a scenario she says is inevitable. She admits that under her stewardship, not only her job, but Canadian content will disappear. "it
will. We know that."

The Canadian government's enthusiastic promotion of free trade
is the final nail in the coffin of Canadian culture. NAFTA's so-called
cultural protection is now widely understood to be toothless. Canada
has lost its key policies to protect its magazine industry after a ruling from the WTO. Trade experts all agree this is a precedent-setting
decision with far-reaching implications for other cultural policies.
U.S. Trade Representative, Charlene Barshefsky, was jubilant, saying
the decision would serve as a useful weapon against other Canadian
cultural practices.

The Canadian Broadcasting Act has been targeted by her office in
a recent report for elimination as a barrier to U.S. exports. The WTO
has scheduled negotiations for the global deregulation of broadcasting for January 1, 2000. Areas for discussion include the definition
of broadcasting, ownership and control of broadcast licensees and
"access and reciprocity to domestic and foreign markets." The
Canadian government is working with the pro-privatization U.S. government and industry to come up with a "common North American
position" to take to the WTO.

And now we have the MAI. To protect culture, the Canadian government is relying on an exemption lodged by the government of
France. But it is badly worded, inadequate to Canada's needs and
unlikely to be granted by the U.S. in any case. Further, the French
really want only to protect their television industry, and it is widely
understood in trade circles that, when negotiations get down to the
wire, France will give up the rest of its exemption for this one safeguard. The Canadian government has not launched its own request
for a full carve-out for culture nor has it mentioned culture in it
reservations.

This means that, as it stands now, only months before final ratifi-
cation of the MAI, none of the practices or policies Canada uses to
promote and protect Canadian culture, including newspapers and
broadcasting, are safe from challenge by the private sector of every
other signatory country to the deal. No subsidy could be given to any
Canadian cultural sector, including the CBC, that is not offered
equally to foreign "private investors." Canadian content law would
be challengeable as discrimination. The ban on setting performance
requirements would mean government couldn't insist that foreign

companies hire Canadian performers, filmmakers, musicians or writers. These companies could take 100 percent of their profits back out of the country and we couldn't say a word.

Under the MAI, a U.S. book publishing giant could buy up a major Canadian publisher and refuse to produce any creative works by Canadians, but still qualify for industrial incentives offered by the Canadian government. Book distribution would be open to continental competition, as would book stores.

The government could no longer require radio stations to play Canadian music, television to air Canadian programs, or film companies to produce Canadian material to qualify for grants and tax breaks. Tax measures to keep Canadian newspapers in Canadian hands would be illegal.

I could, but won't, present the same analysis on education, the other vehicle essential for the creation of our "knowledge nation:" how it has been deeply affected by cuts; how it is under assault by the same ideological forces out to discredit and then privatize and commercialize public education; how the private sector is coming to "rescue" education; how universal public education is put at risk under the MAI. Suffice to say that culture, media and education together are increasingly at risk by very big and very private interests and unless we address this issue, the future of our knowledge nation won't be ours to make.

My vision for the future is simple. I deeply believe in the preservation of an indigenous Canadian culture, grown organically out of the roots, soil and traditions of our own experiences and history. However sophisticated our knowledge technology becomes, we have to keep control of the "software" that must be formed from the dreams and toil of our own heritage. I believe in universal social security and education and the right of every child to equally share the opportunities and resources of our great country. I believe that Canada should become a moral presence on the world stage again.

But I also believe that we have turned our backs on 100 years of history and abandoned our central narrative of sharing for survival. And I fear that, as we lose our identity, our so-called "knowledge" economy may start to reflect a society drowning in information but starved for purpose. Canada as a knowledge nation must reflect *our* history and culture, what *we* know and value. We must move now, to protect our culture, broadcasting, newspapers and education system not only from transnational corporations but domination by the Canadian corporate establishment as well. We must reject the siren call of economic globalization based on the model of privatization and competition; this is anathema to our values.

We must reject the MAI. The world badly needs rules to control global investment, but this badly flawed, one-sided agreement is not the answer. Closer to the mark is the 1974 UN Charter of Economic Rights and Duties of States which stated that member nations have the "inalienable right" to "regulate and exercise authority over foreign investment." It granted nations the right to "regulate and supervise the activities of transnational corporations" in the national interest and declared that "Transnational corporations shall not intervene in the internal affairs of the host State."

Together with the Universal Declaration of Human Rights, this treaty and the UN Covenants on Human Rights established what could be called rights of citizenship—social security, just conditions of work and pay, education, food, housing, medical care and the right to security in the event of unemployment, sickness, disability, old age, or other lack of livelihood beyond the citizen's control. They bound the state signatories to accept a moral and legal obligation to protect and promote human and democratic rights and contained measures of implementation required to do so.

We must restore funding to our cultural community and most particularly, the CBC, and restate our societal commitment to protect indigenous Canadian culture. We must halt the privatization of our universities and place strict controls on big business in our schools. We need legislation to limit and reverse the concentration of media ownership and to encourage diversity of ownership and ensure diversity of content. Canada is alone in the industrialized world in not having legislation to prevent the unprecedented level of newspaper concentration we have reached. Protecting our culture and a diversity of voices in our media is crucial to restoring our democratic rights.

But culture is not just books and films. It is the values by which we live. We must go back and rediscover the roots of universality that we have so readily abandoned. Universal social security was based on an approach to society that included everyone. It was a privilege of citizenship based on the fundamental notion that Canadians have equal social rights and their social, cultural and educational institutions have an obligation to provide them. The Canadian definition of social welfare concerned itself with the well-being of the whole community.

What practical steps must we take to get to my vision? On the

MAI, there is a national coalition in formation. Join us. For the rest, it is more difficult. We need to take more personal responsibility for what is happening seemingly so far away, because it is not far at all. We may all catch the Asian flu before it's over. But the traditional places we have looked to for leadership—partisan politics, the church, academia—are, with some exceptions, failing us. What is needed now is what Indian activist, writer and trailblazer, Vandana Shiva calls "the emerging politics of the new millennium"—a global citizens' movement.

We at the Council of Canadians have launched what we call our Citizens' Agenda for Canada, which serves as both a vision and an action plan for citizens in light of the abdication of responsibility by our government. Central to our agenda is the recognition that Canadians, and peoples around the world, have the right to productive and fulfilling employment, food, shelter, education, pensions, unemployment insurance, health care, universally accessible public services, a safe and clean environment—food, water, and air,—the safe-keeping of our wilderness spaces, and to develop and celebrate our diverse cultures and freely communicate our distinct experiences.

To rebuild democracy means starting back at the roots—in our communities. The only way to fight is together. Across sectors, across countries, across race, gender and age lines, employed and unemployed, city and rural, we must find one another and realize that we are now a movement in opposition to corporate rule and probably the only thing that comes between us and the global feudalism of the new economy. We must not accept the prevailing propaganda of inevitability. To say we have no choice is intellectual terrorism.

Fair trade, full employment, co-operation, cultural diversity, democratic control, fair taxation, environmental stewardship, community, public accountability, equality, social justice: these are the touchstones of our vision and we must celebrate them and each other as we build our alternative world. It will take the rest of our lives even to begin the task before us. But not to try would betray the generations that have come before us and fought so hard for a different world and greatly diminish the dreams of all those who come after.

Chapter Nine: New Media

From carving on stone, to pounding out fibres into paper, to the printing press, communication has had various milestone points in its amazing history. With each new twist, there have had to be changes to incorporate the medium.

In the past five years, the burgeoning of the Internet has created a phenomenal difference to the written word, and one that has to be examined. It has been said that the art of letter-writing has been rejuvenated thanks to electronic mail, or e-mail as we all refer to it. Various magazines also have on-line locations and e-zines have sprouted up everywhere. Advertisers have seen the value of Web sites for products, and private citizens have also discovered the joy of creating "homepages" to show themselves off to the world at large.

What has this new medium done to the writing process? IS there a difference between an article written for a normal magazine and one commissioned by an e-zine? Do we treat e-mail differently from other letters? In a word, YES.

Cyberwriting in all its manifestations should be examined, especially now, as it is evolving. We have to be aware of what is happening and determine what we wish to happen as well. This is a moment of great upheaval, and we as writers and readers have a voice in the process. Additionally, it is a much more democratic field than any previous metamorphosis of the history of language and communication, offering us all a place in its creation.

Let's examine e-mail first of all, since it is the tool that most people will have some practice and experience with, and may indeed be the only online forum that many of us will ever use. E-mail has recreated the urge to write letters. It is an established fact that as soon as you have e-mail, you will reconnect with your penpal from Grade Three, several old chums from high school, and relatives that you usually only write to at Christmastime. E-mails have taken the place of office memos, and also have replaced personal calls home from the office.

The biggest danger to be seen in e-mails is that we seem to compare them to phone calls rather than letters (which we now refer to as "snail-mail"). Instead of allowing for some formality in our language and syntax, we are lax in our quick typing, often pressing the SEND button before even a cursory proofreading. We ignore the need to capitalize the beginnings of sentences, we use ellipses between our thoughts instead of creating new paragraphs, we use acronyms and "emoticons" (☺) rather than proper language. For some reason, we often tend to emulate James Joyce's Molly Bloom in some wild stream of consciousness when we e-mail (though at less poetic and intense levels). This wouldn't be such a problem if the ease and satisfaction of e-mail weren't so prevalent. However, since it is fast becoming a mode of business writing, which has long been characterized by its precise syntax and formality, we must be more wary of how we present ourselves in e-mail.

There are a few things to consider when writing an e-mail. Instead of thinking of it as a separate medium, it is likely better to think of it merely as a form of delivery system. Within that, it is possible to write a love letter, a business letter, or a manifesto. Think of it as the envelope you are putting your missive into, not a format unto itself. After all, whatever arrives on someone's server is an ambassador to your thoughts. You have to remember that at all times. Your words, no matter what filter they are delivered through, will still stand as your thoughts. To be too informal to a professor or an employer can rebound on you. Always consider your audience, instead of relaxing within the ease of the format. As a safeguard, you may even wish to program your e-mail to queue your mail rather than sending it immediately, requiring you to review and proofread your letter before it leaves your desk.

If you tend to wander about the Internet, you will have seen various forms of communication, many of them employing various bells and buttons and wacky backgrounds. It is interesting to see what things people seem to consider necessary to push their company, or product. I am using the term "product" very loosely in this context, as the subject of a Web page may be anything from a children's toy for sale to a province hoping for investors. Even within a personal Web page you are selling something, although in that case it is often yourself as an interesting subject for perusal.

While it is intriguing and seductive to play with all the possibilities that the Internet has to offer, you can deny access to true communication with an overabundance of many of the options. Sometimes less is more. Now, before any computer geeks rise up in protest, let me explain my stance. People accessing your Web page are all coming at it with different browsers, different modems, and idiosyncratic servers. If communication is indeed your aim, it would be wise to consider the lowest common denominator before deciding whether to put a musical WAV file in the background or some exploding java script on your introductory page. If pictures and incidentals keep your page from loading quickly when someone logs on, chances are they will stop the loading and move on to something more accessible. No matter how inventive your page is, and how important your message within, no communication can happen without readers. Creating a bottleneck of time for your viewer is much like writing a plodding and overladen introduction to a written essay. You have to grab your reader from the beginning, and hold him through both the interest level of the material and the speed with which it is delivered.

Another thing to consider is the fact that various computer platforms will read colours differently. It is a wise thing to look for a list of "Web safe" colours—colours that will be seen equally well on all systems of computers—before deciding on your background, text, and links if you want to ensure that what you are creating is going to be seen the way you wish it to be.

After you have come to grips with the mechanical aspects of the Internet, there are still innovations in terms of rhetoric to consider. The link is likely the greatest new invention since MLA documentation formatting. Instead of worrying about unintentionally creating a disjointed argument, you can now place a slightly tangential point into a link. This acts in the same way end- or footnotes work in a more traditional, formal essay. Likewise, instead of expanding upon a certain point, you can create an imbedded link within the text of your argument, offering more background information to an interested reader, but allowing a generalist or already well-informed reader to go on with your argument without having to pursue the background information. (Placing your cursor over a highlighted link will cause the address of the link to appear at the bottom of the reader's browser. This can tell them if it is a link to another page of your text, or whether it is a jump to a background site.) This format can pare down your writing and allow for a stronger focus to your actual argument. The danger, of course, lies in not linking to background and pertinent facts. A naïve reader may read Web-based content and think it sparser than paper-based essays. This can be deceiving, if all the links are not followed. No argument should be offered with only general statements to support it, whatever medium you choose for its publication.

Sometimes a Web writer will take an easy way out, and rather than linking to more information he has himself generated on the topic, will link readers to the reference source itself. This can be good and bad. While it does provide direct proof for the argument, the reader is left to discover the kernel of proof within that full document, rather than having it paraphrased or summarized by the initial writer.

Another concept to play with when creating a Web-based essay, is to decide just how much you intend to put on a page. You may want to divide your argument into several linked pages, and offer the thesis and ensuing topic sentences in a much larger font than the rest of the script. This all helps your reader against eyestrain which can develop when reading an article from the monitor. It also offers the reader yet another button or link to push, which is something to consider, since the attitude of your reader has to be taken into account. Readers who come to you on the Internet are likely to enjoy the whole "surfing" image, and clicking their mouse button is part of the aesthetic. From a completely informal personal poll, clicking beats scrolling in terms of Web approval.

Moving from the layout strategies into the content itself, we have to consider just what we want the world to know about us when we create a homepage. You will find everything from overt confessionals to coy offerings giving you very little information. A homepage can be used for various purposes. Many people have a link to their resumes, in hopes of employers venturing upon them and offering them fantastic jobs. Hobbyists can find like-minded folks on the Internet by proclaiming their collections of Beanie Babies and Pez, or showing pictures of their woodcarving ventures. Many people toss pictures of their children on to their Web pages, for far-flung family members to keep abreast of every lost tooth and gained inch. Some people simply offer a list of links they happen to like, which is one of the least satisfying forms of homepage. While links are fun, and informative, content is much better than mere links. Think of the difference between reading a guide book and the phone book when arriving in a new city. Which offers you more?

While it is possible to create a homespun rumpus room attitude, welcoming people into the very heart of your life, you must remember at all times that complete strangers will happen upon your homepage. Think about how much you would like either a convict or your pastor knowing about your home and life. Decide whether you want the world at large knowing the names of your children, where they go to school, and what your schedule is. Never assume that you are anonymous on the Internet. A very amiable hacker once proved to me that he could find out where I lived from a simple post in an online chatroom (many of these display your IP, or Internet Provider, address). I scoffed, until the phone beside me rang seven minutes later.

This attitude of deciding what you say to whom holds true as well on newsgroups and chat sites. There has been a lot of print generated about strangers who meet on chat sites on the Internet, and fall in love, only to discover that the person whom they've poured their soul out to is not what they seemed to be. A rule of thumb is to presume that everyone on the Internet is a 13-year-old boy until proven otherwise. Think twice before revealing your whereabouts, and it may not be a bad idea to create a nicknamed persona for yourself in these environs.

Don't allow this paranoia to keep you from discovering the joy of communicating in print with others from around the world, though. This is indeed a brave new world, offering us a connection to the world from the comfort of our own terminal. This medium is blurring boundaries and making the world a much smaller place. If anything globalizes us in the 21st century, it will not be multinational corporations or governments; it will be the Internet.

Randy Williams

Randy Williams, a relatively recent immigrant to Canada, was born in Alabama, and grew up in Micronesia. He is a published poet, has written two musicals, and has sung in numerous alternative rock bands. He helped define the voice of the innovative Internet magazine and Web site, *Tripod* (where the following piece was posted), as a writer and editor of several content sections, including Media, Work & Money, and Computers & Internet. He is also a contributing writer to the book *Tripod's Tools for Life: Streetsmart Strategies for Work, Life—and Everything Else.*

He is presently living in Edmonton with his wife and two daughters, where he writes online and multimedia content when not indulging a hellish addiction to maple-dipped doughnuts from Tim Hortons.

Dialling In for Dollars

Over the last several years, North Americans have been subjected to a lot of hype concerning the concept of the virtual office. According to the buzz, the modern employer's ability to sling together space for temporary projects, short-term contract workers, and ad hoc "teams" is serendipitous and beneficial for all. Very cost-effective and organic, don't you know? But while preparing this story, I had occasion to flip through a catalogue of easily assembled desk surfaces and computer tables. The "work positions" snap together like Legos—new surfaces are added to long cubicle-style "walls" as more temp workers are hired. And when a project is completed, the whole enchilada can be broken down and stored in a closet or warehouse somewhere. Cool, except that I kept having a disturbing mental picture of a warehouse full of discarded worker drones—much like the robot graveyards in *Star Wars*.

Thank heavens I've never had to function in that sort of dehumanizing "work hotel." But I am something of an expert on another type of virtual office: while working in the US, as a writer/editor for the Webzine at Tripod.com (located in Williamstown, Massachusetts), I spent about a third to one-half of my time working from my home computer in nearby North Adams. While parked in front of my trusty Mac, pounding out "content," I was linked to my colleagues in Williamstown (and to my columnists and freelancers) only by the slender fibre-optic thread of a dial-up PPP connection.

It should be said at the outset that this arrangement was one largely of my own design. Tripod is a young, dynamic, rapidly-expanding company. That is a polite way of saying that the atmosphere at Tripod World Headquarters often resembles the scene in Francis Ford

Coppola's film, *Bram Stoker's Dracula*, where Renfield and the inmates have taken over the asylum.

Okay, I'm exaggerating. But the fact remained that during my three-year tenure I was surrounded by dozens of young Webserfs, many of them crammed into whatever tiny spaces could just accommodate a computer and a warm body. And each of them had different work ethics and styles. That carnival atmosphere just wasn't, for me at least, conducive to serious, cerebellum-intensive work. Everyone else at the 'Pod seemed perfectly content to thrive and produce in the midst of such friendly and stimulating chaos. But I found that much of my time at the office was spent in frustration, and that I would wind up bringing work home and toiling into the wee hours of the morning just to stay caught up. And that trend came seriously close to obliterating my so-called personal life.

Therefore, I fell into a pattern of spending my mornings at home, producing reams of articles and features in peace and quiet. Then, I would drive over to Williamstown to spend my afternoons in meetings and confabs with my colleagues. I was able to make the transition from cyberspace to meatspace flawlessly. I was more productive, and the time spent alone had me eagerly looking forward to mixing it up with the Tripod gang when I slid into the office. Tripod was forward-thinking enough to trust me—as long as my work got done and I brought my butt (and occasionally my brain) to important planning sessions, everyone was happy.

To this day, I remain a part-time telecommuter. Now that I am living and working in Edmonton, I have been fortunate enough to work out a schedule with my current employer that has me teleworking two afternoons a week, an arrangement which allows me to pick up our two daughters at elementary school while my wife is busy lecturing at the local community college. A little flexibility and trust from my bosses helps ensure that our family doesn't fall prey to the dreaded "latch-key kids" syndrome. The girls, however, have quickly had to learn that Daddy's being in the house doesn't meant that he has time to play with them during those two afternoons; he really will be working after he walks them back home. I help get them hopping on their homework and/or chores until 5:00 rolls around, at which point I can virtually "clock out" for the day. Then, and only then, can we play.

So this is a positive, upbeat story with a happy ending, right? Well, yes and no. You've heard of Warrior Kings? I'm a Worrier King. And there are some details about the whole work-from-home movement that concern me a great deal.

Make no mistake; big businesses are pushing a shiny happy image of teleconferencing and virtual offices with every slick weapon in their advertising arsenals. There are two reasons for this: the very same businesses that want to sell the technology that makes telecommuting possible (and thus make enormous corporate profits) often have huge telework programs themselves (resulting in enormous corporate savings). It's a win-win situation, at least for the big names hyping the supposed revolution.

Telecommuting can also have distinct advantages for many workers—but not all, and that's where problems begin to appear beneath the surface glitz of the digital song and dance routine we're being sold. Independent-minded mavericks with thoughts of ditching the gray confines of the cubicle for the purported freedom of the virtual workplace ought to take a good, hard look at the personal advantages and disadvantages in taking their work home with them for good—or carrying it with them wherever they go. As tempting as it may be to leave Renfield and the other inmates behind at the office asylum, it should also be remembered that, in most classic vampire lore, the victims must invite the bloodsuckers into their home to become truly vulnerable.

THE SET-UP

Think you can jump into telework with your battle-scarred old 386 PC or Mac Classic? Think again. In a 1997 survey conducted by telework advocacy group Telecommute America, 64% of the respondents defined their home offices as "high tech" (Pentium or PowerPC processor, CD-ROM) and another 13% designed their set-ups as "cutting edge" (including videoconferencing and the works). That teleworkers seem to take geeky pride in their home office set-ups is important; such employees must be intimately familiar with both software and hardware—applications, machines, troubleshooting techniques and maintenance requirements. Quite simply, they will not have the luxury of summoning a friendly IS department worker over to figure out what went boom.

A realistic list of the minimum equipment required for an effective home office would look something like this:

- A reasonably high-end CPU (Pentium or PowerPC)
- 16+ MB of RAM, 32 MB or more if the teleworker expects to do conferencing or memory-intensive graphics, video, or number crunching

- No less than a 28.8 modem
- An up-to-date Web browser (Netscape or Internet Explorer)
- Networking software, including PPP, FTP, and Telnet
- 1.5 gigabytes of hard disk storage (more is better, and file sizes are getting enormous)
- A reliable Internet connection
- A work phone line for voice transmissions, preferably with three-way calling and call waiting
- A work phone line for data
- An answering machine (or access to company voice mail)
- PC fax capability or a separate fax machine (a separate machine may require a third work data line of you wish to receive faxes while tying up your primary data line with the modem)
- A fairly high-speed ink-jet or laser printer

Other considerations include the ability to be ready for Web-based conferencing, which will allow far-flung "teams" to share information (including documents, video, audio) and work together. Most of the existing software for such conferencing is still in its infancy but will improve in the very near future; for that reason aspiring teleworkers would be well advised to purchase a computer with top of the line video capabilities and more memory than may be needed immediately.

Obviously, an effective teleworker needs a lot more than two tin cans and a length of string to get the job done. Such a worker also needs a home with plenty of space for equipment and other supplies, whether all of this paraphernalia is installed in a separate "office" or in a vacant corner of a living room or bedroom. If there are to be children, spouses, domestic partners, or roommates wandering through the home while work is being conducted, it is probably foolhardy to expect that anything less than an entire spare room—with a door that can be closed for quiet and privacy—will do the trick.

THE GOOD

PacBell, one of the largest employers of telecommuters in the US, warns new teleworkers to "expect a 30- to 90-day acclimatization period when you start telecommuting" because "it takes a while for even the most organized to figure out how to manage time, space, communication systems and projects while working in two locations."

Once the period of adjustment is over, many teleworkers find themselves happier than pigs in slop. Working from home can provide a more satisfying work/life balance than can be achieved by those who must put in a required number of rigidly-scheduled "face time" hours at the office and scramble to tend to their personal lives in whatever off-hours are left after the commute home. For many, telecommuting is an ideal way to balance work with other aspects of their lives—or at least the best available compromise. It can provide an environment that fosters quiet time for mentally intensive or creative work, or it may be an opportunity to reduce stress and increase productivity.

Such high-minded reasoning aside, the creature comforts can also be powerfully tempting. Responding to Telecommute America's 1997 Survey, 51% of telecommuters said they wear shoes in their home office only occasionally, while 32% said they never bother with footwear at all. Respondents also listed the ability to work with beloved pets at their feet as a big appeal of the work style. A whopping 38% of those surveyed said that they are able to spend more time with family and friends now that they have eliminated the physical commute to and from a traditional office. Asked what it would take to make them give up telecommuting, 39% of respondents said their employer would have to double salaries, 12% said they'd want a free limo for the commute, 9% said they would demand a corner office, and 36% claimed than **nothing** would make them change the way they work.

I can freely attest to the selfish advantages of working in my SOHO (small office/home office—I like that term because it makes me feel like a trendy NYC artist type). I am writing this essay from the comfort of home, and I didn't have to worry about grooming or dressing or high-tailing it to the office at the all-important moment of truth when inspiration hit me like that shot of adrenaline Uma Thurman got in *Pulp Fiction*. I can sip hot cocoa from my vintage 1960s Adam West *Batman* mug, cue up some nice Elvis Costello or John Coltrane on the CD player, and write in a nurturing atmosphere, surrounded by the things that give me pleasure.

And speaking of pleasure, for all you know, I could be wearing nothing but a pair of fuzzy sheepskin chaps and a grin wide as the mighty Mississippi River while these words are being composed. That outfit probably wouldn't so much as raise an eyebrow at most New Media companies, but I could never get away with wearing it to work on Madison Avenue. Those people wear pin-striped chaps.

The increasing popularity of "casual days" at traditional offices has shown that employees hardly need to get gussied up in uncomfortable "business attire" to get their work done; in fact, the inability to feel relaxed can be highly counter-productive. The majority of teleworkers polled in national surveys say that they typically work in jeans, sweatpants, bathrobes, shorts—some proudly report working in nothing at all—or whatever allows them to feel most comfortable and put their emphasis on work, where it belongs. The hours one saves by not "dressing for the part," along with the time saved by eliminating a physical commute, can easily add an hour or two to the truly productive part of the working day.

There are more frustrations associated with the physical commute than just the incredible waste of time and energy. Telecommuters save wear and tear on personal vehicles, avoid cramming into crowded buses or subways, and take a permanent detour around traffic jams and road construction. Next time you're stuck in traffic or standing on a subway platform during peak commuting hours, take a good look around at the stress on the faces of your fellow travellers. Ask yourself if the harried businessman spilling coffee on his tie as he runs to catch the train or the frenzied businesswoman checking her watch and applying her makeup during gridlock will really be able to arrive at the office refreshed and ready to do their best work.

Working from home also allows telecommuters to run personal errands on breaks during the day (you know, when businesses and government offices are actually open), help get the kids off to school and be there to greet them when they return, spend a few more minutes or hours with a spouse or loved one. Telework can provide enormous flexibility; while it may be necessary to make yourself available to clients or colleagues during traditional office hours via phone or e-mail, the meat of the work can be accomplished at one's own pace and on one's preferred schedule. Not all of us are "morning people," and many find that inspiration can strike at odd times. Telecommuting allows one to take advantage of his or her own natural rhythms and thought patterns. In ideal situations—those where managers are chiefly concerned that work be completed by an agreed-upon deadline—the quality of projects completed can represent a significantly improvement over those dutifully pounded out under duress during traditional the conventional 9-to-5 work day.

And, if you're the sort of person who hugs the occasional tree and fondles wildflowers—or if you're just tired of seeing "air" the colour of a burnt sienna Crayola—you can take comfort in the knowledge that telecommuting reduces air pollution at the same time it relieves road congestion.

THE BAD

Telecommuters save firms huge amounts of money in overhead—you know, pesky things like office space, electricity, furniture, equipment, coffee and doughnuts. And companies like to save money—more loot to go around for the big-wigs and the investors that way. Therefore, more and more people are being expected to have a home office from which they can work exclusively, and that can cause several problems—not the least of which is the realisation that one can't relax at home and leave the pressures of the office behind if the office is the home.

There are, of course, also financial considerations. Equipping an off-site employee with a suitable home office costs, on average, between $4000 and $6000. While that's a drop in the bucket to a Hewlett-Packard or AT&T, it can be a pretty daunting figure for many individuals, particularly if they have no way of knowing whether telecommuting will dovetail with their own work habits until they've tried it. Further, the equipment costs will be higher for an individual than the will be for a mega-corporation with buying clout. And the unfortunate truth is that not all companies are willing to lay out the cash to equip telecommuters.

But what of the work itself? While it would be lovely to report that all workers adapt well to telecommuting, there are in fact several distinct traps into which teleworkers are prone to stumble. The first of these has to do with discipline. While the flexibility to establish one's own schedule is one of the primary perks of telecommuting, the self-management required is not to be underestimated. Telecommuting is just peachy for me, probably because I have a Type A (read: lunatic) personality. But many people with whom I've spoken relate horror stories about their inability to adapt to working away from an office hub; they find that the freedom and flexibility of telework makes it all too easy to procrastinate, and they only manage to finish projects at the last minute, under extreme duress. Many such people **need** a work environment that imposes order and discipline, just as they need feedback and input from supervisors and co-workers. Working from home eliminates most job-related human interaction, and that lack of face time leaves many potentially top-notch employees floundering; telecommuters who don't make tough decisions about their work habits often find that moving off-site reduces their productivity instead of improving it.

While it's nice to escape the distractions of the office and work among creature comforts, easy access to all your cool stuff can be just as distracting as workplace hurly-burly. At the office, it's fairly easy to summon the discipline to get back to work after a break—after all, you can see everyone else doing it. At home it can be tricky to chain yourself to the desk again after taking leisure time, especially if you've taken so much leisure time that your energy and concentration levels have plummeted. If you're one of those easily-distracted types who can't stay away from the coffee pot or office gossip about that new hottie over in accounting, just wait until you have 24-hour access to the telephone, TV, stereo, and refrigerator.

Put in simple terms, no one will know whether you've cracked away on your keyboard all day or spent the afternoon playing Nintendo—but when deadlines and productivity reviews roll around, the ensuing panic means you're likely to be a lot less proud of having found the ultra-secret hidden level on that hot new game. Clearly, the motivation for the telecommuter to work responsibly and safeguard his or her employment must come from the individual.

One of the biggest potential productivity drains with which telecommuters struggle is the presence of children in the home. That telecommuting is not a substitute for childcare cannot be overemphasised. While telework can provide chances to spend more quality time with the kids, perhaps by taking them to and from the school or daycare centre, you're fooling yourself if you think you can work effectively while caring for small children. Most established telework programs such as PacBell's require remote workers to provide full-time care for children under six, which means shelling out the dough for a nanny, a baby-sitter, or a daycare centre.

Many of the most successful telecommuters thrive in solitude. People who choose telecommuting for the right reasons are usually highly disciplined, self-starting employees who genuinely enjoy their work and want to give it all they've got. These are exactly the workers who are most susceptible to the equally nasty problem of overwork. Once they start telecommuting, such workers will have 24-hour access to tasks and projects. The simple presence of the computer at dawn, or midnight, or on weekends and holidays, can become an irresistible temptation for these driven types. Consider too that if you start out working too much, it can be difficult to convince a manager who has been spoiled by your amazing level of output that you need to tighten the reins a bit and find a healthier balance—especially since that manager has no way of knowing exactly how many hours you were overworking and may see your attempts to scale back to a reasonable work week as an attempt to slack.

The same 1997 Telecommute America survey that found a majority of telecommuters happily working barefoot, and unwilling to trade that privilege for anything, also hinted at the problem of creeping workaholism. When asked what they do with the time saved by avoiding the physical commute, the popular answer (39%) was that they work more hours. When asked how many days a week they telecommute, 21% said six to seven. That this was the second highest-ranking response is troubling in light of telework's purported "lifestyle advantages."

Pacific Bell's excellent telecommuting guide cautions potential teleworkers that "working too hard causes stress-related illness, burnout and reduced productivity ... The quality and effectiveness of your work are related to factors far more complex than clock hours." That the guide goes on to suggest that "knowing when to stop is essential to good job performance" is encouraging, but the truth is that some managers are counting on precisely this sort of overwork to squeeze every possible nickel's worth of effort from their employees. One respondent in the Telecommute America survey complained that, although management where this person works is "reluctantly permitting some telecommuting during business hours, employees were aggressively encouraged to telecommute during off-hours." In other words, the fact that employees can potentially dial into the office from the comfort of home—after having already worked a full day on-site—is seen as a convenient excuse to suggest extending the total number of hours worked.

Perhaps one of the most troubling side effects of the availability of cheap electronics is that they are increasingly being used in this manner to place an unreasonable demand on many employees—that they are always available, always on-call, always waiting at the other end of a connection to dial in and produce automatic results. Scott Kendrick, a computer programmer an internationally-respected software firm in Huntsville, Alabama, encountered exactly this problem.

"After my wife and I had our first child a few years ago, I put in a home office," says Kendrick. "My wife owns her own business, and she keeps her shop open late one night a week. Because she's not able to pick our daughter up at daycare on that night, I talked my boss into letting me leave early in exchange for agreeing to telecommute a couple hours later that same evening to finish out my work day. He reluctantly agreed, but once he got used to the idea of me being able to dial in from home, he acted like my computer was some kind of beeper. Now this chucklehead sends e-mails with all sorts of questions and requests on nights and weekends—and gets ticked off if I don't respond right away. Somehow I missed the part of this telecommuting deal where I agreed to sacrifice off-hours with my family, and I can't seem to find just the right way to convince my boss that he's being unreasonable. I'm toying with the idea of replying to each e-mail with the same response—'bite me'—but don't expect that to win me any brownie points." The real problem, as Kendrick sees it, is that "this guy, and this kind of manager, is a workaholic who expects no less from his employees."

Which is precisely why labour unions have strongly resisted the rapid growth of an off-site workforce, characterizing home offices as a disguise for virtual sweatshops. But the truth is that organized labour is fighting a losing battle. As Scott Wilton, former Director of Information Technologies at OfficePlus, a provider of executive suites and shared services explains, "So many big companies are 'forcing' their people to work out of their home, there really isn't much of a social stigma against doing it anymore. The prevailing attitude seems to be that it's better than being downsized out of a job."

If Wilton is right, corporations have an unfair advantage in this age of downsizing, rightsizing, and other Orwellian euphemisms for sacrificing all final vestiges of traditional job security and community participation. Because the corporation must look suitably lean and mean for its shareholders and potential investors, the rank and file are highly disposable commodities and the bottom line is God. If it can, a corporation will reduce its outlay for employees support to almost nothing, as long as someone, anyone, will do the work, for whatever real or imagined benefits.

THE PROPER BALANCE

I am hardly a Luddite; in fact, I get rather a geeky thrill from trying out the latest electronic gadgets and gee-whiz software applications. Technological advance is not a bad thing, but some of its implementations border on the inhumane. While the information age allows us to work harder, smarter, faster, it also requires more and more from us to keep up with advances, to constantly improve and refine our work techniques, to stay wired and connected, to merge with the machine. At some point, it really seems that there should be a reward for the workers who are taking on all of this responsibility, a chance to sow the rewards of their endless striving at ultimate efficiency. One such reward, which is entirely possible, is shortening rather than lengthening the work week. Of course, employers will argue that shortening the work week is too costly and would threaten their ability to compete both domestically and abroad. But that need not be so. Many European companies, including Hewlett-Packard in France and BMW in Germany, have used technological advances and increased efficiency to reduce their work week while continuing to pay workers at the same weekly rate. In return, the workers have agreed to work shifts, more of which have been scheduled, resulting in higher output. By operating high-tech work places on a 24-hour basis—rather than expecting employees to be in call around the clock, these companies can double or triple productivity, afford to pay workers the same wages, and still make enormous profits.

In my own life, despite finding occasional telecommuting to be useful, I have worked hard (and thus far been successful) at drawing a line against the idea of constant electronic access. Cell phones, beepers, digital pagers, laptop computers—I've resisted becoming dependent upon these gizmos for many years, largely due to my strong aversion to being too terribly easy to find. Call me paranoid if you like (I prefer Mr. Paranoid), but I treasure the moments when I can leave the pressures of the job behind and have some privacy. I used to be very alarmed by those AT&T adverts in which the yuppie business guy would receive a fax or an important e-mail on the beach in Aruba as a voice-over narrator rhapsodised about the marvels of being wired for input 24/7. I fail to see what's so damned great about that—and if I ever manage to get my happy ass on some of that tropical white sand, I'm going to be harvesting sea shells, not information.

As I said, it's not that I don't get off on gadgetry and convenience as much as the next land mammal—it's just that I think they have their place. And those rare times when I'm able to get away to enjoy nature or the theatre or an art exhibition or the company of good friends—well, that is not an acceptable time or place to interrupt my hard-won serenity. Very few emergencies can't wait a couple of hours until I'm back in work mode.

I am constantly amazed to see people all around me, hunched over their PowerBooks and ThinkPads, functioning like empty vessels awaiting information, always more information. Whenever I fly these days I see folks plugging their laptop computers into phone jacks on the seat in front of them and computing away, oblivious to their surroundings. Sometimes I can almost imagine a guy in a Brooks Brothers suit standing at the head of the galley, cracking a whip over the backs of his worker drone slaves like some brute from an old Viking movie.

That vision may or may not be the result of all that Celestial Seasonings tea I ingested back in the '70s, but it is, nonetheless, more than a little unsettling. I used to enjoy talking to my fellow passengers on planes. Remember that? Conversation without computers? In the age of chat, e-mail, videoconferencing, and the "avatar realm" of the Palace, such a notion probably seems quaint as a horse-drawn honeywagon. But people once enjoyed having conversations with each other, making new friends and acquaintances, debating and probing ideas and issues, perhaps even find ways of doing business together—face to face. Weird, huh? It's hard to imagine these slaves to technology ever relaxing enough to have a meaningful exchange, at home or anywhere else.

Which may explain why I often feel more alive and vibrant during my visits to bustling downtowns, whether they be in New York City, Edmonton, or Toronto. There, among the bums and winos and hipsters, I am reminded that most North Americans still aren't living exclusively in the digital domain. A loud and pungent wave of women and men from all walks of life refuses to be confined to the world that is visible on a monitor. In such surroundings, one has to step lively, to remain alert and aware of the physical surroundings at every moment—but quite frankly, despite the jokes and eye-rolling about the dangers of the city, I find its challenges preferable to being in the company of zombies who can't pry their eyes away from the computer screen for fear of losing their supposed "edge."

In an ideal world, the time we spend working would be proportional to how efficiently we can do our jobs—the less time it takes for us to do our jobs, the more time we should have for leisure activities and family. Perhaps the best way to make that ideal a reality is to become active in one of the fast-growing telework advocacy groups, such as the International Homeworkers Association (http://www.homeworkers.org/iha.htm) or the International Telework Association (http://www.telecommute.org). But for employees working in the home without direct supervision, the real responsibility for striking the right balance between work and private life belongs to the individual. When you become a telecommuter, you are becoming a trailblazing pioneer on a new frontier, the boundaries of which are still being defined.

Make sure you're ready, pardner.

Janice MacDonald

Janice MacDonald is a western Canadian writer who has written everything from musical scores to mystery novels. Her recent book titles include *The Next Margaret* and *The Ghouls' Night Out*. She has served her fellow writers on the boards of the Canadian Authors Association and The WordWorks Society of Alberta. She lectures on Communications and English Literature at Grant MacEwan Community College, in Edmonton.

Enough third person gibberish. This article was commissioned by *Tripod.com*, because the editor had read a personal essay on the topic that I had tossed onto my homepage. The lesson to be had here, I believe, is, while I am leery of placing too much that is not already sold onto the Net, sometimes one has to offer a free sample in order to make a sale.

Brave New Neighbourhoods: Net Communities

Long ago, Marshall McLuhan spoke of the "global village." As a child hearing this, I envisioned a town made up entirely of little geodesic-domed houses. Now, I wonder if he truly foresaw what has come to be, a world in which a woman from Chicago logs on to her computer of an evening to connect with her best friends ... in California, Singapore and Canada. The Internet has brought more than a plethora of information to our home computers; it has brought us the world.

Ann Landers, that purveyor of wet-noodled moral righteousness, has made it clear what she thinks of personal interaction on the Internet. She and her followers hold up evidence of cyber infidelity and castigate the Net as a tool of the Devil. News stories proliferate: of a woman meeting up to discover that her on-line enamorata is not a healthy lusty man, but a dying woman with her chest bound; of people engaging in suicide pacts with folks they've never laid eyes on; of men baring their souls to enchantresses who turn out to be thirteen-year-old boys. While I am sure there are kernels of truth in all these stories (and that alligators roam the sewers of New York City), they strike me as so many wooden shoes thrown in the looms which are weaving the fabric of new societies.

Yes, I love the Internet. I would even go so far to say the Internet has saved my life. And like any zealot, I can trot out myriad examples of the terrific uses of chat rooms and newsgroups. I'm not about to climb into a pair of Nikes and check the comet schedule, though. I know there are misuses of the Net, and pitfalls to any interaction, be it on-line or line dancing at the local saloon. I would like to make a case, however, for the distinction between chat rooms and true Net communities. Each has their place, but the blurring of the two in the minds of non-cyber savvy folk is what causes the confusion (and causes the phone calls from everyone's Aunt Martha who wants to be sure no axe murderer is coming for us the moment we've logged in).

As a fellow chatter once said, "A common URL doesn't constitute community." Some chat sites evolve into such, depending on a special magic that occurs between regulars willing to invest a certain level of honesty and vulnerability to their connections. Some, either because of too large a transient flow, or the negative energy of some participants, never make it past the nightclub stage. And sometimes, regardless of the best intentions of the regulars and volunteer administrators, all it takes is one deviant or two to undermine an entire group. When Jeffrey Dahmer moves in, there goes the neighbourhood.

From what I've experienced, true community on the Net has a frontier mentality to it. People bond for various reasons, the foremost being shared time together. Chatters loyal to one site soon find other regulars to greet with the requisite asterisked action, a *hug,* *smile* or *grin.* As time goes on, they share things: the purchase of a faster modem, or a new car; the arrival of a baby; the decree nisi of a harrowing divorce. These people may initially have nothing more in common than on-line access and a desire to communicate, but eventually they build a history together, and emerge as a diverse and complimentary society. It's a lot like moving into a new neighbourhood, without ever having to carpool.

This concept is throwing anthropologists for a loop, in that the primary definition of "community" is shared location and/or background. Net communities have anything but. We worry about monsoon season in Malaysia, and whether El Niño will stop battering the Eastern Seaboard long enough to give Northern Alberta enough snow for tobogganing. We bemoan the treatment of women in Afghanistan, discuss the relative merit of Dodge Neons over Ford Escorts, and admit to the stupidest clothing fad we've ever succumbed to in the course of an evening's conversation. We celebrate the straight As of children we've never met; we send "virtual chicken soup" to sick friends; and we tease people mercilessly over malapropisms and typos. We send each other zany snail mail cards, birthday presents and Christmas/Hanukkah/Kwanzaa gifts. We observe Yom Kippur,

Ramadan, and Groundhog Day. We are sixteen years old, or maybe we're sixty-three, and it doesn't matter. As long as one can express themselves in an interesting manner, there is a level playing field. In fact, in our town, an ability to punctuate properly wins out over a body that won't quit any day of the week.

Many of us save our money and Air Miles to meet in person. Some of us holiday together. Some of us fall in love. Some of us marry. And while that might sound ludicrous or spooky to the uninitiated, think about this. People who conduct a romance on-line spend on the average about two hours a day (not counting e-mails) talking to each other. Talking. About issues, about feelings, about ideals, about memories, about goals. All the courtship time taken up in the soulful gazing into each others' eyes (which, granted, most on-line couples would give their eye teeth to experience) is used for much more intellectually and emotionally filled communication. I have no doubt that I already know more about the man I am planning to spend the rest of my life with (with whom I have spent more time on-line than off) than the stranger I was married to for eleven years.

The greatest criticism that is levelled at on-line communities is that becoming enmeshed in one somehow isolates you from the real world. The sad response to this argument is that this world is a pretty cold place for a lot of people. You don't have to be stuck in a trapper's cabin to feel the fever. It is just as isolating being a frighteningly clever high school student in a world of party animal drones, or an unappreciated housewife, or a telecommuter without a coffee room to head to on a break. I know an older man who only buys enough groceries for a couple of days at a time, even though he has a car and could get better value buying in greater quantities. Why? Because sometimes the grocery clerk is the only person he speaks to over the course of a day.

Imagine being a newly separated woman with children. Monetarily, you can't afford to get a babysitter and go out for the evening. Psychologically, you can't take the silence, or the need to air your feelings. Morally, you can't talk to people on the phone for fear of your children overhearing something that might paint their father in a bad light. Earlier, I spoke of the Net saving my life. Well, that woman was me. Dazed and lost, and relatively new to the chat experience, I was taken under the wing of two women who knew exactly what I was going through. They consoled, they counselled, and they cajoled me out of my valley. Because they were there, my real-time friends don't cringe when they see me coming, my children have weathered one of life's greater traumas unscathed, and I've saved literally hundreds of dollars in mascara and café lattes.

As a result, and because of the many other wonderful people I've since met on-line, I am a firm believer in the on-line community, the true global village. From where I sit, here in front of my monitor, I am in the centre of a vibrant, brave new world. Who could have imagined that Edmonton, Alberta, would one day be a common reference point for people as far-flung as Cyprus, Melbourne or Massachusetts? Well, I suppose Marshall McLuhan did. After all, he was born right here, in my home town.

Marshall McLuhan

Marshall McLuhan was born in Edmonton, Alberta. He is world-famous as the "guru" of the media age, and his cryptic aphorisms have entered common speech at all levels. While this essay (from the *Antigonish Review*) is not about the Internet, per se, it would be unconscionable to examine this new media without a word from the man who envisioned it all.

The Role of New Media in Social Change

From the Neolithic age until the advent of electromagnetic technology men have been busy extending their bodies technologically. The fragmentation of work and social action that results from specialized extensions of the body has been given close study by Lynn White, in his *Medieval Technology and Social Change*.[1] He opens with a consideration of the stirrup as it modified social organization in the early Middle Ages. As an extension of the foot, the stirrup enabled men to wear armor on horseback. Man became a sort of tank. But armor was expensive. It required the work and skill of a craftsman for a year to turn out a full suit of armor. The small farmer could not pay for such armor. The result was a change in the entire landholding pattern. The Feudal System was spurred into existence by the stirrup, the mere extension of the foot.

The extensions of hand and arm and back that made up the industrial complex of the eighteenth and nineteenth centuries were meshed with Gutenberg technology to create the great team efforts of assembly-line patterns of work and production. But the industrial complex was based on specialist fragmentation of tasks and extensions of the body which carried to an extreme the division of labor that had begun in the Neolithic period in about 3000 B.C.

A totally different kind of extension occurred with the application of electromagnetism to social organization. Electricity enabled us to extend the central nervous system itself. It is a biological kind of event that creates maximal involvement of each of us in the total social process. Electric speed tends to abolish time and space in human awareness. There is no delay in the effect of one event upon another. The electric extension of the nervous system creates the unified field of organically interrelated structures that we call the present Age of

---

[1] Lynn White, *Medieval Technology and Social Change* (Oxford University Press, 1962).

Information. With the reduction of time and space in the pattern of events there is not only a great increase in the amount of data for daily experience, but action and reaction tend to become fused. Whereas in the previous technologies of fragmented extensions of the body there had been typically a considerable gap in time between social action and the ensuing consequences and reactions, this gap of time has almost disappeared. We are confronted with a situation that invites simultaneous or configurational and ecological awareness instead of the older awareness of sequential and linear cause and effect. In the mechanical age of the wheel and the lever, acceleration had expanded and enlarged the sphere of action. At electric or instant speeds the same sphere contracts almost to the dimensions of a single consciousness. Listening to a concert with an eminent psychologist, I happened to mention the highly tactile character of orchestral strings as compared with the other instruments. He seemed quite surprised and asked: "Do you mean that an auditory experience can have a tactile component?" Discussing the matter with him later, it became apparent that many psychologists assume that not only is auditory experience merely auditory, but so with the other senses. Visual experience is merely visual, etc. Thus, in such a view, there would be little difference in the experience and effects of TV and movies. And indeed many students of the media assume that it is the content of media, whether of the sung word, spoken word, the written word, that really matters. It is this sort of assumption that has tended to divert attention away from the forms and parameters of the media themselves. The sensory modalities of the media as such have not been studied. The very idea of "content" which obsesses us, on the other hand, is unknown to non-literate societies. Our Western divisions between form and content occur with literacy and because of literacy. Literacy is itself a work of intense visual stress in a culture. When men begin to translate the speech complex into a visual code they have already opted for a division of labor that affects the whole society. They have become settled and have begun to specialize. Writing is impossible for man the food-gatherer but it is inevitable for Neolithic man, the agriculturalist.

In his monumental study of *The Beginnings of Architecture*, Siegfried Giedion has many occasions to comment on the fact that before script there is no architecture. Until man intensifies the visual parameters of his life by writing, he cannot *enclose* space. Before writing, man resorts to hollowed-out spaces. The parameters of hollowed-out space are mainly tactile, kinetic, and auditory. The visual components of the cave are minimal. Such proprioceptive space is almost like that of clothing, an immediate extension of our bodies. In our own electric age, space for the physicist has become a non-visual thing of complex stresses. It is no longer uniform and continuous but diverse and heterogeneous. On the other hand, when Newton's physics first entered the European ken, Pascal moaned: "The eternal silence of these infinite spaces terrifies me." Before Newton our Western space orientation had had a much smaller visual parameter but the auditory components of space-structure had been very high. With the advent of the printed word, the visual modalities of Western life increased beyond anything experienced in any previous society. The parameters of the visual as such are continuity, uniformity and connectedness. These are not the notes or modes of any of our other senses. Today, when our electric technologies have extended far more than our visual faculties, the parameters of sense experience in the Western world have been radically altered. Our new media—the telephone, the telegraph and radio and television—are extensions of the nervous system.

I suggest that the sensory typology of an entire population is directly altered by each and every new extension of the body or of the senses. Each extension is an amplification that in varying but measurable degrees, alters the hierarchy of sensory preference in ordering daily experience and environment for whole populations.

Thus, it is an ancient observation, that was repeated by Henri Bergson, that speech is a technology of extension that amplified man's power to store and exchange perceptual knowledge; but it interrupted the sharing of a unified collective consciousness experienced by pre-verbal man. Before speech, it is argued, men possessed a large measure of extra-sensory perceptions which was fragmented by speech technology.

Until electro-magnetism over a century ago, all the extensions of man appear as fragmentary. Tools and weapons, clothing and housing, as much as the wheel, or letters, are direct, specialist extensions of our bodies that amplify and channel energies in a specialist and fragmented way. Today much study is being devoted to the micro-climates created for our bodies by clothing. Some measurements indicate that unclad societies eat 40 percent more than those that are clad. As a technology of physical extensions, clothing channels time and energies for special tasks. It also changes the patterns of sensory perception and awareness; and nudity has very different meanings in different cultures. So it is with all the other extensions of ourselves.

The problem of dichotomy between form and content, that troubles and confuses our Western perception of media today, is now beginning to yield to new awareness of structures, of total fields in interplay, and to ecological approaches in general. We still need to develop awareness of the pervasive visual parameters and assumptions that phonetic literacy had imposed upon Western culture for 2000 years. Today, even the physicist is often hampered by his unconscious visual bias. This bias is utterly inhibiting to the physicist since his data are almost entirely non-visual. It is thus not at all accidental that physics is mainly cultivated by men from cultural areas in which visual values are at a minimum. The unfortunate effects of highly literate culture on the state of the physical sciences is a theme of Milic Capek's *The Philosophical Impact of Contemporary Physics*. In the West our intense visual bias and our habit of considering form and content as quite separate derives from the structure of the phonetic alphabet. There is only one such alphabet, among the many kinds of scripts. And the unique property of our alphabet that is unknown to the Chinese or to the Egyptian is its power to separate sound, sight and meaning. The letters of our alphabet are semantically neutral. They can translate the words of any language. But they translate them by semantically meaningless sounds into semantically meaningless visual symbols. This divorce between the visual code and the semantic structure has gradually permeated and shaped all the perceptions of Western literate man.

We have long stressed content and ignored form in communication. But this visual and literate structuring of our perceptions has provided us with very little accompanying immunity to the effects of non-visual form. We were amused in 1900 when the Chinese protested that vertical telegraph poles would upset the psychic equilibrium of their people. We still imagine that the effects of radio depend upon radio programs. Yet such literate assumptions were no protection against Fascism. When radio began in Europe it awakened the ancient tribal energies in their auditory depths, as radio does today in backward countries. The auditory form of radio has, of course, a quite different effect in literate societies from its effect in oral and auditory cultures. Intensely visual and industrial cultures like England and America had few remaining tribal roots and vestiges to be re-energized by the tribal drum of radio. Where such roots still existed as in Ireland, Wales and Scotland, there were marked tribal stirrings and revivals. In the more urban and industrialized England and America radio was mainly felt as a resurgence of the folk arts of jazz and song and dancing. In areas like Germany, where tribal experience had been retained by many linguistic and artistic means, radio meant a revival of mystic forms of togetherness and depth involvement that has not been forgotten.

In the same way, the effect of TV has been very different in Europe and in the U.S.A. The TV image of "mosaic" as it is named by the TV engineers, has a quite different sensory character and effect from the movie and photographic image. The mosaic of the TV image provides, structurally, an experience of what J.J. Gibson calls "active or exploratory touch" as opposed to passive or cutaneous touch.[2]

The TV mosaic created by the "scanning finger" is visually of low definition, making for maximal involvement of the viewer. The painters after Cézanne, in the 1860s, deliberately set about to endow the retinal impression with tactual values.[3] In order to involve their audience maximally they resorted to various low-definition visual effects, many of which anticipated the typical form of the TV image. They achieved an effect described by J.J. Gibson in his experiments when he reports, "The paradox is even more striking, for tactual perception corresponds well to the form of the object when the stimulus is almost formless, and less well when the stimulus is a stable representation of the form of the object. A clear unchanging perception arises when the flow of sense impressions changes most."[4]

At the same time as Monet and Seurat and Rouault were dimming the visual parameters of art in order to achieve maximal audience participation, the symbolists were demonstrating the superiority of suggestion over statement in poetry. The same principle obtains on the telephone as compared with radio. The auditory image of the telephone is of low definition. It elicits maximal attention and cannot be used as background. All the senses rally to strengthen the weak sound of the phone. We even feel the need to be kinetically involved via doodling or pacing. And whereas we complete the strong auditory image of radio by visualizing, we only slightly visualize on the phone.

Dr. Llewellyn-Thomas has used the Mackworth head-camera to study the eye-movements of children watching TV. There is great significance in his discovery that the eyes of the child never waiver

---

[2]J.J. Gibson, "Observations on Active Touch," *Psychological Review* 69, 6 (November, 1962): 477–91.
[3]E.H. Gombrich, *Art and Illusion,* 18.
[4]Gibson, "Observations on Active Touch," 487–88.

from the faces of the actors even in scenes of violence. Maximal involvement is experienced not in the actions of the scene but in the *reactions* of the actors in the scenes. The result is the same as the one recorded by J.J. Gibson concerning tactual perception as most adequate when the stimulus was almost formless. That is, exploratory touch comes into play as the visual parameter is dimmed. It is a normal feature of the comics. Cartoons and comics are visually very dim affairs. The amount of visual data provided is small. But involvement or exploratory touch is at a maximum. Leo Bogart's study of "comic strips and their Adult Readers"[5] observes how comic strip humor seems to produce a grim, unsmiling kind of amusement for the most part. "Genuine hearty laughs seem to be few and far between." Once more, the involvement is high in these forms just in proportion as the intensity of the stimulus is vague and weak. The same comic scenes projected in high visual definition on a movie screen would evoke much more overt response.

Most people were struck by the TV coverage of the Kennedy assassination. We were all conscious of great depth of involvement, but there was no excitement, no sensationalism. When involvement is maximal, we are nearly numb.

One of the notable effects of the TV image on those in the primary grades seems to be the development of near-point reading. The average distance from the page of children in the first three grades has recently been measured in Toronto by Dr. W.A. Hurst. The average distance is 6 1/2 inches. The children seem to be striving to do a psychomimetic version of their relation to the TV image. They seem to be trying to read by proprioception and exploratory touch. The printed page, however, is of high definition visually and cannot so be apprehended.

It isn't only the act of reading that conflicts with habits of TV perception. I wish to suggest that the depth involvement characteristic of TV viewing discourages the traditional habit and need of "seeing ahead." The TV child today cannot see ahead, in a motivational sense, just because he is so deeply involved. He needs a totally new pedagogy and a new curriculum that will accommodate his shifting sensory ratios and his natural drive towards depth participation since TV. This returns us to the theme that our Western preference for considering the content of media instead of their configurational features is itself a bias of perception derived from the form of phonetic

---

[5]In Mass Culture (The Free Press of Glencoe, 1957), 189–99.

literacy. I do not need to be reminded of how much we owe to literacy. It has given us our way of life. It separated the individual from the tribal horde. I suggest that if we value this legacy of literacy, we shall need to take steps to maintain its existence by a fuller understanding of the role of new media in social change. Autonomy and freedom are best secured by a grasp of the new parameters of our condition. I would meet you upon this exponentially, as the mathematicians put it.

1988

CHAPTER TEN: REVIEWS AND CRITIQUES

Being a book reviewer is the best job in the world. You are sent loads of brand new books, and paid to read them. Of course, you are required to sit down and write about them as well, but that is not such an onerous task. It is, however, one that has to be taken seriously, and, as a reviewer, you have certain responsibilities that must be considered. The job of a reviewer is to be the official taster of the court for readers. We have to pre-read books to determine where the unwary reader should spend his hard-earned money. While this sounds relatively simple, there are various things to consider.

For instance, while it is a simple matter to read one book an editor sends you and respond with a review, what happens if you are a reviewer with a column? This means that you have some decision in what gets into that column, and you have to cull five or six titles a month from a shelf of about fifty new releases. What do you choose?

In my column writing days, my decision was to pile up all the Canadian books for sorting, since I wrote for a Canadian newspaper, and we were likely to be the only ones to give those books a chance. I looked as well for books by well-known authors, promising books by unknown authors, books that people would see everywhere and wonder about, books that people might overlook otherwise. Even with those criteria in place, it is impossible to review every book that comes out. One has to hope that, with different reviewers in each newspaper and magazine, most worthwhile books receive mention. Unfortunately, with the homogenization of our newspapers, this is becoming less likely. Book pages are suffering, fewer reviewers are contracted, and both readers and writers are being shortchanged as a result. However, it was a great gig while it lasted, and our house is now rated R40 because of all the bookcases lining the walls.

It is after about sixteen years of professional reviewing that I finally feel qualified to speak about the distinctions between reviews and critiques. In all that time, I only ever received one letter to the editor complaining about a review where I had panned the man's favourite author. It consisted of a death threat because it seemed that I was a "feminist." I was so pleased that someone was actually reading my column that I cut it out and pinned it up on my bulletin board. After all, everyone's a critic, no? In short, no. Some of us are reviewers.

A review is an aesthetic barometer, a gauge by which a potential consumer decides whether to buy a book or CD, or a ticket to a movie or play. A good review will include a brief description of the work which doesn't reveal the surprise ending or any of the really great bits (unless you hated it, in which case it is particularly devilish to reveal the ending). Also useful is a comparison which ranks the work in terms of other works by the same author, or other works in that particular genre ("his best book ever," or "a worthy successor to the noir school of writing created by Hammett and Chandler"); and some indication of how you as a reviewer found the book ("a great beach read," "one of those books you know is good for you, even if it's heavy going," "the greatest coming-of-age novel since *Catcher in the Rye*"). With these indicators, your reader can ascertain whether or not she too will want to read that particular book.

A reviewer whom you trust is worth her weight in gold. Books, while still the most worthwhile item on which to spend your money, are expensive, and having someone who shares your concept of quality is wonderful. It takes time for trial and error to find a useful reviewer. You have to read each consistently, read some of the books they've reviewed, and see how your tastes and rationales align. Most of the best reviewers will reveal a bit of themselves, their own biases and backgrounds, which might explain their take on certain books. This is helpful when we are trying to ascertain, as readers, if we share like interests and yardsticks of excellence. However, no matter whether you think a reviewer accurate or not, if she is consistent, she is still of value to you as a reader/consumer. If you consistently disagree with her choices, you are still ahead of the game, because you know that whatever she likes you can avoid, and whatever she belittles you can safely rush right out and enjoy.

A critique is another thing altogether, although it does share some similarities with a review. It also gives some indication of the story, and occasionally reveals much more than the reviewer would dare. Where a reviewer tends to rate a work, for the public to decide for themselves, a critic contextualizes the work, placing it in a position relative to all other works of that particular art form. It is more useful to read a review PRIOR to seeing or reading the work described; one gets more from a critique AFTER having seen or read the work yourself.

Critics often get called parasites or "wannabe" artists, but this is unkind and truly unfair. A good critic is not a failed artist, or a writer who couldn't make the grade. A good critic is a highly trained reader. Well versed in the artform at hand, a critic has worked diligently to become the ideal reader, the absolute consumer of the work of art; in many ways, the artist is working to communicate with the ultimate critic. We need critics to help us digest and discover the hidden nuances of a work of art, and to give us added insight into works we have enjoyed or puzzled over.

When asked to write a critique, you may assume that your reader has already seen or read the work you are about to dissect. You are free to mention anything pertinent in the book, even the ending, if it is necessary to your argument. Your argument will follow one of various routes. You may argue that this work is unoriginal and adds nothing to the body of work already created. A good way to prove this is to show it as being similar without innovation to other books already existing. Or you may argue that this is going to become a classic of its kind, that it breaks with tradition in ways that shed new light on the topic. In order to prove any critical argument, you must have a background of knowledge in the field, or various expert opinions to draw from. Most often, if a college essay topic requires a "review" of a text, what is really being asked for is a studied critique.

I am, of course, assuming, above, that you are writing a critique of a new title. When you are asked to critique an established work, another thing that has to be considered in your assessment is the works of other critics on the same text. It is still safe to assume that your reader will have read the work in question, but you may have to allow some room to explicate the positions of critics with whom you have decided to either agree or differ. There is a danger of losing sight of the primary text in situations like this, and allowing your critique to segue into an argument with another critic. This is rarely fruitful. Try to stay faithful to your initial intent, which is to bring deeper resonances to the reading of the work to your reader.

Another danger for both reviewers and critics is that it is much easier to write about a bad book than a good book. This is because we are much more able to determine what we didn't like about something than what we enjoyed. Think of someone you dislike. Can you make a list of all the things you dislike about them? They sneer at people, they chew their food annoyingly, they don't bathe. Try to limit yourself to one page in the interest of time. Now, think of someone you love. Why do you love them? It's not easy, is it? It's more than the sum of the parts, there is some amorphous quality that can't be defined.

Now, back to that list of items about the person we despise. As a reviewer or a critic, we have to be sensitive to becoming too caustic about things we don't like. Sometimes, when we have found a particularly biting commentary, it is useful to ask ourselves if we really feel this strongly about the work in question, or whether we have merely fallen in love with our own cleverness. It is sometimes too easy to scribble "trees died needlessly for this book," when what is required is a more thoughtful reasoning behind our distaste. Much like dissecting a problematic argument to determine if all the premises are true, you must search for what it is in particular that disturbs you about the book. Is it the story itself (what is being told)? Or something within the narrative (how it is being told)? Or is there a structural problem? Is it a matter of the quality of the writing (all the characters sound the same, there are obvious inaccuracies in the research, the tone doesn't fit the tenor of the subject matter)? Could it be that the subject matter is one that you personally harbour a distaste for? If that is so, you have to address that within your criticisms of the work, to be fair to the writer, and to your readers.

Conversely, it is difficult to pinpoint what is great about greatness. If a work of art moves you to some strong emotion, logic and reasoning seem to fly out the window. At times like this, it is useful to rummage about in your bag of rhetorical strategies and examine what it was that managed to create the mood you've been left with. Examine the structure of the narrative. See what is underpinning your reaction to the work. Perhaps a dreamlike quality has been evoked. How was that achieved? Through imagery? Through narrative flashbacks? Maybe you identified strongly with the protagonist. Did the writer use a lot of dialogue that allowed you access through a similar vernacular? If the work was disturbing and you found it hard to shake yourself back into the real world after finishing it, how was that created? Was the author allowing himself to be vulnerable through some painful honesties? Were taboos of what it is acceptable to discuss broken? Discussing the work at that level will possibly illuminate the causes of your emotional response, and offer your reader a chance to see the craft behind the magic.

The various reviews and critiques in this section haven't been divided into each camp. It is up to you to determine what purpose they fulfill. Ask yourself if you would glean more from them if you have already read or seen the work discussed. That is the best indicator between the two forms of critical writing. See for yourself which writer would be most useful to you as a barometer of aesthetic judgment. Learn to question the responses and reactions of the writer, given what you know of the work discussed, and what insight you are given into the reviewer's or critic's own makeup.

Start reading the Books section of your local paper. Check out the movie and theatre reviews. Not only will you become a more savvy consumer when it comes to your entertainment budget, you will also be reading some of the best writing around. After all, you don't really believe we writers can survive on our royalties alone, do you?

Rita Donovan

Rita Donovan is a Montreal-born, Ottawa-based writer and editor. She is the author of five award-winning novels: *Dark Jewels* (1990), *Daisy Circus* (1991), *Landed* (1997), *The Plague Saint* (1997), and *River Sky Summer* (1998). She recently edited *Quintet* (Buschek Books, 1998—a collection of prose and poetry by five Ottawa writers). She is also the author of short stories, reviews, and criticism. She is co-editor of *Arc: Canada's National Poetry Magazine*. Donovan was the 1998 recipient of the Canadian Authors Association/Chapters Award for Fiction and has twice (in 1991 and 1993) won the Ottawa Carleton Book Award. She also teaches a creative writing course on the Internet.

Donovan has a BA (Magna cum laude) from Concordia University (Loyola) and an MA from the University of Alberta. She is married with one daughter.

This piece first appeared in *Books in Canada*, Vol. XXI, no. 3, April 1992.

A Fine Romance

The Republic of Love
by Carol Shields

Carol Shields a romance writer? In her latest novel, *The Republic of Love*, Shields takes the reader on a foray into the cold landscape of the late 20th century. Her two protagonists, Fay McLeod and Tom Avery, personably document their respective states: Fay, a recently involved, now single folklorist who is studying the mermaid myth, and Tom, a lonely late-night talk-show host with three failed marriages under his belt. That they will meet and fall in love is inevitable; it is the stuff of romance novels. And, indeed, it is one of the devices Shields purposely adopts from the genre.

Technically, the book is crisply divided into parallel chapters alternating the narratives of Fay and Tom. Their stories progress separately, although minor characters familiar to them both pass from narrative to narrative. Roughly halfway through the book, Fay and Tom meet and fall immediately in love. Interestingly, although their lives now interweave, the narrative threads of their stories are kept separate, presumably to allow the reader to assess Fay through Tom's eyes and Tom through Fay's. This very successfully gives Shields ample room for irony.

Because of these structural decisions, the essential isolation of each character is underlined. Indeed, loneliness is one of the predominant themes in the novel. It contrasts with the longing for independence that several characters exhibit (Fay's father among them), and Shields also explores this duality—the consolatory woman figure and the impenetrable female, the essentially contradictory nature of the psyche—in describing Fay's mermaid research.

We see the loneliness. Tom is afraid of Friday nights. Fay is afraid to go home to an empty apartment. As Tom notes: "Misery does not love company. The lonely can do very little for each other. Emptiness does not serve emptiness."

Is romance possible under these circumstances? And what is romance, anyway? And what is love? These questions plague the citizens of *The Republic of Love*, and they are the basis for what surrounds the bare-boned story of Tom and Fay. No one seems to have definitive answers to these simple questions (simple if you live in a romance novel). Fay asks, "What does it mean to be a romantic in the last decade of the twentieth century?" Her brother Clyde answers "To believe anything can happen to us." Later Fay's father says almost the same thing: "You never know what's going to happen. What's just around the corner." This nicely complements a thought Tom has as he ponders that, despite his problems, "he wakes up most mornings believing that he is about to enter a period of good fortune."

Is this *naïveté*? As if Fay's Tom's own existences aren't enough to convince them, all around they witness the wreckage of love, the compromises that have been made. Fay looks to her parents' settled life and finds it suffocating (yet, ironically, will later be distraught when her father leaves her mother). Fay says, "No one should settle for being half-happy." And her friend answers, "Really?" As Fay later observes: "The lives of others baffle her, especially the lives of couples." Yet despite the evidence of disastrous manifestations of love, Fay and Tom *believe*. This is underlined in Fay's folklore studies, for example, when she describes folk credulity: "Believers ... develop an aptitude for belief, a willed innocence."

This optimism is certainly part of most "romances," and Fay and Tom fall as completely in love as any couple in a romance novel. The *naïveté* seems somehow necessary in order for the couple to begin to love at all. Both characters talk about being "alive" when love comes to them. Fay speaks of "the ballooning sensation of being intensely alive," and Tom notes: "So this is what it feels like. To be coming awake."

They try their best to live up to the old-fashioned versions of love. But Fay and Tom don't live on the pages of a Harlequin romance, and Fay observes that while everyone seems to be searching for love,

love itself is not taken seriously: "It's not respected." And the world intrudes, as it always will.

Theirs, then, must be an "open-eyed" romanticism; they must choose to love, just as they must choose to believe. Contrary to the cynical world around them, and contrary also to the naïve vision in old movies and romance novels, they must create a life that does not deny dead marriages and dying friends, while also not denying the liberating "coming to life" that their love inspires.

Without these qualifications, Shields would have given us a charming tale with little direct bearing on the times. But Fay and Tom earn their right to love. They know the stakes, and they know the odds. So when Shields allows them to honeymoon in Tom's apartment and the storm outside "maroons" them there, the reader feels that they are entitled to their brief stay on their "island," before the world lays claim to them.

Carol Shields has created a sophisticated story in the romance of Fay and Tom. And the "happy ending," so traditional to the romance novel, is here refurbished, updated, and—most happily—earned.

Robertson Davies

Robertson Davies (b 28 Aug 1913; d 2 Dec 1995) was an outstanding essayist and brilliant novelist. His works include: *The Diary of Samuel Marchbanks*, *The Table Talk of Samuel Marchbanks* and *Samuel Marchbanks' Almanack*, *One Half of Robertson Davies*, *The Enthusiasms of Robertson Davies*, *The Well-Tempered Critic*, *Tempest-Tost*, *Leaven of Malice* (which won the Stephen Leacock Medal for Humour), *A Mixture of Frailties*, *Fifth Business*, *The Manticore* (which won the Governor General's Award for fiction), *World of Wonders*, *The Rebel Angels*, *What's Bred in the Bone*, *The Mirror of Nature*, *The Lyre of Orpheus*, *Murther and Walking Spirits*, and *The Cunning Man*.

Celebrated and revered, he was the first Canadian to become an Honorary Member of the American Academy and Institute of Arts and Letters. As well, he received an Honorary D. Litt from Oxford and was a Companion of the Order of Canada.

His piece on *A Christmas Carol* appears in *The Merry Heart: Selections 1980-1995.*

An Unlikely Masterpiece

A Christmas Carol by Charles Dickens

That Dickens's novella *A Christmas Carol* is a masterpiece there can be no doubt. But I have given my address the title "An Unlikely Masterpiece," and you may very well wonder why. It is because the little book offends against every canon of conventional criticism, and if it were to be published today we can imagine the harsh terms with which it would be greeted. "Ill-constructed"; "absurd extravagances of character"; "maudlin sentimentality"; "total failure to find and adhere to a single tone of the authorial voice"; "unmistakable signs of haste in wrapping up the plot"; "vulgarity of diction interspersed with rhetorical wooden thunder"; "total failure to comprehend the economic infrastructure of the modern world"; "an affront equally to labour and management"; "dependent on a world-outlook long abandoned by the majority of readers"; "though rooted in Christmas is chary of Christian forthrightness"; "an absurd and psychologically impossible resolution." And so on. You can hear the heavy newspaper reviewers, the wits of the glossy magazines, and the deep voices of the academic quarterlies—those Rhadamanthine judges of the quick and the dead in the world of literature—searching their hearts for condemnation bitter enough to reflect the greatest possible credit upon themselves.

Nevertheless, the book remains a masterpiece. The latest of Dickens's biographers, Mr. Peter Ackroyd, calls it "this powerful Christmas tale, which has achieved a kind of immortality, born out of the very conditions of the time." Of Dickens's time, and of our time, and of any time, for hardness of heart, avarice, human misery and degradation, are not passing things that can be banished by legislation. Dickens, as so often, seemed to be writing about his own time, but it was one of the splendours of his genius that he wrote for all time, and the abuses he attacked, and the virtues he extolled, have not vanished, but only found new shapes.

The book has been praised extravagantly, and sometimes in terms that quite reasonably arouse the enmity of critics, who are, of course, the most even-handed and moderate of men. Everybody is acquainted with the exuberant judgement of A. Edward Newton who declared that it was "the greatest little book in the world," adding, with generous belligerence, "if you think that rather a large order, name a greater!" A. Edward Newton was not a critic; he was merely a very distinguished collector of books and an ebullient enthusiast for literature of all sorts. Some of the warmest praise has come from contemporaries and fellow-writers who might be expected to be jealous of Dickens. But it was Thackeray who said, with the generosity which was characteristic of him, "It seems to me a national benefit, and to every man or woman who reads it a personal kindness." It is even on record that Carlyle, though a Scot and a philosopher, rushed out after reading it and—bought a turkey!

So, a masterpiece it is. And what is a masterpiece? The production, surely, of a master in his art working at the height of his powers. If it appears to run counter to accepted standards of excellence, may it not be that those standards are not applicable to *A Christmas Carol?* Should we not judge it by other standards, by no means high-flown or contradictory of critical opinion, but simply different from those we have been talking about? That is what I want to talk about tonight.

It is my opinion that in discussing the works of Charles Dickens we should never forget the theatre of his time, to which he was devoted, and in which he first of all hoped to make his career, and whose techniques and characteristics, however he may have seemed from time to time to mock them, determined the form of much of his work and indeed may be discerned even in the later novels, in which his earlier extravagances of plot and character have been moderated.

I come to this opinion as a consequence of sixty years that I have spent in intermittent study of that theatre, and many years in which I have talked to generations of students about it. Much of the popular literature of the nineteenth century leans on this theatrical tradition, but none so plainly or so successfully as Dickens.

It was a theatre, we must remember, that combined in itself all that is shared nowadays among theatre, film, and television. It was popular entertainment ranging between the highest and the lowest taste, incorporating all I have named, and also generous portions of circus and ballet. It was peopled by artists of the highest order, like Dickens's friend Macready, by Edmund Kean (of whom Coleridge said that to see him act was like reading Shakespeare by flashes of lightning), by Samuel Phelps who did the almost impossible task at that time of presenting all but five of Shakespeare's plays, without a penny of subsidy, by the scholarly Charles Kean, and still within Dickens's lifetime, Henry Irving, who compelled the British government to accept the theatre as an art when it knighted him. Below this level were serious artists who brought to the stage qualities of intelligence combined with theatrical insight, who won and held the affection of a huge middle-class audience. And lower still, there were the actors of lesser talent but no less enthusiasm whose rich theatricality delighted Dickens and which he made immortal in Vincent Crummles and his company. Bernard Shaw, who devoted so much of his life to changing this richly emotional theatre into a theatre of ideas and intellect, nevertheless declared that it had been, in its own way, a great theatre, which he had seen when he was a young playgoer, before Dickens died.

The nineteenth century was an age of great acting, and it was Lord Byron—a playwright whose work would be admirably suited to television—who said, "I am acquainted with no immaterial sensuality so delightful as good acting."

We must not think of the nineteenth-century theatre as visually crude or impoverished; at its best it commanded the work of designers and painters of a high order and it had a system of changing scenes which was so rapid that it was done before the eyes of the audience, one scene melting into another with a swiftness that suggests the films rather than the time-consuming scene changes of the early part of this century. It had not our fine versatility of lighting, but it had gaslight which threw upon the scene a magic that was all its own. In those days of painted scenery, many of the effects which are now achieved by lighting were, in fact, painted into the background.

This was the theatre to which Dickens was devoted, and not Dickens alone but such of his contemporaries as George Eliot, Thackeray, Tennyson, and even so stern a critic as Matthew Arnold, who were regular attendants and generous in their praise of what they saw.

What did they see? This is where I have to moderate my enthusiasm for this theatre of the past. There were very few playwrights of even mediocre stature and the repertoire of contemporary plays often makes sad reading. I can speak with knowledge and with feeling, because I have waded through scores of plays which seem to have been written by the same hand, repeating tried-and-true situations and putting in the mouths of the characters such language as has never been uttered elsewhere by human tongue.

If Dickens sometimes makes his theatrical characters speak in this extraordinary language he does not exaggerate. Consider the memoirs of John Ryder, a popular actor of the time who, when he is leaving home as a youth, writes—"I utter valedictory to the author of my being." He means he said good-bye to his mother. There were lots of actors who talked like that. Lines from plays became popular sayings, by no means reverently used. Such a line was "O God, put back thy universe and give me yesterday," from *The Silver King*; another was, "Once aboard the lugger and the girl is mine," from a play called *My Jack and Dorothy*. Many splendid lines are handed down in families where they took on a personal ring; I instance a line from a French Revolution play called *Jacques the Spy*, which became a catchphrase in my wife's family—"She who bathed in milk, and spent a fortune on a single pear." People liked verbal splendour in the nineteenth century, and often I wish it would return. As of course it will; in the theatre, nothing dies.

Nevertheless, verbal splendour divorced from any sort of original thought very soon degenerates into rant, and its intellectual poverty shows through the tinsel. Nineteenth-century theatre delighted in violent incident, improbable confrontations, absurd misunderstandings, and indeed anything at all which provided what was then called "a strong situation." It was the kind of thing we associate with the libretti of operas, but in opera the baldness of the plot and the arbitrary nature of the psychology is disguised, or given another dimension, by the music. Such a popular opera is *Lucia di Lammermoor*, for instance; the musical evocation of the sweetness of youth and the wretchedness of thwarted love conceals from us the violence that the libretto does to Walter Scott's finely psychological novel. The theatre of the nineteenth century was a theatre of feeling, of strong emotion, and it is not always easy for us, who live in an era where that sort of thing has been given over to the movies and to television, to sympathize with it. Our theatre has become almost a coterie entertainment, where we demand intellectual stress, or some reasonable facsimile thereof, and reject naked passion as improbable unless it is cloaked in some Freudian complexity.

It was an accident that Dickens did not join the vivid, rather brainless theatre of his time as an actor. That was his ambition, but Fate determined otherwise, for when he secured an audition with the influential manager Bartley, he was unable to attend because of a disabling cold in the head and deferred his audition for a year—by which time he was too successfully launched as a shorthand reporter to be able to pursue his earlier goal. What we know about his powers as an actor suggests that he would have had a fine career on the stage as a comedian, for he possessed brilliant comic invention, extraordinary powers of impersonation, and a hawklike eye for detail. He did, of course, take the keenest pleasure in amateur theatricals all his life, and scored successes in such dissimilar roles as Captain Bobadil in Ben Jonson's *Every Man in His Humour* and Justice Shallow in Shakespeare's *Merry Wives of Windsor*. It appears also that he could, at need, play tragedy—or at least pathos—with good effect. When he appeared as Richard Wardour in Wilkie Collins's drama of arctic exploration, *The Frozen Deep*, his death scene brought tears not only from the audience but from the actress who was on the stage with him. But his greatest triumphs as an actor were in the readings from his own work with which he occupied so much of his time during the later years of his life. We know that he gave, in all, 427 of these readings to packed audiences in England and in America and there are abundant records of the effect he produced in both comedy and pathos. *The Trial from Pickwick* was apparently irresistible in its evocation of the sleepy, stupid judge, the garrulous Mrs. Cluppins, the ill-prepared but rhetorically overwhelming Sergeant Buzfuz, the irreverent witness Sam Weller, and the deeply affronted Mr. Pickwick. He filled the stage with people, changing from one to another with the uttermost rapidity, and yet never scamping a characterization or a contrast.

From the descriptions that have survived of his readings we learn much about his technique. He had an astonishing range of voice; he could whisper horribly as the surly Creakle in *David Copperfield*, and he could be light, high, and twittering as Mrs. Nickleby; he could be winningly feminine, he could be shrewish, he could be wondrously drink-sodden as Sairey Gamp and her friend Betsy Prig; he could be sonorous and rhetorical as Mr. Micawber and he could be ignorantly pretentious as Wackford Squeers; as socially pretentious characters he was inimitable in his folly, and he could be ironically derisive as Sam Weller. There was nothing, apparently, that he could not do. In the reading which was his greatest success as a piece of sheer sensation, the murder of the harlot Nancy by the brutal Bill Sikes, his screams as the woman who was being beaten to death alternated with the blasphemous roars of her murderer so rapidly that it seemed almost as if they were heard at the same time. This same extraordinary rapidity and variation in what actors call "picking up his cues" was remarked upon in the scene where the reluctant Nicholas Nickleby is being subjected to the enchantments of Miss Fanny Squeers; people swore that both characters seemed to speak at once, in two wholly different voices.

His brilliance as an actor was not confined to vocal dexterity. As Mr. Pickwick he seemed innocent and portly, when his companion Mr. Nathaniel Winkle was slight and notably weak at the knees. The distinction he drew among the three spirits that visited Scrooge—the silvery Ghost of Christmas Past, the ebullient Ghost of Christmas Present, and the veiled Spectre of Christmas Yet to Come—was one of the many wonders of his always popular reading of the *Carol*. In the *Carol*, too, many among his audience commented on the short but important scene where the reformed Scrooge leans from his bedroom window and orders an incredulous small boy to hasten to the poulterer's and buy the prize turkey. The boy has very little to say, but he appeared as a vivid personality to those who saw and heard that reading. Oh yes, Dickens was a very great actor, but great acting does not come simply. How did he do it?

We know from his letters how hard he worked to perfect all his impersonations. It was nothing to him to rehearse a reading two hundred times, in the privacy of his workroom. If that does not astonish you, I suggest that you might try reading a short passage from one of his books *five* successive times, trying to do it as well as you can, and I think you will discover what taxing, wearisome, tedious work it is. Dickens was a mighty man for detail and among actors whom we have seen he seems to me to resemble most the late Laurence Olivier, who was also a great man for detail, leaving nothing whatever to chance, and regarding no trifle of stage work as too trivial for his understanding and his study. I am not vapourizing about that; my wife worked with Olivier and saw what an insatiably curious artist he was in everything that went to make up the totality of a stage production. That was how Dickens worked, and when he appeared on a public platform to read, without any appurtenances except the book he held—but obviously did not need—and occasionally a paper-knife with which he could extend a very few gestures—wearing only conventional evening dress, he was ready to people the stage with the creations of his own fancy, and to make them palpable to audiences of twenty-five hundred people, some of whom on occasions, sat on the platform at his feet. But never, be it noted, behind him.

What he read was not precisely what appeared in the printed texts of his books. He edited, he deleted, he strengthened a passage now and then, he occasionally wrote in a new joke, or an extension of a particularly telling piece of description. But he was able, at need, to do without description. In the *Carol*, for instance, he comes very early to the description of Scrooge: "Oh, but he was a tight-fisted hand at the grindstone, Scrooge; a squeezing, wrenching, grasping, scraping, clutching covetous old sinner." But in the reading all the latter part of that sentence was omitted. Why? Because, as many people have attested, and his manager Dolby, who heard him read the *Carol* scores of times, makes clear, the squeezing, wrenching, covetous old sinner stood before his audience, and the words were superfluous in comparison with the physical presentment.

He could, as it were, conjure up music. When Scrooge goes after his reformation to the house of his nephew Fred to humbly beg pardon for his earlier bearishness and to ask if he may join in the festivities, we are aware that a dance has been in progress—what the Victorians called a "carpet-hop" when the guests simply danced on the tight-stretched carpet to the music of a single piano-player, who might also be a talented guest. Dickens suggested that music by tapping lightly with his fingers on his reading-desk, and that was all that was wanted to call up the simple, domestic music and the happiness that went with it. To explain how he did this is impossible without employing that now seriously overworked word "charisma"; people use it now to mean a particularly attractive personality, but it really means a gift of God not vouchsafed to everyone; a quality which may be refined and enhanced by indefatigable rehearsal, but which cannot be brought into being by any amount of effort.

The story of Dickens's travels and adventures as a reader are of the greatest interest. Undoubtedly he hastened his death by undertaking such efforts at a time when he was oppressed by fears that his creative powers were waning, by the failure of his marriage and the unsatisfactory nature of his relationship with the young woman who became his mistress, but who seems to have taken uncommonly little pleasure in that capacity; by the demands of his large family who must be launched in the world and in the case of the girls whose future must be assured; and by the anxiety of a man who had reached the top of a very high tree and was fearful of a fall. Those 427 nights of extraordinary exertion, achieved after heroic travel, were dearly bought and there were nights when the faithful manager Dolby feared that Dickens might not be able to complete his announced program. But Dickens always came up to scratch; he rallied magnificently when the time came to perform and there is no record of an audience going away disappointed.

Some of the details of how he did it are in themselves Dickensian, in their extravagance and strangeness. All through the nineteenth century actors seem to have recruited their powers during performances by eating and drinking. I am sure some of you know theatrical people, and are aware of their refusal to eat when a performance is near and, in most cases, to drink anything intoxicating. Not so the great ones of the nineteenth century. Edmund Kean, of course, had recourse to the brandy bottle and was sometimes almost incapable of carrying out his evening's work. Not so Dickens's friend Macready, who took his profession with the uttermost seriousness, and always consumed the lean of a mutton chop just before he went on the stage as he was convinced that it lent mellowness and unction to his voice. Not so Henry Irving, who, late in the century, relied on Bovril laced with brandy. But Dickens—well, in the interval in an evening's reading, he regularly ate a dozen oysters and drank a bottle of champagne, and this at times when otherwise he could hardly bring himself to eat at all. Have you ever eaten a dozen oysters and drunk, let us say, three glasses of champagne? Did it put you in form to do a heavy evening's work? But then, you are not a Victorian. They seem in many ways to have been an heroic race.

On Dickens struggled with the readings. He had his reward. In money, of course, they were very satisfactory. When he died his estate was reckoned at £93,000, of which about half had been gained by the readings. What that estate is worth in modern terms I cannot tell, but in 1820 an English pound sterling was worth seven American dollars, and that would bring it up to substantially more than half a million dollars. What would it be today? Perhaps Miss Jackie Collins could tell us. His readings were packed, and at one Liverpool performance alone over 3,000 people were turned away. One significant fact we must bear in mind, when we think of the effort the readings involved, is that this was long before the era of sound amplification. Yet nobody ever complained that they could not hear, even when he spoke in New York's Carnegie Hall. That demands of an actor a vocal technique in no way inferior to that of a great singer.

A notion of the quality and effect of the readings may have been experienced by some of you when the late Emlyn Williams toured the world, reading, in the character of Dickens, what Dickens had read. He enjoyed great success, and was by no means deficient in ranging from the pathetic weakness of little Paul Dombey to the noisy exuberance of Mr. Bob Sawyer. I saw and heard him several times, and I never failed to be deeply moved when, at the end of his performance, he acknowledged the ample applause of his audience and then turned and bowed in appropriate reverence to his reading-desk, which was an exact replica of that which Dickens used. It was a fine acknowledgement, by an artist of distinguished gifts, of the genius to which those gifts had been applied.

But what, you may ask, has this excursion into the nature of the nineteenth-century theatre to do with the novelist and particularly with *A Christmas Carol?* Quite simply, everything, and I want to talk about that now.

If Dickens was so mad for the theatre, you may say, why did he not write plays? Ah, but he did, and of all the keen Dickensians I know, I am myself the only one who has read them. I claim some credit for it. It is not a pleasure. His farces, *The Strange Gentleman* and *Is She His Wife?*, might have been written by any one of a score of Victorian playwrights who turned out such formula work for theatres which were as demanding of material then as television is today. His dramas, *No Thoroughfare* and *The Battle of Life*, are once again without distinction—without indeed a trace of the Dickens touch. As a young man he wrote the libretto for a little operetta called *The Village Coquettes* and I had the experience of inspiring and assisting at a performance of it—I do not think there have been many performances during this century. The music, by John Pike Hullah, was pleasant, but the libretto was clumsy, and any comedy that emerged was provided by the actors. Why do you suppose a man so keen about the theatre failed so utterly when he tried to write for it?

In part I think it was because Dickens, though an original genius in his deployment of traditional forms, was no innovator. His novels are in the great tradition he inherited from his childhood reading of Defoe, Fielding, and Smollett, and even in his mature work he does not stray far from it, though he richly expands it. Now to be a traditionalist in the theatre in his time was to be committed to a worn-out conception of drama, composed of stock situations and mechanical fun, or else tearful pathos straining to achieve the dignity of tragedy. The successful playwrights were hacks whose names have not survived, except in the antiquarian enthusiasm of theatre historians like myself. Great acting could persuade the public that the plays of Sheridan Knowles or John Westland Marston were worthy of attendance, but there is no dramatic vitality in them and they have not lived.

Until late in the century, and after Dickens's death, the nineteenth-century stage did not attract writers of first-rate ability. The reason was simple: the payment was ridiculous. A playwright sold his play outright to a manager, and thereby relinquished all rights to it. Royalties were unheard of Douglas Jerrold's immensely popular drama *Black-Eyed Susan* brought the author fifty pounds, but made a fortune for a variety of managers and actors afterward. I do not know what Dickens got for his farces, but as a beginner it was probably twenty pounds. The rewards of authorship lay in the writing of novels and Dickens was strongly aware of it. Writing plays was a luxury he could not afford, and he was too intelligent a man not to realize that he had little talent for it, working under the restrictions of the theatre as it was during his youth.

Restriction—that is the word. He could not work in such fetters as the theatre put on its writers, though he could, and did, find room for his talent in the restrictions that were involved in publishing his works in monthly parts.

This system of publication involved Dickens with theatre in a way which was of considerable interest, but which is rarely discussed. We are so awed, nowadays, by the immensity of Dickens's genius that we are inclined to forget the keen man of business, who was eager to extract the last shilling from his work. He gained little money from the theatre but he was clever enough to exploit it as a tremendous source of advertisement.

As I have said, the theatre of his time was as greedy for material as modern television, and it was the custom of the day to adapt the popular novels which were appearing in monthly parts for stage presentations. These were often of a crudity that we now regard with astonishment, and many of them preyed upon a popular novel that was not yet completed. We know that Dickens's creating of Mr. Micawber offered such a chance for actors that versions of *David Copperfield* were on the stage before the novel had been finished; indeed, there were versions in which actors who desired to show their versatility "doubled" the roles of Micawber, the richly comic creation, with that of Dan'l Peggotty, the noble and much-wronged uncle of the wayward heroine, Little Emily. It has been recorded that Dickens attended one such version of Copperfield with some friends, and that his anguish at what had been done to his work was so intense that he lay upon the floor of his box and writhed in agony. This was an early, and reversed, version of "rolling in the aisles." But Dickens was a man who could turn misfortune to account during his early days, and that is what he did.

We know now that he made available to playwrights and adapters whom he could trust, advance proofs of his books, revealing the conclusions, so that these favoured adapters could steal an important march on their competitors. Of course it goes without saying that the original author of a novel which had been adapted for the stage received no recompense, but we know that in exchange for these advance proofs money changed hands. And the advertisement value was incalculable.

This was not the case with *A Christmas Carol*, because it was published as a unity. The details of its publishing are, to the modern mind, astonishing: Dickens wrote it in late October and early November of 1843, delivered it to his publishers, Chapman and Hall, by mid-November and by the 19th of December this pretty little book, with its gilt edges and hand-coloured illustrations, was on sale at the price of five shillings, and by December 24 six thousand copies had been sold, and it has sold pretty briskly ever since. The modern author, who thinks himself lucky if his publisher gets his book before the public in six or seven months, is left with his mouth hanging open. As early as possible in 1844 there were four dramatizations on the London stage. One of these, called *The Miser's Warning*, was the work of C.Z. Burnett, and it was advertised as being sanctioned by Dickens; whether he received any money for that sanctioning we do not know, but certainly he did so for later works. Burnett's *Carol*, which is a clumsy and impudently altered version of the book, offered the celebrated actor O. Smith as Scrooge; Smith was the most famous "villain" of his time, and was the first actor of the Monster in *Frankenstein* when it was adapted for the stage. We have records of his performance, which was criticised as being too gloomy and villainous.

This is interesting. The public has never been ready to accept Scrooge as a villain. He is essentially a comic character, and the exuberance of his avarice is positively refreshing. His cries of "Bah" and

"Humbug" sometimes find an echo in our own hearts when we are battered with demands for charities at Christmas. We are repelled by his oppression of his clerk, Bob Cratchit, but we never doubt for an instant that Scrooge is the greater man, and that Bob—decent, good fellow that he is—nevertheless must be reckoned as one of Nature's losers. It takes ghosts and disembodied spirits to get the better of Scrooge; he is in the most powerful sense an active agent in the story, not a passive one, and his conversion is brought about by apparitions that are, when we look at them carefully, elements of himself.

Now we come to my point. We cannot really know the essence of Scrooge, or the magic of his story, unless we meet it in Dickens's book, and that is because the book is in its deepest bones a theatrically conceived, theatrically written story. It is in this and in his other novels that Dickens shows himself to be not only a very great novelist but immeasurably the greatest dramatist of his time, and one might well say the greatest dramatic author in English since Shakespeare.

Drama, yes. But drama is what is left of great theatre when you have drained all the fun out of it. Drama is what serious people are ready to accept as worthy of their distinguished consideration. Theatre is the exuberance, the exaggeration, the invention, the breathtaking, rib-tickling zest of theatrical performance at its peak. There is plenty of theatre in Shakespeare as well as the dramatic essence. There is theatre in all the great playwrights, including even such unlikely figures as Ibsen. When the drama domineers, or drives the theatrical element out altogether you get the plays of Goethe —always excepting *Faust* in which he spoke most truly—and the plays of Schiller, of Racine—plays which we regard with profound respect but which perhaps we do not rush to see when deeply serious companies offer them.

The powerful theatrical element in Dickens's writing has been deplored by critics. Edmund Wilson writes disparagingly of what he calls the ham element in Dickens. But what is ham? May not a great ham still be a great artist? Is it not an element of excess, of—no, not too much, but more than the rest of us are able to rise to in our lives and our creations? My dictionary gives as one definition of excess "over-stepping due limits." But whose due limits? Those of critics, who are always afraid of excess because they are at best classically restrained minds, and on the average crotch-bound, frightened people who fear that if they abandon themselves to the Dionysian excess of a great artist they may never again be able to retreat to their cosy nests? Do they not fear excess because it makes nonsense of their confined world? But the general public loves excess because it feeds upon the energy and invention of the great man, and thus it makes heroes of excessive characters, some worthy and many, it is to be feared, unworthy.

Dickens's excess was an abundance of theatrical device in his writing. His books, and especially the early ones before adulation and misfortune had combined to sadden him, vibrate with his excess. He infects us as readers with his marvellous excess; he even infected his early illustrators, Cruikshank and Leech. Have you ever noticed how theatrical the light is in their illustrations? How it seems to come almost entirely from the front and often from below, as if from footlights? That was how nineteenth-century stage light was. His books—the *Carol* as much as any—are full of effective touches of the kind that actors call "business." Consider the appearance of Marley's face in the knocker of Scrooge's house, illumined with a ghostly radiance like a bad lobster in a dark cellar; have you observed how, when he has opened the door, Scrooge looks to see if Marley's pigtail is sticking backward through the wood? Sheer theatre. Do you recall how, when the Ghost presents himself in Scrooge's chamber, the light flares up in the fire, as if to say "Marley's Ghost!" Now why do you think that was? I think it was because actors of the era of the *Carol* had a trick of stamping on the stage at crucial moments, because the stamp made the gaslights in the footlights flare up, giving a special emphasis, and that is what an actor playing the Ghost—and the actor was Dickens, don't forget—would have done. And when the Ghost retreats toward the window, and at every step the window rises a little higher—what an effective piece of stage management! You can go through the book looking for these stage effects, and you will find plenty of them. And from the nineteenth-century stage derives also the Ghost's elaborate rhetoric— "O captive, bound and double-ironed," it begins in its culminating address to Scrooge, and he, with brilliant comic utterance, undercuts the rhetoric as a great comedian might, saying, "Don't be flowery Jacob, pray." The mingling of pathos and terror is extraordinary, but the interjection of comedy is no less powerful, and it is achieved by means that Dickens had seen in the theatre, given fresh lustre by the splendour of his own invention.

I began by calling *A Christmas Carol* "an unlikely masterpiece." I have shown you, I hope, how unlikely it is as being one of the most powerfully *theatrical* creations in the whole of English literature. It invites us to take part in its nineteenth-century theatricality, becoming ourselves actors, directors, scene painters, gaslight controllers, and also audience as the play unfolds. It is unusual for a book to require this of us; most often a book allows us to sit back, as it were, as the story unfolds, and to judge it by the experience we bring to it. We agree with the new insights the author reveals, and we take pleasure in the characters he describes and the plot in which they are displayed. But how often are we asked so compellingly to be participators in what happens as we are asked to do by Dickens?

I think this is why stage and film versions of Dickens's books are so rarely completely satisfactory. I have seen many of them, ranging from the innocent adaptations of Dickens Fellowship groups to elaborate musical shows in which Dickens's verve and breadth of spirit is supposed to be offered in a musical form—and isn't. Mr. Pickwick singing is not Mr. Pickwick. Films have been more successful, though my gorge rises when I am asked to accept the archetypal con-man W.C. Fields as the high-minded Wilkins Micawber. Many films have been made of *A Christmas Carol* and one of them, in which the part of Scrooge is played by the great Alistair Sim, comes commendably near to the mark. But to know the *Carol* in its essence you must read it, abandon yourself to it, and personally body it forth with whatever theatrical skill you may command.

That surely is what makes the *Carol* unusual. But—a masterpiece? Why?

In his observations on literature the late Vladimir Nabokov put the matter succinctly. He says: "An original author always invents an original world, and if a character or action fits into the pattern of that world, then we experience the pleasurable shock of artistic truth, no matter how unlikely the person or thing may seem if transferred into what book reviewers, poor hacks, call 'real life.' There is no such thing as real life for the author of genius; he must create it himself and then create the consequences."

The author of genius who brings us artistic truth. Is that not Charles Dickens, and is it not its artistic truth, as opposed to the kind of truth that stands up in a court of law, that makes *A Christmas Carol*, however unlikely, an undoubted masterpiece?

Janice MacDonald

Janice MacDonald is a mystery writer and reviewer. Her column "If Words Could Kill" (from which the following piece comes) ran for several years in *The Edmonton Journal*.

Murder Most Foul Ball

Prairie Hardball by Alison Gordon

There is just something mystical about baseball. Alison Gordon's *Prairie Hardball* (McClelland & Stewart, 282 pges, $26.99) capitalises on our love of the game we all know how to play. This is Alison's fifth Kate Henry mystery. Kate, that intrepid sports journalist and erstwhile detective who follows the Toronto Titans, has dragged her policeman boyfriend home to Indian Head, Saskatchewan for a trip down memory lane. There is the requisite view of western small town from the viewpoint of the big city dweller, but to her credit, it is filtered through Kate, who is fiercely protective and amusingly self-conscious.

It is a memory trip for Kate's mother as well, as she is to be inducted, along with other former members of the All-American Girls Professional League, into the Saskatchewan Baseball Hall of Fame in Battleford. Helen Henry, the straight-laced minister's wife, was once Helen "Wheels" Maclaren, a Racine Belle. Kate, who is still aware of her mother's tacit disapproval of all her choices ("You're forty-five years old, Kate." "Not in this house, I'm not."), learns quite a few things about her mother on this trip.

While several of the women making the trip to the reunion are from other teams, like the Rockford Peaches, someone has targeted the Racine Belles for threatening letters. When one of the Belles is discovered murdered in the Hall of Fame, Andy's statement that "Kate attracts murderers the way other people attract mosquitoes" rings true once again.

Andy is asked to help with the interviewing; and as everyone cools their heels in the hotel, Kate decides to research a piece about the women already immortalized in the movie A League of Their Own. The story of these amazing sportswomen, often shy country girls who found themselves emblazoned on the cover of Life Magazine while the men were off to war, has a far more mythical and romantic hue to it than the average Rosie the Riveter tale. Melded as it is with the sport of baseball, there is something heart-stirring even without it being in the hands of a master-storyteller.

Gordon is a master, however, and she goes one better than just giving women their due; she opens the portals to all the Canadian women who watched Penny Marshall's inspiring movie and allows us to feel some of that glow as well. In the same way as the Blue Jays winning the World Series allowed us all to say "it's our game too," *Prairie Hardball* allows us to stand tall, hold our caps to our hearts and say "those were our girls too." God bless 'em.

Robert Kroetsch

Robert Kroetsch was born in Heisler, Alberta, and received his BA from the University of Alberta, and his PhD from the University of Iowa. He has published nine novels and numerous volumes of poetry and essays, and a travel book. His titles include: *The Studhorse Man* (Governor General's Award, 1969), *The Stone Hammer Poems*, *Seed Catalogue*, *The Sad Phoenician*, *Field Notes*, *Badlands*, *The Words of My Roaring*, *What the Crow Said*, *Excerpts from the Real World*, *The Lovely Treachery of Words*, *The Puppeteer*, *A Likely Story* (from which this piece comes), and *The Man from the Creeks*. His writing continues to influence the direction of Canadian literature.

He has taught literature and creative writing at the State University of New York and the University of Manitoba. He now lives with his wife in Victoria, B.C.

Sitting Down to Write: Margaret Laurence and the Discourse of Morning

The Diviners by Margaret Laurence

Early morning is the time of the mind's revisioning. In the turn from dream toward daylight it finds the crack in everything of which Leonard Cohen sings. It is the time of disconnection and connection, a dangerous time, a liberating time, as Margaret Laurence shows us in the opening of her novel *The Diviners*. In the third paragraph on the first page, morning having announced itself, we read:

> *Pique had gone away. She must have left during the night. She had left a note on the kitchen table, which also served as Morag's desk, and had stuck the sheet of paper into the type-writer, where Morag was certain to find it.*

We persist in the conviction that the author begins from a blank sheet of paper. This assumption has held among writers and readers at least since the beginning of the Romantic Period. *Tabula rasa. Ab ovo.* Sprung full-grown, from the brow of Zeus. Making something out of nothing. The writer as creator. Virgin Mother or Big Bang … The very notion bestows upon the author a kind of godhead.

Morag Gunn, sitting down to her typewriter—sitting down to begin—finds she has already begun. Uncannily, the sheet of paper in her typewriter is written upon. The first page of her narrative is written. Morag is presented with characters and an action. In structuralist terms, she is confronted by—and she confronts—a double violation; an unexpected disordering of the world; an unexpected disordering of authorial control.

Morag Gunn, sitting down to begin, finds not only that she has begun. She has been begun. She has been positioned. Contrary to the assumption of authorial freedom, she has been left with almost nowhere to turn. She has been told that if Gord phones, "Tell him I've drowned and gone floating down the river, crowned with algae and dead minnows, like Ophelia."

To begin with, that is not where Pique has gone at all. If Morag delivers the message, she lies. If she does not deliver the message, she fails.

At first glance, then, Morag seems to be caught between lying and failing. She is in between a rock and a hard place. Life—or at least art—has got her, as Christie Logan might say, by the short hairs. Forced to act, she cannot avoid complicity. By that complicity she is empowered. By that same complicity, she is relegated.

Morag Gunn, sitting down to write, finds she has been written to. Intending to send a message, she has received one instead. She is being told what to do by someone who has up and cleared out. If writing is a god-game, then the power appears to reside with the one who is absent, not with the one who is present. But that is the way with gods. Presence announces not the writers sacred but rather her profane condition. She is in the here and now of time present, place present; she is in a world of contingency, surprise, short-sightedness. Her assignment is not simply to begin; it is to begin from the impossibility of beginning.

"Now please do not get all uptight, Ma," Pique writes, constructing the person to whom she writes. Thanks to Pique, Morag is indeed all uptight. She's wired. She's a wreck. Consider, Pique says, what your writing has done to your Ma-ness. And before you take your Ma-ness too seriously, remember that you are one of Shakespeare's myriad and perishing children.

Morag, by way of response, first off reads Pique's message as writing. She, as much as her daughter, confronts the question of agency. "Slightly derivative," Morag thinks, feebly, bravely, lovingly, of Pique's message.

To announce one's intention to write a novel is to announce one's intention to write what is already written. We are, as writers, always in the predicament of Goldilocks: "Someone has been sitting in my chair."

The chances of being original are less than slim. They don't exist.

It is because they don't exist that one can be original. But that is a Kroetschian argument, not a Laurentian argument.

Morag Gunn sits down at her kitchen table to a typewriter. The kitchen table is one of the marks of her own self-construction— part of what we might call her signature—and the problem of writing what already exists is a problem in signing. Perhaps, then, the kitchen table is not only a mark of Morag Gunn's signature; it is also a mark of Margaret Laurence's signature. But let us avoid that question.

The typewriter signals a technology of writing that offers grave resistance to signatures of any sort. Some of us are old enough to remember a time when one did not write personal letters on a typewriter. To do so would have contradicted one's very intention.

The typewriter signals the Foucauldian technology by which we construct the act of writing—and by which we construct literature. The writer is part of an apparatus that produces the texts that society and culture require in order to be society and culture.

Morag Gunn counters that force—that power—with the kitchen table. With kitchen talk. The busy writer, avoiding work, works by gossiping. She gossips with herself. She brings to bear an alternate technology of production—feminine technology, one might wish to say—that engages the typewriter in dialogue. She talks around the subject until the talking around becomes the subject.

With her positioning herself at a kitchen table that serves as a desk, she enters into a dialogue with the positioned self created by Pique. By placing her typewriter on that table become desk, Morag at once accepts a technology, and asserts her own agency within the elaborate apparatus that is going to establish her and use her as a writer. She lays claims to gender, to class, to social relationships of her own. But let us avoid those questions.

How does one begin if the page in the typewriter is already written? How does one read that page? How does one write with and against that page? Is it one's own writing that constitutes the intertextuality?

It is the very fullness of the page inserted by someone else in her typewriter that compels Morag Gunn. Tradition has created much of the fullness. But she, too, by the writing of her novels, has done some of the filling. It is the fullness of that page, its overflow, not its emptiness, that enables Morag Gunn to write, even as she is threatened with a silencing.

By sticking that page "into" Morag's typewriter, Pique became the first enabler. In her own devious way, Pique is muse. "Am going west," she writes, the "I" not yet invented for that sentence. "Am going west." "Am" becomes a noun. Almost a proper name. To go west is to find "I" and to lose it in the finding. It is to turn "I" into a continuous exchange of resolving image and fading trace, of disappearance and innuendo and encompassing presence.

Pique's going forward in time carries Morag back into the genealogy of her own writing, and by that process forward, too. Pique's note on the first page of the novel becomes the first page of the novel.

One is able to write one's absence, and in a way that is what Pique does. She writes a one-paragraph novel, and in the process lays claim to all the huge explanatory footnote that her mother will write as a consequence.

But there is another side to the story. The moment of loss invites silence, yes. But it also creates both the site for a speaking and a speaking out. When and where does the pained speaker erupt into words? More to the point—when does the pained body erupt into words? Perhaps it is in the pained body that both Morag and Margaret find signature. But let us avoid that question.

Perhaps there is always another side to the story. The note that Pique sticks into the typewriter positions Morag between two discourses. Morag confronts the contingent and autobiographical moment. Yet Pique, shrewdly, to get to that moment, perhaps to control and shape it, invokes in her own writing the colonializing paradigm implicit in the notion of canonical writing. Perhaps Pique herself has internalized the paradigm. More probably, she reads her mother, that Ma from the West, as someone whose uprightness derives in part from a submission to the inhibiting paradigm that enables a daughter to conclude an abrupt message with the word *Ophelia*.

Morag is caught up elaborately in pedagogy. Pedagogy becomes, obviously, an element in society's technological project. Morag's husband, as an agent of that technology, would diminish and even erase the autobiographical (at least for Morag if not for himself). He would have her embrace the discourses of truth we now associate with modernism and with empire.

Morag, in her resistance to the idea of Artist with a capital A, tries out other discourses. She quickly tells us that she is doing work, hard work, and that she is a tradesperson. ("Don't knock the trade.") And yet from Royland's talk she has learned to venture beyond mere work. From the talk and silence of Christie and Prin she has learned to listen so totally that she is able to risk erasure as well as realization.

Sitting down to her kitchen table and to words, she sits down as an established and experienced writer—but also as a novice, as someone learning again and again, in a postmodern sense, not how to end, but rather how to begin.

Morag Gunn begins her novel by reading. This time she reads a message left in her typewriter, not by past generations, but by the next generation. She positions herself between—among—conflicting discourses. By that positioning she becomes a spokesperson for a Canadian poetics. It is the strategy of a preemptive cultural or political or social or economic force to have one discourse dominate. In Canada, the writer refuses the resolution into dominance. That resistance, that wariness of power, portrays itself in the various discourses at work, and at play, on the first page of Laurence's *The Diviners*.

We as readers, approaching the table, approaching the typewriter on the kitchen table become a desk, approaching the writer at work, discover that the writer at work is not writing at all but rather that she is reading. We as readers reading the text, first of the novel, then of the paragraph in the typewriter in the novel, discover that the first paragraph of the text could not have been the first paragraph of the text because the first paragraph is already there on the sheet of paper in the typewriter in the text, and it was not written by the writer who is writing the novel. Or perhaps it was.

Now we know we are Canadian readers reading a Canadian text about a Canadian poetics of fictional prose. It is, it turns out, necessary, after all, to refer to the description of morning in Margaret Laurence's text. In that description we find the phrase so dear to our students, and now so reassuring to our critic—"apparently impossible contradiction."

And now we are prepared to leap again over the first and second paragraphs, and over the third and fourth paragraphs as well. I see I have said nothing about Pique's having left at night. What is the discourse of night in *The Diviners*? How does that painful discourse engage in equal and balanced and Canadian dialogue the discourse of morning? But let me avoid those questions.

Now we can begin to read the apparently impossible contradictions included in paragraph five: "Pique was eighteen. Only. Not dry behind the ears. Yes, she was, though. If only there hadn't been that other time when Pique took off, that really bad time."

Yes, it is not a difficult text to read. But no, it is though.

She is not here. We miss her. She is here.

Candace Fertile

Candace Fertile received her PhD on the work of Lawrence Durrell from the University of Alberta. An avid reader from an inordinately young age, she jokes that she found the perfect job as a book reviewer. She has been a reviewer for various publications in the past twenty years. She is also a lecturer in the Department of English at the University of Victoria, in Victoria, British Columbia.

Alberta Author Creates a Buzz

A Recipe for Bees by Gail Anderson-Dargatz

Writing a novel after the huge success of *The Cure for Death by Lightning* had to be a monumental task for Gail Anderson-Dargatz, and she only partially succeeds in creating the charm of her first novel.

A Recipe for Bees, according to interviews that Anderson-Dargatz has given, is based loosely on her own family history, and it is possible to see where life intersects with fiction. The meeting is infelicitous as it's too contrived, and it's likely that the author has not gained sufficient distance on the events to write about them in a convincing manner.

Using the motif of the beehive, Anderson-Dargatz tells the life story of Augusta and her husband, Karl Olsen. They now reside on Vancouver Island after a very hard life on a farm in the B.C. interior. Augusta's only daughter, Joy, and Joy's husband Gabe also live on the island, and the cast of characters is rounded out by Rose, another retiree. It takes time to sort out the characters as the novel shuffles back and forth in time and place for no apparent reason except to cause confusion. In the present time line of the novel, Augusta, Karl, Rose, and Joy are waiting for news of the results of Gabe's brain surgery.

In the flashbacks, Augusta's life is delineated, and the hardships of farm life are made painfully clear. The separated worlds of men and women are also made evident, and while women appear to be accorded little regard, they do enormous amounts of work in keeping families going.

Anderson-Dargatz's sparkling style is evident from the first line, "Have I told you the drone's penis drops off during intercourse with the queen bee?", but it is not maintained with any consistency.

I suspect the publisher wanted to capitalize on the success of Anderson-Dargatz's last novel. This one has an excellent premise, but needs refining.

Female farm fiction seems to be coming into vogue, and no doubt many wonderful stories are out there to be shaped and told. This novel, however, while offering some perkiness is a tad limp in terms of characterization. The prose is serviceable, with occasional flashes of delight, but generally I sense the feeling that the characters just keep slipping away from their author, and the result is an annoying superficiality.

What is quite lovely about the book is all the information about bees, and Anderson-Dargatz matches with success the lives of the bees with the lives of her characters. While the human counterparts are groping for love, and acceptance, and understanding, and even mere survival, the bees go about their instinct-ordained lives, perhaps just like the human characters.

The novel also includes family snapshots from the authors' parents photo album, and while they are interesting artifacts, they don't add anything to the narration. If the book is a crossover between novel and biography, it needs much more clarification. Certainly, Anderson-Dargatz is not doing what Frank McCourt did in *Angela's Ashes*, but neither is she writing straight fiction—and the result is a smeared mirror.

A Recipe for Bees will not be a huge disappointment to fans of *The Cure for Death by Lightning*, but it is a falling-off. Anderson-Dargatz's new novel is competent, but it is not a prize-winner.

Dr. Kelly Hewson

Dr. Kelly Hewson received her MA from the University of Waterloo and her PhD from the University of Alberta. She is a lecturer in the Faculty of Arts & Communications at Mount Royal College, Calgary, Alberta, teaching courses in the English Department, the Professional Writing Certificate Program, and in the Applied Communications Degree. In her spare time, she chairs the judging panel for the Canadian-Caribbean Region of the Commonwealth Writers Prize 1998 and 1999. "To Dream the Authentically Canadian Dream" was originally presented at the Southwestern Association of Canadian Studies Conference held in Lafayette, Louisiana, February 1992.

To Dream the Authentically Canadian Dream and Other Desires in Jane Urquhart's The Whirlpool

The Whirlpool by Jane Urquhart

My maternal grandmother is a descendant of United Empire Loyalists. It was she who first took me to Niagara Falls, Ontario, and implanted this opinion: "we" have the better falls. I recall her asserting this energetically, then insisting a stranger take a picture of the two of us in front of the bigger, better Horseshoe Falls. On that same trip Gran informed me and the air around her, often, that those falls over there, the ones being eaten up by rock, only to be but a trickle in time, were American. "And don't let anybody tell you different," she admonished.

I begin with this anecdote because it uncovers a cast of mind which influenced mine and probably many other Canadians' with Southern Ontario connections. Some of its elements—a competitiveness or obsession with "over there"; the need to claim ownership and to protect something, anything from presumed takeover; a blind spot due to a failure to acknowledge its historical roots—led me into this discussion of Urquhart's text through a figure who, to a large and comic extent, plays out my grandmother's mentality.

"Ah yes, ... She came to me in a dream [Laura Secord did] ..., saying *Remind them, remind them*. I was in college at the time studying anything but Canadian history. I was dreaming a lot too. Don't dream anymore for some reason."[1]

---

[1] Jane Urquhart, *The Whirlpool* (Toronto: McClelland & Stewart Ltd., 1986), p. 83. Subsequent references to the text will follow the quotation in parentheses.

So explains Major David McDougal, a war historian in whom the locale of Niagara Falls, Ontario, the setting of Urquhart's *The Whirlpool*, excites an industrial-strength, wrap-yourself-with-the-flag kind of Canadianisation. "Our" Falls' proximity to that "other" Niagara Falls, New York; the fact of the border, an "interval of resonance"[2] between spaces which can't be seen but is felt; and all those historical scripts overwritten by the more titillating ones of daredevils, honeymooners, and the desperate make the site a challenge for a figure like McDougal whose duty and desire it is to remind Canadians to think Canadian thoughts, dream Canadian dreams, and most urgently to repossess Canadian historical moments—particularly the victorious outcome of the War of 1812—from "those arrogant bastards," the Americans.

This, admittedly crudely, is what being authentically Canadian means to McDougal—that you're 100% Canadian content, unconsciously as well as consciously. Anything from that site of culture to the south is to be viewed with great suspicion, even paranoia. You'd best be on guard because somewhere "out there" is something American waiting to pounce. Other figures in the text's desires have little to do with creating or defending a national identity. Rather, considered in the light of Robert Kroetsch's broad formulation that "the Canadian" is not a noun but a verb, they share, ultimately, the desire of searching for, if not necessarily finding, the right place.[3] While the Major's search for an enemy beyond the walls of the garrison is a paradigmatic one in Canadian Letters, the searches of others in the text are less conventional.

Urquhart sets her novel in 1889, the year of Robert Browning's death in Venice. (The last day of Browning's life, as imagined by Urquhart, acts as a frame story to the inner stories). Her Niagara Falls is "a geography of fierce opposites. Order on one side and, nearer the water, sublime geological chaos" (31). It is kind of a dream, admits a character, "all this wild landscape and the American factories just around the bend where you can't see them" (100). Further, within this geography of opposites, Urquhart locates Fleda, McDougal's wife, intriguingly, by the whirlpool, "the only part of the river that is entirely Canadian", according to her husband. His proprietary asser-

---

[2]Marshall McLuhan, "Canada: The Borderline Case" in *The Canadian Imagination*, ed. by David Staines (Cambridge, Mass: Harvard University Press, 1977), p. 226.

[3]From a talk Robert Kroetsch gave in Calgary, Alberta, at the Memorial Library, April 1992.

tion means nothing to her. What she loves is the silent flux, the circular swirl of the whirlpool and the natural chaos that implies; she seems "chained ...to the whirlpool" (108), living in a tent near it, waiting for David, who spends most of his time in town lamenting the quickness with which Canadians bury their history and struggling to dig it up, to build their house.

Fleda is positioned in a middle ground between the town and the wilderness proper, outside and around culture, (though an old world form of culture is with her, embodied in the books she takes with her and pours over in a real landscape: Robert Browning's poetry, including The Ring and the Book (a domestic tyrant irritated by his wife's virtues) and the book her husband gave her, Patmore's Angel in the House (the ideal wife). Urquhart's placing of Fleda in what can be conceptualised as a "pseudo-wilderness", to use Heather Murray's term, might encourage certain questions.[4] For one, is the woman in the clearing in the forest of nature going to be ascribed a mediating role? That is, will she have to perform some sort of synthesis between nature and culture because of her "in-between" position? Or will she be granted the freedom to create an action that will discover its own consequences?

What Fleda initially desires while living in this clearing by the whirlpool is a reconciliation of opposites, a "spiritual marriage of romance and domesticity" (30), a desire which is to some extent achieved by her reading of poetry and her keeping of a diary, both which act as devices "for distancing synchronised response" and allow her to live out of time and the ordinary apprehension of experience (31). In living the way she does, in a tent that responds to the elements, near a whirlpool that she doesn't understand but studies, she's begun to unpack herself from convention, particularly from her definition of marriage as "an accumulation of objects" (105). Out in the open, she is mostly solitary, taking pleasure in reading Browning's poetry, writing in her diary, attending to small domestic details, dreaming of and watching the whirlpool. She does not realise that she herself is being watched.

Enter Patrick, the tormented poet, who, "[u]nable to deal effectively with either the body or the soul of the new country" (69), has

---

[4]Heather Murray, "Women in the Wilderness" in *A Mazing Space: Writing Canadian Women Writing*, eds. Shirley Neuman and Smaro Kamboureli (Edmonton: Longspoon/Newest Press, 1986), p. 75.

constantly been in search of "an often elusive inspiration" which evades him. It evades him because he has learned the wrong language, the language of the British Romanticists, and hence has real problems understanding where he actually is. On one of his obsessive quests for poetic content, for instance, Patrick wades through the hip-deep snow of the Gatineau Hills in search of "Wordsworth's daffodils" (69), which, not surprisingly, are nowhere to be found among the rock of the Shield, the cedars and scotch pine. He shares this trick of imposing imported conventions on a new land with Fleda who regards the landscape of Niagara County as an absence as she compares it to the "undulations of the Tuscan countryside" and "the hill country of England" (31): there is nothing of that here, she notes in her diary.

Patrick has been sent to the edges, so to speak, from his civil service job in the metropolitan centre, to recover from a breakdown which left him almost languageless. On one of his rambles through the wild, he spots Fleda in the clearing. At first he is puzzled that a figure would enter one of "his landscapes"; then he finds she is a more interesting specimen than the birds he has been watching (37). He approaches her, only to get a better view from a distance. He "could not believe she was real, could not, at first, cope with the fact of her being there" (38), yet later desires "an utter comprehension of the forces that had moved her into the forest" (107). The image that immediately captures him, the one in which he freezes her, is "the way her body relaxed into the landscape ... as if her environment were an extension of herself" (40). How did she come to be so comfortable with the landscape, he wonders. How was it that she turned herself so fearlessly to the open? He wants to "[learn] the woman" (81). Figure out how she became unhoused. He thinks he does so by watching her, often, through his instruments of distance. He does not have to venture nearer nor does he want her any closer; he prefers to remain a voyeur, surmising the key to her ecological politics from this vantage.

To ensure Fleda remains who he desires her to be, he poeticises her. She is not simply a woman in a clearing; she is "like a woman in a painting, as though she had been dropped into the middle of the scene for decorative purposes, or to play a part in a legend" (39). She is an art object. Further, he transforms her, in order to keep her at bay and under his control, into "a child at play" (107). That way she remains whole, is not "fragmented into consideration of self and other" (107).

Fleda notices Patrick watching her. She has heard about the Canadian poet from her husband. She is flattered, delighted, that a poet would be interested in her and does not let on she knows she is being watched. She dresses for him, dreams about him, and silently, imaginatively, reciprocates his poeticisation of her. Browning has been her image-maker, so she frames her experience of Patrick in Browning's words and lets this literary representation shape and over-whelm her idea of Patrick. He becomes, to her, what she has read about: "I only knew one poet in my life/And this, or something like It, was his way," she quotes from "As It Strikes A Contemporary" in her journal after her first view of Patrick (131).

Both become obsessed with the other, before ever actually having met; succumb to the urge to interpret, imagine and invent; and end up with a "fixed idea" of the other. It's the major who aids in their respective constructions, serving as an unwitting mediator between the two, answering Patrick's questions about Fleda and Fleda's about Patrick. It is through him that each discovers the other is fascinated by the whirlpool.

Wanting to know more about this poet who wants to swim the whirlpool and why, desiring his friendship, for a start, Fleda drops her reticence: she initiates a conversation, their first beyond small talk, tentatively, about some of her musings, including a remark about "the veil [Patrick] was creating, the one that separated her from the present" (158). Clearly fearful of the subjective mode, Patrick dis-misses her overture by snapping "the imagination is a trap", fully aware that his chosen perception of Fleda is an imaginative one, one that won't withstand the eruption of the real, and one, presumably, he knows won't last. For he has dreaded meeting her; he knows that "one more step on his part and she would leave, forever, the territory of his dream and he would lose something, some power, some privacy, some control" (98). She is forcing him to do something he cannot: surrender the security of distance.

Patrick is "looking away" from the flesh-and-blood Fleda, "always looking away" because he has consciously chosen to operate at the level of subject/object experience:

> He didn't want her to have a voice, did not wish to face the actuality of her speech, how words would change the shape of her mouth, stiffen the relaxed bend of her neck which he had seen when he watched her read. (98)

Her subjectivity is simply not relevant to him: the real, more mundane Fleda, the woman of mind and words, the independent questioner, the wife, is not who he wants in his story. He does not want her to exist in the here and now but in a symbolic dimension. A bad poet, he mistakes image for ornament.

When Patrick denies her desire for intimacy by asserting his fear of closeness, she challenges him by admitting she knows he has been watching her, and that must mean he wants to be close to her. Their only face-to-face confrontation, their only real intercourse, is this: and this is when the real erupts for Patrick; to think that she may have been performing for him sickens him, his fantasy has been contaminated, dragged into "the mundane architecture of fact." (182) Fleda becomes now "... everything he had tried to escape from ... the smudge of the news on his fingers, the ink from his employment on his hands, the ugly red brick of his small house" (186). She is no longer a thing of beauty.

So it is on the middle ground, in the pseudo-wilderness that archetypically functions in much English-Canadian literature as a field for transformation and change, that each confronts the other.[5] And the recognition which follows from this confrontation—that they are subjects, that they exist and desire outside the other's control and definition—stuns them both. Their awareness of self and other comes without any joy, for what both have desired is a desire for what is not.[6] Clearly such a desire is an impediment to ever reaching the other. It's a desire that's at odds with the meeting of minds, bodies, subjects because in Patrick's case, it's a kind of addiction to the ideal, in Fleda's, an addiction to ambiguity.

Because of this encounter, the pseudo-wilderness in which it occurs can also be conceived of as an "intersubjective sphere", where what happens *between* individuals and *within* the individual in the presence of others is important as opposed to what happens within the individual psyche.[7] Perceived this way, something striking occurs

---

[5]Murray, p. 76.

[6]Juliet Mitchell, introduction to *Feminine Sexuality; Jacques Lacan and the "Ecole Freudienne*," eds. Mitchell and Rose, trans. Rose (New York: Norton, 1982), pp. 1-26.

[7]Jessica Benjamin, "A Desire of One's Own: Psychoanalytic Feminism and Intersubjective Space" in *Feminist Studies/Critical Studies*, ed. Teresa de Lauretis (Bloomington: Indiana UP, 1986), p. 92.

between the two. Each destroys the others' fantasy, yes, and in so doing Fleda becomes aware of and Patrick cannot sublimate the space between the I and the you. No trustworthy connection is made; neither language nor imagination can span the space between the woman and the poet. However, while each discovers or has reaffirmed that space, at the same time each discovers, as part of a continuum, "an inner space", wherein desire, constituted for and of the self, resides.[8] After this thwarted meeting of two subjects in the clearing, a recognition of intentions, an ability to express them through action, and the confidence that they are their own evolves in Patrick and Fleda. They realise their own notions of agency and desire.

After Fleda has asserted herself as an independently existing subject, Patrick reformulates his desire. He realises he has "dislocated and mixed categories ... [has confused] fear with desire, desire with quest, quest with fear" (192) and the result has been chaos. So he casts himself in an orderly script that will lead him to a definite resolution. His desire, he acknowledges, is not for Fleda but for the land: "It was landscape that he wanted and needed, uncomplicated setting, its ability to function in a pure, solitary state" (192). So the poet, who knows that he has never in his life acted as he wished, in whom every fibre of his being longed for and feared magnificent dramas, experiences a kind of Sartrean special moment, discovers a real belief, and swims the whirlpool.

Set on distance between himself and Fleda, he is not afraid of "merging" with the whirlpool, demonstrating an almost erotic love for water: "Submerge. To place oneself below and lose character, identity, inside another element" (80). For Patrick, swimming is an act which will renew the imagination and offer an escape from the "world above". It is also Romantic: an address to death, the ultimate communion with the natural world. And much more than an action designed to impress Fleda, the swim becomes a symbolic casting-off of the shackles of an old, inappropriate language, and the entrance "into another country, a journey he would choose to make in full knowledge that he hardly spoke the language" (221). He knows the whole space is alien to him; still he chooses it, and the physical goes back to the elemental.

For Patrick, the whirlpool is the right place, a place where chaos and order are synonymous. Swimming it is his battle and his strength. (Such a test is what he has been searching for.)

---

[8]Benjamin, 95.

Just as Fleda destroyed his fantasy, so Patrick destroyed hers. She felt, after their encounter, "like an abandoned house" (193); he demolished her dream; she was no longer part of the creation of poetry. Gone was erotic ambiguity: "the complex symbolism that had described the meaning behind the meaning" (194). She reads his poetry but is chilled by the absence of figures in its grey landscape. She has nothing left to interpret. As much as she wants, she cannot speak her anger to him. Instead, she resorts to actions—writes bitter notes to herself on torn pieces of paper; cuts her hair shorter and begins dressing in men's clothes as if she, her sexuality, were to blame. She tries to forget her dream poet and his denial of her, but her body won't let her. She's been sexually awakened. Her desire has not diminished, it's just less centralised, and an idea forms: the idea of departure.

Fleda leaves the clearing, the site no longer of her dream home but of McDougal's statement on the landscape. She rejects the geometry of squares, the architecture of order, the life of convention and containment his house represents. Further, she rejects submission to his sexual desires, desires which aren't generated by her but by Laura Secord, the Loyalist version of a pin-up girl. (To tickle his fancy, The Major requires that Fleda wear Laura's calico dress, complete with mud on the hem, as a prelude to intercourse.) Just as Patrick has to her, David poeticises Laura Secord and projects that image onto Fleda. Throughout their marriage, the transaction he has urged upon her is to read Laura Secord as mythic and emblematic, decoration and ornament. In his reading—remember, he's a war historian susceptible to mythologising history—Laura Secord takes on a national posture: she is woman as national muse. Because of her heroic twelve mile walk through enemy territory—feet shod in thin leather slippers and accompanied by a cow to fool the sentries—to inform Fitzgibbon of the American's position, "we" won and a colony formed an idea of itself as a nation. Fleda has intuited all along that once the idea of a nation influences the perception of a woman then that woman is suddenly and inevitably simplified. But only now does she actively disobey the Major's reading; she has her own ideas, about Laura Secord and about herself.

Determined neither to live a "closeted life" restrained by David's rules that "she had learned so well" nor endure the "soundless, heavy, seemingly endless" landscape, she leaves. Nobody's angel. In her diary, she says of Laura Secord's famous walk, "Nobody understood. It wasn't the message that was important. It was the walk. The journey. Setting forth" (219). So with her writing in hand, Fleda sets forth, following Laura Secord's route, only to assert her difference from her.

Where many Canadian novels end with the writing woman writing, alone, Urquhart breaks this pattern by ending at least the inner story of her novel with the writing woman walking, alone, with her writing.[9] It's worth contemplating what Fleda is walking away from. She's certainly walking away from a gendered sphere, from a marriage and dependence, from, she admits, her "recent past"; in doing so she is operating from drives she feels are her own and that come from within her. Whether or not she can bear them without losing herself is left to question. Might she also be walking away from Canada, from the idea of a nation as formulated by the Major? And, what, exactly, is she walking into? Into the disorder of over there? Is the wilderness into which she is heading a liberatory space, a new world where she can begin again or a desert?

In setting forth, Fleda takes possession of her desire and sees it her duty to fulfill. She feels the need to initiate a beginning. Perhaps the right place for her, the place she is walking to and searching for, is imaginary, an inner place where, rather than waiting to be found by an explorer, she can give herself the opportunity to explore as a creative activity. And perhaps there she can begin to see herself—not as others in the text have seen her—but as careful readers have—as an artist herself.

For David McDougal, Fleda's disappearance can have nothing voluntary about it. He is convinced that "something American" has happened to her—that at this moment she is being interrogated and tortured "by an American military historian who had heard about his work and was even now trying to obtain, by God knows what terrifying means, information concerning his views on the Siege of Fort Erie" (228). His worst fears have been realised—the republican rabble have broken down his door and, unspeakably, violated his wife. Momentarily he feels the world evaporating before his eyes, but he only allows chaos to penetrate his mind briefly. Anything implying disorder is unacceptable to him, something that should not be in the world and ought to be conquered, by violence if necessary. He has always envisioned himself "as being a center of calm in the thick of imagined chaos" (133). So after being deserted by Fleda, he

---

[9]Robert Kroetch, "Beyond Nationalism: A Prologue" in *The Lovely Treachery of Words: Essays Selected and New* (Toronto, Oxford UP, 1989), p.70.

compensates by going to the war museum. This is the place, like the whirlpool for Patrick, where opposites are reconciled. Ironically, "there was peace [at the museum], and the major knew it" (231). For David war is "bullets, gunflints, cannon-balls, caged and harmless in their glass cabinets" (231). No further statements to make, no more journeys to embark on. For David, war is peace.

CHAPTER ELEVEN: NUTS AND BOLTS
(OR SURVIVING ESSAY WRITING)

The bulk of this book has been aimed at demonstrating and explaining various rhetorical strategies, much of which can be considered basic building blocks of your argument when creating an essay. However, whether or not you've been out of school for one summer break, or for a few dozen years while pursuing another career, there is nothing quite so frightening as sitting down to write that first essay. As you can see demonstrated in the pages of this book, there are myriad ways to write an essay, to phrase an argument, to nail a point. What this chapter will offer you is a safety net, a surefire way to create an essay that will do all that is required of you. The more practice you have, the less you will look down to see if the net is indeed there to catch you. You will find yourself experimenting, combining, and inventing ways to make your argument fly. In the meantime, let's just make sure you never plummet. You must understand, however, that while this "recipe" for an essay will give you a solid essay every time, you will likely not win an essay writing bake-off without adding ingredients of your own.

The rule of thumb in every essay has been summed up in an age old phrase: "Tell them what you're going to tell them, tell them, and then tell them what you told them." This may sound somewhat redundant, and lord knows that is not what any of us want, but it for the most part holds true. Your readers do require a road map to navigate your essay, and that is what a strong opening paragraph, complete with thesis statement, will give them.

How do you come up with a strong opening paragraph? First of all, you require a strong outline. Once you have determined what you intend to argue, and the three strongest points that will make your case, you can synthesize the skeleton of your outline into your opening paragraph.

Did you notice I said three strongest points? There is a reason for three. Writing is very much like Zen, where groups of three and five are considered to be the most tranquil and aesthetic for consideration.

A thousand-word essay requirement should take you no more than three points to create. Any more major points and you will either be in danger of running over your maximum word length, or short-changing your argument. Each paragraph of the body of your essay should focus on one major point of your argument, delineating it in a topic sentence, and then bolstering it with proof, expert witnesses, and explanation.

Much like every cell of a living organism is a complete entity, each paragraph in your essay should be organized much the same way as your essay. Lead off with your thesis statement, so your reader knows where you are taking him. Bolster your point with three solid bits of proof. Tie up your point before moving on to the next bit of your argument. Create a link from one paragraph to the next, so that your reader can wend her way from point to point rather than leaping heroically across ice floes to reach the concluding far shore.

Your conclusion (tell them what you told them) is vital, because as we've said in other places in this book, readers cannot be trusted to give their undivided attention to every word of your essay. They will drift in places. They need you to tie up the whole argument into a clearly defined capsulized package. If you are following this recipe closely, you will see that what you have will be five paragraphs consisting of introduction, three paragraphs of body, and conclusion. It really isn't all that hard once you're started.

So you now have an introduction, a body, and a conclusion. Pat yourself on the back. All right, now back to work. What you have is a first draft. You are still miles away from having something you will want to submit for someone else's eyes to see. Remember, that when other people actually read your work, you cannot be there to explain, or highlight, or answer any questions they might have. Your words will have to stand on their own. They are ambassadors from your brain. As such, it is always best to make them the best you can possibly make them.

The first rule, which is never followed by students writing to deadline, but I'll say it anyway, is to give yourself enough time to be able to put the essay away for at least twenty-four hours. The information and arguments you have been working with are like food in a microwave. Even after you've taken them out of the microwave and put them on paper, they'll continue to cook for a while. When you return to your first draft, you may spot holes in your argument, or discover another way of ordering the points to create a more impressive whole. You may just have come up with some better phrasing, or even one particular word that was lying at the back of your consciousness which you couldn't dredge up at the initial time of writing. Without some preplanning, this additional ruminating time will be lost to you. There is a reason why instructors hand out topics well before the deadline. It's in your best interest not to leave your essay till the last minute.

Once your paper is as ready as you think it can be, you are still not ready to turn it in. Just as you wouldn't want to meet your new inlaws with a piece of parsley on your teeth, you need to check your paper over for correctable flaws. Proofreading something that you've been submerged in for some time is not easy. Your own words there in black on the pristine white paper tend to look terrific, and your eye somehow skips over the fact that you've typed out an entire sentence twice or missed a word. Take a ruler to keep your eye trained on the line of type, and read your paper backwards, beginning from the last line, and going back through the entire text. This will not make any sense thematically, but misspelled words and improper punctuation will stand out. You will begin to see the trees for the forest. You will also find sentence fragments when you read your paper backward, line by line. Every sentence should be able to stand on its own sensibly. A formal essay is no place for a fragment, however stylistic it might seem. Get in there and find that verb. After reading it through backwards, reread your essay from the beginning. See if there is anything else you haven't caught. At this moment your eyes will be as fresh to the words as they can be, having been disoriented by the backward glance.

Another proofreading technique that will help your paper is to read the entire work aloud. You needn't have an audience for this. In fact, if you are embarrassed, lock yourself in the bathroom and turn on the tap to cover your actions. However, you must listen to your own words. Do they flow well? Are you having trouble with any particular sentence? If you need to read it twice for it to make sense, perhaps you should rewrite it for clarity. If you are out of breath reading a sentence, it might get tagged "run on" by a marker. You will discover wayward commas and semicolons in this way as well.

If you have someone you can read your essay to, who will not try to rewrite the entire argument for you, it would be helpful to buy this person a coffee and do so. If she understands the concepts you are presenting and can follow your argument as you've laid it out, it is a worthwhile exercise. Combined with reading it aloud, you will see if your argument holds water as well as if your sentences flow properly.

If your colleague begins to argue with you, take a careful look at whether you've left holes in your argument. It could be you've merely created a beautifully controversial position, and you have nothing to fear. However, if you find yourself having to explain a particular point for the entire argument to make sense to your listener, perhaps you need to go back into the essay and work on that section.

If you know you are a bad speller, be very careful and check any word you are not absolutely sure of. It is not enough to rely on any "spell checker" that comes with your word-processing program, since most of them will not recognize homonyms. *Eye cheque aver thyme, and eye right whale.* (That sentence wasn't lit up at all by my spell checker as I typed it.) There are various words that are commonly misspelled, and most handbooks and some dictionaries will have lists of them. See if any of them are regular problems for you. The difference between a good speller and a bad speller is sheer memory, nothing more. There are anachronisms in the English language that defy logic. Likewise, there are words that, through ages of slurring or dialectical differences, seem to sound wrong when spelled properly. My own nemesis of a word is "separate." The first "a" in there still looks wrong to me, since, when I speak, it is flattened into an "e." However, I've learned to knuckle under and spell it the way the rest of the world wants to see it. Bad spelling is detrimental to your argument. No matter how many cogent points you make, if your words are misspelled it works to undermine your intelligence in the mind of your reader, and you will be arguing from behind the eight ball.

The most common error I've come across in years of marking papers is the misuse of the apostrophe in "its" and "it's." The simplest way to correct this, if this is one of your problems, is to always remember that an apostrophe is there to indicate that a letter is missing, so that two words can be contracted and joined together. It's a good thing to remember. See that apostrophe? It is standing in for the "i" in "It is." It is being used properly in this case. However, if I were to write, "The dog gnawed on its bone," there would be no need for an apostrophe, since one cannot read that sentence as "The dog gnawed on it is bone" and have it make sense. If you are ever in doubt, try putting in the letters the apostrophe should replace, and determine if the sentence still makes sense. Some people, when trying to overcompensate for their trouble with "its," decide to eliminate apostrophes from all possessives. In that case, you have to decide whether the apostrophe is there to denote that the attached "s" means there is an object that belongs to the person or thing you are speaking of, or whether you want to indicate that there is more than one person or thing. For instance, do you mean to refer to "radio's blaring," (a commentary on the sound from the medium of radio), or are you talking about "radios blaring" (a commentary on the sound heard at the public beach, with many radios all turned on at once). One apostrophe can change the meaning of an entire sentence.

Before the advent of word processors, there was an inclination by desultory typists to leave second-rate paragraphs standing, rather than cleaning them up. Now, with such lovely tools as "cut and paste," and the ability to delete and add bits in to your work in progress, there is really no excuse not to submit work that is always proving your potential.

While we're on the topic, there is absolutely no excuse any more to submit non-typewritten assignments. Your paper should arrive with margins of about an inch on all sides, on 8 1/2 x 11" white bond paper. Your essay should be double-spaced, which allows for ease of reading and room for edit marks. A title page covering it with the title, your name, and the course number is also useful. If you put a "submitted to" line on your title page, make sure you spell the instructor's name correctly. Number your pages, in case they get shuffled in some accidental blizzard of paper. Attach them together with a paper clip or a staple, rather than any fancy plastic cover.

Determine from your particular instructor or editor what form of documentation they require. If they have no preference, either the MLA or the APA format are the most widely acceptable. Haul out your handbook and follow the rules. Consistency is everything when documenting. Check your Reference or Works Cited page as you proofread.

There is a final comment to make and that concerns what to do when your essay is returned to you, graded. Chances are there are more marks on it than just the letter or percentage grade scrawled at the bottom. Pay attention to commentary on consistent problems or some queries in the margins of your text. You may never again receive such constructive criticism (for free) on your writing. Learn and grow from errors you've made, and correct them in future essays. The clearer your writing becomes, the clearer your thoughts will be. That may sound backward to you, and in some ways clear thinking does create clear writing. However, an ability to express yourself clearly and to formulate and set down a clear thought somehow enables the next thought to appear less muddled in your head.

396 ❈ *Chapter Eleven*

The root of all writing is always communication. If the lines of communication are clear, the world becomes a better place. In other words, as you sit down to start that first essay, you're not only fulfilling an arbitrary requirement for a specific class, you're helping to foster peace in our time. There, doesn't that take the pressure off? Good luck.

Appendix

This section is a collection of essays from beyond the borders of Canada and beyond the spectrum of contemporary timelines. The authors of these essays have long been renowned for their skills as essayists, and this selection is meant to give you some indication of the scope and power of the essay as a rhetorical and aesthetic tool.

There is also something to be gained in seeing the lineage from which today's essays spring. No writer appears out of a vacuum. Anyone with anything to say has spent his lifetime reading and watching the world. Chances are very good that every single writer in this volume has also read these five essayists, if not these particular essays by them.

Jonathan Swift's "A Modest Proposal" has become a classic to show how satire can be used for political purposes. George Orwell, whose predictions of "newspeak" were dealt with in his infamous novel *1984,* writes cautionary words for writers in "Politics and the English Language," which hold as true today as they did for the time he wrote them. E.B. White, while now likely more famous for his children's books *Charlotte's Web* and *Stuart Little,* was also an essayist of renown and shows that the eye of a writer must be open to all the nuances of both adult and child in "Once More to the Lake."

Dorothy Parker, a member of the American writing elite of the Algonquin Roundtable set, was one of the most wittily urbane writers to have ever graced the planet. To read her is akin to eating fancy hors d'oeuvres—tantalizingly tasty, but not something with which one could ever make a balanced meal. And James Thurber, who gives us a taste of the days when there were scores of magazines brimming full of delightful writings, is someone whose writing, pinned specifically as it is to a set period in history, stands the test of time. The serene humanity he offers in his work makes his ponderings universal in their staying power.

All these writers provide samples of the various rhetorical strategies we've been isolating and examining through this book. Including them here is an attempt to offer you both a scaffolding on which to position the more contemporary essays you've been digesting, and an exhortation for you to go forth and both discover and uncover essays, new and old, which speak to your heart, your intellect, and your soul. Above all information, above all reportage, an essay should be an aesthetic experience. Demand from what you read a sensual and stimulating encounter. Moreover, when you write, use words well, and lovingly. You are joining your words to a magnificent tradition. Go forth, and write beautifully.

Jonathan Swift

Jonathan Swift is considered one of the world's great satirists. *Gulliver's Travels*, which is often mistakenly seen as a simple children's story, is actually a condemnation of the various petty characteristics of mankind. His famous essay about the "Irish Problem" has long been misunderstood by naïve readers.

A Modest Proposal

First Published in 1729

A MODEST PROPOSAL FOR PREVENTING THE CHILDREN OF POOR PEOPLE IN IRELAND FROM BEING A BURDEN TO THEIR PARENTS OR COUNTRY, AND FOR MAKING THEM BENEFICIAL TO THE PUBLIC

It is a *melancholy object to those who walk through this great town or travel* in the country, when they see the streets, the roads, and cabin doors, crowded with beggars of the female sex, followed by three, four, or six children, all in rags and importuning every passenger for an alms. These mothers, instead of being able to work for their honest livelihood, are forced to employ all their time in strolling to beg sustenance for their helpless infants: who as they grow up either turn thieves for want of work, or leave their dear native country to fight for the *Pretender in Spain*, or sell themselves to the *Barbadoes*.

I think it is agreed by all parties that this prodigious number of children in the arms, or on the backs, or at the heels of their mothers, and frequently of their fathers, is in the present deplorable state of the kingdom a very *great additional grievance*; and, therefore, whoever could find out a fair, *cheap, and easy* method of making these children sound, useful members of the commonwealth, would deserve so well of the public as to have his statue set up for a preserver of the nation.

But my intention is very far from being confined to provide only for the children of professed beggars; it is of a much greater extent, and shall take in the whole number of infants at a certain age who are born of parents in effect as little able to support them as those who demand our *charity in the streets*.

As to my own part, having turned my thoughts for many years upon this important subject, and maturely weighed the several schemes of other projectors, I have always found them grossly mistaken in the computation. It is true, a child just dropped from its dam may be supported by her milk for a solar year, with little other nourishment; at most not above the value of 2s., which the mother may certainly get, or the value in scraps, by her lawful occupation of begging; and it is exactly at one year old that I propose to provide for them in such a manner as instead of being a charge upon their parents or the parish, or wanting food and raiment for the rest of their lives, they shall on the contrary contribute to the feeding, and partly to the clothing, of many thousands.

There is likewise another great advantage in my scheme, that it will *prevent* those voluntary abortions, and that horrid practice of women murdering their bastard children, alas! too frequent among us! sacrificing the poor innocent babes I doubt more to avoid the expense than the shame, which would move tears and pity in the most savage and inhuman breast.

The number of souls in this kingdom being usually reckoned *one million and a half*, of these I calculate there may be about two hundred thousand couple whose wives are *breeders*, from which number I subtract thirty thousand couples who are able to maintain their own children, although I apprehend there cannot be so many, under the present distresses of the kingdom; but this being granted, there will remain an hundred and seventy thousand breeders. I again subtract fifty thousand for those women who miscarry, or whose children die by accident or disease within the year. There only remains one hundred and twenty thousand children of poor parents annually born. The question therefore is, how this number shall be reared and provided for, which, as I have already said, under the present situation of affairs, is utterly impossible by all the methods hitherto proposed. For we can neither employ them in handicraft or agriculture; we neither build houses (I mean in the country) nor cultivate land: they can very seldom pick up a livelihood by *stealing*, till they arrive at six years old, except where they are of towardly parts, although I confess they learn the rudiments much earlier, during which time, they can however be properly looked upon only as probationers, as I have been informed by a principal gentleman in the county of Cavan, who protested to me that he never knew above one or two instances under the age of six, even in a part of the kingdom so renowned for the quickest proficiency in that art.

I am assured by our merchants, that a boy or a girl before twelve years old is no salable commodity; and even when they come to this age they will not yield above three pounds, or three pounds and half-a-crown at most on the exchange; which cannot turn to account either to the parents or kingdom, the charge of nutriment and rags having been at least four times that value.

I shall now therefore humbly propose my own thoughts, which I hope will not be liable to the least objection.

I have been assured by a very knowing *American* of my acquaintance in London, that a young healthy child well nursed is at a year old a most delicious, nourishing, and wholesome food, whether stewed, roasted, baked, or boiled; and I make no doubt that it will equally serve in a fricassee or a ragout.

I do therefore humbly offer it to public consideration that of the hundred and twenty thousand children already computed, twenty thousand may be reserved for breed, whereof only one-fourth part to be males; which is more than we allow to *sheep, black cattle or swine*; and my reason is, that these children are seldom the fruits of *marriage*, a circumstance not much regarded by our savages, therefore one male will be sufficient to serve four females. That the remaining hundred thousand may, at a year old, be offered in the sale to the persons of quality and fortune through the kingdom; always advising the mother to let them suck plentifully in the last month, so as to render them plump and fat for a good table. A child will make two dishes at an entertainment for friends; and when the family dines alone, the fore or hind quarter will make a reasonable dish, and seasoned with a little pepper or salt will be very good boiled on the fourth day, especially in winter.

I have reckoned upon a medium that a child just born will weigh 12 pounds, and in a solar year, if tolerably nursed, increaseth to 28 pounds.

I grant this food will be somewhat dear, and therefore very proper for landlords, who, as they have already devoured most of the parents, seem to have the best title to the children.

Infant's flesh will be in season throughout the year, but more plentiful in March, and a little before and after; for we are told by a grave author, an eminent French physician, that fish being a prolific diet, there are more children born in *Roman Catholic* countries about nine months after Lent than at any other season; therefore, reckoning a year after Lent, the markets will be *more glutted than usual*, because the number of popish infants is at least three to one in this kingdom: and therefore it will have one other collateral advantage, by lessening the number of papists among us.

I have already computed the charge of nursing a beggar's child (in which list I reckon all cottagers, laborers, and four-fifths of the farmers) to be about two shillings per annum, rags included; and I believe no gentleman would repine to give ten shillings for the carcass of a good fat child, which, as I have said, will make four dishes of excellent nutritive meat, when he hath only some particular friend or his own family to dine with him. Thus the squire will learn to be a good landlord, and grow popular among his tenants; the mother will have eight shillings net *profit*, and be fit for work till she produces another child.

Those who are more thrifty (as I must confess the times require) may flay the carcass; the skin of which artificially dressed will make admirable gloves for ladies, and summer boots for fine gentlemen.

As to our city of Dublin, shambles may be appointed for this purpose in the most convenient parts of it, and *butchers* we may be assured will not be wanting; although I rather recommend buying the children alive, and dressing them hot from the knife, as we do roasting pigs.

A very worthy person, a true lover of his country, and whose virtues I highly esteem, was lately pleased in discoursing on this matter to offer a refinement upon my scheme. He said that many gentlemen of this kingdom, having of late destroyed their deer, he conceived that the want of venison might be well supplied by the bodies of young lads and maidens, not exceeding fourteen years of age nor under twelve; so great a number of both sexes in every country being now ready to starve for want of work and service, and these to be disposed of by their parents, if alive, or otherwise by their nearest relations. But with due deference to so excellent a friend and so deserving a patriot, I cannot be altogether in his sentiments; for as to the males, my American acquaintance assured me, from frequent experience, that their flesh was generally tough and lean, like that of our schoolboys by continual exercise, and their taste disagreeable; and to fatten them would not answer the charge. Then as to the females, it would, I think, with humble submission be a loss to the public, because they soon would become breeders themselves; and besides, it is not improbable that some scrupulous people might be apt to censure such a practice (although indeed very unjustly), as a little *bordering upon cruelty*; which, I confess, hath always been with me the strongest objection against any project, however so well intended.

But in order to justify my friend, he confessed that this expedient was put into his head by the famous Psalmanazar, a native of the island Formosa, who came from thence to London above twenty years ago, and in conversation told my friend, that in his country when any young person happened to be put to death, the executioner sold the carcass to persons of quality as a prime dainty; and that in his time the body of a plump girl of fifteen, who was crucified for an attempt to poison the emperor, was sold to his imperial majesty's prime minister of state, and other great mandarins of the court, in joints from the gibbet, at four hundred crowns. Neither indeed can I deny, that if the same use were made of several plump young girls in this town, who without one single groat to their fortunes cannot stir abroad without a chair, and appear at playhouse and assemblies in foreign fineries which they never will pay for, the kingdom would not be the worse.

Some persons of a desponding spirit are in great concern about that vast number of poor people, who are aged, diseased, or maimed, and I have been desired to employ my thoughts what course may be taken to ease the nation of so grievous an encumbrance. But I am not in the least pain upon that matter, because it is very well known that they are *every day dying* and rotting by cold and famine, and filth and vermin, as fast as can be reasonably expected. And as to the young laborers, they are now in as hopeful a condition; they cannot get work, and consequently pine away for want of nourishment, to a degree that if at any time they are accidentally hired to common labor, *they have not strength to perform it*; and thus the country and themselves are happily delivered from the evils to come.

I have too long digressed, and therefore shall return to my subject. I think the advantages by the proposal which I have made are obvious and many, as well as of the highest importance.

For first, as I have already observed, it would greatly lessen the number of papists, with whom we are yearly overrun, being the principal breeders of the nation as well as our most dangerous enemies; and who stay at home on purpose with a design to deliver the kingdom to the Pretender, hoping to take their advantage by the absence of so many good Protestants, who have chosen rather to leave their country than stay at home and pay tithes against their conscience to an episcopal curate.

Secondly, The poorer tenants will have something valuable of their own, which by law may be made liable to distress and help to pay their landlord's rent, their corn and *cattle* being already seized, and money a thing unknown.

Thirdly, Whereas the maintenance of an hundred thousand children, from two years old and upward, cannot be computed at less than ten shillings a-piece per annum, the nation's stock will be thereby increased fifty thousand pounds per annum, beside the profit of a new dish introduced to the tables of all gentlemen of fortune in the kingdom who have any refinement in taste. And the money will circulate among ourselves, the goods being entirely of our own growth and manufacture.

Fourthly, The constant breeders, beside the gain of eight shillings sterling per annum by the sale of their children, will be rid of the charge of maintaining them after the first year. Fifthly, This food would likewise bring great custom to taverns; where the vintners will certainly be so prudent as to procure the best receipts for dressing it to perfection, and consequently have their houses frequented by all the fine gentlemen, who justly value themselves upon their knowledge in good eating: and a skillful cook, who understands how to oblige his guests, will contrive to make it as expensive as they please.

Sixthly, This would be a great inducement to marriage, which all wise nations have either encouraged by rewards or enforced by laws and penalties. It would increase the care and tenderness of mothers toward their children, when they were sure of a settlement for life to the poor babes, provided in some sort by the public, to their annual profit instead of expense. We should see an honest emulation among the married women, which of them could bring the fattest child to the market. Men would become as fond of their wives during the time of their pregnancy as they are now of their mares in foal, their cows in calf, their sows when they are ready to farrow; nor offer to beat or kick them (as is too frequent a practice) for fear of a miscarriage.

Many other advantages might be enumerated. For instance, the addition of some thousand carcasses in our exportation of barreled beef, the propagation of swine's flesh, and improvement in the art of making good bacon, so much wanted among us by the great destruction of pigs, too frequent at our tables; which are no way comparable in taste or magnificence to a well-grown, fat, yearling child, which roasted whole will make a considerable figure at a lord mayor's feast or any other public entertainment. But this and many others I omit, being studious of brevity.

Supposing that one thousand families in this city would be constant customers for infants flesh, besides others who might have it at merry meetings, particularly weddings and christenings; I compute that Dublin would take off annually about twenty thousand carcasses, and the rest of the kingdom (where probably they will be sold somewhat cheaper) the remaining eighty thousand.

I can think of no one objection that will possibly be raised against this proposal unless it should be urged that the number of people will be thereby much lessened in the kingdom. This I freely own, and it was indeed one principal design in offering it to the world. I desire the reader will observe, that I calculate my remedy for this one individual Kingdom of Ireland, and for no other that ever was, is, or, I think, ever can be upon earth. Therefore, let no man talk to me of other expedients: Of taxing our absentees at five shillings a pound: Of using neither clothes, manufacture: Of utterly rejecting the materials and instruments that promote foreign luxury: Of curing the expensiveness of pride, vanity, idleness, and gaming in our women: Of introducing a vein of parsimony, prudence, and temperance: Of learning to love our country, wherein we differ even from Laplanders, and the inhabitants of Topinamboo: of quitting our animosities and factions, nor act any longer like the Jews, who were murdering one another at the moment their city was taken: Of being a little cautious not to sell our country and consciences for nothing: Of teaching landlords to have at least one degree of mercy towards their tenants. Lastly, of putting a spirit of honesty, industry, and skill into our shopkeepers, who if a resolution could now be taken to buy only our native goods, would immediately unite to cheat and exact upon us in the price, the measure and the goodness, nor could ever yet be brought to make one fair proposal of just dealing, though often and earnestly invited to it.

Therefore, I repeat, let no man talk to me of these and the like expedients, till he hath at least a glimpse of hope that there will ever be some hearty and sincere attempt to put them in practice. But as to myself, having been wearied out for many years with offering vain, idle, visionary thoughts, and at length utterly despairing of success, I fortunately fell upon this proposal, which, as it is wholly new, so it hath something solid and real, of no expense and little trouble, full in our own power, and whereby we can incur no danger in disobliging England. For this king of commodity will not bear exportation, the flesh being of too tender a consistence to admit a long continuance in salt, although perhaps I could name a *country* which would be glad to eat up our whole nation without it.

After all, I am not so violently bent upon my own opinion as to reject any offer proposed by wise men, which shall be found equally innocent, cheap, easy, and effectual. But before something of that kind shall be advanced in contradiction to my scheme, and offering a better, I desire the author or authors will be pleased maturely to consider two points. First, as things now stand, how they will be able to find food and raiment for an hundred thousand useless mouths and backs. And secondly, there being a round million of creatures in human figure throughout this kingdom, whose whole subsistence put into a common stock would leave them in debt two millions of pounds sterling, adding those who are beggars by profession to the bulk of farmers, cottagers, and laborers, with their wives and children who are beggars in effect: I desire those politicians who dislike my overture, and may perhaps be so bold as to attempt an answer, that they will first ask the parents of these mortals, whether they would not at this day think it a great happiness to have been sold for food, at a year old in the manner I prescribe, and thereby have avoided such a perpetual scene of misfortunes as they have since gone through by the oppression of landlords, the impossibility of paying rent without money or trade, the want of common sustenance, with neither house nor clothes to cover them from the inclemencies of the weather, and the most inevitable prospect of entailing the like or greater miseries upon their breed for ever.

I profess, in the sincerity of my heart, that I have not the least personal interest in endeavoring to promote this necessary work, having no other motive than the public good of my country, by advancing our trade, providing for infants, relieving the poor, and giving some pleasure to the rich. *I have no children by which I can propose to get a single penny, the youngest being nine years old, and my wife past child-bearing.*

George Orwell

George Orwell was born in Motihari, Bengal, India. He attended Eton, where he published his first writings in college periodicals. In 1922 he went to Burma to serve in the Indian Imperial Police and later recounted his experiences in *Shooting an Elephant* and *A Hanging*. His subsequent experiences as a beggar in Europe gave him material for *Down and Out in Paris and London*.

In the 1930s Orwell adopted socialistic views and travelled in Spain to report on the Civil War. The war made him a strong opposer of communism. From this and further political musings sprang the famous *Animal Farm* and *1984*.

Politics and the English Language

Most people who bother with the matter at all would admit that the English language is in a bad way, but it is generally assumed that we cannot by conscious action do anything about it. Our civilization is decadent and our language—so the argument runs—must inevitably share in the general collapse. It follows that any struggle against the abuse of language is a sentimental archaism, like preferring candles to electric light or hansom cabs to aeroplanes. Underneath this lies the half-conscious belief that language is a natural growth and not an instrument which we shape for our own purposes.

Now, it is clear that the decline of a language must ultimately have political and economic causes: it is not due simply to the bad influence of this or that individual writer. But an effect can become a cause, reinforcing the original cause and producing the same effect in an intensified form, and so on indefinitely. A man may take to drink because he feels himself to be a failure, and then fail all the more completely because he drinks. It is rather the same thing that is happening to the English language. It becomes ugly and inaccurate because our thoughts are foolish, but the slovenliness of our language makes it easier for us to have foolish thoughts. The point is that the process is reversible. Modern English, especially written English, is full of bad habits which spread by imitation and which can be avoided if one is willing to take the necessary trouble. If one gets rid of these habits one can think more clearly, and to think clearly is a necessary first step toward political regeneration: so that the fight against bad English is not frivolous and is not the exclusive concern of professional writers. I will come back to this presently, and I hope that by that time the meaning of what I have said here will have become clearer. Meanwhile, here are five specimens of the English language as it is now habitually written.

These five passages have not been picked out because they are especially bad—I could have quoted far worse if I had chosen—but because they illustrate various of the mental vices from which we now suffer. They are a little below the average, but are fairly representative samples. I number them so that I can refer back to them when necessary:

(1) I am not, indeed, sure whether it is not true to say that the Milton who once seemed not unlike a seventeenth-century Shelley had not become, out of an experience ever more bitter in each year, more alien [*sic*] to the founder of that Jesuit sect which nothing could induce him to tolerate.

Professor Harold Laski
(Essay in *Freedom of Expression*)

(2) Above all, we cannot play ducks and drakes with a native battery of idioms which prescribes such egregious collocations of vocables as the basic *put up with* for *tolerate* or *put at a loss* for *bewilder*.

Professor Lancelot Hogben (*Interglossa*)

(3) On the one side we have the free personality: by definition it is not neurotic, for it has neither conflict nor dream. Its desires, such as they are, are transparent, for they are just what institutional approval keeps in the forefront of consciousness; another institutional pattern would alter their number and intensity; there is little in them that is natural, irreducible, or culturally dangerous. But *on the other side*, the social bond itself is nothing but the mutual reflection of these self-secure integrities. Recall the definition of love. Is not this the very picture of a small academic? Where is there a place in this hall of mirrors for either personality or fraternity?

Essay on psychology in Politics (New York)

(4) All the "best people" from the gentlemen's clubs, and all the frantic fascist captains, united in common hatred of Socialism and bestial horror of the rising tide of the mass revolutionary movement, have turned to acts of provocation, to foul incendiarism, to medieval legends of poisoned wells, to legalize their own destruction of proletarian organizations, and rouse the agitated petty-bourgeoisie to chauvinistic fervor on behalf of the

fight against the revolutionary way out of the crisis.

Communist pamphlet

(5) If new spirit is to be infused into this old country, there is one thorny and contentious reform which must be tackled, and that is the humanization and galvanization of the B.B.C. Timidity here will bespeak canker and atrophy of the soul. The heart of Britain may be sound and of strong beat, for instance, but the British lion's roar at present is like that of Bottom in Shakespeare's *Midsummer Night's Dream*—as gentle as any sucking dove. A virile new Britain cannot continue indefinitely to be traduced in the eyes, or rather ears, of the world by the effete languors of Langham Place, brazenly masquerading as "standard English." When the Voice of Britain is heard at nine o'clock, better far and infinitely less ludicrous to hear aitches honestly dropped than the present priggish, inflated, inhibited, school-ma'amish arch braying of blameless bashful mewing maidens!

Letter in *Tribune*

Each of these passages has faults of its own, but, quite apart from avoidable ugliness, two qualities are common to all of them. The first is staleness of imagery; the other is lack of precision. The writer either has a meaning and cannot express it, or he inadvertently says something else, or he is almost indifferent as to whether his words mean anything or not. This mixture of vagueness and sheer incompetence is the most marked characteristic of modern English prose, and especially of any kind of political writing. As soon as certain topics are raised, the concrete melts into the abstract and no one seems able to think of turns of speech that are not hackneyed: prose consists less and less of *words* chosen for the sake of their meaning, and more and more of *phrases* tacked together like the sections of a prefabricated henhouse. I list below, with notes and examples, various of the tricks by means of which the work of prose-construction is habitually dodged:

Dying metaphors. A newly invented metaphor assists thought by evoking a visual image, while on the other hand a metaphor which is technically "dead" (e.g., *iron resolution*) has in effect reverted to being an ordinary word and can generally be used without loss of vividness. But in between these two classes there is a huge dump of worn-out metaphors which have lost all evocative power and are merely used because they save people the trouble of inventing phrases for themselves. Examples are: *Ring the changes on, take up the cudgels for, toe the line, ride roughshod over, stand shoulder to shoulder with, play into the hands of, no axe to grind, grist to the mill, fishing in troubled waters, on the order of the day, Achilles' heel, swan song, hotbed.* Many of these are used without knowledge of their meaning (what is a "rift," for instance?), and incompatible metaphors are frequently mixed, a sure sign that the writer is not interested in what he is saying. Some metaphors now current have been twisted out of their original meaning without those who use them ever being aware of the fact. For example, *toe the line* is sometimes written *tow the line.* Another example is *the hammer and the anvil,* now always used with the implication that the anvil gets the worst of it. In real life it is always the anvil that breaks the hammer, never the other way about: a writer who stopped to think what he was saying would be aware of this, and would avoid perverting the original phrase.

Operators or verbal false limbs. These save the trouble of picking out appropriate verbs and nouns, and at the same time pad each sentence with extra syllables which give it an appearance of symmetry. Characteristic phrases are *render inoperative, militate against, make contact with, be subjected to, give grounds for, have the effect of, play a leading part (role) in, make itself felt, take effect, exhibit a tendency to, serve the purpose of,* etc., etc. The key-note is the elimination of simple verbs. Instead of being a single word, such as *break, stop, spoil, mend, kill,* a verb becomes a *phrase,* made up of a noun or adjective tacked on to some general-purpose verb such as *prove, serve, form, play, render.* In addition, the passive voice is wherever possible used in preference to the active, and noun constructions are used instead of gerunds (*by examination* of instead of *by examining*). The range of verbs is further cut down by means of the *-ize* and *de* – formations, and the banal statements are given an appearance of profundity by means of the *not un* – formation. Simple conjunctions and prepositions are replaced by such phrases as *with respect to, having regard to, the fact that, by dint of, in view of, in the interests of, on the hypothesis that;* and the ends of sentences are saved from anticlimax by such resounding commonplaces as *greatly to be desired, cannot be left out of account, a development to be expected in the near future, deserving of serious consideration, brought to a satisfactory conclusion,* and so on and so forth.

Pretentious diction. Words like *phenomenon, element, individual* (as noun), *objective, categorical, effective, virtual, basic, primary, promote, constitute, exhibit, exploit, utilize, eliminate, liquidate,* are used to dress up simple statements and give an air of scientific impartiality to biased judgments. Adjectives like *epoch-making, epic, historic, unforgettable, triumphant, age-old, inevitable, inexorable, veritable,* are used to dignify the sordid process of international politics, while writing that aims at glorifying war usually takes on an archaic color, its characteristic words being: *realm, throne, chariot, mailed fist, trident, sword, shield, buckler, banner, jackboot, clarion.* Foreign words and expressions such as *cul de sac, ancien régime, deus ex machina, mutatis mutandis, status quo, gleichschaltung, weltanschauung,* are used to give an air of culture and elegance. Except for the useful abbreviations *i.e., e.g.,* and *etc.,* there is no real need for any of the hundreds of foreign phrases now current in English. Bad writers, and especially scientific, political, and sociological writers, are nearly always haunted by the notion that Latin or Greek words are grander than Saxon ones, and unnecessary words like *expedite, ameliorate, predict, extraneous, deracinated, clandestine, subaqueous,* and hundreds of others constantly gain ground from their Anglo-Saxon opposite numbers.[1] The jargon peculiar to Marxist writing (*hyena, hangman, cannibal, petty bourgeois, these gentry, lackey, flunkey, mad dog, White Guard,* etc.) consists largely of words and phrases translated from Russian, German, or French; but the normal way of coining a new word is to use a Latin or Greek root with the appropriate affix and, where necessary, the *-ize* formation. It is often easier to make up words of this kind (*deregionalize, impermissible, extra-marital, nonfragmentary* and so forth) than to think up the English words that will cover one's meaning. The result, in general, is an increase in slovenliness and vagueness.

Meaningless words. In certain kinds of writing, particularly in art criticism and literary criticism, it is normal to come across long

---

[1] An interesting illustration of this is the way in which the English flower names which were in use till very recently are being ousted by Greek ones, *snapdragon* becoming *antirrhinum, forget-me-not* becoming *myosotis,* etc. It is hard to see any practical reason for this change of fashion: it is probably due to an instinctive turning away from the more homely word and a vague feeling that the Greek word is scientific. [Orwell's note]

passages which are almost completely lacking in meaning.[2] Words like *romantic*, *plastic*, *values*, *human*, *dead*, *sentimental*, *natural*, *vitality*, as used in art criticism, are strictly meaningless, in the sense that they not only do not point to any discoverable object, but are hardly ever expected to do so by the reader. When one critic writes, "The outstanding feature of Mr. X's work is its living quality," while another writes, "The immediately striking thing about Mr. X's work is its peculiar deadness," the reader accepts this as a simple difference of opinion. If words like *black* and *white* were involved, instead of the jargon words *dead* and *living*, he would see at once that language was being used in an improper way. Many political words are similarly abused. The word *Fascism* has now no meaning except in so far as it signifies "something not desirable." The words *democracy*, *socialism*, *freedom*, *patriotic*, *realistic*, *justice*, have each of them several different meanings which cannot be reconciled with one another. In the case of a word like *democracy*, not only is there no agreed definition, but the attempt to make one is resisted from all sides. It is almost universally felt that when we call a country democratic we are praising it: consequently the defenders of every kind of régime claim that it is a democracy, and fear that they might have to stop using the word if it were tied down to any one meaning. Words of this kind are often used in a consciously dishonest way. That is, the person who uses them has his own private definition, but allows his hearer to think he means something quite different. Statements like *Marshall Pétain was a true patriot*, *The Soviet press is the freest in the world*, *The Catholic Church is opposed to persecution*, are almost always made with intent to deceive. Other words used in variable meanings, in most cases more or less dishonestly, are: *class*, *totalitarian*, *science*, *progressive*, *reactionary*, *bourgeois*, *equality*.

Now that I have made this catalogue of swindles and perversions, let me give another example of the kind of writing that they lead to. This time it must of its nature be an imaginary one. I am going to translate a passage of good English into modern English of the worst sort. Here is a well-known verse from *Ecclesiastes*:

---

[2]Example: "Comfort's catholicity of perception and image, strangely Whitmanesque in range, almost the exact opposite in aesthetic compulsion, continues to evoke that trembling atmospheric accumulative hinting at a cruel, an inexorably serene timelessness. ... Wrey Gardiner scores by aiming at simple bull's eyes with precision. Only they are not so simple, and through this contented sadness runs more than the surface bittersweet of resignation." *(Poetry Quarterly.)* [Orwell's note]

I returned and saw under the sun, that the race is not to the swift, nor the battle to the strong, neither yet bread to the wise, nor yet riches to men of understanding, nor yet favor to men of skill; but time and chance happeneth to them all.

Here it is in modern English:

Objective consideration of contemporary phenomena compels the conclusion that success or failure in competitive activities exhibits no tendency to be commensurate with innate capacity, but that a considerable element of the unpredictable must invariably be taken into account.

This is a parody, but not a very gross one. Exhibit (3), above, for instance, contains several patches of the same kind of English. It will be seen that I have not made a full translation. The beginning and ending of the sentence follow the original meaning fairly closely, but in the middle the concrete illustration—race, battle, bread—dissolve into the vague phrase "success or failure in competitive activities." This had to be so, because no modern writer of the kind I am discussing—no one capable of using phrases like "objective consideration of contemporary phenomena"—would ever tabulate his thoughts in that precise and detailed way. The whole tendency of modern prose is away from concreteness. Now analyze these two sentences a little more closely. The first contains forty-nine words but only sixty syllables, and all its words are those of everyday life. The second contains thirty-eight words of ninety syllables: eighteen of its words are from Latin roots and one from Greek. The first sentence contains six vivid images, and only one phrase ("time and chance") that could be called vague. The second contains not a single fresh, arresting phrase, and in spite of its ninety syllables it gives only a shortened version of the meaning contained in the first. Yet without a doubt it is the second kind of sentence that is gaining ground in modern English. I do not want to exaggerate. This kind of writing is not yet universal, and outcrops of simplicity will occur here and there in the worst-written page. Still, if you or I were told to write a few lines on the uncertainty of human fortunes, we should probably come much nearer to my imaginary sentence than to the one from *Ecclesiastes*.

As I have tried to show, modern writing at its worst does not consist in picking out words for the sake of their meaning and inventing images in order to make the meaning clearer. It consists in gumming together long strips of words which have already been set in order by someone else, and making the results presentable by sheer humbug. The attraction of this way of writing is that it is easy. It is easier— even quicker, once you have the habit—to say *In my opinion it is not an unjustifiable assumption that* than to say *I think*. If you use ready-made phrases, you not only don't have to hunt about for words; you also don't have to bother with the rhythms of your sentences, since these phrases are generally so arranged as to be more or less euphonious. When you are composing in a hurry—when you are dictating to a stenographer, for instance, or making a public speech—it is natural to fall into a pretentious, Latinized style. Tags like *a consideration which we should do well to bear in mind* or *a conclusion to which all of us would readily assent* will save many a sentence from coming down with a bump. By using stale metaphors, similes, and idioms, you save much mental effort, at the cost of leaving your meaning vague, not only for your reader but for yourself. This is the significance of mixed metaphors. The sole aim of a metaphor is to call up a visual image. When these images clash—as in *The Fascist octopus has sung its swan song, the jackboot is thrown into the melting pot*—it can be taken as certain that the writer is not seeing a mental image of the objects he is naming; in other words he is not really thinking. Look again at the examples I gave at the beginning of this essay. Professor Laski (1) uses five negatives in fifty-three words. One of these is superfluous, making nonsense of the whole passage, and in addition there is the slip—*alien* for akin—making further nonsense, and several avoidable pieces of clumsiness which increase the general vagueness. Professor Hogben (2) plays ducks and drakes with a battery which is able to write prescriptions, and, while disapproving of the everyday phrase *put up with*, is unwilling to look *egregious* up in the dictionary and see what it means; (3), if one takes an uncharitable attitude towards it, is simply meaningless: probably one could work out its intended meaning by reading the whole of the article in which it occurs. In (4), the writer knows more or less what he wants to say, but an accumulation of stale phrases chokes him like tea leaves blocking a sink. In (5), words and meaning have almost parted company. People who write in this manner usually have a general emotional meaning— they dislike one thing and want to express solidarity with another— but they are not interested in the detail of what they are saying. A scrupulous writer, in every sentence that he writes, will ask himself at least four questions, thus: What am I trying to say? What words will express it? What image or idiom will make it dearer? Is this image fresh enough to have an effect? And he will probably ask himself two more: Could I put it more shortly? Have I said anything that is avoidably ugly? But you are not obliged to go to all this trouble. You can shirk it by simply throwing your mind open and letting the ready-made phrases come crowding in. They will construct your sentences for you—even think your thoughts for you, to a certain extent—and at need they will perform the important service of partially concealing your meaning even from yourself. It is at this point that the special connection between politics and the debasement of language becomes clear.

In our time it is broadly true that political writing is bad writing. Where it is not true, it will generally be found that the writer is some kind of rebel, expressing his private opinions and not a "party line." Orthodoxy, of whatever color, seems to demand a lifeless, imitative style. The political dialects to be found in pamphlets, leading articles, manifestoes, White Papers and the speeches of undersecretaries do, of course, vary from party to party, but they are all alike in that one almost never finds in them a fresh, vivid, home-made turn of speech. When one watches some tired hack on the platform mechanically repeating the familiar phrases—*bestial atrocities, iron heel, blood-stained tyranny, free peoples of the world, stand shoulder to shoulder*—one often has a curious feeling that one is not watching a live human being but some kind of dummy: a feeling which suddenly becomes stronger at moments when the light catches the speaker's spectacles and turns them into blank discs which seem to have no eyes behind them. And this is not altogether fanciful. A speaker who uses that kind of phraseology has gone some distance towards turning himself into a machine. The appropriate noises are coming out of his larynx, but his brain is not involved as it would be if he were choosing his words for himself. If the speech he is making is one that he is accustomed to make over and over again, he may be almost unconscious of what he is saying, as one is when one utters the responses in church. And this reduced state of consciousness, if not indispensable, is at any rate favorable to political conformity.

In our time, political speech and writing are largely the defense of the indefensible. Things like the continuance of British rule in India, the Russian purges and deportations, the droppings of the atom bombs on Japan, can indeed be defended, but only by arguments which are too brutal for most people to face, and which do not square with the professed aims of political parties. Thus political language has to consist largely of euphemism, question-begging, and sheer cloudy vagueness. Defenseless villages are bombarded from the air, the inhabitants driven out into the countryside, the cattle machine-gunned, the huts set on fire with incendiary bullets: this is called *pacification*. Millions of peasants are robbed of their farms and sent trudging along the roads with no more than they can carry: this is called *transfer of population* or *rectification of frontiers*. People are imprisoned for years without trial, or shot in the back of the neck or sent to die of scurvy in Arctic lumber camps: this is called *elimination of unreliable elements*. Such phraseology is needed if one wants to name things without calling up mental pictures of them. Consider for instance some comfortable English professor defending Russian totalitarianism. He cannot say outright, "I believe in killing off your opponents when you can get good results by doing so." Probably, therefore, he will say something like this:

> While freely conceding that the Soviet régime exhibits certain features which the humanitarian may be inclined to deplore, we must, I think, agree that a certain curtailment of the right to political opposition is an unavoidable concomitant of transitional periods, and that the rigors which the Russian people have been called upon to undergo have been amply justified in the sphere of concrete achievement.

The inflated style is itself a kind of euphemism. A mass of Latin words falls upon the facts like soft snow, blurring the outlines and covering up all the details. The great enemy of clear language is insincerity. When there is a gap between one's real and one's declared aims, one turns as it were instinctively to long words and exhausted idioms, like a cuttlefish squirting out ink. In our age there is no such thing as "keeping out of politics." All issues are political issues, and politics itself is a mass of lies, evasions, folly, hatred and schizophrenia. When the general atmosphere is bad, language must suffer. I should expect to find—this is a guess which I have not sufficient knowledge to verify—that the German, Russian, and Italian languages have all deteriorated in the last ten or fifteen years, as a result of dictatorship.

But if thought corrupts language, language can also corrupt thought. A bad usage can spread by tradition and imitation, even among people who should and do know better. The debased language that I have been discussing is in some ways very convenient. Phrases like *a not unjustifiable assumption*, *leaves much to be desired*, *would serve no good purpose*, *a consideration which we should do well to bear in mind*, are a continuous temptation, a packet of aspirins always at one's elbow. Look back through this essay, and for certain you will find that I have again and again committed the very faults I am protesting against. By this morning's post I have received a pamphlet dealing with conditions in Germany. The author tells me that he "felt impelled" to write it. I open it at random, and here is almost the first sentence that I see: "[The Allies] have an opportunity not only of achieving a radical transformation of Germany's social and political structure in such a way as to avoid a nationalistic reaction in Germany itself, but at the same time of laying the foundations of a co-operative and unified Europe." You see, he "feels impelled" to write —feels, presumably, that he has something new to say—and yet his words, like cavalry horses answering the bugle, group themselves automatically into the familiar dreary pattern. This invasion of one's mind by ready-made phrases (*lay the foundations*, *achieve a radical transformation*) can only be prevented if one is constantly on guard against them, and every such phrase anaesthetizes a portion of one's brain.

I said earlier that the decadence of our language is probably curable. Those who deny this would argue, if they produced an argument at all, that language merely reflects existing social conditions, and that we cannot influence its development by any direct tinkering with words and constructions. So far as the general tone or spirit of a language goes, this may be true, but it is not true in detail. Silly words and expressions have often disappeared, not through any evolutionary process but owing to the conscious action of a minority. Two recent examples were *explore every avenue* and *leave no stone unturned*, which were killed by the jeers of a few journalists. There is a long list of flyblown metaphors which could similarly be got rid of if enough people would interest themselves in the job; and it should also be possible to laugh the *not un* – formation out of existence,[3] to reduce the amount of Latin and Greek in the average sentence, to drive out foreign phrases and strayed scientific words, and, in general, to make pretentiousness unfashionable. But all these are

---

[3]One can cure oneself of the *not un* – formation by memorizing this sentence: *A not unblack dog was chasing a not unsmall rabbit across a not ungreen field.* [Orwell's note]

Appendix

minor points. The defense of the English language implies more than this, and perhaps it is best to start by saying what it does *not* imply.

To begin with it has nothing to do with archaism, with the salvaging of obsolete words and turns of speech, or with the setting up of a "standard English" which must never be departed from. On the contrary, it is especially concerned with the scrapping of every word or idiom which has outworn its usefulness. It has nothing to do with correct grammar and syntax, which are of no importance so long as one makes one's meaning clear, or with the avoidance of Americanisms, or with having what is called a "good prose style." On the other hand it is not concerned with fake simplicity and the attempt to make written English colloquial. Nor does it even imply in every case preferring the Saxon word to the Latin one, though it does imply using the fewest and shortest words that will cover one's meaning. What is above all needed is to let the meaning choose the word, and not the other way about. In prose, the worst thing one can do with words is to surrender to them. When you think of a concrete object, you think wordlessly, and then, if you want to describe the thing you have been visualizing you probably hunt about till you find the exact words that seem to fit it. When you think of something abstract you are more inclined to use words from the start, and unless you make a conscious effort to prevent it, the existing dialect will come rushing in and do the job for you, at the expense of blurring or even changing your meaning. Probably it is better to put off using words as long as possible and get one's meaning as clear as one can through pictures or sensations. Afterward one can choose—not simply *accept*—the phrases that will best cover the meaning, and then switch round and decide what impression one's words are likely to make on another person. This last effort of the mind cuts out all stale or mixed images, all prefabricated phrases, needless repetitions, and humbug and vagueness generally. But one can often be in doubt about the effect of a word or a phrase, and one needs rules that one can rely on when instinct fails. I think the following rules will cover most cases:

   (i) Never use a metaphor, simile, or other figure of speech which you are used to seeing in print.
  (ii) Never use a long word where a short one will do.
 (iii) If it is possible to cut a word out, always cut it out.
  (iv) Never use the passive where you can use the active.
   (v) Never use a foreign phrase, a scientific word, or a jargon word if you can think of an everyday English equivalent.

(vi) Break any of these rules sooner than say anything outright barbarous.

These rules sound elementary, and so they are, but they demand a deep change of attitude in anyone who has grown used to writing in the style now fashionable. One could keep all of them and still write bad English, but one could not write the kind of stuff that I quoted in those five specimens at the beginning of this article.

I have not here been considering the literary use of language, but merely language as an instrument for expressing and not for concealing or preventing thought. Stuart Chase and others have come near to claiming that all abstract words are meaningless, and have used this as a pretext for advocating a kind of political quietism. Since you don't know what Fascism is, how can you struggle against Fascism? One need not swallow such absurdities as this, but one ought to recognize that the present political chaos is connected with the decay of language, and that one can probably bring about some improvement by starting at the verbal end. If you simplify your English, you are freed from the worst follies of orthodoxy. You cannot speak any of the necessary dialects, and when you make a stupid remark its stupidity will be obvious, even to yourself. Political language—and with variations this is true of all political parties, from Conservatives to Anarchists—is designed to make lies sound truthful and murder respectable, and to give an appearance of solidity to pure wind. One cannot change this all in a moment, but one can at least change one's own habits, and from time to time one can even, if one jeers loudly enough, send some worn-out and useless phrase— some *jackboot, Achilles' heel, hotbed, melting pot, acid test, veritable inferno,* or other lump of verbal refuse—into the dustbin where it belongs.

E.B. White

Although he is best known for his children's books, including *Charlotte's Web* and the *Trumpet of the Swan*, author E.B. White's primary trade was the personal essay. In his seventy-year career, most of his essays found their way into the prestigious *New Yorker* magazine. Each essay demonstrates an incredible ability to describe ordinary events vividly, as well as the melancholy and sentimental perspective that dominated White's life.

Once More to the Lake

One summer, along about 1904, my father rented a camp on a lake in Maine and took us all there for the month of August. We all got ringworm from some kittens and had to rub Pond's Extract on our arms and legs night and morning, and my father rolled over in a canoe with all his clothes on; but outside of that the vacation was a success and from then on none of us ever thought there was any place in the world like that lake in Maine. We returned summer after summer—always on August 1st for one month. I have since become a salt-water man, but sometimes in summer there are days when the restlessness of the tides and the fearful cold of the sea water and the incessant wind which blows across the afternoon and into the evening make me wish for the placidity of a lake in the woods. A few weeks ago this feeling got so strong I bought myself a couple of bass hooks and a spinner and returned to the lake where we used to go, for a week's fishing and to revisit old haunts.

I took along my son, who had never had any fresh water up his nose and who had seen lily pads only from train windows. On the journey over to the lake I began to wonder what it would be like. I wondered how time would have marred this unique, this holy spot—the coves and streams, the hills that the sun set behind, the camps and the paths behind the camps. I was sure the tarred road would have found it out and I wondered in what other ways it would be desolated. It is strange how much you can remember about places like that once you allow your mind to return into the grooves which lead back. You remember one thing, and that suddenly reminds you of another thing. I guess I remembered clearest of all the early mornings, when the lake was cool and motionless, remembered how the bedroom smelled of the lumber it was made of and of the wet woods whose scent entered through the screen. The partitions in the camp were thin and did not extend clear to the top of the rooms, and as I was always the first up I would dress softly so as not to wake the others, and sneak out into the sweet outdoors and start out in the canoe, keeping close along the shore in the long shadows of the pines. I remembered being very careful never to rub my paddle against the gunwale for fear of disturbing the stillness of the cathedral.

The lake had never been what you would call a wild lake. There were cottages sprinkled around the shores, and it was in farming country although the shores of the lake were quite heavily wooded. Some of the cottages were owned by nearby farmers, and you would live at the shore and eat your meals at the farmhouse. That's what our family did. But although it wasn't wild, it was a fairly large and undisturbed lake and there were places in it which, to a child at least, seemed infinitely remote and primeval.

I was right about the tar; it led to within half a mile of the shore. But when I got back there, with my boy, and we settled into a camp near a farmhouse and into the kind of summertime I had known, I could tell that it was going to be pretty much the same as it had been before—I knew it, lying in bed the first morning, smelling the bedroom, and hearing the boy sneak quietly out and go off along the shore in a boat. I began to sustain the illusion that he was I, and therefore, by simple transposition, that I was my father. This sensation persisted, kept cropping up all the time we were there. It was not an entirely new feeling, but in this setting it grew much stronger. I seemed to be living a dual existence. I would be in the middle of some simple act, I would be picking up a bait box or laying down a table fork, or I would be saying something, and suddenly it would be not I but my father who was saying the words or making the gesture. It gave me a creepy sensation.

We went fishing the first morning. I felt the same damp moss covering the worms in the bait can, and saw the dragonfly alight on the tip of my rod as it hovered a few inches from the surface of the water. It was the arrival of this fly that convinced me beyond any doubt that everything was as it always had been, that the years were a mirage and there had been no years. The small waves were the same, chucking the rowboat under the chin as we fished at anchor, and the boat was the same boat, the same color green and the ribs broken in the same places, and under the floor-boards the same freshwater leavings and débris—the dead helgramite, the wisps of moss, the rusty discarded fishhook, the dried blood from yesterday's catch. We stared silently at the tips of our rods, at the dragonflies that came and went. I lowered the tip of mine into the water, tentatively, pensively dislodging the fly, which darted two feet away, poised, darted two feet back, and came to rest again a little farther up the rod. There had been no years between the ducking of this dragonfly and the other one—the one that was part of memory. I looked at the boy, who was silently watching his fly, and it was my hands that held his rod, my eyes watching. I felt dizzy and didn't know which rod I was at the end of.

We caught two bass, hauling them in briskly as though they were mackerel, pulling them over the side of the boat in a businesslike manner without any landing net, and stunning them with a blow on the back of the head. When we got back for a swim before lunch, the lake was exactly where we had left it, the same number of inches from the dock, and there was only the merest suggestion of a breeze. This seemed an utterly enchanted sea, this lake you could leave to its own devices for a few hours and come back to, and find that it had not stirred, this constant and trustworthy body of water. In the shallows, the dark, water-soaked sticks and twigs, smooth and old, were undulating in clusters on the bottom against the dean ribbed sand, and the track of the mussel was plain. A school of minnows swam by, each minnow with its small individual shadow, doubling the attendance, so clear and sharp in the sunlight. Some of the other campers were in swimming, along the shore, one of them with a cake of soap, and the water felt thin and clear and unsubstantial. Over the years there had been this person with the cake of soap, this cultist, and there he was. There had been no years.

Up to the farmhouse to dinner through the teeming, dusty field, the road under our sneakers was only a two-track road. The middle track was missing, the one with the marks of the hooves and the splotches of dried, flaky manure. There had always been three tracks to choose from in choosing which track to walk in; now the choice was narrowed down to two. For a moment I missed terribly the middle alternative. But the way led past the tennis court and something about the way it lay there in the sun reassured me; the tape had loosened along the backline, the alleys were green with plantains and other weeds, and the net (installed in June and removed in September) sagged in the dry noon, and the whole place steamed with midday heat and hunger and emptiness. There was a choice of pie for dessert, and one was blueberry and one was apple, and the waitresses were the same country girls, there having been no passage of time, only the illusion of it as in a dropped curtain—the waitresses were still fifteen; their hair had been washed, that was the only difference—they had been to the movies and seen the pretty girls with the clean hair.

Summertime, oh summertime, pattern of life indelible, the fade-proof lake, the woods unshatterable, the pasture with the sweetfern and the juniper forever and ever, summer without end; this was the background, and the life along the shore was the design, the cottages with their innocent and tranquil design, their tiny docks with the flagpole and the American flag floating against the white clouds in the blue sky, the little paths over the roots of the trees leading from camp to camp and the paths leading back to the outhouses and the can of lime for sprinkling, and at the souvenir counters at the store the miniature birch-bark canoes and the post cards that showed things looking a little better than they looked. This was the American family at play, escaping the city heat, wondering whether the new-comers in the camp at the head of the cove were "common" or "nice," wondering whether it was true that the people who drove up for Sunday dinner at the farmhouse were turned away because there wasn't enough chicken.

It seemed to me, as I kept remembering all this, that those times and those summers had been infinitely precious and worth saving. There had been jollity and peace and goodness. The arriving (at the beginning of August) had been so big a business in itself, at the railway station the farm wagon drawn up, the first smell of the pine-laden air, the first glimpse of the smiling farmer, and the great importance of the trunks and your father's enormous authority in such matters, and the feel of the wagon under you for the long ten-mile haul, and at the top of the last long hill catching the first view of the lake after eleven months of not seeing this cherished body of water. The shouts and cries of the other campers when they saw you, and the trunks to be unpacked, to give up their rich burden. (Arriving was less exciting nowadays, when you sneaked up in your car and parked it under a tree near the camp and took out the bags and in five minutes it was all over, no fuss, no loud wonderful fuss about trunks.)

Peace and goodness and jollity. The only thing that was wrong now, really, was the sound of the place, an unfamiliar nervous sound of the outboard motors. This was the note that jarred, the one thing that would sometimes break the illusion and set the years moving. In those other summertimes all motors were inboard; and when they were at a little distance, the noise they made was a sedative, an ingredient of summer sleep. They were one-cylinder and two-cylinder engines, and some were make-and-break and some were jump-spark, but they all made a sleepy sound across the lake. The one-lungers throbbed and fluttered, and the twin-cylinder ones purred and purred, and that was a quiet sound too. But now the campers all had outboards. In the daytime, in the hot mornings, these motors made a petulant, irritable sound; at night, in the still evening when the afterglow hit the water, they whined about one's ears like mosquitoes. My boy loved our rented outboard, and his great desire was to achieve singlehanded mastery over it, and authority, and he soon learned the trick of choking it a little (but not too much), and the adjustment of the needle valve. Watching him I would remember the things you could do with the old one-cylinder engine with the heavy flywheel, how you could have it eating out of your hand if you got really close to it spiritually. Motor boats in those days didn't have clutches, and you would make a landing by shutting off the motor at the proper time and coasting in with a dead rudder. But there was a way of reversing them, if you learned the trick, by cutting the switch and putting it on again exactly on the final dying revolution of the flywheel, so that it would kick back against compression and begin reversing. Approaching a dock in a strong following breeze, it was difficult to slow up sufficiently by the ordinary coasting method, and if a boy felt he had complete mastery over his motor, he was tempted to keep it running beyond its time and then reverse it a few feet from the dock. It took a cool nerve, because if you threw the switch a twentieth of a second too soon you would catch the flywheel when it still had speed enough to go up past center, and the boat would leap ahead, charging bull-fashion at the dock.

We had a good week at the camp. The bass were biting well and the sun shone endlessly, day after day. We would be tired at night and lie down in the accumulated heat of the little bedrooms after the long hot day and the breeze would stir almost imperceptibly outside and the smell of the swamp drift through the rusty screens. Sleep would come easily and in the morning the red squirrel would be on the roof, tapping out his gay routine. I kept remembering everything, lying in bed in the morning—the small steamboat that had a long rounded stem like the lip of a Ubangi, and how quietly she ran on the moonlight sails, when the older boys played their mandolins and the girls sang and we ate doughnuts dipped in sugar, and how sweet the music was on the water in the shining night, and what it had felt like to think about girls then. After breakfast we would go up to the store and the things were in the same place—the minnows in a bottle, the plugs and spinners disarranged and pawed over by the youngsters from the boys' camp, the fig newtons and the Beeman's gum. Outside, the road was tarred and cars stood in front of the store.

Inside, all was just as it had always been, except there was more Coca-Cola and not so much Moxie and root beer and birch beer and sarsaparilla. We would walk out with a bottle of pop apiece and sometimes the pop would backfire up our noses and hurt. We explored the streams, quietly, where the turtles slid off the sunny logs and dug their way into the soft bottom; and we lay on the town wharf and fed worms to the tame bass. Everywhere we went I had trouble making out which was I, the one walking at my side, the one walking in my pants.

One afternoon while we were there at that lake a thunderstorm came up. It was like the revival of an old melodrama that I had seen long ago with childish awe. The second-act climax of the drama of the electrical disturbance over a lake in America had not changed in any important respect. This was the big scene, still the big scene. The whole thing was so familiar, the first feeling of oppression and heat and a general air around camp of not wanting to go very far away. In midafternoon (it was all the same) a curious darkening of the sky, and a lull in everything that had made life tick; and then the way the boats suddenly swung the other way at their moorings with the coming of a breeze out of the new quarter, and the premonitory rumble. Then the kettle drum, then the snare, then the bass drum and cymbals, then crackling light against the dark, and the gods grinning and licking their chops in the hills. Afterward the calm, the rain steadily rustling in the calm lake, the return of light and hope and spirits, and the campers running out in joy and relief to go swimming in the rain, their bright cries perpetuating the deathless joke about how they were getting simply drenched, and the children screaming with delight at the new sensation of bathing in the rain, and the joke about getting drenched linking the generations in a strong indestructible chain. And the comedian who waded in carrying an umbrella.

When the others went swimming my son said he was going in too. He pulled his dripping trunks from the line where they had hung all through the shower, and wrung them out. Languidly, and with no thought of going in, I watched him, his hard little body, skinny and bare, saw him wince slightly as he pulled up around his vitals the small, soggy, icy garment. As he buckled the swollen belt suddenly my groin felt the chill of death.

Dorothy Parker

An American critic, satirical poet, and short story writer, Dorothy Rothschild Parker is remembered as much for her flashing verbal exchanges and malicious wit as for the disenchanted stories and sketches in which she revealed her underlying pessimism. Starting her career as *Vanity Fair*'s drama critic (1917-20) and continuing as the *New Yorker*'s theatre and book reviewer (1927-33), Parker enhanced her legend in the 1920s and early 1930s through membership in the Algonquin Hotel's celebrated Round Table.

Parker published her first light verse in *Enough Rope* and *Death and Taxes*. These were followed by the short-story collections *Laments for the Living* and *After Such Pleasures*, containing her single most famous story, "Big Blonde." Parker scripted films in Hollywood from 1933 to 1938 and in 1937 covered the Spanish Civil War as a reporter. In collaboration with others she also wrote two Broadway plays: *Close Harmony*, with Elmer Rice, and *Ladies of the Corridor*, with Arnaud d'Usseau.

Good Souls

Their Characteristics, Habits, and Innumerable Methods of Removing the Joy from Life.

All about us, living in our very families, it may be, there exists a race of curious creatures. Outwardly, they possess no marked peculiarities: in fact, at a hasty glance, they may be readily mistaken for regular human beings. They are built after the popular design; they have the usual number of features, arranged in the conventional manner; they offer no variations on the general run of things in their habits of dressing, eating, and carrying on their business.

Yet, between them and the rest of the civilized world, there stretches an impassable barrier. Though they live in the very thick of the human race, they are forever isolated from it. They are fated to go through life, congenital pariahs. They live out their little lives, mingling with the world, yet never a part of it.

They are, in short, Good Souls.

And the piteous thing about them is that they are wholly unconscious of their condition. A Good Soul thinks he is just like anyone else. Nothing could convince him otherwise. It is heartrending to see him, going cheerfully about, even whistling or humming as he goes, all unconscious of his terrible plight. The utmost he can receive from the world is an attitude of good-humored patience, a perfunctory word of approbation, a praising with faint damns, so to speak—yet he firmly believes that everything is all right with him.

There is no accounting for Good Souls.

They spring up anywhere. They will suddenly appear in families which, for generations, have had no slightest stigma attached to them. Possibly they are throw-backs. There is scarcely a family without at least one Good Soul somewhere in it at the present moment —maybe in the form of an elderly aunt, an unmarried sister, an unsuccessful brother, an indigent cousin. No household is complete without one.

The Good Soul begins early; he will show signs of his condition in extreme youth. Go now to the nearest window, and look out on the little children playing so happily below. Any group of youngsters that you may happen to see will do perfectly. Do you observe the child whom all the other little dears make "it" in their merry games? Do you follow the child from whom the other little ones snatch the cherished candy, to consume it before his streaming eyes? Can you get a good look at the child whose precious toys are borrowed for indefinite periods by the other playful youngsters, and are returned to him in fragments? Do you see the child upon whom all the other kiddies play their complete repertory of childhood's winsome pranks— throwing bags of water on him, running away and hiding from him, shouting his name in quaint rhymes, chalking coarse legends on his unsuspecting back?

Mark that child well. He is going to be a Good Soul when he grows up.

Thus does the doomed child go through early youth and adolescence. So does he progress towards the fulfillment of his destiny. And then, some day, when he is under discussion, someone will say of him, "Well, he means well, anyway." That settles it. For him, that is the end. Those words have branded him with the indelible mark of his pariahdom. He has come into his majority; he is a full-fledged Good Soul.

The activities of the adult of the species are familiar to us all. When you are ill, who is it that hastens to your bedside bearing molds of blanc-mange, which, from infancy, you have hated with unspeakable loathing? As usual, you are way ahead of me, gentle reader—it is indeed the Good Soul. It is the Good Souls who efficiently smooth out your pillow when you have just worked it into the comfortable shape, who creak about the room on noisy tiptoe, who tenderly lay on your fevered brow damp cloths which drip ceaselessly down your neck. It is they who ask, every other minute, if there isn't something that they can do for you. It is they who, at great personal sacrifice, spend long hours sitting beside your bed, reading aloud the continued stories in the *Woman's Home Companion*, or chatting cozily on the increase in the city's death rate.

In health, as in illness, they are always right there, ready to befriend you. No sooner do you sit down, than they exclaim that they can see you aren't comfortable in that chair, and insist on your changing places with them. It is the Good Souls who just *know* that you don't like your tea that way, and who bear it masterfully away from you to alter it with cream and sugar until it is a complete stranger to you. At the table, it is they who always feel that their grapefruit is better than yours and who have to be restrained almost forcibly from exchanging with you. In a restaurant the waiter invariably makes a mistake and brings them something which they did not order—and which they refuse to have changed, choking it down with a wistful smile. It is they who cause traffic blocks, by standing in subway entrances arguing altruistically as to who is to pay the fare.

At the theater, should they be members of a box-party, it is the Good Souls who insist on occupying the rear chairs; if the seats are in the orchestra, they worry audibly, all through the performance, about their being able to see better than you, until finally in desperation you grant their plea and change seats with them. If, by so doing, they can bring a little discomfort on themselves—sit in a draught, say, or behind a pillar—then their happiness is complete. To feel the genial glow of martyrdom—that is all that they ask of life.

Good Souls are punctilious in their observation of correct little ceremonies. If, for example, they borrow a [one-penny] postage stamp, they immediately offer two pennies in return for it—they insist upon this business transaction. They never fail to remember birthdays—their little gift always brings with it a sharp stab of remembrance that you have blissfully ignored their own natal day. At the last moment, on Christmas Eve, comes a present from some Good Soul whose existence, in the rush of holiday shopping, you have completely overlooked. When they go away, be it only for an overnight stay, they never neglect to send postcards bearing views of the principal buildings of the place to all their acquaintances; to their intimates, they always bring back some local souvenir—a tiny dish, featuring the gold-lettered name of the town; a thimble in an appropriate case, both bearing the name of their native city; a tie-rack with the name of its place of residence burned decoratively on its wood; or some such useful novelty.

The lives of Good Souls are crowded with Occasions, each with its own ritual which must be solemnly followed. On Mothers' Day, Good Souls conscientiously wear carnations; on St. Patrick's Day, they faithfully don boutonnieres of shamrocks; on Columbus Day, they carefully pin on miniature Italian flags. Every feast must be celebrated by the sending out of cards—Valentine's Day, Arbor Day, Groundhog Day, and all the other important festivals, each is duly observed. They have a perfect genius for discovering appropriate cards of greeting for the event. It must take hours of research.

If it's too long a time between holidays, then the Good Soul will send little cards or little mementoes, just by way of surprises. He is strong on surprises, anyway. It delights him to drop in unexpectedly on his friends. Who has not known the joy of those evenings when some Good Soul just runs in, as a surprise? It is particularly effective when a chosen company of other guests happens to be present— enough for two tables of bridge, say. This means that the Good Soul must sit wistfully by, patiently watching the progress of the rubber, or else must cut in at intervals, volubly voicing his desolation at causing so much inconvenience, and apologizing constantly during the evening.

His conversation, admirable though it is, never receives its just due of attention and appreciation. He is one of those who believe and frequently quote the exemplary precept that there is good in everybody; hanging in his bedchamber is the whimsically phrased, yet vital, statement, done in burned leather—"There is so much good in the worst of us and so much bad in the best of us that it hardly behooves any of us to talk about the rest of us." This, too, he archly quotes on appropriate occasions. Two or three may be gathered together, intimately discussing some mutual acquaintance. It is just getting really absorbing, when comes the Good Soul, to utter his dutiful, "We mustn't judge harshly—after all, we must always remember that many times our own actions may be misconstrued." Somehow, after several of these little reminders, there seems to be a general waning of interest; the little gathering breaks up, inventing quaint excuses to get away and discuss the thing more fully, adding a few really good details, some place where the Good Soul will not follow. While the Good Soul, pitifully ignorant of their evil purpose, glows with the warmth of conscious virtue, and settles himself to read the Contributors' Club, in the *Atlantic Monthly*, with a sense of duty well done.

Yet it must not be thought that their virtue lifts Good Souls above the enjoyment of popular pastimes. Indeed, it does not: they are enthusiasts on the subject of good, wholesome fun. They lavishly patronize the drama, in its cleaner forms. They flock to the plays of Miss Rachel Crothers, Miss Eleanor Porter, and Mr. Edward Childs Carpenter. They are passionate admirers of the art of Mr. William Hodge. In literature, they worship at the chaste shrines of Harold Ben Wright, Gene Stratton-Porter, Eleanor Hallowell Abbott, Alice Hegan Rice, and the other triple-named apostles of optimism. They have never felt the same towards Arnold Bennett since he sprung "The Pretty Lady" on them; they no longer give "The Human Machine" and "How to Live on Twenty-four Hours a Day" as birthday offerings to their friends. In poetry, though Tennyson, Whittier, and Longfellow stand for the highest, of course, they have marked leaning toward the later works of Mrs. Ella Wheeler Wilcox. They are continually meeting people who know her, encounters of which they proudly relate. Among humorists, they prefer Mr. Ellis Parker Butler.

Good Souls, themselves, are no mean humorists. They have a time-honored formula of fun-making, which must be faithfully followed. Certain words or phrases must be whimsically distorted every time they are used. "Over the river," they dutifully say, whenever they take their leave. "Don't you cast any asparagus on me," they warn, archly; and they never fail to speak of "three times in concussion." According to their ritual, these screaming phrases must be repeated several times, for the most telling effect, and are invariably followed by hearty laughter from the speaker, to whom they seem eternally new.

Perhaps the most congenial role of the Good Soul is that of advice-giver. He loves to take people aside and have serious little personal talks, all for their own good. He thinks it only right to point out faults or bad habits which are, perhaps unconsciously, growing on them. He goes home and laboriously writes long, intricate letters, invariably beginning, "Although you may feel that this is no affair of mine, I think that you really ought to know," and so on, indefinitely. In his desire to help, he reminds one irresistibly of Marcelline, who used to try so pathetically and so fruitlessly to be of some assistance in arranging the circus arena, and who brought such misfortunes on his own innocent person thereby.

The Good Souls will, doubtless, gain their reward in Heaven; on this earth certainly, theirs is what is technically known as a rough deal. The most hideous outrages are perpetrated on them. "Oh, he won't mind," people say. "He's a Good Soul." And then they proceed to heap the rankest impositions upon him. When Good Souls give a party, people who have accepted weeks in advance call up at the last second and refuse, without the shadow of an excuse save that of a subsequent engagement. Other people are invited to all sorts of entertaining affairs; the Good Soul, unasked, waves them a cheery good-bye and hopes wistfully that they will have a good time. His is the uncomfortable seat in the motor; he is the one to ride backwards in the train; he is the one who is always chosen to solicit subscriptions and make up deficits. People borrow his money, steal his servants, lose his golf balls, use him as a sort of errand boy, leave him flat whenever something more attractive offers—and carry it all off with their cheerful slogan. "Oh, he won't mind—he's a Good Soul."

And that's just it—Good Souls never do mind. After each fresh atrocity they are more cheerful, forgiving and virtuous, if possible, than they were before. There is simply no keeping them down—back they come, with their little gifts, and their little words of advice, and their little endeavors to be of service, always anxious for more.

Yes, there can be no doubt about it—their reward will come to them in the next world.

Would that they were even now enjoying it!

James Thurber

Humorist James Thurber is remembered for his *New Yorker* essays and cartoons, for such short stories as "The Catbird Seat" and "The Secret Life of Walter Mitty," for children's books including *The Thirteen Clocks*, and, as coauthor (with Elliot Nugent), for the witty Broadway play *The Male Animal*. Thurber portrayed the modern world, in all its confusions and frustrations, most successfully in two books illustrated by himself—*Fables for Our Time* and *Further Fables for Our Time*. Aping Aesop, Thurber scripted stories about animals who talked and acted much like his contemporaries, offering such morals as "It is better to have the ring of freedom in your ears than in your nose."

University Days

I passed all the other courses that I took at my University, but I could never pass botany. This was because all botany students had to spend several hours a week in a laboratory looking through a microscope at plant cells, and I could never see through a microscope. I never once saw a cell through a microscope. This used to enrage my instructor. He would wander around the laboratory pleased with the progress all the students were making in drawing the involved and, so I am told, interesting structure of flower cells, until he came to me. I would just be standing there. "I can't see anything," I would say. He would begin patiently enough, explaining how anybody can see through a microscope, but he would always end up in a fury; claiming that I could *too* see through a microscope but just pretended that I couldn't. "It takes away from the beauty of flowers anyway," I used to tell him. "We are not concerned with beauty in this course," he would say. "We are concerned solely with what I may call the *mechanics* of flars." "Well," I'd say. "I can't see anything." "Try it just once again," he'd say, and I would put my eye to the microscope and see nothing at all, except now and again a nebulous milky substance—a phenomenon of maladjustment. You were supposed to see a vivid, restless clockwork of sharply defined plant cells. "I see what looks like a lot of milk," I would tell him. This, he claimed, was the result of my not having adjusted the microscope properly, so he would readjust it for me, or rather, for himself. And I would look again and see milk.

I finally took a deferred pass, as they called it, and waited a year and tried again. (You had to pass one of the biological sciences or you couldn't graduate.) The professor had come back from vacation brown as a berry, bright-eyed, and eager to explain cell-structure again to his classes. "Well," he said to me, cheerily, when we met in the first laboratory hour of the semester, "we're going to see cells this time, aren't we?" "Yes, sir," I said. Students to the right of me and left of me and in front of me were seeing cells; what's more, they were quietly drawing pictures of them in their notebooks. Of course, I didn't see anything.

"We'll try it," the professor said to me, grimly, "with every adjustment of the microscope known to man. As God is my witness, I'll arrange this glass so that you can see cells through it or I'll give up teaching. In twenty-two years of botany, I —" He cut off abruptly for he was beginning to quiver all over, like Lionel Barrymore, and he genuinely wished to hold onto his temper; his scenes with me had taken a great deal out of him.

So we tried it with every adjustment of the microscope known to man. With only one of them did I see anything but blackness or the familiar lacteal opacity, and that time I saw, to my pleasure and amazement, a variegated constellation of flecks, specks, and dots. These I hastily drew. The instructor, noting my activity, came from an adjoining desk, a smile on his lips and his eyebrows high in hope. He looked at my cell drawing. "What's that?" he demanded, with a hint of squeal in his voice. "That's what I saw," I said. "You didn't, you didn't, you *didn't*!" he screamed, losing control of his temper instantly, and he bent over and squinted into the microscope. His head snapped up. "That's your eye!" he shouted. "You've fixed the lens so that it reflects! You've drawn your eye!"

Another course that I didn't like, but somehow managed to pass, was economics. I went to that class straight from the botany class, which didn't help me any in understanding either subject. I used to get them mixed up. But not as mixed up as another student in my economics class who came there direct from a physics laboratory. He was a tackle on the football team, named Bolenciecwcz. At that time Ohio State University had one of the best football teams in the country, and Bolenciecwcz was one of its outstanding stars. In order to be eligible to play it was necessary for him to keep up in his studies, a very difficult matter, for while he was not dumber than an ox he was not any smarter. Most of his professors were lenient and helped him along. None gave him more hints, in answering questions, or asked him simpler ones than the economics professor, a thin, timid man named Bassum. One day when we were on the subject of transportation and distribution, it came Bolenciecwcz's turn to answer a question. "Name one means of transportation," the professor said to him. No light came into the big tackle's eyes. "Just any means of transportation," said the professor. Bolenciecwcz sat staring at him. "That is," pursued the professor, "any medium, agency, or method of going from one place to another." Bolenciecwcz had the look of a man who is being led into a trap. "You may choose among steam, horse-drawn, or electrically propelled vehicles," said the instructor. "I might suggest the one which we commonly take in making long journeys across land." There was a profound silence in which everybody stirred uneasily, including Bolenciecwcz and Mr. Bassum. Mr. Bassum abruptly broke this silence in an amazing manner. "Choo-choo-choo," he said, in a low voice, and turned instantly scarlet. He glanced appealingly around the room. All of us, of course, shared Mr. Bassum's desire that Bolenciecwcz should stay abreast of the class in economics, for the Illinois game, one of the hardest and most important of the season, was only a week off. "Toot, toot, too-tooooooot!" some student with a deep voice moaned, and we all looked encouragingly at Bolenciecwcz. Somebody else gave a fine imitation of a locomotive letting off steam. Mr. Bassum himself rounded off the little show. "Ding, dong, ding, dong," he said, hopefully. Bolenciecwcz was staring at the floor now, trying to think, his great brow furrowed, his huge hands rubbing together, his face red.

"How did you come to college this year, Mr. Bolenciecwcz?" asked the professor. "*Chuf*fa chuffa, *chuf*fa chuffa."

"M'father sent me," said the football player.

"What on?" asked Bassum.

"I git an 'lowance," said the tackle, in a low, husky voice, obviously embarrassed.

"No, no," said Bassum. "Name a means of transportation. What did you *ride* here on?"

"Train," said Bolenciecwcz.

"Quite right," said the professor. "Now, Mr. Nugent, will you tell us —"

If I went through anguish in botany and economics—for different reasons—gymnasium work was even worse. I don't even like to think about it. They wouldn't let you play games or join in the exercises with your glasses on and I couldn't see with mine off. I bumped into professors, horizontal bars, agricultural students, and swinging iron rings. Not being able to see, I could take it but I couldn't dish it out. Also, in order to pass gymnasium (and you had to pass it to graduate) you had to learn to swim if you didn't know how. I didn't like the swimming pool, I didn't like swimming, and I didn't like the swimming instructor, and after all these years I still don't. I never swam but I passed my gym work anyway, by having another student give my gymnasium number (978) and swim across the pool in my place. He was a quiet, amiable blonde youth, number 473, and he would have seen through a microscope for me if we could have got away with it, but we couldn't get away with it. Another thing I didn't like about gymnasium work was that they made you strip the day you registered. It is impossible for me to be happy when I am stripped and being asked a lot of questions. Still, I did better than a lanky agricultural student who was cross-examined just before I was. They asked each student what college he was in—that is, whether Arts, Engineering, Commerce, or Agriculture. "What college are you in?" the instructor snapped at the youth in front of me. "Ohio State University," he said promptly.

It wasn't that agricultural student but it was another a whole lot like him who decided to take up journalism, possibly on the ground that when farming went to hell he could fall back on newspaper work. He didn't realize, of course, that that would be very much like falling back full-length on a kit of carpenter's tools. Haskins didn't seem cut out for journalism, being too embarrassed to talk to anybody and unable to use a typewriter, but the editor of the college paper assigned him to the cow barns, the sheep house, the horse pavilion, and the animal husbandry department generally. This was a genuinely big "beat," for it took up five times as much ground and got ten times as great a legislative appropriation as the College of Liberal Arts. The agricultural student knew animals, but nevertheless his stories were dull and colorlessly written. He took all afternoon on each one of them, on account of having to hunt for each letter on the typewriter. Once in a while he had to ask somebody to help him hunt. "C" and "L," in particular, were hard letters for him to find. His editor finally got pretty much annoyed at the farmer-journalist because his pieces were so uninteresting. "See here, Haskins," he snapped at him one day, "why is it we never have anything hot from you on the horse pavilion? Here we have two hundred head of horses on this campus—more than any other university in the Western Conference except Purdue—and yet you never get any real low-down on them. Now shoot over to the horse barns and dig up something lively." Haskins shambled out and came back in about an hour; he said he had something. "Well, start it off snappily," said the editor. "Something people will read." Haskins set to work and in a couple of hours brought a sheet of typewritten paper to the desk;

it was a two-hundred word story about some disease that had broken out among the horses. Its opening sentence was simple but arresting. It read: "Who has noticed the sores on the tops of the horses in the animal husbandry building?"

Ohio State was a land grant university and therefore two years of military drill was compulsory. We drilled with old Springfield rifles and studied the tactics of the Civil War even though the World War was going on at the time. At 11 o'clock each morning thousands of freshmen and sophomores used to deploy over the campus, moodily creeping up on the old chemistry building. It was good training for the kind of warfare that was waged at Shiloh but it had no connection with what was going on in Europe. Some people used to think there was German money behind it, but they didn't dare say so or they would have been thrown in jail as German spies. It was a period of muddy thought and marked, I believe, the decline of higher education in the Middle West.

As a soldier I was never any good at all. Most of the cadets were glumly indifferent soldiers, but I was no good at all. Once General Littlefield, who was commandant of the cadet corps, popped up in front of me during regimental drill and snapped, "You are the main trouble with this university!" I think he meant that my type was the main trouble with the university but he may have meant me individually. I was mediocre at drill, certainly—that is, until my senior year. By that time I had drilled longer than anybody else in the Western Conference, having failed at military at the end of each preceding year so that I had to do it all over again. I was the only senior still in uniform. The uniform which, when new, had made me look like an interurban railway conductor, now that it had become faded and too tight made me look like Bert Williams in his bellboy act. This had a definitely bad effect on my morale. Even so, I had become by sheer practice little short of wonderful at squad manoeuvres.

One day General Littlefield picked our company out of the whole regiment and tried to get it mixed up by putting it through one movement after another as fast as we could execute them: squads right, squads left, squads on right into line, squads right about, squads left front into line, etc. In about three minutes one hundred and nine men were marching in one direction and I was marching away from them at an angle of forty degrees, all alone. "Company, halt!" shouted General Littlefield, "That man is the only man who has it right!" I was made a corporal for my achievement.

The next day General Littlefield summoned me to his office. He was swatting flies when I went in. I was silent and he was silent too, for a long time. I don't think he remembered me or why he had sent for me, but he didn't want to admit it. He swatted some more flies, keeping his eyes on them narrowly before he let go with the swatter. "Button up your coat!" he snapped. Looking back on it now I can see that he meant me although he was looking at a fly, but I just stood there. Another fly came to rest on a paper in front of the general and began rubbing its hind legs together. The general lifted the swatter cautiously. I moved restlessly and the fly flew away. "You startled him!" barked General Littlefield, looking at me severely. I said I was sorry. "That won't help the situation!" snapped the General, with cold military logic. I didn't see what I could do except offer to chase some more flies toward his desk, but I didn't say anything. He stared out the window at the faraway figures of co-eds crossing the campus toward the library. Finally, he told me I could go. So I went. He either didn't know which cadet I was or else he forgot what he wanted to see me about. It may have been that he wished to apologize for having called me the main trouble with the university; or maybe he had decided to compliment me on my brilliant drilling of the day before and then at the last minute decided not to. I don't know. I don't think about it much any more.